WORK AND SOCIETY

Work and Society is an important new text about the sociology of work and employment. It aims to provide both undergraduate and postgraduate students of sociology, business and politics, with a firm and enjoyable foundation to this fascinating area of sociology, giving comprehensive coverage of traditional areas of the sub-discipline as well as new trends and developments.

The book is divided into three complementary and interconnected parts – Investigating work, Work and social change, and Understanding work. These parts allow readers to explore themes, issues and approaches by examining how sociologists have thought about and researched work and how the sub-discipline has been influenced by the wider society itself. Novel features include separate chapters on researching work, domestic work, unemployment and work, and the representation of work in literary and visual media.

Tim Strangleman is a Reader in Sociology at the School of Social Policy, Sociology and Social Research, University of Kent, where he teaches and researches the sociology of work. Areas of interest include work identity and meaning, deindustrialisation, nostalgia, and visual methods and approaches.

Tracey Warren is Associate Professor and Reader in Sociology, University of Nottingham. Her research interests lie in the sociologies of work and employment, and of social divisions.

WORK AND SOCIETY

Sociological approaches, themes and methods

Tim Strangleman and Tracey Warren

Routledge
Taylor & Francis Group

LONDON AND NEW YORK

First published 2008 by Routledge
2 Park Square, Milton Park, Abingdon, Oxon, OX14 4RN

Simultaneously published in the USA and Canada
by Routledge
711 Third Avenue, New York, NY 10017

Routledge is an imprint of the Taylor & Francis Group,
an informa business

Typeset in Garamond by Graphicraft Limited, Hong Kong

British Library Cataloguing in Publication Data
A catalogue record for this book is available from the British Library

Library of Congress Cataloging in Publication Data
Strangleman, Tim, 1967–
Work and society : sociological approaches, themes and methods / Tim
Strangleman and Tracey Warren.
p. cm.
Includes bibliographical references and index.
ISBN 978-0-415-33648-2 (hbk.) – ISBN 978-0-415-33649-9 (pbk.)
– ISBN 978-0-203-93052-6 (electronic)   1. Industrial sociology.
2. Work – Social aspects.   I. Warren, Tracey.   II. Title.
HD6955.S8745 2008
306.3′6–dc22
2007041453

ISBN 13: 978-0-415-33648-2 (hbk)
ISBN 13: 978-0-415-33649-9 (pbk)
ISBN 13: 978-0-203-93052-6 (ebk)

CONTENTS

ILLUSTRATIONS

FIGURES

TABLES

TEXT BOXES

ACKNOWLEDGEMENTS

In writing this book we have incurred a number of debts. Thanks go first to Alan Felstead, Marek Korczynski and Satnam Virdee for providing us with advance copies of their publications, and also to Alan for permission to use the photograph in Chapter 5. Tim would like to thank friends and colleagues in no particular order: Mike Savage, Ian Roberts, Miriam Glucksmann, John Russo, Sherry Linkon, Jack Metzgar, Jeff Cowie, Dawn Lyon, Iain Wilkinson, Chris Wall, Sarah Vickerstaff, Richard Brown, Jim Daniels and Chris Coates. Tracey would like to thank her colleagues/friends who provided general support and advice about the writing of the book: Fiona Devine, Sam Hillyard, Helen Jarvis, Stephanie Lawler, Julia O'Connell Davidson, Janice McLaughlin, Gemma Metcalfe and Alison Stenning. A period of study leave granted to Tracey by Nottingham University helped towards the book. We would like to thank the many undergraduate students on the sociology of work modules that we have taught over the years, at the universities of Kent, Newcastle, Nottingham and Sheffield.

Finally, Tim and Tracey would like to acknowledge the debts they owe to Claudia, Max and Maddy, and Derek, Kai and Esme respectively.

CHAPTER 1

Introduction

WHAT IS WORK?

The answer to this basic question, 'What is work?' may seem a simple one. Work is what we do for a living, we work to earn a living, to purchase the things we need, food, clothing, heat, light, power, shelter and hopefully have something remaining to enjoy ourselves. Easy, right? Well, we also work for other reasons such as self-respect, tradition, we feel forced to work by norms and values, or people are literally coerced into working for others. Some people love their work; others hate it with a passion. For some, work is inextricably bound up with who they are; it defines their identity not only for themselves but also in their family and community. Work can divide people and can unite them.

So as soon as we try to pin down what work 'is' we run in to problems of definitions as to what counts as work and what is not work. Work could simply mean effort or labour. We could extend this to include mental as well as physical labour. We could simply define work in terms of effort which is rewarded by the payment of money. But this would exclude all sorts of work not formally recognised by the payment of cash – much domestic labour and care work, voluntary work, and a variety of hidden work.

This question of what is work is made more complex still if we reflect back on the 'historical meanings of work'. In the ancient world, to work was to occupy a dishonourable position in society. Indeed, it was the mark of the common mass or even the slave. Leisure was the defining principle of the élite in ancient Greece and Rome. In later Christian societies, work was viewed as the curse of Adam and Eve, the punishment of God for humans having eaten from the tree of knowledge in the Garden of Eden. Much later, Protestants began to view hard work as a sign that they were part of an elect to be saved on the Day of Judgement. This gospel of hard work, the Protestant work ethic, developed in many western societies during the eighteenth, nineteenth and into the twentieth centuries. In liberal political thought, to be a worker, to be economically *independent* was seen as the mark of a citizen, a fully adult member of society. To be *dependent* on the work of others was to be less than a full citizen.

In socialist and communist states in the middle of the twentieth century, the worker was lionised and fêted. Countries in Eastern Europe, Asia and Latin America defined themselves as workers' states. Still later, debates about work and the work ethic have been renewed in welfare states in many developed countries where politicians fear that generations of men and women have 'lost the work ethic'. Policies are devised to make employment central to people's lives, work being seen as the answer to almost every social problem from community cohesion to education. At the same time, these debates are occurring against a background where work has changed and is continuing to change profoundly. Within a generation, we have seen the growth of service industries, globalisation, an explosion in the use of information technology, and deindustrialisation or huge reductions in manufacturing industry in the West and massive industrialisation in other parts of the world. With these processes has come a huge shift in the social relations around work with important consequences for the individual, the family and communities. Some commentators now openly talk about a 'crisis in work', or even the 'end of work'. Others suggest that work now has no meaning for the people who undertake it. Where once what one 'did' defined one's character, identity is now supposedly derived from what one consumes or wears. While some celebrate this liberation from the 'dogma of work', others detect nostalgia for the perceived certainties of a work-based past.

So the question, 'What is work?' becomes even more difficult to answer. It is made complex to define at any one point in history, shifting in its meaning across cultures. In some societies work is or has been what defines the individual, it is what makes them a fully adult citizen, in others it is the definition of an absence of citizenship. In turn, it is a curse, or a sign of being saved, something to be cherished and embraced or discarded and avoided at all costs.

WHAT IS THE SOCIOLOGY OF WORK?

The varying definitions of work raise important questions about how we should study work. How do we make sense of the historical and changing meaning of work? What analytical, theoretical and methodological tools can we bring to bear in understanding the world of work? What do the changes witnessed in the world of work over the past thirty or forty years mean for such a study? And what will happen to work in the future?

There are lots of ways to answer these questions and the study of work is one that exercises a great many academic disciplines – history, economics, political science, social policy, geography, industrial relations, anthropology, management, theology, philosophy as well as literature. In this book we attempt to examine work from a sociological perspective, one that brings what C. W. Mills (1959) described as the 'sociological imagination' to bear. Work has exercised this sociological imagination from the very beginnings of the discipline in the nineteenth century. Each of sociology's founding fathers was concerned with the transition from a largely rural society to one defined by industry and the urban environment. They were interested in understanding different aspects of what this transition meant for individuals, families, communities and wider society. Karl Marx, Emile Durkheim and Max Weber asked a set of questions about this new society and the way people were to live in it – how is order possible in mass society?; how is work to be organised and allocated?; what does work mean to people now and in the past?; what happens if people do not have enough or any work?; how do people adapt to greater levels of specialisation?; and how is paid work supported and underpinned by other social structures? What is striking about the questions posed by nineteenth-century sociologists is how central and relevant they still are today. In the twenty-first century, we still need to ask these same questions about work and those who do it.

Of course, sociologists do not have all the answers to these questions and to some extent the intellectual divide between those who study work is an accidental or arbitrary one. So what is distinct about the sociology – or perhaps that should be the sociologies – of work? Both authors of this book are sociologists with a distinct set of interests and training in the discipline, and in the production of this book have thought long and hard about what a sociology of work looks like. So here goes. First, sociology is a subject underpinned and shot through by theoretical understandings of how society is created, reproduced and changes over time. Sociology has a series of concepts and analytical tools for understanding society and the work that goes on inside it such as the division of labour, the employment relationship, alienation, rationalisation, gender, 'race' and class, and so on. Through these formal and abstract concepts we examine the empirical world of work. Sociology at its best does this historically and comparatively. It is also capable of looking at the world of work simultaneously at the macro, mezzo and micro levels so that we can make intelligible large-scale shifts in industry alongside small-scale interaction on the floor of a workplace or in the domestic arena. Sociologists of work can also draw on a remarkable range of methodological approaches to examine the world of work at these different levels. These range from the compiling and interrogation of quantitative data sets about trends in and experiences of work, through a wide variety of qualitative approaches such as oral history, ethnography and visual techniques.

In *Work and Society*, we want to describe and celebrate how sociologists have studied work but this will not be an uncritical evaluation. *Work and Society* offers the reader a critical account of what the sociology of work has looked at as well as pointing out absences. We want the reader to gain a sense of why work sociology has chosen to examine certain aspects of working life and not others at different times. We also want the reader to come out of each chapter with a sense of where current debates are within work sociology as well as suggesting where sociology might usefully develop in the future. In doing so, we are deliberately catholic in our choice of literature drawn on from outside sociology which could be integrated in to future analysis.

HOW COULD THE SOCIOLOGY OF WORK CHANGE?

In the spirit of this disciplinary self-criticism we want to suggest a variety of ways in which the sociologies of work could develop and expand. This can be seen in terms of approaches, themes and methods. In this book we present a variety of areas which should be the subject of greater sustained attention by sociologists of work. This is not to say that sociologists have not looked at them already but rather their integration into the mainstream of work sociology has been problematic. We could cite the examples of domestic work, unemployment, 'race' and work, and visual approaches and material in this respect. The reasons for this neglect are involved and complex but in part they are due to the way that the sociology of work has been defined and reproduced over time. In the past what counted as the sociology of work was often defined by the employment relationship, namely, paid work often carried out by men in large industrial organisations. While there are understandable and fascinating reasons for this that tell us much about the history of sociology, it is important that the future of the discipline is not held captive by this past structure. Equally it is important that where new issues emerge, we do not simply bolt them on to our existing frameworks. Rather, we argue here that a novel and vibrant sociological study of work is one that genuinely integrates and embeds approaches to issues like gender and 'race'. Importantly, though sociologists equally need to be aware of the rich tradition of sociological research and the way the sociological imagination has tackled a variety of perennial issues and questions, we try to encourage here the development of a robust historical depth to the study of work. We want also to encourage sociologists to be unafraid to look outside the sociological canon when trying to understand what is happening to work. Of course, sociologists have always done this to some extent but we are keen to give licence to the reader to study beyond the obvious close subject matters to also draw on approaches such as literature, art, photography, film and cultural studies. We are not suggesting that these are a substitute for sociological analysis, rather that they help us shed light on new or even old issues: they offer a different cut in to our subject. Finally, we want the reader to be aware of the variety of research methods which can be brought to bear in the study of work. We cover here both established and relatively new methodologies in various chapters.

What we want to argue in *Work and Society* is that a revival of the sociology of work emerges from a subject which is both ready to learn from other areas, happy to adopt and adapt ideas, but is also secure in its own self-knowledge, aware of its own history and specific trajectory.

PHILOSOPHY OF THE BOOK

The argument we have outlined above has obviously had an important influence on the design and philosophy behind *Work and Society*. We have written is a book that can be used in a variety of different and complementary ways. It combines a discussion of theory, method and substantive issues alongside a history of the development of those issues. We try to make links between different themes across the book. We deliberately take a very broad view both about what sociology is as well as what counts as work. The book, if it takes a line, is designed to offer the reader the sense of possibility in a plural sociology of work, arguing that no one method, theory, approach or set of evidence can capture the dynamic of work. We need to develop a plural sociological literacy towards work. In doing so, we outline below the structure and organisation of the book.

ORGANISATION OF THE BOOK

The book is divided into three parts – 'Investigating Work', 'Work and Social Change', and 'Understanding Work'. Part I contains three chapters which show how sociologists think about, research and conceptualise work. We are interested in the theories adopted; the method used and, finally, in the ways that work is represented in a variety of cultural media. In Chapter 2, we look at the question of 'Theory and Work', examining how and why sociologists have used theory in the way they have, explain how useful theory can be, and look at how sociological theories of work have developed over time. Chapter 3 looks at how sociologists 'Research Work', how they have gone about answering some of the questions posed by the theories outlined in the previous chapter. In Chapter 4, 'Representations of Work', Strangleman has written a novel account of the way work is represented in a variety of artistic media, including visual, literary, and aural formats. His aim is to encourage the reader to broaden their ideas about what counts as sources for the sociological study of work.

Part II, 'Work and Social Change', contains two chapters which map the development of modern industrial society and the way this has been challenged by the developments over recent decades. Chapter 5, 'Work and Industrial Society', takes the reader from the Industrial Revolution up to the 1970s, examining how industrial society evolved and how sociologists made sense of it. In Chapter 6, 'Work and Post-Industrial Society and Globalisation', we look at the changes in society over the last four decades. We examine what has changed about work as well as the way sociologists have interpreted these changes.

The final and longest part, Part III, 'Understanding Work', develops the sociological understanding of work by examining key themes and questions around work and working life. We start in Chapter 7 by looking at 'Divisions and Work', and specifically look at questions of class, gender and 'race'. How have these shaped the way work is organised? How have sociologists worked with these concepts? Chapter 8 on 'Control and Resistance at Work' follows, asking how control has changed with the development of capitalism. We show how a distinctly sociological understanding of control emerged from the work of the classical theorists. Chapter 9 is concerned with ideas of 'Time and Work' demonstrating the centrality of time for the organisation, experience and control of work. Chapter 10 is concerned with 'Domestic Work' in a variety of settings. It offers a critique of mainstream work sociology for largely disregarding this area in the past. Chapter 11 concerns 'Unemployment and Work', which, like domestic work, has often been marginal to the sociology of work. The final substantive chapter, Chapter 12, looks at the related themes of 'Culture, Emotion and Identity at Work'. We look at how the level of interest in these issues, which has emerged over the past twenty years, often ignores a longer sociological tradition. Finally, we offer a Conclusion in Chapter 13.

INTERNAL STRUCTURE OF CHAPTERS

In each of the chapters we have tried to follow a similar structure, although there is some variety between them. Each begins with an *Overview* followed by an *Introduction* where the reader will quickly see what the chapter covers. A section called the *Sociological Mission*, where we outline why sociologists of work have been and should be interested in the topic under discussion, follows. We sensitise the reader to some of the main sociological themes and issues in the field. In the *Foundations* section, we offer a summary of how the theme of the chapter was understood and developed by the classical theorists of sociology, it looks at what they studied (or ignored) and the kinds of questions which emerged from their work. In *Later Developments*, we see how these issues were discussed by sociology and how this process shaped work sociology. This section takes the reader from the era of the foundations of the subject up to the 1970s or 1980s. In *Contemporary Issues and Future Trends*, we bring the story up to date and examine the current thinking on the subject and the trajectory debates are likely to take in the future. We conclude each chapter with a short summary. Several sections aimed at stimulating the reader to explore the topic in greater depth follow this. We include useful resources and key further readings, websites and finally suggest student projects and essay questions.

As we said at the beginning of this chapter, we intend this book to be used in a variety of ways. It can be read as a comprehensive account of what sociologists have made of work. It covers many of the accepted core concepts and issues. In addition, it adds discussions on researching work, the representation of work as well as dealing with issues of domestic work and unemployment in a way that is rare in a book such as this.

Our second aim was to provide a book that rooted current thinking about a topic within an historical account. We believe it is essential that the reader understands where, how and why a concept has emerged in the way it has. We have included as much historical and comparative material as possible. The chapters are designed to be read as stand-alone essays but we cross-reference topics and themes, and some knowledge is assumed in later chapters.

Our third aim was to encourage students reading this text to explore topics further for themselves and, hopefully, to carry out their own research on work, workplaces and workers in the future. We hope you enjoy *Work and Society*.

Part I

Investigating Work

Theory and Work

OVERVIEW

This chapter will:

- Give an understanding of why sociologists are interested in work.
- Consider how and why they attempt to theorise work.
- Explore the big questions sociologists have asked about work.
- Analyse how these have developed down the years.
- Examine how classic concepts have been revisited.

INTRODUCTION

In this chapter we look at how sociologists have tried to theorise work. We want to explore why it is that we need theories of work at all, how is it that theoretical approaches can offer an understanding of work? It examines what is distinct about the kind of theoretical approaches to work that sociologists have compared to other social scientists. Throughout this chapter you will see that sociological theory has grown up in a variety of different and distinct ways over the years and there is not one coherent body of 'theory' that can be pulled from the shelf and applied to real-life problems. Rather, we argue here that theory and the questions that have been asked in the past provide a set of resources which we can draw upon to understand the world of work. We start by looking at why sociologists have looked at work through a theoretical lens. We chart the big questions they have asked about work starting with the classical theorists before going on to look at later sociologists working in the field. In particular, we are interested as to how later theorists operate within, and transgressed the boundaries laid out by the classical theorists. Finally, we look at the contemporary ways in which sociologists theorise work and draw attention to the way much of this analysis draws on the classical tradition. In this chapter we want the reader to gain both an understanding of, and confidence in, applying and using theory in the workplace and work. We want the reader to think of theory as a toolbox which can be drawn on selectively to aid understanding of events, problems and issues.

THE SOCIOLOGICAL MISSION

So why should sociologists be interested in theory? The short answer is that sociology is essentially a theoretical subject. It is an attempt to understand the social world systematically and as such it deploys theory in going beyond simple description of that world. If, for example, we were simply to describe a workplace we might well produce some very interesting accounts. These might include the numbers of workers, their backgrounds, the technology used, the size of the workplace, and so on. What theoretical approaches enable us to do is look beyond this type of description to understand the deeper significance of patterns, social norms and values. They also let us compare and contrast different types of work across time and space by allowing us to study in abstract distinct components of labour.

The classical theorists – Karl Marx, Emile Durkheim and Max Weber – laid the foundations of sociological theorisation about work. Each was trying to understand the complexity of social change in modernity and central to this project was the transformation of work, organisations and social structures. They shared a concern about the impact of industrialisation on individuals and their communities and these issues were explored through issues of power, rationalisation, alienation, the development of class society and increasing specialisation.

What then distinguishes sociological approaches to the theorisation of work? As we will see later in this chapter and at other points in this book, sociology is not a homogenous whole, rather, it is made up of different approaches, sometimes complementary, often contradictory to one another. But it is possible to see something distinctly sociological when compared to other disciplines. First, sociology allows us to combine a study of small-scale social interaction with an analysis of much larger communities – be they factories, industries or countries. Sociologists take as their starting point the idea of the social relationship as being fundamental to the understanding of industrial society. Central to much of this is the concept of the employment relationship under capitalism which, put simply, is the interface between capital and labour in the context of paid work. Sociologists attempt to understand how this relationship is played out in an infinite variety of settings across time and space.

Second, sociology is a critical discipline which tries to understand why things are as they are. Unlike, say, management, sociology as a subject is not concerned with trying to perfect organisations or to take sides necessarily, rather, its purpose is to identify deeper structural forces which shape work patterns. Third, central to a sociological account is that social forms are the product of historical processes. In order to understand any contemporary situation, it is necessary to examine its history. Finally, what is distinct about sociology in relation to work are the ways in which it can combine a variety of theoretical approaches to the empirical study of work. In many ways, the argument of this book is that sociology works best when it combines theoretical insights with empirical research to produce what some people call grounded theory. But our focus on classical theory in informing the study of work does not mean that little of value has emerged since the nineteenth and early twentieth centuries. There have been a series of challenges to the assumptions and positions adopted by the founding fathers. Most recently we have seen the rise of postmodern and post-structural theories which fundamentally challenge many of the assumptions made by earlier generations.

FOUNDATIONS

For sociologists, the foundations of theorisation about work are usually associated with the writing of Karl Marx, Emile Durkheim and Max Weber. In what follows we will look at each of these theorists in turn, examining their main contribution to the area. In a book such as this we can do little more than alert the reader to some of the major themes and encourage them to read and think further about these ideas.

Karl Marx (1818–1883)

Biography:

- Born in Trier in the Rhineland of Jewish descent.
- Educated at the universities of Bonn and Berlin – studied philosophy and law.
- Career as independent scholar, journalist and revolutionary.

Theoretical concerns about work:

- Understanding the development of the capitalist system.
- Studying it by way of a fusion of history, politics, philosophy and economics.
- Writing as the combination of French socialist theory, German philosophy and British political economy.
- Theory forged out of meticulous research, political activism and journalism Most famous for *Communist Manifesto* of 1848; *Capital* (3 vols).
- Saw work as crucial in understanding social development.

Marx was a product of a rich intellectual background that included classical philosophy, legal studies, economics, politics and history. Like the other members of the triumvirate, his work spanned a vast array of interests which was common in European intellectual life at that time. Essentially Marx was attempting to understand the developing capitalist system which was unfolding around him as he studied and wrote. In doing this, he drew on French socialist theory, German philosophy and British political economy. The socialist theory had emerged out of the French Revolution that had rocked Europe in 1789 where the absolutist monarchy had been deposed by a violent revolution. German philosophy was largely the work of Hegel, an idealist philosopher who saw history as an unfolding of a rational logic of societal development. Finally, the British political economy element of Marx's thinking was centred on intellectuals such as Adam Smith and others who had attempted to understand the working of industrial society and its markets.

While Marx found much of value in each of these traditions, he forged his own distinct ideas about industrial society. Marx's ideas about work have to be understood as a complete system for thinking about and analysing capitalism. He was engaged upon the construction of elaborate models and conceptual apparatus in order to do this. For Marx, work was central to any understanding of human existence and the social relations in society. Marx saw human uniqueness as rooted in their productive capacity. What made them distinct from other animals was the way in which humans produced their own subsistence. They acted on the world in order to live – unlike animals that merely lived off the world. This has two important implications. First, through this process humans became conscious of themselves and the world in which they lived and worked. They perceived themselves as distinct from the world upon which they acted. Second, they quickly came to co-operate with others – family or tribes – in the process of creative work. Therefore, work was fundamentally a social activity – requiring organisation and co-operation between humans. What Marx did was to take this conceptualisation of social relations and use it to analyse how in more complex societies such social relations underpinned economic links.

Marx saw the process of economic development as evolving through distinct stages – primitive, feudalism, capitalism and, finally, socialism. Each stage had its own social system which was closely related to the economic system, or base. For example, a feudal society only works if there is a peasantry tied to land from which they produce a surplus for a lord. In turn, a lord has certain roles and duties to those vassals in his care. Importantly, for Marx, this was not a static system but a dynamic one where advances in one area brought changes to another. So the social relationships that pertained under feudalism could not be sustained in the early stages of capitalism. For Marx, the underlying base of a society and its patterns of ownership explained the social relationships and hierarchies at a particular stage in history. There is great debate as to the extent to which there is autonomy between the economic base and what Marx called the superstructure. In the narrowest interpretation, Marx is portrayed as believing that the base always directly determines the superstructure – change in the former will have a direct consequence in the latter. A more nuanced interpretation would suggest that there is far more autonomy in the relationship between these two elements, that the social relationships of a given society always have scope to take action independent of the economy and its forces.

As society developed, the social relations became increasingly polarised between the owners of what Marx called the means of production (such as the machinery deployed and the raw material used in production) and those who were increasingly dependent on cash wages to survive, as opposed to being able to make a living by various means. Marx believed that through-out history that societies had contained different social classes which were the social manifestations of underlying structural inequalities. In capitalist society he saw the creation of a proletariat and a bourgeoisie – or simply workers and capitalists. It was the antagonism between these two classes which created movement in the system, which eventually Marx believed, would bring about its downfall. But why was this so? As societies developed from primitive to feudal, and then on to capitalist stages, they developed an ever more sophisticated division of labour and with this shift there was a change in the social relationships within society.

TEXT BOX 2.1 DIVISION OF LABOUR

The division of labour is the way in which a particular society organises and allocates work. Usually the more complex and advanced a society, the greater the division of labour into ever more specialist functions.

Following on from the writers in the political economy tradition such as Adam Smith, Marx recognised that capitalism needed to increase specialisation in order to become more efficient. Instead of a craft worker being able to create an object from start to finish, a greater division of labour meant that tasks would increasingly be broken down and that individuals would concentrate on these routines rather than generalise. The advantage for the employer was that the pace of production could be increased and individuals could be substituted with less disruption as there was less skill in each task. Here is Adam Smith's classic account of the process applied to the manufacture of pins:

> One man draws out the wire, another straights it, a third cuts it, a fourth points it, a fifth grinds it at the top for receiving the head; to make the head requires two or three distinct operations; to put it on, is a peculiar business, to whiten the pins is another; it is even a trade by itself to put them into paper; and the important business of making a pin is, in this manner, divided into about eighteen distinct operations, which in some manufactories, are all performed by distinct hands.
>
> (Adam Smith, *The Wealth of Nations*, 1776, quoted in Thomas 1999: 109)

Marx believed that in the modern capitalist economy the nature of this work was being transformed – degraded, dehumanised and increasingly specialised. This process led to a state of alienation, an estrangement between the worker, the objects they worked on and those around them. Marx believed that under such conditions workers became increasingly alienated in a variety of ways:

- alienation in the sense of absence of control by producer of the product;
- alienation in the sense of greater division of labour – degradation of work, loss of intrinsic interest;
- alienation in the sense of marketisation of relations – reduction of humanity to exchange value;
- alienation in the sense of work becoming mindless and repetitive – distinction between humans and animals becomes less clear.

Marx was also interested in mapping the details of the relationship between capital and labour at the level of the shop floor as well as at greater levels of abstraction. In doing so he broke down the individual elements of work processes and the relationships that underpinned them. This can be seen in his discussion of the labour process.

TEXT BOX 2.2 THE LABOUR PROCESS

The process by which products are created by human labour for satisfaction of human need.

Marx identified the components of the labour process as:

* purposeful action (work);
* the object upon which work is performed;
* the instruments of that work.

Marx believed that in the modern era the capitalist system of production would revolutionise work and work organisation. As capitalists sought increased profits they would invest in capital equipment. As this process took place, so capitalists monopolised the ownership of the means of production and thus workers could do little but offer their labour to the highest bidder. The relationship between capital and labour would be more apparent than ever but the nature of this exploitation would be more hidden than ever – the laws of capital appearing as natural. By this he meant that what appeared as a simple transaction – the buying and selling of labour was in fact the manifestation of a complex social and economic process – not a value-free exchange of equal partners.

Crucially, what Marx identified was that what capital bought was labour power, not labour. Capital made its profit from the surplus value between the cost of labour and raw materials and the price of the goods when sold on. Thus capital was not rewarding labour fully for the value labour added to the raw material. This is why Marx saw capitalism as an exploitative system as it derived its wealth from the abstraction of this surplus value.

Central to Marx's theorisation of modern society is the relationship between capital and labour – the employment relationship. This is both an abstract concept and one that in turn can be applied to any given form of (paid) work. At its simplest this relationship can be expressed as the tension between employers on the one hand, who wants to buy as much labour as possible for as little money as possible, and on the other the employee who wants to sell their labour for the highest price. For the political economists, this was a simple market transaction carried out between equals. For Marx, it was overlaid with a variety of social inequalities and power relations than meant that the exchange was far from neutral. It did, however, appear to be a neutral or natural system rather than one constructed by human action.

There was, therefore, a fundamental contradiction at the heart of capitalism. It was a system that was built on the inequality between capital and labour and it was this very contradiction that provided the motive power for change to occur. This was in the historic tendency for capital to demand ever-greater returns on its investment. As greater and greater levels of capital were invested in the productive process, labour would be pressed ever harder for greater returns. The result, Marx believed, would be the eventual overthrow of the capitalist system by the proletariat so over-worked that they no longer had anything to lose in creating revolution.

There are four points to make about Marx's writing:

1 Social relationships are embedded in economic systems; one should understand society in terms of its productive development.
2 Capital purchases labour power – not labour – therefore there is a need for management; labour needs to be managed in order to maximise a return, managers are not simply purchasing a block of labour.
3 This in turn means that there is a fundamentally antagonistic relationship between capital and labour; the interests of worker and capitalist are not the same and this creates tensions between them that are embedded in the very system itself.
4 Market forces, not individual wishes, create change; the capitalist system is impersonal in that, however caring an employer may wish to be, ultimately they need to act in a certain way in order to survive.

Taken together, these points provide us with an important base for thinking about any form of paid work within capitalist society, the questions they imply are as relevant today as they were when Marx was writing in the middle of the nineteenth century.

Emile Durkheim (1858–1917)

Biography

- French.
- First sociologist to hold an academic post.
- Social democratic politics.

Theoretical concerns about work

- Division of labour in society.
- Forms of attachment.
- Professional groups and their ethics.

Like Marx, Emile Durkheim was concerned about the transition of society from feudalism to capitalism. He sought to understand the effect that such a transition had on people and the social groups of which they formed a part. He was interested in what was distinctive about modernity and its social forms and social order. Sociologically Durkheim is important because he is one of the first to use the term sociology (after Comte) and he held a sociological professorship in the French university system. His work attempted to find the collective social, rather than psychological, reasons why people acted as they did. In doing so, Durkheim analysed both traditional and modern society, comparing and contrasting the way in which they were organised.

As in Marx's work, we need to see Durkheim's theory as representing a whole, but it contains conceptual tools which we need to understand. One of the most important elements here is the interest in the division of labour (Durkheim [1893] 1964). Like Marx and others, Durkheim saw the increasing division of labour as one of the most important aspects of modernity. This specialisation was an unavoidable consequence of industrialisation but it was one that he recognised as having important consequences for individuals and their communities. In order to understand the role of the division of labour in Durkheim's work we need to see the way in which he characterised the distinct stages of development.

In traditional societies, Durkheim believed that social order was realised through what he called mechanical solidarity. This referred to the very basic and simple links between people living and working in small-scale communities. Villages and towns could function because of the proximity of one person to another; the division of labour was basic because what was produced and the services given were themselves basic. The division of labour within such communities was not complex. A blacksmith, for example, could service the entire community's need from chains, horseshoes to nails. In modern urban social systems such a division of labour was impossible so that, to extend the model of the blacksmith, each product created in a smithy in the small-scale community was now produced in greater volumes in a specialist manufactory. Now one group of workers would make the chains, another would make the horseshoes and a third would make the nails. Indeed, as we saw with the quote from Adam Smith on p. 16, even the seemingly most basic product was itself subject to ever greater specialisation.

For Durkheim, the consequences of such a trend were profound. The mechanical solidarity characteristic of earlier times was changing into what he called organic solidarity. Using a biological metaphor, Durkheim believed that modern societies were marked by a more complex specialisation which resembled that in the natural world. In industrial societies, communities would achieve social solidarity through a greater interdependence of one part on another. The division of labour necessary for industrial efficiency meant that individuals were more dependent on others than in the past. In mechanical solidarity there was a superficial sense in which existence was more human but Durkheim argued that this was at the expense of suppressing individuality to the needs of the community. In organic solidarity there was the potential for an ethical individualism. By this, Durkheim meant that people could achieve a greater sense of individual freedom but that this was dependent on society. People could achieve this freedom only by being part of a collective endeavour that was socially coherent.

This model of the transition from one form of society to another was an ideal. In reality, Durkheim recognised that societies could develop a division of labour that did not adequately reflect the individual talents of its membership. For Durkheim, the ideal society and its division of labour were based on meritocratic principles. In other words, people were able to find a niche that best suited their abilities and qualifications. Unfortunately society, as presently constructed, meant that this did not always occur and that there was a forced division of labour where people occupied the wrong position because of social inequality. If forced into a specific division of labour, or if jobs were allocated inappropriately, then the result would be a lack of social cohesion. This lack of cohesion is how Durkheim explained tension and conflict within society. The danger of an imperfectly realised division of labour was that such a situation would lack a moral authority over both individuals and groups. Durkheim called this *anomie* or a lack of attachment. There are parallels to Marx's notion of alienation but these concepts are not interchangeable.

For Durkheim, then, social order in modernity was potentially problematic because of the risk that people felt socially isolated as a result of what he called abnormal division. He recognised that in modernity there was a greater distance between the individual or family and the state. Society was more remote from the individual than in traditional societies where, superficially, it was all encompassing. His solution to this is to see the importance of occupational and professional groups which mediate between the needs of the state on the one hand, and the individual on the other (Durkheim 1992). Fundamental to such groups was the understanding that they were essentially democratic in that the ethics of the groups were emergent from them. Actors were constrained by these ethics precisely because they were the products of the collective. Guilds had been a model for this type of group but the difference was that the latter were re-imagined as dynamic rather that static and unchanging. So work and the occupational groups based on them played a crucial role in Durkheim's theories about modernity.

Max Weber (1864–1920)

Biography

- German.
- Liberal conservative.
- Historian, economist, sociologist.
- Eclectic thinker/writer.

Theoretical concerns about work

- Sociology as the study of social action.
- Pessimistic view of modernity.
- Rationality.

- Bureaucracy.
- Origins and specificity of capitalism.

Weber was interested in the way modern capitalism had developed in the West rather than in other places or points in history. He wanted to know what was distinct about the experience of Western Europe in its transition to modernity. Weber wanted to account for why industrialism occurred in the form and place it had and to find out what combination of factors had caused this to happen. He was not seeking to claim that Europe was special, the elements of industrialisation had, after all, existed in other societies at other points in history. Rather Weber was interested in the range of factors which had combined at a certain point – these included technical development and intellectual trends. Like the other theorists, Weber's ideas have to be seen as relational – so his theory of industrial development has to be seen in relation to his ideas on rationalisation, ideal types as well as other elements. Fundamental to making sense of Weber is his idea of the ideal type.

TEXT BOX 2.3 IDEAL TYPE

An analytical model which represents a pure concept against which the 'reality' of the world may be measured. This method allows the classification and comparison between phenomena. For example, when studying the organisation, Weber developed an ideal type of bureaucracy which the modern organisation would need to display in order to function. Empirical study then compares that ideal with reality.

When we look at or use Weber's concepts, we need to bear in mind that they are often these idealisations that are used to conceptualise rather than describe a reality. The important role of ideal typology is that it allows comparison between historical periods or between different examples of the same phenomena – thus we can compare and contrast bureaucracy in ancient China with that in modern organisations. We will return to these ideal types in what follows.

The development of 'Western' capitalism

Weber, as we have seen, was interested in why it was that capitalism developed in the West and at the time it did. He argued that this was because of a series of interlinked factors coupled with the belief systems and actions of societies. So the technological advance that made industrial development possible was underpinned by cultural factors. In particular, Weber thought that the distinct work ethic pertaining within parts of Europe in the eighteenth century provided the spark for other developments. Weber identified the so-called Protestant work ethic as a crucial factor in capitalist development because of the effect of its ideology. To understand this we need to understand what was distinct about Protestantism.

In Catholicism, which had been the dominant religion in Europe until the Reformation of the sixteenth century, people sinned and then repented and they could be saved right up to the point of death. In Protestantism, however, this was not the case as there was a group of people, already chosen by God to enter heaven, called the elect. If you were not one of the elect, you would not be saved and would go to hell. The problem for the faithful was that they could not know if they were part of the elect or not. What developed was a culture in which people tried to reassure themselves as to their position in the afterlife by acting well and working hard in their life on earth. One aspect of this was a moral conservatism especially over conspicuous consumption. Weber believed that Protestants adopted an ascetic lifestyle dominated by self-denial. The consequences of this were rigid self-discipline and a belief in hard work and commitment to a craft or work role. To be a good worker was a possible sign of being part of the elect. This combination of factors laid the foundations of capitalism in that it provided a disciplined workforce; it legitimised individual profit-seeking since this was willed by God; it legitimised the division of labour as specialised labour was a duty and led to the creation of a surplus which in turn was invested rather than consumed. Weber's point here is not that Protestantism set out to create capitalism, nor that this made Protestants better than other religions. Rather, Weber tried to analyse what such a culture did in combination with other factors. In many ways, he claimed that the rise of capitalism was an unintended result of this religious belief rather than its intended aim. One of the important factors he identified was the process of rationalisation within the West with a greater emphasis on calculability.

Rationality

Another theme in Weber's work is that of rationality. Weber believed that industrial societies, as part of their development, were marked by increasingly rationalised and calculated action. Making use of his ideal type model, Weber believed that sociology's mission was to understand why actors acted in the way they did. He believed that fundamentally all action could be viewed as being rational from the point of view of the individual. As Weber wrote: '[A] thing is never irrational in itself, but only from a particular . . . point of view. For the unbeliever every religious way of life is irrational, for the hedonist every ascetic standard' (Weber, cited in Brubaker 1991: 35). So sociologists had to pay careful attention to individual and group belief in order to understand why people acted as they did. Very broadly, Weber identified four different types of action – traditional, affective, value and instrumental.

- traditional – where a person is carried along by habit and custom;
- affective – where someone is carried along by feeling;
- value (*wertrational*) – a conscious belief in the value of acting in a particular way;
- instrumental (*zweckrational*) – consciously calculating attempt to achieve desired ends with appropriate means.

The first two types of action were, Weber believed, those of pre-modern society where people were driven by custom and patterns of hierarchy based on an unquestioning belief or on emotion. These forms of action, while rational, lacked a sense of reflexivity – they were not subject to a great deal of calculation and reflection. The second two types were those more likely to be found in modernity. In modern societies, action was subject to far more reflection and calculation. Indeed, there was a trend towards ever greater levels of rationalisation in all aspects of society and its institutions. Weber saw this as an inevitable consequence of the development of capitalist society. Those earlier types of action were simply not those that would support modern society and its division of labour. This rationalisation process can be seen at different levels within the institutions of the modern state, in organisations and in the relationships between groups and individuals. For example, the division of labour, which we saw was a theme in the work of both Marx and Durkheim, was a manifestation of this rationalising process for Weber. The greater division of labour allowed increased production and the creation of mass markets. Work was subject to calculation and design in order to make it more efficient. At its most extreme, each aspect of the work process is broken down and designed to make it as efficient as possible regardless of tradition, custom or sentiment (see later chapters on industrial control and Taylorism).

Perhaps the best illustration of the process of rationalisation was in Weber's discussion of bureaucracy. In modernity, capitalism would only work if its organisations were run along ordered lines with specialised functions drawn up along technical lines and hierarchies. Older forms of industrial organisation – those, say, where an owner manager could control every aspect of their business, were impossible to replicate in large-scale manufacturing on multiple sites. Again, Weber using his ideal typologies drew up the characteristics that such a modern organisation would need:

- organisational tasks are distributed among various positions as official duties – clear-cut division of labour/specialisation, expertise of staff, technical qualifications;

- hierarchy – position of offices clear, lines of responsibility below and above;
- formal establishment of rules and regulations – govern official decisions and actions;
- continuity in spite of changes to personnel – impersonal;
- specialised administrative staff – dealing directly with keeping the organisation going – not directly making things;
- officials expected to assume an impersonal orientation in their contacts with clients and other officials: clients as cases, disregard of personal considerations, designed to stop personal considerations clouding rational judgements;
- employment in an organisation constitutes a career for officials – full-time official looks forward to job for life, based on technical qualification rather than political or family connection, qualification tested by exam.

The major features to emphasize in these six points are that this 'ideal' is impersonal – one's place in the bureaucracy is won through qualification, and is essentially meritocratic. Decisions are made with regard to rule, not personal decision or connection. Therefore, a decision is carried out because of rules and regulations which have been arrived at through a formal process of reflection. Bureaucracy has come to have very negative connotations and Weber was aware of its weaknesses but he was also aware of the positive features. The impersonality of modern organisations is their strength as well as their weakness. They are impersonal in that they are fair, with all decisions and appointments subject to rules and with the decision-making transparent. But equally they are impersonal in the sense that they are inhuman. Weber is often viewed as the most pessimistic of the founding fathers because he viewed modernity as an ambiguous process where human individuality and creativity would be progressively squeezed out, modern society would become dehumanised and soul-less.

Classical theory and theories of work

As we have seen, the classic period of sociology provides a rich set of theoretical approaches on which we can draw. Essentially the classical theorists were attempting to make sense of societies undergoing the trauma of industrialisation and urbanisation. These were entirely new experiences. Each in their own way created a framework in order to understand these events and processes. In each, the key feature of this transition is work and the workplace.

It should be apparent to the reader that sociology was founded on a concern with the world of production, class and state, and that each of the three founding fathers discussed here was inspired by industrial and political revolutions, and by the emergent industrial capitalism. These are very much 'public sphere' concerns: that is, they are to do with civil, economic and political society. The historical period that led to the birth of sociology was characterised by the emerging separation of the public from the private arena of the home and family as industrialism was advancing. The founding fathers' overriding concern with the former sphere was inherently gendered since men dominated public life and women were increasingly being relegated to the private sphere (see Chapter 5). Influential discourses of men and women at the time very much saw men as naturally rational creatures, active and competitive and thus suited to public life, while women were seen as irrational, closer to nature, more emotional and passive – suited for the private sphere of the home. This so-called natural woman/cultured man dichotomy (Sydie 1987) impacted on the interests and ideas of the three theorists: they were far less interested in the private arena and their ideas were shaped by a belief in natural differences between women and men. In Durkheim's *The Division of Labour*, for example, although he does provide a short analysis of changing relations between women and men towards more complex forms of marriage, he suggests that women and men are 'carrying out their own nature' (Evans 2003: 19).

It was Frederick Engels, who wrote with Marx, who was best known of the early 'fathers' for exploring historical changes in the private sphere of the family and for relating these to public sphere developments in state and production. Most famously, in his (1884) *The Origin of the Family, Private Property and the State*, Engels links the growth in private property to the decline in matriarchal societies – and the emergence of women's subordination to men – as men sought to establish ways to pass newly privatised property to their own (i.e. biological) offspring. Ideas from Engels' work were to be picked up in the 1970s by Marxist-feminists who were looking for new ways to explain gender inequalities in society, to link private and public spheres, and to interweave theoretical explanations for relations of reproduction and of production.

Throughout the book we look to the three founding fathers for their profound influence on the sociology of work. No doubt many readers will already be asking about the absence of founding mothers, and this is a question that vexes feminist sociology (Delamont 2003; Evans 2003; Lengermann and Niebrugge-Brantley 1998). Part of this is because women were indeed writing on issues pertinent to sociology in and prior to this historical period, but their impact on the sociological canon has been minimal. For example, Harriet Martineau (1802–1876), who could be described as one of the first founding mothers of sociology, rarely features in mainstream books or courses on sociological theory. She wrote about positivism and method (translating Comte's writings into English), slavery, capital and labour; and the degradation of women, among other issues. On class, she suggested, reflecting Marx's analysis of the agency of the working class. 'The progression or emancipation of any class usually, if not always, takes place through the efforts of individuals of that class' (1837; *Society in America*, III, III, II, II) (Hoecker-Drysdale 1992). And Marianne Schnitger Weber (1870–1954) wrote sociological texts in her own right as well as a biography of her sociologist husband, Max. The earlier work of Mary Wollstonecraft has been more widely recognised historically. Her *The Vindication of the Rights of Woman* (1792) attacked the cultural conditioning of girls in childhood, arguing that women's subordination was neither inevitable nor natural. If women were brought up like boys, Wollstonecraft argued, they would be more assertive and better able to enter employment. Despite this pioneering critique of natural woman/cultured man, this dichotomy (though see Text box 2.4) was to remain dominant and it very much influenced the early development of sociology.

TEXT BOX 2.4 A PROBLEMATIC DICHOTOMY

It should be noted that the natural/cultured, irrational/rational, female/male distinction was also classed and 'racialised'. Wollstonecraft herself only spoke about emancipatory opportunities for upper middle-class women since working-class women were seen as more debased. And in 1851 an influential speech by freed slave Sojourner Truth (1797–1883) showed that black women were not seen as passive, delicate creatures in need of male protection:

> That man over there says that women need to be helped into carriages, and lifted over ditches, and to have the best place everywhere. Nobody ever helps me into carriages, or over mud-puddles, or gives me any best place! And ain't I a woman? Look at me! Look at my arm! I have ploughed and planted, and gathered into barns, and no man could head me! And ain't I a woman?
>
> (Stanton *et al.* 1889: 114–17)

Women's voices were rendered largely invisible in early sociology and women's lives were ignored on the whole by its founders. As a result, the sociological mainstream classical tradition has been termed the 'malestream'. Ann Oakley critiqued the malestream (1974: 4) as follows:

[M]ale orientation may so colour the organization of sociology as a discipline that the invisibility of women is a structured male view, rather than a superficial flaw. The male focus, incorporated into the definitions of subject areas, reduces women to a side issue from the start.

In this context in our book, while we take our start from the three founding fathers and look to how later writers have worked within the boundaries they laid out, we are also keen to show how the boundaries have been critiqued and transgressed. As feminist sociologist Dorothy Smith (1988) advises, we need to see the everyday as problematic. In the next section, 'Later developments', we hope to do just this.

LATER DEVELOPMENTS

How did the classical tradition develop in later discussions of work? Here it is important to stress the fragmentary nature of the development of sociological theory around work and also understand the ways in which sociological ideas were used. Equally, it is important to understand the way theorisation about work, and the workplace in particular, are not the sole preserve of sociologists. Arguably one of the most important disciplines to look at in terms of development of theory about paid work is management. One of the earliest exponents of such a discipline was Fredrick W. Taylor who developed what has been called scientific management, and sometimes Taylorism. Taylor was born into a reasonably wealthy family but decided to undertake an apprenticeship in pattern-making and machining. He later joined the Midvale Steel Company and worked his way up the company. He noted the poor, sometimes brutal, management techniques coupled with the slack way in which workers went about their tasks. Taylor was obsessed with rationalising the productive process by creating a perfect system for undertaking any particular task. His idea was that if the machinery could be run at its greatest efficiency with the workers operating them in a rational manner then the company would thrive and could reward the worker well. Taylor believed that his scientific management, once understood by both management and labour, would be adopted as it was a neutral system which benefited both sides – the one with greater output and efficiency, the other with increased pay and bonuses.

Taylor will crop up at other points in this book but for our purposes here he is important in terms of his attempt to theorise and analyse work processes, albeit in an applied rather than more abstract way. At the heart of his theory was a model of human behaviour with regard to work, the idea of economic man. This is a concept usually associated with economists who suggest that (male) workers can be understood as rationally motivated. If you offer them more pay, they will work harder. This is a theory that strips away or largely ignores other motivations and ideas about why and how people work. It ignores the norms and values within a particular workplace as it sees motivation as entirely explained by monetary reward (see Kanigel 1997; Rose 1988).

Neo-Durkheim approaches: structural functionalism and the study of work

One of the earliest influences theoretically on the study of work sociology was structural functionalism. The origins of this school can be found in Durkheimian sociology but it also draws on the writing of Pareto, and anthropologists such as Malinowski and Radcliffe-Brown. Later this approach was popularised by the US sociologist Talcott Parsons. At the heart of structural functionalism is the concept that society is made up of a series of intelligible structures which are differentiated but interdependent.

TEXT BOX 2.5 STRUCTURAL FUNCTIONALISM

A theoretical approach to the world where societies are conceived of as social systems. The social structures within these systems are seen to have a functional role in contributing to the creation and reproduction of parts and the whole of the social system.

The role of the sociologist is to identify these structures and the nature of the functions they perform. Structural functionalism greatly influenced a number of sociological studies of work and was attractive to those trying to understand modern organisations. This was because industrial organisations could readily be envisaged as social systems. Initially the most prominent of these was the group of researchers engaged on the Hawthorne experiments in the Western Electric Company in Chicago between 1927 and 1932. Their studies examined the relationship between output and variations in the inputs to production – factors such as lighting, heating and payments systems. The team made the distinction between formal and informal aspects of the organisation. The 'formal' are systems, policies, rules and regulations of the plant as well as those patterns of human interaction which are supposed to exist. The informal aspects by contrast are all those social aspects and relationships which are not formally recognised. These latter features may or may not be functional to the firm in question.

As Brown (1992) and others have argued, structural functionalism was the dominant social theory of the 1940s and 1950s and as such had an important influence, whether explicit or implicit, on many early industrial sociological studies. This is particularly true of organisational sociology and parts of industrial sociology. While dominant theoretically for a time, structural functionalism was never unchallenged within sociology generally or particularly in the field of work. The two most basic criticisms are that such an approach tends to reify the organisation wherein it is seen to have needs and aims independent of the people who make it up. Second, functionalism has difficulty in explaining conflict within organisations. As an approach, it views order or equilibrium as the normal state and claims that disharmony or conflict is the result of factors which need to be ameliorated or excluded. Thus, whereas Marxists saw conflict as fundamentally part of capitalism, functionalists viewed it as a system in disequilibrium.

Functionalism was also influential in other parts of the sociology of work such as ethnography. Harper and Lawson (2003) argue that the cultural sociological study of work shares much with anthropology and especially its roots in functionalism. Here it is important to note the influence of the Chicago School, the group of sociologists at the University of Chicago's sociology department. Early figures such as Everett Hughes sought to understand the effect of different social systems on professions and occupations. Hughes became editor of the *American Journal of Sociology* in the early 1950s and devoted his first issue to the cultural aspects of work, including classic examples of work ethnography such as Donald Roy and Eli Chinoy (Harper and Lawson 2003: xii–xiii).

TEXT BOX 2.6 SYMBOLIC INTERACTIONISM

Symbolic interactionism explains social action and interaction as the outcome of meaning emerging from social processes. These meanings do not reside in things but are interpreted and constructed through social interaction.

Another aspect of the Chicago School in relation to work sociology is in terms of the development of symbolic interactionist and ethnomethodological traditions. Both these related strands conceptualise micro interactions in social settings and thinking through how they relate to wider social forms. While not exclusively concerned with work settings, clearly their ideas are applicable to a number of organisational environments such as hospitals in the case of Strauss and his colleagues (1963), or prisons and mental hospitals in the case of Goffman (1961).

TEXT BOX 2.7 ETHNOMETHODOLOGY

The idea that actors are skilled and knowledgeable about their role in the social world. Ethnomethodologists are interested in the tacit knowledge that actors have and how they go on in the world seeking to show how people use this knowledge in everyday interaction with others.

Neo-Weberian approaches – affluent workers, identity and action

Functionalist theorists were clearly influenced by Durkheim but during the 1960s various writers drew upon Weber's ideas on work and organisations. In the UK the most famous and influential was the Affluent Worker study (Goldthorpe *et al.* 1968a, 1968b, 1969). This research was originally designed to test the idea that working-class people were gradually becoming more like those in the middle class in terms of behaviour and attitudes. Goldthorpe and his colleagues set about testing this hypothesis in the context of work organisations in Luton in Bedfordshire. In part, the study rejected a systems approach because it failed to adequately recognise the point of view of the actors themselves. Weber's sociology had at its heart the idea of meaningful understanding. This was the idea that you had to take seriously what people themselves understood about the situation they found themselves in, in order to interpret their actions and beliefs. Although it was never the intention of the study, the team developed a conceptualisation of so-called 'orientations to work' which were ideal typologies for understanding the ways in which groups of workers would choose to work for particular companies and not others.

Weber's ideas have also continued to be influential within organisational sociology and business school approaches. His ideas on bureaucracy and the nature of industrial organisation have been reassessed partly in the wake of shifts within organisational practice over the last two or more decades (see, for example, Albrow 1997; Du Gay 2000, 2005; Ray and Reed 1994).

The reassertion of Marxian ideas and the labour process

If the affluent worker studies were an attempt to revive Weberian approaches to industrial sociology, then the late 1960s and early 1970s also saw the revival in Marxian concepts in analysing work. In 1974, Harry Braverman wrote his seminal book, *Labor and Monopoly Capitalism*. This book has become a classic in discussions of work, particularly for those writers working within a Marxist tradition. Braverman reinvigorated Marx's discussion of the labour process by suggesting that capitalists systematically tried to deskill work by means of the separation of conception and execution of work processes. Put simply, management attempted to monopolise the knowledge about how work should be carried out. They would design the machinery, specify the way in which it was operated and its pace. The worker would be left to undertake a simplified function. As should be apparent, Braverman was drawing not only on Marx but also on Taylor and his ideas of rational scientific management. Braverman's book became a best seller and is still in print. His work and the debate it spawned are one of the major theoretical trends within the sociology of work. But this is not to say that it has not been heavily criticised. There are a number of problems identified in Braverman's work. First is the idea that it makes sweeping generalisations about work over the past century. Second, there is a lack of consideration of the role of resistance against these trends. Third, there is the criticism that it implies that management are obsessed with deskilling rather than production. Finally, some criticise the book for its lack of consideration of subjectivity, rather, what is stressed are the structural trends underpinning deskilling. In a wider sense, Braverman's work had a detrimental effect on work sociology in that it narrowed the focus of what the focus of the discipline could be, neglecting other methods and approaches (see Epstein 1990).

There were a range of more fruitful developments within the sociology of work in the 1960s and 1970s and these have worked with a variety of theoretical traditions. While we have limited space to consider these fully, it is worth noting studies such as Michael Burawoy's *Manufacturing Consent*, which is clearly a Marxian-influenced ethnography of workplace culture. Equally there were a number of sociologists in the UK writing in the 1960s who developed classical sociology in the context of work. Notable examples of this can be seen in writers such as Alan Fox, John Eldridge, Huw Beynon and Richard Brown. What is interesting about these writers is that their work has a place outside the immediate area of the sociology of work, and to some degree can be seen as representing what Savage has labelled 'the Golden Age' of work sociology in Britain (see Savage 2000a).

Feminist theory and work

Feminist theorists began to make a real impact on the sociological understanding of work in the 1970s. It is important first to stress the heterogeneous nature of theories that have been termed feminist since versions emerged that focused on different explanations of gender inequalities: the family, the labour market, sexual violence, and so on. Indeed, it is more useful to talk about *feminisms* than about one over-arching feminism. Nevertheless, it is still useful to highlight how writers labelled feminist have influenced sociological theorising on work.

Some second-wave feminists (Text box 2.8) looked to explain gender differences in work by drawing on and adapting existing theories of work. Marxist ideas were particularly influential, with the class analysis retained and gender incorporated into class accounts. For example, Veronica Beechey (1977) and Irene Breugel (1979) re-worked Marx's reserve army of labour: that capitalism needs a reserve army of labour that it can draw on in times of boom and lay off in slumps. Women provided a flexible and disposable reserve army since the home is their first priority and employment is secondary. Engels' writing on private property and family was also re-examined with Marxist-feminists looking to his argument that women's oppression was derived from class exploitation; that once they were involved in the labour market alongside men, women would unite with men to work for a socialist future of equality (see Sayers *et al.* 1987).

TEXT BOX 2.8 FIRST- AND SECOND-WAVE FEMINISM

First-wave feminism is associated with nineteenth- and early twentieth-century campaigns for, for example, female emancipation and access to education, while second-wave feminism emerged in the 1970s in the USA and Europe.

For other feminist theorists, such Marxist accounts were limited by the over-domination of class. Sociologist Sylvia Walby (1986) argued that gender must be seen to stand apart from class as an independent source of inequality, and that gender needed its own theory. Building on early models of patriarchy, including those of Heidi Hartmann (1979) and of Christine Delphy (1977), Walby argued that key patriarchal relations are found in domestic work, paid work, the state, male violence, sexuality and cultural institutions, and these six come together to form a complex system of patriarchy. Walby went on to develop her model of patriarchy still further, suggesting 'differentiated patriarchies' to recognise that the forms and intensity of women's subordination to men are not uniform across time or place. In 'private patriarchies', for example, men exploit women mainly within the private sphere of the home, and in 'public patriarchies' the public sphere of the labour market is the main site of women's oppression. Although gender must be seen to stand apart from class, for Walby, the system of patriarchal relations does need to be articulated alongside a system of capitalist relations. It is for this reason that Walby – and Hartmann too – earned the title of a dual systems theorist.

The difficulties in combining two already complex large-scale structural theories of capitalism and patriarchy to explain both gender and class work inequalities (never mind bringing in other inequalities like 'race') were not insubstantial. Hartmann herself lamented in 1979 'the unhappy marriage of Marxism and Feminism' that was resulting. This lament links us to the final section on contemporary issues in theory and work in which we refer to post-modern and post-structural developments in sociology that were to critique any attempt at providing such large-scale theories.

CONTEMPORARY ISSUES AND FUTURE TRENDS

So what are the current trends that have emerged in the past few years in theory and work and what is likely to be the direction of future theorisation? As in the past, it is important not to see these as representing a completely homogenous body of work.

Ritzer and McDonaldization

George Ritzer's (1998) *The McDonaldization of Society* has become important shorthand for many who talk about work. Ritzer uses the ideas of both Weber and Marx to portray contemporary developments in social and economic life. Essentially this is the ever-greater rationalisation of every aspect of modern life, including work. Using the management techniques and processes employed by the fast food chain as a metaphor, Ritzer suggests that much of today's work processes are similarly being broken down, simplified and rationalised. Work is increasingly subject to control, supervision and simplification. Ritzer's book is brilliantly seductive at offering a theory not only of the future of work but of industrial society. Perhaps, however, it is too neat and tidy and we need to be alive to the contradictions in the work-place that have always interested sociologists such as how workers resist control, or examining the real-world problems managers and supervisors have in controlling staff.

Post-structural and postmodern developments

In opposition to the above attempts to develop theories of large-scale structural change, sociology has also been influenced by various 'post-' developments. The best known, postmodernism is based on the belief that social reality is socially constructed. Large theories of social change – or meta-narratives – like Marxism that dominated modernism have failed to realise that society is fragmented, for many postmodernists. Postmodernism instead heralded an 'incredulity towards meta-narratives' (Lyotard 1984: xxiv), with a new emphasis on, among other issues, the fragmentation of social classes; the emergence of new interest groups; and consumption replacing work as a source of identity, as Bauman puts it: 'Postmodernism is maintained by a view of the human world as irreducibly and irretrievably pluralistic, split into a multi-tude of sovereign units and sites of authority, with no hierarchical or vertical order' (1992: 35). The critique of meta-accounts impacted on theoretical ap-proaches to gender inequalities too. As an over-arching theory, patriarchy was already being critiqued within feminism for failing to account for heterogeneity in women's lives, changes over time and variations across place. A more recent alternative to patriarchy has been the emergence of 'middle level' theorising of gender inequalities. In place of discussions of patriarchy and patriarchies in cross-national analyses of gendered work, in the sociology of work cul-tures, and in the sociology of embodied work, and so on, we have seen the formulation and use of ideas such as gender systems and gender contracts (Hirdmann 1998); gender régimes (Connell 2002); and gender arrangements (Pfau-Effinger 1998). These all attempt to explain how a range of institu-tions (including the family, industrial relations, emotional relationships) come together in different ways – at different times and in different places – to shape gendered work patterns in the home and the labour market.

The writings of French theorist Michael Foucault have influenced many work and organisational sociologists. His work has allowed contemporary thinkers to develop ideas on power and surveillance at work as well as ideas of discipline, especially self-discipline. Foucault's work is not uncontroversial within the field, as is the case with postmodern and post-structural positions more generally. These divisions boil down to disagreements over the nature of knowledge about the world. For those who reject the 'post-' developments, there is a fear that there is a danger that a critical faculty will be lost. If social scientists can no longer appeal to an objectively intelligible world, all knowledge becomes relative and asking critical questions of powerful groups and individuals is undermined. For the supporters of a 'post-' position, the strength of this approach lies in its ability to deal with nuance and difference. It can help understand ideas of subjectivity and identity in a way that older approaches do not allow for. A good illustration of this debate can be seen in the clashes within the labour process tradition between the supporters of post-structuralism – Knights and Willmott (1989, 1990) – and the detractors Thompson (1993) and Thompson and Smith (1998). The problem with this discussion is that it often falls back onto caricatures of the position of one side of the other. What the postmodern turn has allowed is a shift in focus onto some important questions for the sociology of work which arguably had been ignored. We discuss briefly here the emotions and identity at work

Emotional labour and the sociology of the emotions

Emerging from the critique of an over-focus on the material and the econ-omic in the sociology of work, one of the most interesting trends in the past two decades has been the interest in so-called emotional labour as well as a wider interest in emotions more generally. American sociologist Arlie Hochschild in her book, *The Managed Heart*, coined the phrase 'emotional labour'. Hochschild theorises the role of emotions in work and especially the idea that service workers increasingly had to manage their own emotions in order to provoke a particular response in customers or clients. Partly in response to Hochschild's work, there has been an expansion in interest in the emotions in work, workplaces and organisations. There has also been a reflection on what an interest in the emotions can help us understand about the experience of unemployment and deindustrialisation. There is a tendency in much of this work to claim that the field is relatively new, or that sociology has neglected the emotional aspects of work in its pursuit of other themes (see, for example, Fineman 1993). In reality, sociologists and sociology have long looked at subjective aspects of work, Marx on alienation and Weber on depersonalisation are two longstanding manifestations of this. However, Hochchild's work, in breaking down analytically the elements involved in the study of work, has allowed sociologists to think and theorise about emotions in the workplace in a far more systematic way.

Identity at work

Identity and work is another area which has seen more attention theoretically and is likely to continue to do so in the future. In many ways, identity has long been a concern in sociology but what has renewed interest here have been the changes in the social organisation of work, deindustrialisation and the impact these have had on the way individuals and groups talk about work. For many writers, as we will see later in the book, work in contemporary societies has lost its ability to be a major source of meaning and identity (see Casey 1995; Du Gay 1996; Strangleman 2007). This view is often built upon an assumption that work was of central importance in the past, and invariably that work meant paid employment. The result has been a debate about the so-called end of paid work and the ways in which people look outside of the workplace in order to gain meaning in their lives. This debate is likely to continue to be a significant area of discussion in future years and is interesting as it draws on and develops sociological theory in relation to the past, present and future of work.

One aspect of this area of interest has been the way there is a desire to understand more fully work identity in the past. This can be seen in a number of studies of de-industrialised communities (see Cowie and Heathcott 2003; Dudley 1994; Linkon and Russo 2002). A series of sociological accounts of attachment to work emerged, witnessed in the writing of Michele Lamont (2000) and Randy Hodson (2001). Both these authors tackle theoretically the issue of dignity at work and develop frameworks to do so. In France,

Pierre Bourdieu (Bourdieu *et al.* 1999) also focused on the different feelings and attachments workers had for employment. What all these studies have in common is recognition of the importance of taking seriously workers' own ideas and feelings about the work they do, without doing so at the exclusion of wide social and economic forces. What this writing also displays is an appreciation of generational, gendered, 'racial' and historical difference and the way this structures and informs identity of both individuals and communities over time.

Total Social Organization of Labour (TSOL)

Another welcome development in the sociology of work is the attempt to take up the challenge of considering how we can best explain the organisation and distribution of, and the interconnections between, all types of work. This challenge has been boosted in the UK by Miriam Glucksmann's (1995, 2006) development of her *Total Social Organization of Labour* (TSOL). Here, her aim was to provide an examination of the interconnections between different kinds of work activities, including paid work, informal and formal work and domestic labour; as well as different temporalities and spatialities of work and place. The links between work and non-work have also been an emerging concern. Glucksmann's conceptualisation very much captures how we approach work in this book – we argue that a holistic sociology of work needs to study all forms of work: forms that are not waged as well as those that are waged. Accepting the fundamental links between all forms of work is the only way to reach a full understanding of who does what work, why and with what consequences.

Work–life articulation

Glucksmann's concern with extending the TSOL to also explore the links between work and non-work feeds into current theorising of work–life balance, articulation or reconciliation. Although the term itself has been criticised for problematically contrasting 'work' against 'life', it does reflect academic and policy concerns over how we can achieve better quality lives and not just good jobs. The relationship between 'work' and the rest of people's lives is not a new interest for the sociology of work, of course. Writers have explored the impact of long hours employment on workers' family lives and on their health, for example, they have examined the impact of a lack of paid work on unemployed men's self and identity, and the relationship between women's housework and their opportunities for leisure time has provided fascinating insight into the notion that 'a woman's work is never done'. Similarly, the precursor to work–life articulation; 'work–family' balance, has already framed much of the sociology of women's and men's work. For example, Feldberg and Glen (1979) argued that a 'gender model' was invariably employed to explain women's working lives: in which their personal and family characteristics were used to account for their employment behaviour. In contrast, a 'job model' was used to explain men's lives: a man's paid work not only accounted for his labour market behaviour but his home life, his community interactions and his identity too. Recent moves towards 'work–life' articulation reject the bi-polar picture in which workers (and these are usually female workers) try to reconcile only their family-caring and paid work (Lewis and Lewis 1996). Women, and men, have lives that include many other important spheres, such as leisure and health (Warren 2004). In this way, the study of work can be located more explicitly within peoples' broader daily lives.

CONCLUSION

In this chapter we have attempted to look at the ways in which sociology and sociologists have theorised work and society. We started by looking at the importance of theory when examining work, arguing that, without a theoretical understanding, sociology would be an impoverished empirical approach that would add little to our knowledge of work. The power of sociological approaches to work is in its approach and ambition to both study work at a number of levels to contextualise, compare and contrast; and ask important questions about structural inequality and culture. Throughout this chapter we have suggested that theory needs to be treated and used creatively. Work and the social world are complex systems and we need a range of ways in which to interrogate them. Theory can be thought of as a toolbox which can be creatively drawn on in thinking about the world of work sociologically. While there is nothing wrong with abstract theorisation, some of the best sociology can be seen in the marriage of theoretical insight with empirical research where there is a constant dialogue between the two elements.

FURTHER READING

Korczynski, Hodson and Edwards' *Social Theory at Work* (2006) is an excellent advanced introduction to theoretical approaches to work. It covers both individual theorists as well as wider schools and trends in thought.

Richard Brown's *Understanding Industrial Organisations: Theoretical Perspectives in Industrial Sociology* (1992) is a very good overview of the main approaches adopted by sociologists. It is weaker on more contemporary trends.

Rosalind A. Sydie's *Natural Women, Cultured Men: A Feminist Perspective on Sociological Theory* (1987) is a classic feminist account of sociological theoretical concerns.

WEB SOURCES

Dead sociologists index:
http://www2.pfeiffer.edu/~lridener/DSS/INDEX.HTML

Famous sociologists:
http://www.sociosite.net/topics/sociologists.php

In the classical tradition: modern social theorists, critics and prophets:
http://www.faculty.rsu.edu/~felwell/Theorists/Tradition/index.html

Illuminations:
http://www.uta.edu/huma/illuminations/kell.htm

STUDENT PROJECTS AND ESSAY QUESTIONS

1 Why do we need theories of work?
2 How and in what ways are the classical sociological theorists still important to the sociology of work?
3 What are the strengths and weaknesses of abstract theory in relation to work and employment?
4 Examine your current or a former workplace through a theoretical lens.

Researching Work

▌ OVERVIEW

This chapter will:

- Examine how sociologists go about researching work.
- Raise questions as to the strengths and weaknesses of quantitative and qualitative research methods, approaches, techniques and assumptions, highlighting the growth of combined accounts.
- Stress the central role of ethics in researching work.

▌ INTRODUCTION

In the previous chapter, we looked at how sociologists theorise work. Here we ask the linked question of how sociologists research work. And how, if at all, this differs from other researchers who examine work and society. There are clearly areas where sociologists have much in common with others but we need to consider what is distinct about our focus. We want to argue in this chapter that a sociological approach to the study of work allows a breadth and depth to the examination of work that no other discipline has. How do we back up that claim?

The sociology of work allows us to look at various levels at which work is carried out and organised. At the micro level, sociologists study detailed social interaction between, for example, different groups of workers; workers and their managers; and carers and breadwinners. We examine work relationships, employment relationships, work culture, power and gender, class and 'race'. At the mezzo level, sociology allows us to think about the characteristics of places where work is carried out: firms, factories, homes, and shops. At the macro level, sociological research allows us to investigate the differences and similarities in work between societies. And sociology also allows us to compare and contrast societies at these different levels across time using historical and comparative frameworks.

In this chapter we also ask why sociologists are interested in research methods. We start by stressing the fundamental link between theory and methodology, as well as looking at research questions in sociology and what lies behind them. We then examine how sociologists of work first went about researching work and economic life, how work has been researched since then, and conclude with recent innovations in the study of work. We stress the importance of formulating the right kind of research question and reflecting on the right kind of approach to that question. Throughout, we hope to encourage the reader to reflect on how work, in its myriad forms, can be studied well and imaginatively.

THE SOCIOLOGICAL MISSION

Why is sociology so interested in research and in how it is carried out? Well, methodology is essential for sociologists. This is because methodology is not just about which techniques we use to gather data but refers in addition to how we view the world that we live in. Theory and methodology are linked inextricably: in sociology we 'collect data which initiate, refute or organise our theories' (May 2001: 32). This fundamental connection goes right back to the birth of the discipline and to the writings of the founding fathers of sociology (see next section). Two central concepts represent the link between theory and research: (1) epistemology, which concerns what is appropriate knowledge about the social world; and (2) ontology, which relates to how the social world is viewed – is it external to individuals or do they create it? (Bryman 2004; see Text box 3.1).

TEXT BOX 3.1 POSITIVISM AND INTERPRETIVISM

There are two major epistemological positions: positivism and interpretivism. To differentiate, albeit rather simply, between the two, we can look at how they would answer the following questions: can and indeed should the social world be studied by the social sciences in the same way that the natural sciences study the natural world? The epistemological position traditionally associated with the natural sciences, positivism, would answer yes, while interpretivism would answer no. This is because the latter sees the subjects of the social sciences (people) as so different to the objects of the natural sciences (atoms, waves), that they must be studied in very different ways. These two epistemological positions relate to two broadly differing onotologies. The ontological position associated with positivism is that social reality is objective and external to individuals. For interpretivism, social reality is shifting and is emergent from the actions of individuals (Bryman 2004).

One of the most exciting challenges for any sociologist planning research into work is determining what question to try to answer. What we have to ensure as sociologists is that our research is sociological: the purpose of sociological research is to gather quality information in a systematic way, drawing upon and/or feeding into sociological theorising. Accordingly, a fundamental question for sociologists is how to identify appropriate methods with which to carry out research into various aspects of work and society. In this chapter, we hope to show how sociologists of work have approached this question in diverse and innovative ways. You will see a distinction made between qualitative and quantitative methods in most sociological research texts, and we make this distinction here too, but we will also show how researchers have usefully 'mixed' their methods. The remainder of the chapter will show how the sociology of work has examined the various levels at which work is carried out and organised, using a diverse range of techniques.

FOUNDATIONS

Auguste Comte devised the term 'sociology' and he, followed by Emile Durkheim, is accredited with developing its positivistic tradition. Reflecting fundamental tenets of positivism, outlined above, both theorists believed that sociology could be a 'positive' science of society and that it could, just like the natural sciences, generate causal laws to explain social phenomena. In Durkheimian theory, society was a *sui generis*, a thing in itself that stood apart from and shaped individuals. So, according to Durkheim, we could study social phenomena: 'in the same state of mind as the physicist, chemist or physiologist when he (*sic*) probes into a still unrecognised region of the scientific domain' (1964: xiv).

In his research into work that we saw in the previous chapter, Durkheim asked what keeps people together in society. He set out to demonstrate that the expanding industrial division of labour engendered a higher form of solidarity than existed before, comparing the mechanical solidarity of pre-industrial times with the organic solidarity of industrialism. Solidarity is a highly complex concept to research. Durkheim looked at indirect indicators of it in the form of social arrangements such as law and religion. He undertook comparative macro-level historical analysis. Durkheim is also associated with the analysis of official statistics in his broader work, most notably because he compared suicide statistics from differing societies to inform his research into social solidarity.

The theorist most strongly associated with establishing an interpretivist tradition within sociology is Max Weber. Weber's use of the concept of *Verstehen*, or interpretive understanding, has been highly influential within the discipline, shaping the ethnographic tradition that we discuss later. He emphasised understanding social action, and this reflected his theoretical stress on the importance of ideas in society as opposed to an over-focus on the material that he critiqued in Marx's work. Weber's theoretical standpoint is reflected clearly in his influential research into the significance of religious ideas in the historical development of capitalism: *The Protestant Ethic and the Spirit of Capitalism*. One of his research questions here concerned the role of the Protestant work ethic – a belief in work as an indicator of salvation – in the development of economic systems. His study was based largely on cross-national comparative and historical analysis. In it, Weber also drew upon the 'ideal type' methodological approach (see Text box 2.3), whereby researchers construct simplified types or models of an issue/phenomenon to identify its essence and so facilitate its comparative analysis. Weber sought to identify and analyse the characteristics of an ideal typical capitalist and an ideal typical Protestant ethic. Finally, Weber also entered into and influenced discussions over how 'value-free' or objective and neutral research could be, arguing in particular that the choice of a subject area for study by researchers is inherently 'value full'.

In thinking about Karl Marx in terms of sociological research, we face a problem. Marx was a very different type of scholar than Durkheim or Weber. He did not write in the context of a university post but was a combination of journalist and political activist whose immense contribution to sociology can be found in his development of his theory of historical materialism which he developed alongside his lifelong collaborator Engels. Historical materialism could be seen as a method or approach to the study of work and economic life. It combines economics, politics, philosophy and, of course, history which allows us to understand the development of the capitalist system. The strengths of this approach are that it allows for a simultaneous analysis of work and working life at a number of levels and, further, that the conditions of work are always placed in historical context.

Of these three founders, Durkheim and Weber are more associated with establishing the methodological foundations of the discipline of sociology than Marx. In this chapter, we trace their influence on later developments in the growth of quantitative and qualitative approaches to the sociology of work respectively. But this is not to say that Marxists have not developed methodological understandings of the research process.

LATER DEVELOPMENTS

Quantitative research in the sociology of work

The positivist tradition of Comte and Durkheim in sociology has been most closely linked to quantitative research methodology, and a preoccupation with measurement, causality, generalisation and replication (see Bryman 2004). The quantitative approach in sociology has had a powerful impact on the ways in which we study and understand work today. The insights gained from quantitative research into large numbers of workers, non-workers, managers and workplaces – in different countries and over the years – have vastly increased our knowledge of work and economic life. Quantitative sociology has told us about what work entails; who carries it out, for whom and with what rewards (if any); when workers do it, where and alongside whom; and how workers and non-workers feel about their work or lack of it.

Quantitative research may have its roots in the positivist deductivistic tradition but for many researchers who undertake quantitative data collection and analysis, its philosophical foundations are far less relevant than are its technical strengths. The strengths of the questionnaire-based survey, the most prevalent quantitative method used in sociology, are rooted in its means for accessing large – often very large, indeed – numbers of respondents. These people are commonly representative of a population, in terms of class, gender, ethnic group, age, and so on, and the surveys provide a substantial amount of information from them. This is done relatively quickly, and it offers the capacity for sophisticated statistical analysis of the responses.

There are challenges involved in carrying out surveys of course, including obtaining a good response rate, and being confident that respondents understand the questions that they are answering (see Text box 3.2). But an impressive array of influential surveys have been carried out on work and society. There are far too many to detail here, even if we were to narrow our focus to the UK, but we draw on the findings of many throughout the book.

TEXT BOX 3.2 DEVISING QUESTIONNAIRES

In a follow-up study to the 'Fourth Survey of Ethnic Minorities', a team of UK-based researchers devised a questionnaire to explore in more depth self-employment among the four main South Asian groups in Britain (Pakistanis, Bangladeshis, Indians, and East African Asians). The research was thus carried out across cultures and across languages, and it was important to try to ensure that researcher and respondent did not attach different meanings to survey questions. For the research team, the greater the cultural divide between the two, the greater the risk. To reduce the potential of misinterpretation, the questionnaire was translated from its initial English into five Asian languages. Other translators then checked the first translations. Finally, interviewers and respondents were ethnically matched (Metcalf *et al.* 1996).

Quantitative research can be split into two main forms: primary data analysis and secondary. Secondary data analysis has been defined as: 'any further analysis of an existing data-set which presents interpretations, conclusions or knowledge additional to, or different from, those presented in the first report on the inquiry as a whole and its main results' (Hakim 1982: 1). Primary analysis is the first analysis.

Primary analysis

Many sociologists have researched work quantitatively by devising their own surveys specifically on the topic of work. To give an example of the magnitude of some of these survey-based projects, the *Social Change and Economic Life Initiative* (SCELI) of 1986–87 by Duncan Gallie and a range of colleagues, consisted of three surveys, each carried out in six locations of England and Scotland (Aberdeen, Coventry, Kirkcaldy, Northampton, Rochdale and Swindon; UK Data Archive 2007). Its purpose was to explore the attitudes of the population to changes in employment, including in the occupational structure; in the gender composition of the workforce; and increases in unemployment and casual labour. A 'Work Attitude and Work Histories' survey of 6,111 people was carried out, followed by a 'Household and Community Relations' survey of a third of the original respondents (1,816 respondents), and then a survey of their employers in the 'Employer Work-force Policies' survey (1,308 employers). A range of related in-depth studies followed. The team encompassed 35 researchers and a broad range of publications has resulted exploring, for example, gender segregation in work, unemployment levels and the experience of unemployment, skills and occupations, support for trade unionism, and both household and employer work strategies. All in all, it provided a depth and breadth of information on economic life in Britain that few studies have achieved.

Researchers have also carried out general surveys that incorporate sub-sections on work. A highly influential example is provided by the Policy Studies Institute (PSI) series into the lives of minority ethnic groups in Britain (Brown 1984; Daniel 1968; Jones 1986; Modood *et al.* 1997; Smith 1977). The most recent research team (led by sociologist Tariq Modood) analysed their data on work to tap any changes and continuities in the working lives of minority peoples over the years; to discuss the importance of trade unions for black and minority ethnic workers; and to explore the extent of racial harassment and discrimination in the workplace and its form for differing minority groups (Virdee 1995), among many other topics. The survey of around 8,000 people showed strong ethnic disparities in levels of employment, for example, with most minority ethnic men under-represented in higher level occupations, and high proportions of Indian female workers in manual jobs (see Figure 3.1). The PSI research has provided the most influential survey results on the work experiences of large numbers of the different minority groups living in Britain, that we draw on more in Chapter 7.

In addition to these very large studies, researchers have carried out smaller dedicated surveys of work. As an example, Rosemary Lucas' (1997) research into part-time working of undergraduate students at Manchester

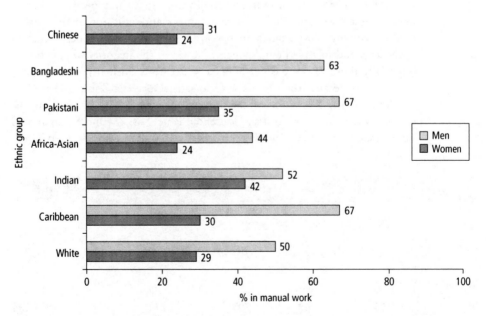

Figure 3.1 Proportion of manual workers by ethnic group; employees and self-employed
Source: Derived from Modood *et al.* (1997), Tables 4.10 and 4.13.

Metropolitan University included a survey of just over 1,000 students. A third had part-time jobs during the university term and 92 per cent had also worked during the holidays. The bulk of their jobs were in the hotel, catering and leisure and retail sectors, mainly in bar and shop work.

Secondary analysis

Sociologists have analysed work and economic life using a variety of secondary data sources too. As with primary analysis above, these include surveys specifically into work as well as general surveys that incorporate work sub-sections. A prominent example of a large survey that focuses on work is the UK Women and Employment Survey (WES) carried out in 1980 by the Office of Population Censuses and Surveys. This was innovative because it focused on women's work and as it asked about work experiences inside and outside the home, as well as attitudes to working lives. Jean Martin and Ceridwen Roberts produced a substantial report entitled *Women and Employment: A Lifetime Perspective* in 1984, and a range of researchers went on to re-analyse the data. Shirley Dex, an economist who has been influential on the sociology of work, carried out secondary analysis to examine women's employment patterns and their attitudes towards work, influencing sociological debates over heterogeneity among women workers and the role of choices and preferences in shaping gender differences in work experiences (Dex 1987, 1988). As an example, she showed that the typical number of hours women work in their jobs is an important indicator of the quality of their employment: women in part-time jobs were over-concentrated in lower-level and low-paid employment. However, the majority of part-timers (especially those working 8–30 hours a week) were satisfied with their jobs, in large part because their hours were so satisfactory (see Table 3.1).

Along similar lines, one of the authors (Warren 2001) has carried out secondary analysis of the British Household Panel Survey (BHPS), an annual survey that began in 1991 with approximately 10,000 individuals interviewed.

Table 3.1 Women workers' satisfaction with usual hours worked

	Usual hours worked per week					
	<8	*8–<16*	*16–30*	*31+*	*Vary*	*All*
% satisfied	71	80	87	67	79	74
N	133	366	795	1,811	99	3,204

Source: 1980 'Women and Employment Survey' data. Taken from Dex (1988), Table 5.8, p. 131.

She contrasted findings from the BHPS with those from the WES to examine changes in the proportions of female employees working part-time in Britain after 1980, concluding that younger cohorts of female employees were becoming less likely to work part-time than older cohorts in their peak years of child-rearing.

Special sources of secondary data are administrative records. One useful example is data on employee profiles from workplaces. For example, Mike Savage (2001) examined careers in the banking industry via the analysis of thousands of corporate staff records of bank employees, from 1880 to 1960. In another study Savage and colleagues made use of the extensive public record of railway workers held in the national archives in Kew, South-West London. This contains hundreds of thousands of files on railway company employees and gives details of their careers (Savage 1998). A further example of this type of material is the employee records of the Ford Motor Company (Detroit Area) for 1918–47 that are lodged at the UK Data Archive (see later) and contain work histories for each employee including their wage rates, occupation, dates of hire, length of time on the job, reasons for leaving, and job performance ratings, as well as background demographic information such as date of birth, gender, 'race', ethnicity, place of birth, citizenship, and English language ability.

Finally, government data are an important secondary source of information on work. Examining ethnic differences in women's employment, Angela Dale and Clare Holdsworth (1998) carried out secondary analysis of the Office for National Statistics' Longitudinal Survey (based on Census data). They found just over a third of women aged between 16 and 50 were in employment in 1981, with slightly higher proportions of Black women, and slightly lower figures for Indian, Chinese and Other-Asian women. Very few Pakistani and Bangladeshi women were in jobs.

A very useful example of government surveys on paid work is the Labour Force Survey (LFS) of Britain and Northern Ireland, a household survey carried out four times a year by the Office for National Statistics with a remit to provide information on the labour market to develop and evaluate government policies. The enormity of the LFS – fully 57,000 households are sampled annually – makes it really useful for analysis of sub-groups of workers, say, by ethnic group or by region. Findings from the survey are available in the regular publication *Labour Market Trends* that is available free via a governmental web-site (see end of chapter). *Social Trends* similarly provides regular, more simplified, figures from the LFS, with a chapter on the labour market in each edition. *Social Trends* number 36 (ONS 2006) displays LFS data to show, for example, employment rates in the EU, with the highest rates in Denmark and the Netherlands (see Table 3.2). As an other example, we can see employment rates by age in the UK over the ten-year period 1994–2004, with the figure showing a gradual increase in employment over time for those aged 50–64 (Figure 3.2).

Table 3.2 Employment rates, EU, 2004	
Country	(%)
Denmark	75.7
The Netherlands	73.1
Sweden	72.1
United Kingdom	71.6
Cyprus	68.9
Austria	67.8
Portugal	67.8
Finland	67.6
Ireland	66.3
Slovenia	65.3
Germany	65.0
Czech Republic	64.2
France	63.1
Estonia	63.0
Latvia	62.3
Luxembourg	61.6
Lithuania	61.2
Spain	61.1
Belgium	60.3
Greece	59.4
Italy	57.6
Slovakia	57.0
Hungary	56.8
Malta	54.1
Poland	51.7
EU-25 average	63.3

Source: Labour Force Survey, *Social Trends* 36, 2006: Table 4.4.

The variety of high quality information available is one of a number of advantages of secondary analysis for researchers. Others include that it is cheaper and often far quicker to use such pre-collected data. The researcher is then able to dedicate more time to looking at the theoretical aims of the project. The data are often useful in the analysis of trends in work over time, and research can be replicated to check the findings of earlier research projects.

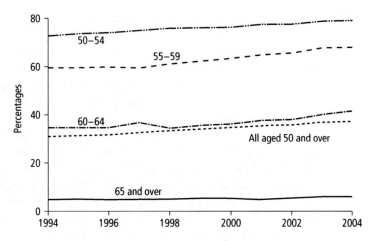

Figure 3.2 Employment rates of older people, UK
Source: Labour Force Survey, *Social Trends*, 36, 2006, Figure 4.9.

Finally, it is one of the least intrusive of methodologies available to social researchers, since many research projects can analyse the same data, the respondents answering the questions are not 'over-researched' (Dale *et al.* 1988). Problems do exist with secondary analysis, of course. The questions asked and the detail provided are already set, for example, and they might be restricting. Perhaps the major warning is that it is vital to consider how the data were constructed, and to analyse all findings taking this into account. Text box 3.3 uses a rather notorious example of how to interpret official figures on unemployment levels in the UK.

TEXT BOX 3.3 UNEMPLOYMENT STATISTICS

In Christina Beatty *et al.*'s (2002) *The Real Level of Unemployment*, the researchers were surprised to find that the regional level of official 'claimant unemployment' was little changed after large-scale closure of mines. The researchers found this was because claimants for unemployment-related benefits were being encouraged to switch to sickness benefits or off benefits altogether and into early retirement. Their research cast serious doubts on the validity – or integrity – of government statistics on unemployment. It also highlighted concerns about comparing trends in unemployment levels over time if who we are classifying as 'unemployed' changes, and we don't know about this change.

Qualitative research in the sociology of work

The Weber-inspired interpretivist tradition in sociology is more closely linked to qualitative methods and focuses upon understanding the subjective meaning of social action. Its preoccupations are with seeing how people interpret their own world; providing detailed description; locating research within its social context; stressing processes; and flexibility (Bryman 2004). Qualitative approaches to researching the sociology of work are extremely varied, ranging from interview techniques, through ethnography to visual approaches. What unites this very different set of interests is their focus on the meanings attached to behaviour and attitudes. In qualitative research sociologists are interested in getting at the motives and understanding people have about their work, the way they do it and the links to family and community. As we saw above, Weber's notion of *Verstehen* or meaningful understanding implies that it is important to appreciate action and understanding from the point of view of those being researched.

Approaches to interviewing

One of the most common ways in which to research the experience of work is by interviewing people. As in most forms of research, there is a range of ways of doing this. Rather than one form of interview, it is better to think of a continuum with structured, or semi-structured, interviews at one end and oral histories at the other. The approach adopted largely depends on the type of research and the form of material the researcher wants to generate about a particular topic.

The structured/semi-structured approach is usually adopted when researchers want to generate data about a set of people who share similar characteristics, for example male workers over 50 years of age, or South Asian homeworkers. Before undertaking the interview, the researcher will create an interview schedule of questions designed to access the kinds of material of interest. The important difference within this type of interviewing is the extent to which structuring occurs. For instance, some researchers may go into an interview armed with a long list of detailed questions. This highly structured approach offers the advantage of producing a large number of factual type answers which make it easier to compare across the sample as a whole. In some ways, this approach is like a quantitative survey. Alternatively, semi- or even unstructured interviewing can be employed, and this involves a more open approach. Here the object is to encourage the interviewee to open up about their working life, or an aspect of it. The advantage of such a stance is that it allows the subject of the interview to construct their own narrative and to reflect on what is important to them, potentially producing rich and deep accounts of working life. Qualitative interviewers can also use a variety of prompts as part of the process such as the use of photographs and other pieces of material which may stimulate conversation. We will discuss photo elicitation, where photography is used as part of the interview process, later in the chapter.

To demonstrate, here is a short extract from an interview carried out by Tim Strangleman with Walter Mulligan, a retired train driver from Newcastle. At the end of the interview, Walter began to speak in quite emotional terms about his attachment to his former job and the memory of what he saw from the cab of his train travelling up and down the east coast of Britain:

> The best part was when it was day shift, or through the night even, and you saw, that's the one thing always sticks in my mind, the job was part and parcel of what you did, but the change in scenery, the sights you saw, people can't describe. Like geese coming from Alaska or wherever they came from landing at Lucker, and the whole fields were black with these black-backed geese, that sort of thing. You saw lambs just been born, running about, you only saw a glimpse of them, you didn't stop, but you got a glimpse of them as you went past. The sight of Alnmouth when the tide was in, that sort of thing, you can't forget.

The next extract is from a study of casino workers in Australia, New Zealand, the USA and the UK by Austrin and West (2005). The research identified a very high level of surveillance in the workplace, and what is expressed vividly in the (shortened) quotation from a new card dealer are the complexities of having to control your body in the work:

> They taught us step by minute step and went around and they showed us themselves and you would deal for ages and they would come round and tell you: no, do this, put this down, change this . . . dealing a card involves pulling out of a shoe with this finger with having the rest of your arm straight like this, don't have your elbow too high, don't turn your hand on the side, keep your fingers together, which I could never do, keep this thumb showing, take it down, flip it up, you put your thumb just like that and you have to practise where to put the card so that you are not holding the card and if you lifted the card off the pressure of the table it would drop, and at the same time wiggle your thumb around so that the card comes in a straight line with those fingers keeping your hand like this.
> (Female Maori dealer, aged *c.* 28, Austrin and West 2005: 315)

Oral history

Oral history is clearly related to semi- and unstructured interviewing in that it puts an emphasis on collecting the subject's personal reflection about their life or aspects of it. Again there is a wide variation in the amount of structuring that occurs in such interviews and some would argue that there is little or no difference between oral history and semi-structured interviewing. One of the best examples of an oral history approach in the study of work is *Working* by Studs Terkel. Terkel is probably the best-known oral historian in the world and has produced a number of books on a variety of subjects, including work. His open style and self-deprecation disguise his skill at producing in his interviewees a willingness to talk in great depth. In the Introduction to *Working*, he reflects on his approach:

> I realised quite early in this adventure that interviews, conventionally conducted, were meaningless. Conditioned clichés were certain to come. The question-and-answer techniques may be of some value in determining favoured detergents, toothpaste and deodorants, but not in the discovery of men and women. There were questions, of course. But they were causal in nature – at the beginning: the kind you would ask while having a drink with someone; the kind he would ask you. The talk was idiomatic rather than academic. In short, it was conversation. In time, the sluice gates of dammed up hurts and dreams were opened.
>
> (Terkel 1972: xxv)

The real strength of this type of interviewing is the quality of the material rendered. From good interviews it is possible to obtain wonderfully rich accounts of work and the meanings that are attached to it. A good interview or oral history will produce a highly reflexive account of life, rather than the kind of cliché answers that Terkel mentions. But it is important to recognise the weakness of oral history techniques too. Memory is always a selective account of past events and the interviewee for many different reasons may change key facts in any story. Importantly, oral historians do not necessarily see this as a huge problem. For many the style of the narrative told is as important as the content of what is being said. Here Italian oral historian Alessandro Portelli explains why this is the case:

> The oral sources used in this essay are not always fully reliable in point of fact. Rather than being a weakness, this is however, their strength: errors, invention and myths lead us through and beyond facts to their meanings.
>
> (2001: 2)

This is quite a step for many academics to take. What is being highlighted here is that there is a whole level of meaning that needs to be taken seriously if sociologists are to fully understand work, or any set of social relations. In their collection *The Myths We Live By*, social historians Raphael Samuel and Paul Thompson talk about the importance of taking myth seriously and that 'what is forgotten may be as important as what is remembered' (Samuel and

Thompson 1990: 7). Thompson has been one of the most influential figures in the oral history movement. His *The Voice of the Past: Oral History* is both an intellectual argument for oral methods to be taken seriously as well as representing a manual on how to carry out studies (Thompson 1978; see also Perks and Thomson 1998).

Ethnographic research

Within the sociology of work there has been a long tradition of ethnographic or observational research. Some of the classic 'shop floor' studies took this form – see, for instance, Huw Beynon's (1973) *Working for Ford*, Michael Burawoy's (1979) *Manufacturing Consent*, Miriam Glucksmann's (writing as Ruth Cavendish 1982) *Women on the Line*, Anna Pollert's (1981) *Girls, Wives, Factory Lives*, and Sallie Westwood's (1985) *All Day, Every Day*. It is possible to argue that ethnography is one of the most important forms of qualitative research of such workplaces because it allows access to hidden parts of work. Ethnography takes two broad forms: participatory and non-participatory. As the name suggests, participatory ethnography is where the researcher actively takes part in the work group, rather than simply watching. Such research can also be categorised in terms of being either overt or covert. Overt ethnography is when those being studied are fully aware of the role and purpose of the researcher. The researcher may or may not be a participant in the work carried out. Huw Beynon's *Working for Ford* is an example of non-participant observation. In covert ethnography the researcher joins the work team as a full member and does not reveal their true identity as an academic. Glucksmann's *Women on the Line*, published under a pseudonym of Ruth Cavendish, was based on a seven-month period of covert participant observation in 1977–78 during which time she was employed full-time in a motor components factory. There are ethical issues involved in such an approach (see later) but this type of work has produced some excellent accounts of shop floor life. Ethnography explores workplace culture by describing in detail and analysing the actions of workers and work groups. Here Donald Roy describes his growing awareness of the hidden meaning of workplace culture:

> Banana time followed peach time by approximately an hour. Sammy again provided the refreshments, namely one banana. There was, however, no four-way sharing of Sammy's banana. Ike would gulp it down by himself after surreptitiously extracting it from Sammy's lunch box, kept on a shelf behind Sammy's work station. Each morning, after making the snatch, Ike would call out, 'Banana time!' and proceed to down his prize while Sammy made futile protests and denunciations.
>
> (Roy, 1958, reprinted in Harper and Lawson 2003: 298)

What Roy did was describe the complex interaction within a small group of workers. He makes sense of a mass of seemingly meaningless shop floor banter and behaviour. In doing so, he reveals the inner working of shop floor culture and its own logic. Banana time, for instance, was understood as part of an elaborate game by which workers made the day pass more quickly. It also acted as a powerful bond between workers, introducing humour, routine, and tradition. Similarly, Cavendish describes routine manual work in her ethnography:

> The women ran the line, but we were also just appendages to it. Its discipline was imposed automatically through the light, the conveyor belt and the bonus system. We just slotted in like cogs in a wheel. Every movement we made and every second of our time was controlled by the line; the chargehands and supervisors didn't even have to tell us when to get on.
>
> (Cavendish 1982: 107)

A more recent example of work ethnography can be found John Bone's (2006) research in the direct selling industry and in Ben Fincham's study of bicycle messengers. As part of his research, Fincham worked as a messenger on the streets of London and Cardiff. His study includes a reflection on the danger of the job:

> Rush hour on Oxford Street was absolutely thrilling, but my inexperience definitely resulted in a couple of heart-stopping moments. Getting wedged between two buses going in opposite directions being the highlight. Actually that did scare me (field diary, 09.05.2003).
>
> (Fincham 2006: 198)

This quote, and Fincham's other reflections on his work as a messenger, highlight the advantage of this type of method, namely the researcher's ability to get under the skin of those doing the work. While researchers will only be doing a job for a short period, they can experience work in a way that is not really available to other approaches. In carrying out this type of investigation, sociologists need to be aware of the dangers of 'going native' where they drop their critical stance and become one of the researched (see Brewer 2000).

There is a long tradition of workplace ethnography by academics but it seems to be less common than in the past, although there are exceptions (see Bone 2006). The reasons for this are not clear, but it may reflect a lack of willingness or ability on the part of academics to spend the time embedding themselves in the workplace. Gaining access to a particular workplace and then embedding oneself in it for any meaningful period can take a great deal of time and effort. American work ethnographer Laurie

Graham, for instance, took six months to gain access to the car plant she worked in before spending a further six months undertaking a covert study (Graham 1995).

Visual methods in sociology

In many ways the use of visual methods in the social sciences in general, and in the study of work in particular, are not new. Douglas Harper (1986), an American sociologist who has written widely on visual methods and work, pointed out visual images had been used in the *American Journal of Sociology* since 1896 but that this tradition had largely died out after the First World War. More recently there has been an explosion of interest in the use of the visual within the social sciences, but what do we mean by the visual and in what ways can it be used in researching work? There are a number of ways in which we can research with and through the visual:

- Illustration
- As evidence
- Content analysis
- Semiotics
- Photo elicitation
- Visual ethnography.

Illustration/evidence. First, visual material can be used 'simply' as illustration, if, say, you wanted to show Henry Ford's production line at his River Rouge plant or women workers in nineteenth-century agriculture. But what is clear when we look in more depth at work and the visual is that there is nothing 'simple' about a picture. There are always questions to be asked about what a picture shows, why it was taken, who took the picture and who paid for it. It is therefore vital to be critical in using pictures as evidence, just as we would be with any other sources.

Content analysis is a technique that is less common in visual approaches. Here the idea is that the researcher would look at a series of images from a source and chart the instances of a particular feature. For example, one might want to know how often minority ethnic workers appeared in a company magazine. One could choose to look through the entire run or select an edition from one month every year for a decade. Content analysis is one method in which we might consider quantitative statements about our findings (Rose 2001).

Semiotics. Semiology is a fairly technical way of interrogating images, their meaning and their construction. The approach offers a range of tools for deconstructing a picture and 'tracing how it works in relation to broader systems of meanings' (Rose 2001: 69).

Photo elicitation is perhaps one of the most popular forms of visual research. It can take a number of related forms but essentially it involves using images in qualitative interviews as a way opening up the process and allowing the interviewee to be more involved. In some cases, photo elicitation involves the use of archive photographs which workers are asked to talk about, while in others the images may have been generated by the researcher as part of the project. Harper has used both techniques in his writing. In his *Working Knowledge* (1987), he took photographs of a worker in a small engineering shop. He did not simply take the photos, however, but allowed Willie, his respondent, to tell him when and where to take a picture. When the images were developed, Harper then interviewed Willie getting him to talk about his work and the importance of what he was doing. As Harper explains, the advantage of this method is that:

> The researcher gains a phenomenological sense as the informant explains what the objects in the photograph mean, where they have come, or developed from, and what elements may be missing, or what photographs in a sequence may be missing. This method provides a way in which the interview can move from the concrete (a cataloguing of the objects in the photograph) to the socially abstract (what the objects in the photograph mean to the individual being interviewed).
>
> (Harper 1986: 25)

In a later book, *Changing Works*, Harper (2001) used archive photographs of agricultural work and life in the USA from the *Standard Oil* collection taken just after the Second World War. Harper passed these pictures around groups of farmers who had started their working lives at the time the original photos had been taken. By a judicious mixture of careful listening and prompting, Harper collected a rich and detailed account of a lost world. Often his respondents would move on to the next photo with a throwaway line about the content of the previous one. Harper would ask them to expand on what they had said and pull out a far more complex account of work that the workers themselves took for granted.

Perhaps an even more radical step can be seen in a recent study where Bolton *et al.* (2001) gave child workers disposable cameras and asked them to photograph their workplaces. The research produced a fascinating account of work itself, the relationship between academics and their subjects, as well as illustrating power structures in the workplace – as the authors noted: 'several young people had earlier decided to opt out of the photographic stage of research for this very reason, fearing that taking photographs might jeopardise their employment' (ibid.: 512). The authors make the point that this type of analysis adds a different dynamic to the research process as well as producing a different order of data. The attraction for many researchers in using the photo elicitation technique is that it involves those being researched in a way that arguably few other approaches do.

Visual ethnography is another popular approach and one that lends itself to researching work. Like other visual techniques, it can take several forms. The most notable division would be between researchers who use still images and those who use moving images through video. There are a number of excellent examples of work in this area. Cynthia Cockburn and Susan Ormrod (1993) combined several techniques, including visual ethnography, in their study of technology and gender. They trace the way a technological artefact, the microwave oven, is gendered at each stage of the design, production, testing, selling through to its eventual use in the home. The book would have been a fascinating account of the gendering process without visual illustration but the photographs used, taken by Cockburn, bring the text alive by 'simple' illustration but also by a more complex process where the reader starts to look critically at the pictures in relation to the text. They challenge everyday assumptions about social life.

A second major strand of visual ethnography is through the use of video. This has often been used in the contexts of control rooms or in the study of the medical profession. These workplace studies make a point of actually examining the work done rather than the social context or other issues that other forms of sociology focus on. There are many examples of this work including Heath *et al.*'s (2002) study of a London Underground control room; and Whalen *et al.*'s (2002) research on telesales work.

Mixed methods in the sociology of work

Splitting research methods into qualitative and quantitative approaches as we have in this chapter does not mean that all research projects only employ one set of techniques. Many studies explicitly use a combination of quantitative and qualitative techniques: so-called between method 'triangulation' (Denzin 1989). For philosophical purists who believe that epistemology determines choice of methods, researchers will choose only quantitative or qualitative methods, and the two methods are necessarily incompatible. For non-purists, however, the issue is which methods are technically superior for the particular research project to be undertaken: what are the strengths of the data collection?; and which analysis options are available? Hence the two approaches can be compatible, with each one making up for the shortfalls of the other.

To show some examples, Paul Willis' (1977) classic largely qualitative research into young non-academic working-class boys as they made the transition from school to work demonstrates the potentially multi-faceted nature of a project. He employed a main case study of 12 'lads' from the working-class 'Hammertown Boys' school in the Midlands, and indeed has often been criticised for his use of a small sample. But as well as interviewing the boys, Willis interviewed their parents and teachers and, later, their foremen (*sic*), managers and shop stewards in the workplace. He carried out individual and group interviews with the boys, diary analysis as well as observation of their school and work lives. Willis also researched a range of other groups of boys, differentiated by class, academic achievement and school, to allow him to make comparisons with his main group.

A range of techniques was also used by Arlie Russell Hochschild (1983) in her influential project on working in the US airline industry. She carried out interviews with managers, undertook overt participant observation of training courses for flight attendants, and carried out open-ended interviews with attendants too. Randy Hodson's (2001) *Dignity at Work* adopted an approach whereby he collected approximately one hundred workplace ethnographies carried out over a number of decades. He then coded these and analysed quantitatively. Using this technique he claimed he yielded more information than other approaches, allowing him to make more generalisable observations from qualitative material than might otherwise be the case.

Mixing methods like this is not without its problems. One potential challenge is how to integrate the different data if inconsistencies emerge in the project. Fiona Devine and Sue Heath (1999) discuss how Nicky Gregson and Michelle Lowe's (1994) research into domestic labour in the UK, *Servicing the Middle Classes*, analysed job adverts for nannies and cleaners in magazines and newspapers; carried out surveys of middle-class dual-employed households in Reading and Newcastle, and interviewed nannies, cleaners and their employers. They found more job adverts for nannies than for cleaners but the survey showed that cleaners were used much more frequently in middle class homes. Julia Brannen and Peter Moss's (1991) *Managing Mothers: Dual Earner Households after Maternity Leave* also shows how their quantitative and qualitative data were at odds at times. In the survey component, for example, women expressed low levels of dissatisfaction with their partners' roles in their dual-earner lifestyle, even though most partners were not taking an equal role in domestic work. But the qualitative data suggested more criticism or ambivalence, albeit usually veiled (see Chapter 10 on domestic work):

> *How do you feel about what he does?* I'm quite happy. I'd be pleased if he did more . . . Perhaps if he picked up his clothes off the floor and made the bed. But no, he's very good.
>
> (Brannen and Moss 1991: 200–1)

Rather than seeing the contradictions in the two sets of data as a problem, the researchers were inspired by the differences and used them to shape the analysis and to identify processes 'by which dissatisfaction was played down and explained away' (ibid.: 20).

In Linda Hantrais' (2005) review of multi-methods in cross-national research projects, she identifies the strengths and the challenges faced by researchers carrying out this type of comparative research. When research teams were composed of researchers from different countries, she shows that although language problems often arose, there was the real potential for the 'intensive discussion of concepts' and the 'scrutiny of interpretations by other teams' members, research subjects and users' (2005: 416).

To end, it is safe to say that, despite these challenges, the combined approach dominates much sociological research into work, producing studies that are wide-ranging and innovative. Text box 3.4 shows just how well diverse methods can be used.

TEXT BOX 3.4 MULTIPLE METHODS

Alan Felstead *et al.*'s (2005) *Changing Places of Work* book is a result of two linked projects into the spatial organization of work that were based on a combination of the analysis of secondary and primary quantitative surveys, qualitative data derived from case studies of organizations, and qualitative and quantitative data derived from interviews with workers. The list of techniques used in the projects is remarkable, ranging from telephone polling of organizations, interviewing managers and employees, photographing workstations and communal spaces and making a video film in organizations, carrying out a photo-elicitation study in which respondents were given disposable cameras for photographing their working environments, distributing questionnaires at motorway service stations and on trains, as well as researchers shadowing workers as they went about their jobs (see Figure 3.3).

Ethics

Ethics are central to all good sociological research projects. Ethics are concerned with how we should treat the people on or with whom we are conducting our research. The main ethical issues that concern us as researchers are: avoiding harm to the participants (though see Text box 3.5 on researchers' safety in the research process too), obtaining informed consent, avoiding invasion of privacy, and deception (Bryman 2004). Informed consent is one of the most complex of the four since there are fundamental theoretical and philosophical debates over what it actually means, as well as more practical debates over how to obtain it. Obtaining informed consent is often seen as part of the commitment that we have as sociological researchers to protect our respondents. One of the major problems for many sociologists of work is that by its very nature the organisations and social forms they look

Figure 3.3 Working 'under the arches', while waiting for a delayed train.
Source: Felstead *et al.* (2005).

at are political and contested. In carrying out a study, sociologists have to negotiate a whole series of power relationship which, at times, beg import-ant questions about ethics. Probably the most heated debates around ethics in sociological research have focused on covert ethnographic techniques in workplaces since here the researcher, rather than try to obtain informed con-sent, deliberately conceals their identity from those being researched.

TEXT BOX 3.5 SAFETY OF RESEARCHERS

Debates on ethics in sociological researching largely concern those being researched. But researchers themselves have come to the forefront in recent discussions, particularly issues relating to their own safety when they are 'in the field'. Boosted by feminist researchers and others examining sensitive areas (Lee 1993), there is increasing awareness of the potential dangers (including of physical threat and psychological trauma; Craig *et al.* 2000) for researchers, influenced by factors of class, gender and 'race'. A 'risk assessment' now plays a central part in the planning of most soci-ological research projects.

There are many examples of covert participant observation in industrial sociology where both organisations and the workforce were unaware of the research process. Despite the clear ethical issues it raises, two main reasons have been proposed for adopting such a strategy. First, the researcher may want those being researched to be unaware that they are being studied in order that they may act 'naturally', thus avoiding the so-called Hawthorne effect.

TEXT BOX 3.6 THE HAWTHORNE EFFECT

This describes the way in which a group of workers at the Western Electric factory in the USA in the 1930s studied by social researchers responded differently as a result of knowing they were being researched, and because of the particular régime of supervision they were subject to. Six female workers were placed in an isolated test room and were subject to various changes in terms of condition. Researchers noted an increase in productivity but, crucially, rates continued to rise when these improvements were withdrawn. The researchers concluded that social contexts and workplace cultures had to be taken into account as well as working conditions. The effect raises important questions about the unintended consequences of the research process (see Gillespie 1991).

The second reason is that gaining access to organisations may be impossible if the researcher was completely open with 'gatekeepers'. Researchers of workplaces have to negotiate a range of power relations that might prevent or seriously curtail the story that they are able to tell. Such pressures include the management and supervisors in workplaces who may object to the version of the story being told; local governments who might object to negative images of an industry being portrayed; and trade unions who may object to researchers on the ground both of threats to the workplace or the negative portrayal of the unions. Huw Beynon (1988), writing on the politics of the research process, looks back on *Working for Ford* and tells of the hostility from management to his book to the point where Ford attempted to discredit him, but also from the leader of the Transport and General Workers Union who objected to part of Beynon's account which focused on the role of the union.

Nichols and Cam (2005) tell of how their research into the global white goods industry was nearly ruined by failing to gain access to a series of factories because of management refusal. In Fiona Devine's (1992) research into Vauxhall workers in Luton, re-visiting the 'Affluent Worker' 1968–69 studies of Goldthorpe *et al.* in the same location, the company refused to generate a sample of employees. In the context of redundancies and tricky negotiations between employer and trade unions over a new shift system: 'the board did not want to whip up unwarranted fears and expectations among its workforce, nor to see the company presented in a bad light' (1992: 33). Devine had to access her initial sample via a trade union official and the regional 'Worker's Educational Association' instead.

Another good example of covert ethnographic research in a factory is provided by the American sociologist Laurie Graham (1995) whose book, *On the Line at Subaru-Isuzu,* is an account of her doctoral research into Japanese car assembly in the USA. Her book describes the process by which she was recruited, selected, trained and socialised into the company over a period of a year while she was doing her fieldwork. She kept her real status hidden from both employer and her fellow co-workers throughout her time on the line and she discusses the ethical dilemmas she faced.

It is important to note, however, that being overt or covert is not an all or nothing decision. Julia O'Connell Davidson's research into prostitution is very useful because it shows up the complexities of the 'overt versus covert' choice that researchers make. She was overt with the prostitutes that she was observing and with their receptionists, but she did not reveal her role as a researcher to the clients. O'Connell Davidson was very open about her decision regarding the clients:

> I have a professional obligation to preserve their anonymity and to ensure that they are not harmed by my research, but I feel no qualms about being less than frank with them and no obligation to allow them to choose whether or not their actions are recorded.
>
> (O'Connell Davidson and Layder 1994: 215)

O'Connell Davidson's statement on protecting from harm and preserving anonymity brings us back to the other ethical issues that began this section. 'Protecting the researched from harm' usually incorporates maintaining the confidentiality and protecting the privacy of respondents. One popular way to maintaining confidentiality is to use pseudonyms when writing up findings, be it for firms or individuals. Virinder Kalra (2000) used a combination of pseudonyms and real names for his minority ethnic self-employed men, at respondents' requests (see Text box 3.7 too), while Nickie Charles and Emma James (2003a, 2003b) studied the experiences of workers in the South Wales firms 'BureauGen', 'Make-a-Lot' and 'BigShop'. Ruth Cavendish's *Women on the Line* is a good example of a study where not only are the workers' identities disguised but also where the author had to disguise the factory, its location as well as what it actually made for legal reasons.

TEXT BOX 3.7 ETHICS

Kalra's (2000) study of minority ethnic self-employed men shows how he faced a range of ethical issues: potential risk to the participants, informed consent, and invasion of privacy because:

> My interests in issues of employment, pay and times of working were especially sensitive when it came to research in the area of taxi driving and working in the take-aways. These areas of the economy have long operated on a 'cash' payment basis and as such are open to intense scrutiny from tax and benefit agencies . . . I was . . . as explicit as possible about the aims of the project and the extent to which it was for a University degree rather than for the local authority.
>
> (2000: 49)

A classic example of what can go wrong when our strategies to maintain confidentiality are confounded is provided by the so-called 'British Association Scandal'. Here, David Morgan's research into female factory workers inadvertently attracted the attention of the British tabloid press who, using the few details that Morgan had provided about the factory to contextualise his research, managed to track down the factory and identify his key respondents (Morgan 1972).

The professional association of sociologists in Britain, the British Sociological Association (BSA), its American equivalent (ASA) and the Social Research Association provide valuable guidelines on ethics on their web-sites (see useful resources).

Non-sociological influences on researching work

We have traced the influence of classical sociology on developments in researching work, but it is important to note that the ways in which sociologists study work and employment have also been shaped by research taking place outside academia, by journalists, philanthropists, as well as those concerned with industrial efficiency (F. W. Taylor, for example). From Henry Mayhew (1851), a lawyer turned journalist who researched the conditions of the poor in London; through Joseph Rowntree's (1901) and Charles Booth's (1889) maps of the occurrence of poverty in London and York, as well as Jacob Riis' (1890) studies in the United States, and the ethnographic work of journalists Polly Toynbee (2003), Fran Abrams (2002) and Barbara

Ehrenreich (2001), the borders between sociology, social policy, journalism and other academic traditions are not always straightforward. We will return to this issue later in the book.

CONTEMPORARY ISSUES AND FUTURE TRENDS

We end this chapter by reflecting on current innovations in how sociologists research work, while remembering at the same time how these still build on the foundations discussed already.

Feminist research methods

Feminism has had an impact on sociological researching into work (as well as theorising as we saw in the previous chapter), but there is both a debate over whether there is a distinct feminist methodology (Harding 1987), and no necessary agreement among feminists on the best methodological approaches to take. For some feminists, research is only feminist when women researchers carry out qualitative research with (as opposed to 'on') women with the express political aim of improving women's lives. The first feminist-inspired research projects into work in the 1970s invariably did use qualitative methods, reflecting the close links between academic sociology and women active in the feminist movement and the commitment to write for all women rather than in specialised academic language[1] using obscure methods. Harriet Bradley (2004) discusses how this approach reflected a distrust of mainstream science – for early feminist research, any hint of the positivistic model was critiqued, especially any positioning of researchers as powerful and the researched as 'objects' to be studied (Roberts 1989). So, while espousing qualitative research, feminists critiqued the 'paradigm of the proper interview' with its appeal to values like objectivity, detachment, hierarchy and science. Ann Oakley (1981) was very influential in these early debates, criticising, for example, the masculine imagery which pervaded textbook descriptions of the interview process in which an interviewer was to remain detached, distant, dominant and in control (contrast this text-book approach with French sociologist Pierre Bourdieu's account in Text box 3.8). In Oakley's (1979) research into first-time mothers, *Becoming a Mother* (published again in 1986 as *From Here to Maternity*), she made the decision to share her own experiences with the women she was interviewing rather than remain detached. She had noticed 'the tendency of the interviewed to ask questions back' (1986: 310): how do you clean the baby's nails?; how do you cook an egg for a baby?; and so on. As a mother of three children herself, Oakley shared her knowledge of early motherhood and child-rearing.

TEXT BOX 3.8 PIERRE BOURDIEU

Pierre Bourdieu (1999) explored the complexity of the relationship between the researcher and the researched. His essay calls for a highly reflexive position to be adopted by the former and suggests an almost spiritual relationship between the two, 'that the interview can be considered a sort of spiritual exercise that through forgetfulness of self, aims at a true conversion of the way we look at other people in the ordinary circumstances of life' (Bourdieu *et al.* 1999: 614).

Perhaps one uniting interest for feminist – and indeed other – researchers today is to bring the voices of the researched more firmly into the research process. One technique employed is to provide respondents with transcripts of their interview, and ask for their input into its interpretation. In Jane Holgate's (2005) study of a union's attempt to organise minority ethnic workers in a London sandwich factory, because the voices of black and minority research subjects have been especially silenced, Holgate asked participants to discuss and debate the research findings to both improve her analysis and to help feed into policy-making within the trade union.

In recent years, research has been identified as feminist by reference to its theoretical framework rather than by its techniques or indeed the gender of the researcher or the researched. Part of this development is that quantitative techniques have become more accepted by feminist researchers. They have been seen to provide valuable information on 'big picture' gender inequalities in work and economic life such as the extent of the gender wage gap at national levels (Walby and Olsen 2004), cross-national similarities and differences in gendered work patterns (Crompton 2006), and the gender gap in who carries out the bulk of housework (Sullivan 1997). The secondary analysis of quantitative data has also been seen to be one of the least intrusive methodologies, and so a way to protect the women being researched. For Angela Dale and colleagues (1988), in qualitative interviews in which a rapport is built up between interviewer and interviewee, respondents have confided personal information which they later regretted. The depersonalised large-scale survey provides more protection, as well as almost guaranteed anonymity.

Cross-national comparative research

Comparing issues in different countries has been central to sociology from its birth, with the three founders Marx, Weber and Durkheim all looking across borders to understand social change. Nevertheless, it is useful to take a moment to reflect on the real strengths of cross-national comparisons for the sociology of work. Cross-national, comparative research focuses on particular issues or phenomena which are studied in two or more countries, with the aim of comparing the issues in different socio-cultural settings (Hantrais 1989: 10). Jan Windebank's (2001) qualitative analysis of dual-earner couples in Britain and France looked at the impact of the two different societies on equality in the working lives of women and men. Duncan Gallie's (2003) quantitative analysis of work quality in Europe used the 1996 'Employment in Europe' survey and explored questions that asked workers to rate how far, for example, 'there is a lot of variety in my work', 'I have a lot of say over what happens in my job', 'My job requires that I keep learning new things'. Comparing data from 15 countries in Europe, he concluded that workers in Denmark and Sweden were the most advantaged in terms of the quality of their work tasks as well as their involvement in decision-making in the workplace.

As with all methods, cross-national research has its limitations. If there is an over-focus on exploring cross-national differences, important similarities between countries might be lost. And a stress on inter-country difference may serve to under-emphasise within-country diversity too, by region, say, or by class or ethnicity (Duncan 1995). But the real strength offered by the comparative cross-national approach – to help us question the 'taken for granted' within a society, is fundamental for sociology.

Longitudinal studies

If we are interested in examining changes over time, or indeed lack of change, in any aspect of work, then we look towards longitudinal methods. We might be concerned with whether classed work identities have faded or intensified since the 1970s, whether men have increased their share of domestic work over a certain period, or whether women from different minority ethnic groups spend longer periods of their lives outside the labour force than their white peers. Developments over time are fundamental to many such sociological research questions. A range of options exist for sociologists to carry out longitudinal quantitative research into work (Menard 1991). There are now a number of large-scale surveys that are dedicated to tracking change in social and economic life. These include 'trend studies' where the same topics are asked of comparable samples over time and 'panel studies' where the same people are researched over time. Cohort panels trace cohorts over time, asking respondents about their lives at intervals. And retrospective studies are collected via life history methods, covering the whole life course of individuals, thus allowing researchers to link changes in work with changes in other aspects of people's lives. The 1980 Women and

Employment Survey that was mentioned earlier incorporated a life history method. Qualitative longitudinal research has also contributed to the sociology of work. In Oakley's (1979) research into first-time mothers, she returned to interview the women on separate occasions, before and after the birth (and during the birth for some!). Ray Pahl's in-depth study of work in the Isle of Sheppey, Kent, *Divisions of Labour* took place over a period of five years.

Secondary analysis of qualitative data

We discussed the secondary analysis of quantitative data earlier. There is now much more interest in re-using qualitative data, for many of the same reasons, not least the high costs of carrying out primary qualitative work (Procter 1993). Recent examples of researchers who have gone back to carry out reanalysis of classic studies include Mike Savage, who has re-examined a number of work studies from the 'golden age' of British industrial sociology (Savage 2000a, 2005). John Goodwin and Henrietta O'Connor (2005) have carried out a large-scale re-evaluation of Norbert Elias' study of young people's transition into work in the early 1960s. They studied original field work data and then followed up some of the original participants to see what had happened to them over the course of their working life.

A new Qualidata archive in Britain has been funded to promote the archiving of data from qualitative studies (Corti *et al.* 1995). At the time of writing, Goldthorpe *et al.*'s Affluent Worker studies are archived here, as are Pahl's research on the Isle of Sheppey and the SCELI studies. The secondary analysis of qualitative data has been facilitated by developments in computing assisted analysis of qualitative data (CAQDAS; Fielding and Lee 1991). Indeed, for those engaged in interviews of various types there has been a trend towards the use of software to aid analysis of qualitative material. This involves coding of responses to questions. Arguably this type of analysis is more useful at the more structured end of interviewing and there are those who would argue that this type of software goes against the spirit of this type of research (see Bryman 2004).

Participative research

Participative or action research 'is associated with attempts to bring about emancipation and social justice based on the desires and direct involvement of ordinary people' (Todhunter 2001: 1). It is used to promote the empowerment of disadvantaged groups (Kemmis and McTaggart 1988). While not widely used in the sociology of work yet, a useful example is Stephan Gaetz and Bill O'Grady's (2002) participatory action research into the economy of young homeless people in Toronto. Exploring how they made money to survive, the project involved the young people in the design, implementation and analysis of the project. Six people were trained in research design and then helped to develop a survey questionnaire as well as select research sites in which to interview homeless people.

Auto/biographical writing

An important and often overlooked source of data on work can be found in auto/biographical writing which reflects on a working life. While it is often élites who write published autobiography, there is a wide and extensive range of material from ordinary people. It is worth making some distinction about this type of material as it varies considerably. There are a series of autobiographies focusing on working life that are very professionally written. An example is Ben Hamper's (1986) *Rivethead* which is an account of his life as a production line worker at a General Motors plant in the USA. Another example would be Theriault's (1995) book *How to Tell When You're Tired.* There are also a wide set of autobiographies by workers in other trades and professions. Some of these have been published in collections such as *Useful Toil* edited by John Burnett (1994a), which traces working life from the 1820s to the 1920s and his *Idle Hands* (1994b) examining unemployment from 1790 to 1990. Others have been published in a variety of other ways, ranging from university presses to local histories. Some occupations are better represented than others; the railway industry, for example, has generated hundreds of worker autobiographies, while in others published accounts are virtually nonexistent. It is important to note that these accounts may be useful sources for understanding the changing nature of work across the years (Strangleman 2005). Each autobiography can tell us something important about work and the meaning workers attach to their labour. As was the case with oral history, we need to be alert when reading autobiography to what is being added and what is being left out, but again as was the case with oral history, this is part of the usefulness of this kind of material.

Internet research

There are a growing number of potential uses of the internet for researchers. Alan Bryman (2004) has listed these as: web-sites as the objects of analysis; ethnographic studies of the internet; qualitative research using online focus groups; qualitative research using online personal interviews; and quantitative social surveys via email or a web-site questionnaire. The internet can also be a wonderful instrument for visual researchers. There are many sites specifically holding content on work, from trade union banners, through fine art to photography. The use of search engines with image search can yield many useful results. Try, for example, searching for the work of American photographer Lewis Hine. There are over 6,000 examples of his work on the web. Of course, you need to be aware of copyright law when using the images. More generally, there are problems involved in researching the internet. The BSA states:

> Members should take special care when carrying out research via the Internet. Ethical standards for internet research are not well developed as yet . . . Members who carry out research online should ensure that they are familiar with ongoing debates on the ethics of Internet research, and might wish to consider erring on the side of caution in making judgements affecting the well-being of online research participants.

(2002: 41)

CONCLUSION

This chapter has explored how sociologists go about researching work. It identified a diverse range of techniques that have been employed over the years, in isolation and in various combinations, from ethnographies to interviewing to large-scale surveys. These techniques are not exclusive to sociology but we have argued that the breadth and depth of sociological researching, combined with its necessary links to sociological theorising, set apart our discipline.

NOTE

1   Ann Oakley's research into house-work was published for an academic audience as *The Sociology of Housework* (1974) and later for a more general readership as *Housewife* (1974).

FURTHER READING

Fiona Devine and Sue Heath's *Sociological Research Methods in Context* (1999) provides useful reviews of the methodologies employed in a number of classic sociological studies, a number of which concern work including Nicky Gregson and Michelle Lowe's (1994) *Servicing the Middle Classes* on domestic work; Janet Finch and David Mason's *Negotiating Family Responsibilities*, and Annie Phizacklea and Carol Wolkowitz's (1995) *Homeworking Women*.

A range of very good textbooks on different aspects of research methods exist for sociologists including:

Alan Bryman's *Social Research Methods* (2004).

Alan Bryman and Emma Bell's *Business Research Methods* (2007) has much useful material for the sociologist of work.

Martin Bulmer's (ed.) *Sociological Research Methods* (2000).

Sandra Harding's *Feminism and Methodology: Social Science Issues* (1987).

WEB SOURCES

The British Sociological Association: http://www.britsoc.co.uk/. See its ethics guidelines in its 'Statement of Ethical Practice'.

CASS Question bank: http://qb.soc.surrey.ac.uk/. Based at the University of Surrey, it is a free online resource which helps users find and view questionnaires from the main UK social surveys, view commentary on social measurement in specific topics, and find books and resources.

ESDS Qualidata. http://www.esds.ac.uk/qualidata/about/introduction.asp. Part of the UK Data Archive (UKDA). It promotes and facilitating use of qualitative data in research, learning and teaching.

European Foundation for the Improvement of Living and Working Conditions http://www.eurofound.eu.int/. Provides free (largely quantitative) reports on working lives from throughout Europe, including results from the 'European Working Conditions Survey' carried out every five years since 1990.

Mass-Observation Archive. http://www.massobs.org.uk/. At the University of Sussex, the Mass-Observation Archive contains material from the original Mass-Observations in 1937 to early 1950s, as well as newer material collected since 1981.

Office for National Statistics (ONS). http://www.statistics.gov.uk. National Statistics Online provides free summary statistics and detailed data on Britain's economy, population and society at national and local levels. See it for publications such as *Labour Market Trends* and *Social Trends* too.

Social Research Update. http://www.soc.surrey.ac.uk/sru/index.html. An online publication, quarterly, by the Department of Sociology, University of Surrey, reviewing research issues in Sociology.

UK Data Archive (UKDA). http://www.data-archive.ac.uk/. Holds the largest collection of digital data in the social sciences and humanities in the UK at the University of Essex.

STUDENT PROJECTS AND ESSAY QUESTIONS

1   Focusing on either qualitative or quantitative methodologies, in what ways has this methodological approach contributed to our understanding of work? Draw on sociological studies to inform your answer.

2   Can sociologists of work be value-free in the research that they carry out? Should they be?

3   How would you go about researching the following broad research topics? How would you develop the focus of the topic to have a 'do-able' and sociologically relevant project? What methodological approach or combination of approaches would you utilise? Can you identify the limitations of your approach? How would you obtain access to a sample? What ethical issues might you face and how would you deal with these? What practical considerations would be pertinent for your project?

1   The work experiences of migrant domestic workers to the UK.

2   Control and surveillance in call centres.

Representations
of Work

▮ OVERVIEW

This chapter asks:

- Why should sociologists be interested in representations of work?
- What do we mean by representations?
- What does the sociology of work tell us about representations of work in different societies?
- How do we make use of representations of work as sociologists?

▮ INTRODUCTION

In this chapter, Strangleman examines how work has been represented in a variety of media. This chapter has two main aims. First, it aims to understand the variety of ways in which work and employment figure in a range of art forms and other media. We want to look at how work is presented in visual media (fine art, photography, film, sculpture); in written form (novels, diaries, autobiography and poems) and also in song. The second aim is to suggest how such material can be used by work sociologists to add to our understanding of the topic. As you will see, this current chapter links directly to our discussion of the use of visual methods in the previous chapter, where we looked at how sociologists use images as part of their research. It is also our intention that the reader goes forward from this chapter with a wider sense of the resources and approaches available in studying work. For instance, in the next two chapters we will discuss industrialisation and post-industrial society where many of the themes covered are addressed in the current chapter. The format of this chapter is slightly different from the others in this book because of the subject matter under discussion.

THE SOCIOLOGICAL MISSION

There will be an obvious tension running through this chapter. On the one hand, we want to argue that there has been a long tradition of drawing on the kinds of resources that we are describing here. On the other, we want to suggest that there is still a resistance in seeing such resources as legitimate ones for sociologists of work (see Harper 1998). Our argument here is that the sociology of work should not be scared to experiment with the different types of material, techniques and methods. We are not suggesting that this kind of approach is 'better' than more conventional and traditional areas of sociological inquiry, but rather that the use of such resources would broaden and deepen our knowledge of work in the past, present and future. We argue that the sociology of work needs to develop a capacity and language to deal with the variety of representations of work.

FOUNDATIONS

Before we go on to look in detail at specific examples, we want to ask some basic questions about the approaches and materials we are dealing with here. First, what do we mean by representations? It could be argued that all accounts of work, be they by academics or others, are representations of a reality. Sociological accounts of the workplace or of working life are in many ways like that of an artist, a reflection of a truth. This is a position that postmodernist thinkers would adopt whereby the description of the world offered by sociologists is just one more narrative among many other competing accounts (see Chapter 2). Where the distinction can be made is in the systematic and rigorous way in which social scientists go about trying to find the answers to their questions. They apply a method to this process and have to potentially defend in public what they do. In the realm of art, however, these pressures are not the same. The artist, be they visual or non-visual, are engaged in a self-conscious process of creation in which the imagination, the fictional takes central place. While they may be aiming at getting at a 'truth', it is a truth mediated through their own artistic talents and understandings. For the sociologist attempting to draw on art in their research, this distinction represents both a weakness and strength. The weakness is that we need to be careful when we look at art or other forms of representation in that they are acts of fiction and creativity, they do not pretend to be the truth, or tell the whole story, they are dramatisations which emphasise particular parts of a story while excluding or downplaying other elements. The strength, on the other hand, is that works of art highlight particular aspects of their subject, and that these allow us new insights into particular problems and conditions. Through their work artists may be exploring a whole range of issues that are difficult or impossible to explore through conventional methods of research and writing in written social scientific prose. In this book we are suggesting that the world of work and employment is a complex and multifaceted order. No one method or approach can ever really do justice to the complex and multi-level relationships of work. What we are arguing here is that art and other forms of representative media allow us to highlight, or offer us a different cut into a particular problem, issue or place. The artifice, or dramatisation, may throw light on a problem in a different way which in turn helps us to develop our sociological analysis of the issue.

What a consideration of representation offers us is a variety of possibilities for exploring the world of work. On one level in looking at the artistic representation of work across time and space, we understand more fully what different societies made of work; the place and hierarchy of different forms of labour; and how these were mediated through the artistic imagination. Therefore, at a basic level, we can use representations as reflections on the social meaning of work. We can ask questions about what work is being represented and how, what types of work are excluded, who commissions and pays for the representation, who makes the work of art and who is the intended audience for the representation? Of course, these are a complex set of questions which we need to examine critically.

A second approach is to recognise the power of art to allow us access to the subjective and sensual world. Later in this book we look at questions of identity, culture and emotion. While it is possible to use more established techniques within the social sciences to gain access to these subjective understanding the realm of art allow a deeper and richer insight at crucial moments. In their paper on the use of art to explore organisations Cohen *et al.* use the ideas of the sociologist Theodore Adorno:

> [R]ather than succumbing to the forced identity of concept and object that characterises the instrumental logic of linguistic representation, autonomous art by virtue of its mimetic relationship to the object of its interest is capable of exploring and exposing characteristics of the

external world; characteristics that are frequently obscured or obfuscated by the web of conceptual relations which mediate our everyday experience and communicative actions.

(Cohen *et al.* 2006: 111)

Put simply, Adorno is suggesting that it is precisely *because* art stands outside our normal framework of interpretation that it is able to tell us something new. It offers a different set of understandings and tools to gain access to the object of study, in our instance, work.

An example of this can be seen in Tim Edensor's research concerned with the aesthetics of deindustrialisation. In the Introduction to his book, *Industrial Ruins*, Edensor argues specifically in terms of the power of photography in exploring abandoned workplaces:

> Photographs are never merely visual but in fact conjure up synaesthetic and kinaesthetic effects, for the visual provokes other sensory responses. The textures and tactilities, smells, atmospheres and sounds of ruined spaces, together with the signs and objects they accommodate, can be empathetically conjured up by visual material in the absence of any realistic way of conveying these sensations, other than through words and images.

(Edensor 2005: 16)

Thus the reflection on art gives the sociologist access to levels of emotion, meaning and feeling which are often difficult to come by in more traditional and mainstream social science. Lucie-Smith and Dars (1977) touch on this sensibility in their discussion of the paintings of the nineteenth-century artist Millet:

> Millet particularly seems to make an enormous effort to gather all sensations felt by the worker – earthbound peasant or straining quarryman – to create from these an image which puts us in the very midst of the work situation. He makes us feel the ache in the muscles and the sweat on the brow of the brutish, almost animal-like creature who leans upon his hoe to take a moment's respite.

(ibid.: 32)

We must also acknowledge another set of issues and limitations in the artistic portrayal of work – that artists and often their audiences were themselves middle and upper class. Their portrayal of labour and workplaces is refracted through a whole set of ideas, ideologies and prejudices so in no sense can we see the various artistic representations of work as objective accounts from which we can simply read off the 'truth'. But rather we need to reflect upon what they can tell us about. As Lucie-Smith and Dars put it: 'what gives them their value as historical evidence is precisely this lack of objectivity. They show us how men of the period tried to deal with evidence that, in many cases, they found difficult to accept' (1977: 44).

It is worth noting here and elsewhere in this chapter the highly gendered nature of both representations and the discussion of such representations of work. Indeed, in reflecting on what is absent as well as what is present in such representations we come to understand much about a society's relationship to work and the value placed on it. Writing in the context of oral history and its lack of objectivity, Italian oral historian Alessandro Portelli (2001) argues that the myths that are perpetuated within the genre allow us access to a different layer of meaning, we understand more about the belief and value system of the individuals and the societies we study. To stretch Portelli's point further, we can see the value in studying the art of a particular era in understanding what is both present and absent.

THE VISUAL REPRESENTATION OF WORK

Humans have been representing work in various art forms since the beginning of art itself. Think, for instance, of cave paintings. What counts as work in such societies, hunting and gathering, is there portrayed on the walls. Through the centuries work has been a part of the artistic landscape. Given the potential breadth of this field, this chapter can only focus on a limited number of examples. Art of course is a reflection of the age in which it is produced and during the nineteenth century there were a whole series of attempts to capture new forms of work emerging as part of industrialisation and those forms of labour or life which were disappearing as part of the same process. Often artists would portray work and the workplace by chance as they sought to capture another aspect of the emerging industrial society they witnessed before them (see Lucie-Smith and Dars 1977). In Francis Klingender's (1947) ground-breaking study, *Art and the Industrial Revolution*, we can see work graphically portrayed within the context of a wider canvas reflecting the Industrial Revolution. During the Victorian period, work was reflected in many different styles, and the messages sent out by artists were varied. For some, modernity was an exciting expansive period, others chose to portray the negative effects of industrialisation and urban development. Another trend can be witnessed in the way some artists reflected back on older types of work and community which were being lost as part of this process. We will try and reflect this range in what follows.

In 1872, France's most celebrated graphic artist Gustave Doré produced a remarkable series of drawings of London. In showing life on the streets Doré also represented many of the trades and occupations carried out. His drawings, published in *London: a Pilgrimage*, comprise 180 plates and illustrate all levels of Victorian society (Figure 4.1). His most famous images are of working-class communities and street life. These tell us much about the very

Figure 4.1 Warehousing in the City
Source: Gustave Doré, 1872.

public life led on the street, including the gendered division of labour, the nature of child labour, and work dress (Jerrold and Doré 2005).

Henry Mayhew in his *London Labour and London Poor* employed the services of an illustrator to provide engravings of his 'types of labour'. These are an important source of information about the variety of labour within the London labour market as well as providing a stylised representation of particular trades, occupations and crafts (Figure 4.2).

Figure 4.2 'Dark House Lane – Billingsgate'
Source: Gustave Doré, 1872.

A far more positive reading of work can be seen in the art of the Pre-Raphaelites Brotherhood in the mid-nineteenth century. In his book, *Men at Work: Art and Labour in Victorian Britain*, Tim Barringer (2005) looks at the way Victorian art and artists reflect a whole series of questions about the meaning and status of labour in nineteenth-century society. For instance, how was modern factory employment to be understood? As drudge labour or celebrated as vibrant and progressive? There were also debates played out on canvas about the moral status of work, or types of work, the dignity of labour as well as notions of duty and calling. We can see the obvious parallels between artists and contemporary sociologists. Barringer illustrates his thesis by a detailed reading of the painting 'Work' by Ford Madox Brown, painted between 1852 and 1865. This painting reflects a powerful narrative about the Victorian attitude to work and the status of manual, masculine labour (Figure 4.3). The picture is dominated by three central figures of the labourers. While working hard, the men are portrayed as healthy and dignified, their employment as necessary, useful and honourable. The picture is a powerful social commentary on wider Victorian society and reflects many prevailing attitudes towards the employment of men and women of all social classes.

Often the dignity of labour which is a feature of the Pre-Raphaelite School is portrayed within rural settings and as such is seen as a backward-looking, at times nostalgic, account of work. The portrayal of women within this artistic school is very instructive of mid-Victorian social attitudes with female labour carried out largely in the domestic sphere. Art critic John Ruskin, with his stress on the value of craft and skill, was very influential on the Pre-Raphaelites who shared his disquiet at the problems of industrial society. This tension between work as negative and positive is reflected in other genres of Victorian art in Britain, Europe and the USA. For instance, social realism as a genre of illustration in Europe tends to reflect on the negative aspects of working conditions in industrialisation can be contrasted with American Impressionism where work and labour are often celebrated and idealised (see Larkin 2005; Treuherz 1987). In European social realism, women's (and children's) role in the public as well as the domestic division of labour is portrayed (see Sayer 1995; Treuherz 1987).

Figure 4.3 'Work', Ford Madox Brown (1852–65)
Source: © Manchester Art Gallery.

One of the most important developments in the portrayal of work in the nineteenth century came with the invention and widespread use of photography. This created a rival way of illustrating the world which was at the time seen as more objective and accurate (Jeffery 1981). From quite early on, photographers recorded images of work either by design or as part of a wider social scene. Importantly photography as a medium was very early on pushed into the service of social reportage and propaganda. In the United States two photographers' portfolios became synonymous with the representation of work – Jacob Riis and slightly later Lewis Hine.

Jacob Riis (1849–1914) was a pioneering photographer of the conditions of the poor in New York during the late nineteenth century. Riis, a Danish immigrant, began taking photographs in New York after being hired by the Tribune and Associated Press as a reporter in 1877. He was quickly promoted to police reporter, gaining access to the ghettoes on the city's lower East Side. Ten years later Riis developed a lecture series that highlighted the wretched conditions of his subjects which he began to illustrate with lantern slides. These pictures, alongside a series of essays, were published in 1890 in his *How the Other Half Lives* (see also Yochelson 2001).

A second major figure in the tradition of photography of labour is Lewis Hine (1874–1940). Hine obtained a Master's degree in sociology at Columbia University. Socially committed, Hine spent his time taking photographs for a series of socially aware magazines and later for the National Child Labor Committee (NCLC). The NCLC used his photography in a very direct way as evidence of child exploitation (Langer 1998). But there was another side to Hine's work, as he himself explained: 'There were two things I wanted to do. I wanted to show the things that had to be corrected. I wanted to show the things that had to be appreciated' (Hine, quoted in Langer 1998: 20).

This second aspect of his studies celebrated work and the worker in industrial society, subverting the notion that in an industrial age humans became mere appendages to their machines. Rather, Hine lionised heroic workers and labour, most famously in his series of photographs recording the construction of the Empire State Building in New York (Langer 1998; see also Orvell 1995).

There are various parallels with documentary and socially active photographers in the UK and elsewhere. One early example is in the publicity material and reporting of the sweated trades and in particular the famous match girls strike of 1888 in London's East End. Here photography and engravings were used to mobilise public support for the strikers by showing the graphic poverty associated with match manufacture (Figure 4.4) (Smith 1997).

But just as trade unions and social activists could harness the power of photography so too could governments and corporations. From the late nineteenth century onwards there developed a widespread use of corporate photography for a variety of reasons. These uses could include advertising and promotion of product, the recording of new organisational developments, the capturing

Figure 4.4 'Match Workers at the Bryant and May Factory', London, 1888
Source: © TUC Library Collections.

of new trades and occupations or marking those which were in the process of dying out. There is now a growing literature on corporate use of photography. David Nye's (1985) book, *Image Worlds*, for example, examines the use of photography in the ideological construction of the General Electric Company in the USA. In turn, Nye looks at the way the company recorded its workforce, managers, products, factories, engineers, publicity and consumers.

Henry Ford, as in so many other respects, was a pioneer in the use of photography for corporate purposes. Having purchased a camera for personal use in 1896, he later set up the Ford Motor Company motion picture department in 1914. His moving and still pictures record every aspect of the organisation and its workforce. These images were used for internal training purposes as well as to promote the company to its customers and a wider public. The scale of this endeavour can be seen in the fact that in 1963 the company presented the US National archives with approximately 1.5 million feet of silent film and the collection of more than 75,000 stills from the company's Rouge plant taken from its opening in 1917 to 1941 (Bryan 2003: 246).

Elspeth Brown's (2005) *The Corporate Eye* is a fascinating study of the rather different purposes that photography was put to from the mid-1880s to 1930. In particular, she looks at the way early management theorists used photography to help identify types of workers by reference to their physiognomy. Essentially this involved creating a theory of reliable or unreliable facial and bodily types against which a job applicant could be judged. In another chapter, Brown looks at the pioneering use of photography by scientific management theorists Frank and Lillian Gilbreth. Here photography was used in time and motion studies to identify and design work processes.

During the inter-war period in the United States, there were important developments in the use of so-called documentary photography. This was stimulated by the creation of a series of photo magazines, newspapers and the state sponsorship of photographers during the Depression years of the 1930s through the Works Progress Administration (WPA) and later the Farm Security Administration (FSA). The FSA photography division provided pictures which would support the work of the Resettlement Administration. Under the directorship of Roy Stryker, dozens of photographers recorded conditions of farmers and the working poor across America (Hurley 1972). The resultant images, which have become icons of part of American life during this time, were made available to magazines and newspapers. Importantly the wide range of subjects covered by photographers included 'race', gender, domestic work as well as paid employment. The FSA collection was later housed in the US Library of Congress and amounts to 165,000 prints, a further 265,000 negatives, as well as 1,600 colour slides (Daniel *et al.* 1987; Orvell 2003). Aside from these stunning pictures of working life and social conditions, the photographers were important as many went on to produce further images of work and labour in a variety of genres including corporate and propaganda settings.

It is important that in discussing photography and work that we do not neglect the continued production of paintings and drawings by artists. Indeed, some of the finest art associated with the representation of work was produced in the inter-war period. In the United States, for example, Mexican artist Diego Rivera produced a stunning celebration of industry in his Detroit murals which cover the walls of the City's Institute of Art (Figure 4.5). These were commissioned and financed by Henry Ford's son Edsel in 1932 (Downs 1999). Elsewhere in the USA, New Deal Federal Government

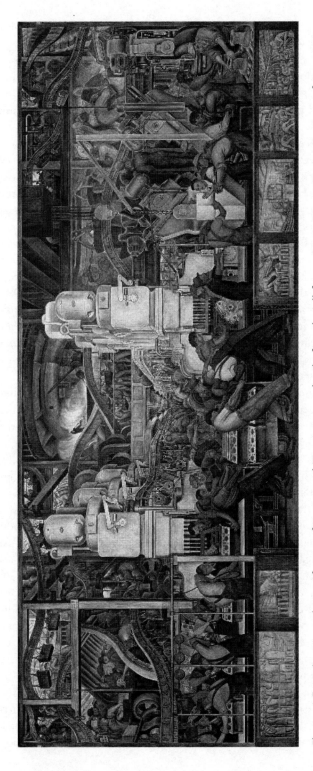

Figure 4.5 Production and Manufacture of Engine and Transmission, detail of north wall fresco, Diego Rivera, Detroit Institute of Art, 1933

Source: © The Detroit Institute of Art.

funding stimulated the creation of hundreds of examples of visual art celebrating workers (Doss 2002).

Mixing both photography and other forms of visual art, it is important
to acknowledge the literature on propaganda likewise offers an account of
the social meaning of labour. In the wake of the Russian Revolution in 1917,
art and propaganda became a very important source of communication for
the new Soviet government first under Lenin and later under Stalin. These
régimes developed a form of representation of work and labour which often
portrayed workers as heroic and dignified. This socialist realist style put the
ordinary worker at its centre, although often in a highly stylised way, and
reflected a political ideology of a state based on the importance of the
worker. All types of labour are seen in such art including female construction workers on the Moscow Underground, steelworkers and coalminers to
electrical engineers. Work and the working class were portrayed in progressive and positive light, highlighting their role in modernising a new country.
Brown and Taylor's (1993) *Art of the Soviets* includes several essays on the
portrayal of labour in the former USSR while Clark's (1997) *Art and
Propaganda* offers many illustrations of the promotion of heroic labour in
Soviet and Nazi art. Outside the context of totalitarian régimes, Foner
and Schultz's (1985) *Art and the Labour Movement in the United States* is a
fantastic collection of images of American labour from fine art through
photography and the cartoons of ordinary working people.

In the UK, the state representation of work and workers often takes on a
more benign aspect. This can be seen in the various documentary films we
touch upon below but is also witnessed in art work produced for government departments and bodies. One illustration of this among many is the
artwork produced for the Empire Marketing Board, established in 1926.
Through a series of high quality posters designed by some of the leading artists
of the day, the Board portrayed a powerful message about the British Empire
and its trade links – essentially producing a narrative of interdependence between
the colonies, the suppliers of raw materials, and Britain, where industrial products would be forged from these same materials (Figure 4.6). Posters such as
these again tell us much about how the division of labour on a global scale
was seen from the perspective of the metropolitan economies of the world.
As a by-product, many of the posters portray industry, labour and work and
what is especially noteworthy is the portrayal of race and ethnicity. These
images were widely distributed and could at the time be purchased by
schools and the general population (Constantine 1986).

One element of writing on representation can be found in the analysis of
trade union banners and memorabilia. Here one could cite the work of John
Gorman (1986) and his classic *Banner Bright*, originally published in 1973,
or more recently Rodney Mace's (1999) *British Trade Union Posters*. Both deal
in slightly different ways with the issue of the iconography of labour. The
labour movement across the world has often produced art which portrays labour

Figure 4.6 Colombo, Ceylon, Empire Marketing Board, 1928, K. D. Shoesmith
Source: © The National Archives.

and work. Like the Soviet art discussed above, the art of trade unions seeks to promote positive images of collective organisations, or, as was often the case with craft unions, it sought to stress unique skills and attributes of a particular occupation. Thus, in many older trade union banners, we can see the tools of the trade or even a worker at work.

A contemporary example of socially informed photography of labour can be seen in the work of the Brazilian photographer Sebastião Salgado, whose touring exhibitions have been seen by hundreds of thousands across the world and have been reproduced as fine art collections (Salgado 1993). Salgado's photography often features as illustrations in, and on the covers of, sociological volumes on work. Salgado's work and its iconographic status in reflecting the contemporary nature of labour have spawned a number of review essays which examine the meaning and intention behind the images. Both Orvell (1995) and Stallabrass (1997) explore the tension in Salgado's work between documentary photography and its status as fine art. Both critics also dwell on the way his photographs celebrate or even mourn the passing of industrial work, his images capturing or projecting dignity and heroic features of labour.

Before ending this section it is important that we at least mention cartoons and their portrayal of work. The selection here could be vast as work is so often a target of the cartoonist's pen so we will focus on just two examples. First, the Dilbert strip drawn by US cartoonist Scott Adams. Adams developed the strip having worked in a series of offices and his Dilbert character is a composite of many of his former co-workers. The Dilbert strip, which is syndicated across the globe, reflects the absurdity of modern office life and especially corporate culture and managerial rhetoric.

Finally, a range of feminist-inspired cartoons, including, in the UK, Jackie Flemming's work, reflects on the subject of work and especially the domestic divisions of labour. Through humour, Flemming explicitly targets established and taken-for-granted aspects of the labour market and the engendering of roles (Figure 4.7).

FILM AND TV

Like the other media we are discussing as part of this chapter, moving images in film and TV offer a wide and potentially rich source for the study, reflection and representation of work. Film, like photography, reflected work virtually from its infancy. Early film-makers would often use the new media to record crowd scenes of people at leisure and work; this can be seen in the films of Mitchel and Keynon, a pair of early British cinematographers. As we noted before, this section could be expanded into a book in itself so what

Figure 4.7 'Rubbish'
Source: © Jackie Flemming.

we present here is just a flavour of this material. Corporations were early adopters of film for a variety of purposes – advertising, training and public relations. There are countless examples of this type of film-making on both sides of the Atlantic as well as in other parts of the globe. Henry Ford was a pioneer of film for a variety of purposes and in the process of recording events has left an important legacy about life and work in his plants (Bryan 2003).

In the UK, documentary films, often explicitly featuring work, grew up in the 1920s and 1930s. One of the main stimuli of a series of films produced by the so-called Documentary Film Movement (DFM) was the funding provided by a series of film boards created as parts of large public corporations such as the Empire Marketing Board, the Shell Film Unit and the General Post Office (GPO) Film Unit. A group of young socially com-mitted film makers coalesced around John Grierson and produced films on work groups and industries such as fishermen (*Drifters* 1929), the tea trade (*Song of Ceylon* 1933–4), coalmining (*Coalface* 1935), railways and the Post Office (*Night Mail* 1936) (see Aitken 1998; Hardy 1979; Swann 1989). The DFM were important in a number of ways both at the time and subsequently for the influence individual members of the group had on both document-ary and later feature films. One of the most important members of this group was Humphrey Jennings who was involved in a number of films about or around work. Arguably his best work can be seen in the wartime propaganda films he made which are dominated by scenes of work and often working-class life – see, for example, *Fires Were Started* (1943) about the work of the auxiliary fire service tackling fires in the London Blitz where the gendered division of labour is most apparent.

After the Second World War, members of the DFM moved into a variety of other film-making forms including feature films as well as continuing to produce corporate work including training and promotional material for pub-lic and private bodies. One of the best examples and most easily available is the work of British Transport Films. As well as numerous training films made for internal audiences, the unit also produced dozens of high quality award-winning short films about the whole field of transport in the UK at the time, including mainline and underground railways, shipping and buses (Reed 1990). Documentary films such as these tell us a great deal about work and organ-isation in the post-war period and much about the attitudes to workers them-selves. Perhaps their most important feature is that they do record, however partially, work practices and places that have either been revolutionised or eradicated in the passing years. They can also tell us something about how work was done and what people felt about their work. We see the special and gendered division of labour and what infuses all of the films mentioned here is to importance of class and the way this is embedded in work cultures. The films also tell us a great deal about the film-makers and the values which informed their art. Take, for example, the members of the Documentary Film Movement whose films often reflect heroic work in traditional industries. One of their number, Edgar Anstay wrote: 'the workingman can only be a heroic figure. If he's not heroic, he can't be a workingman' (Swann 1989: 88). Clearly, the DFM had a developed political as well as highly gendered notion of what work was, what types of work were important and, by implication, what was not worthy of portrayal and attention.

While so far we have considered documentary factual films, there has equally been a long tradition of feature films which examine work in a way in which sociologists can make use of. As with other visual arts, we can distinguish between films as artistic reflections of the mood and mores of the period in which they are made and, second, in terms of their content film and TV programmes can be used as a way in to understanding detail of work, especially subjective and inter-subjective experience. In looking at films about work we are presented with an enormous field. Starting with Charlie Chaplin's *Modern Times* (1936), a satire on modern factory work, we can trace films from all over the world that reflect aspects of working life. In the 1960s, in Britain we could look at *I'm Alright Jack* (1959), the relationship between unions and employers as well as hinting at 'race' tensions around immigrant labour; *Saturday Night, Sunday Morning* (1960) (individuality and mundane work); through to films like *Blue Collar* (1978) which is a graphic portrayal of Fordist production and workplace tension, especially along class and 'race' lines; to films such as *Brassed Off* (1996) and *The Full Monty* (1997) and *Billy Elliot* (2000) which examine deindustrialisation. There have also been a number of films which portray the work of women such as *Working 9 to 5* that deals also with sexual harassment; or more recently *A Good Girl* (see Hassard and Holliday 1998; Rowbotham and Beynon 2001; Stead 1989; Zaniello 2003). How women reconcile the competing demands of work and home is a recurring theme, in films such as *Baby Boom* and in TV shows such as *Sex and the City*.

Equally in the context of television, programme makers have often reflected on the workplace in serious and comedy programme – *On the Buses, Taxi, The Rag Trade, Boys from the Black Stuff, Clocking Off, Dinnerladies, Cutting It* and more recently *The Office*. This last example has become a worldwide hit and portrays very mundane clerical white-collar work. *The Office*, apart from being very funny, is important as it allows us access to a series of themes in modern work such as emotion in the workplace, office politics, gender, 'race' and sexuality. The comedy is as far removed from the heroic workers portrayed in the documentary films discussed above as it is possible to be.

Some occupations obviously gain more attention from programme makers so medical workers have been reflected in programmes such as *ER* and *Casualty*, or earlier still in *Angels*, featuring the lives of nurses, *Dr Finlay's Casebook* and *Dr Kildare*. The police are an obvious parallel to this. In addition, on both sides of the Atlantic there has been a rash of docu-soaps often based on the workplace (Rowbotham and Beynon 2001). Finally, it is worth thinking about the ways in which children's' programmes represent work now and in the past. In the UK, we could point to the *Trumpton, Chigley* and *Camberwick Green* in the 1960s, or more recently to *Fireman Sam, Postman Pat* and *Bob the Builder*. Clearly strong messages about work are portrayed in a variety of such programmes and these also tell us about the type of stories adults want to tell children about the world of work. Importantly, all these examples have embedded within them very powerful gendered messages about a division of labour and the separation of work tasks, with a far more restricted range of roles on offer to girls. Note the absence of Firewoman Sam and Postwoman Pat. Bob the Builder's business partner Wendy has brick-laying skills but her 'real strength is organization' (Bob the Builder web-site 2007 http://www.bobthebuilder.com/uk/meet_bob_the_builder_and_his_whole_gang.htm). What is of interest is the continual relevance of work-based identity in media targeted at children.

SCULPTURE

It is worth noting very briefly that work has been portrayed in another artistic medium, that of sculpture. As in other visual media the portrayal of labour in sculpture is a long-standing tradition going back to classical times if not before, but perhaps unlike other art forms the commentaries on this aspect of art in relation to work are less common. The real exception to this is Melissa Dabakis (1999) and her ground-breaking book *Visualising Labor in American Sculpture*. Dabakis' study reveals the complex history of the ways in which labour is memorialised within a period of American public art. More often than not, the sculpture sought to celebrate masculine manual labour rather than that by women or white-collar workers. She argues that the study of such monuments tell us much about those who commissioned and the intended audience for the art.

Another dimension of this discussion can be seen in the public art of the former communist régimes. Here in self-proclaimed workers' states, the purpose of art was at times largely to celebrate work and the worker. Throughout the former Eastern bloc, statues to various types of workers were erected (see Brown and Taylor 1993).

Much art tends to reflect on ideas of the past and memory and this is particularly true of public sculpture. One of the interesting phenomenon of the past twenty of so years has been the way in which attention has been turned to the memorialisation of forms of work, workplaces and whole industries which have been lost as part of the process of deindustrialisation (Figures 4.8 and 4.9). It is interesting to reflect on what is memorialised and what is not. It is also worth noting the ways in which the public art come to be erected and how the public interact with them (see Linkon and Russo 2002).

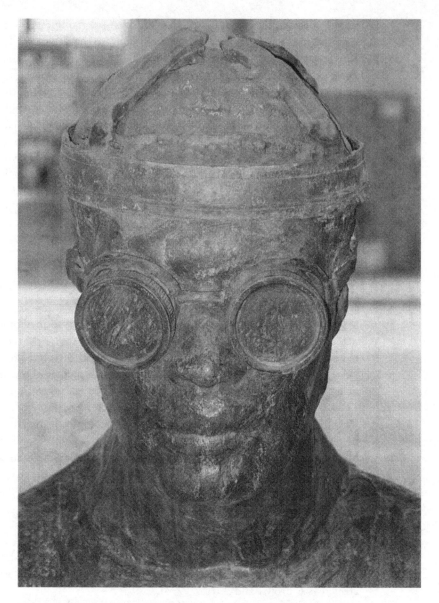

Figure 4.8 Steelmakers, sculpture, George Segal, 1980
Source: Photograph Tim Strangleman.

▌ AURAL

Another sense in which we can think of work being represented is in terms of music and song. While the sociological material on this area is much more limited than that on the visual, it is a substantial and growing area. There

Figure 4.9 The Building Worker, sculpture, Alan Wilson, London, 2006
Source: Photograph Chris Wall.

is an important set of writing about the presence of music within the workplace which examines the way workers use, enjoy or even loath sound. While this is strictly outside the theme of this chapter, it is worth recognising that this is an important and neglected area and one worth further investigation. As Marek Korczynski notes: 'Despite the potential importance of music, *there is a huge gap in the sociological knowledge of the role of music within work.* This means, therefore, that there may be important gaps in our understanding of work' (2003: 314; emphasis in original).

As Korczynski and others have pointed out, music offers us a clue as to how workers think about their work, how they pace their labour and often how they cope with boredom. Often folk songs have emerged out of work, which are themselves a reflection on the workplace itself.

Songs which reflect on work go back centuries and are part of a long-established oral tradition. American musicologist Ted Gioia has attempted to trace this tradition across many centuries, continents and types of work. In his *Work Songs* (2006), he writes about the commonality of songs about work in pre-industrial and industrial societies, drawing on industries and sectors such as hunting, agricultural, textiles, fishing, industrial work, and mining. Music, he argues, is embedded within workplace culture. It both helps us understand work itself, its rhythms, norms and customs, but also helps us in understanding people's attitudes to their labour, the workmates and employers (see also Green 1993). As Korczynski puts it:

> Music is, therefore, a potentially rich medium through which to explore people's experiences of work. This is doubly so because we know that music can be a transgressive medium of communication, allowing the expression of sentiments that would not be permitted in other formats. For instance, sailors could sing out grievances to the ship's captain in the words of shanties . . . and slaves could mock figures of power in their songs.
>
> (2004: 257–8)

Songs about work can therefore be seen as a way in which workers subvert, or de-subordinate the power relations in firms alongside other tactics such as humour, satire and sarcasm (see Ackroyd and Thompson 1999).

A fascinating example of the way work can be represented in a form of song can be seen in *The Radio Ballads* produced by the BBC during the 1950s and 1960s in the UK. These were a series of programmes created by folk singers Ewan MacColl and Peggy Seeger and produced by Charles Parker. Between 1957 and 1964, the team produced eight programmes, five of which were explicitly about work – railway workers, road building, fishing, coal mining and boxers. The programmes took the form of narrative documentaries with interviews with workers spliced with song and music which reflected the work they did. These interviews were originally obtained purely for background context for the songs but such was the richness of the material they recorded the team decided to incorporate it as part of the recording. MacColl and Seeger were respected folk musicians and drew on a number of influences including American Blues, country and jazz music alongside the domestic folksong of parts of the UK. *The Radio Ballads* tended to be based on male-dominated traditional industries which were easy to portray as heroic. *The Radio Ballads* are interesting for us in that they both draw on and contribute to powerful images of work in society (MacColl 1990). In 2006, a further series of *Radio Ballads* was produced, including two explicitly about work. Interestingly these were again male-dominated traditional industries, this time shipbuilding (*The Ballad of the Big Ships*) and steel-making (*The Song of Steel*).

Another sense in which we can see the workplace reflected in song and music is in the genre of the company song. El-Sawad and Korczynski (2007) have researched the specific case of IBM and its Songbook, which was used by the company for over fifty years, and comprising of over a hundred songs. The songs themselves are divided into two groups, those about the company and those in tribute to individual workers and managers. Now while it would be easy to poke fun at company songs, it is important that we acknowledge that they can tell us something about organisations, the way they are led and the people in them.

Before we finish this section on song, it is worth looking at the way more contemporary music reflects on work. While many songs in multiple genres reflect work and employment, one of the singers whose work has attracted the most attention is Bruce Springsteen. What makes Springsteen so interesting is the way throughout his career his music and lyrics have reflected on work and work cultures. His early songs reflected his own blue-collar background of New Jersey but as he has matured as an artist his music now reflects on a far wider range of labour, including Mexican migrants (*Across the Border* 1995) and those experiencing deindustrialisation *My Home Town* (1984) and *Youngstown*. In his song *Youngstown* (1995), Springsteen tells the story of the creation, operation and destruction of the steel industry in Youngstown, Ohio, in a song which is little over four minutes long, he captures the way in which industry both creates and destroys communities, the way it forges cultures and loyalties and the sense of betrayal when big business moves on and abandons plants. A variety of scholars have written about Springsteen's songs in connection with industrial society including Rhodes (2004), on the utopian aspects of work; Cowie and Boehm (2006), on the way his lyrics reflect working-class identity through and around work; and Linkon and Russo (2002), who draw on Springsteen's work in interpreting a community's response to economic change.

WRITTEN REPRESENTATIONS OF WORK

Finally, in this chapter we turn our attention to written forms of art, these could include novels, poetry and also autobiography. This latter source has been discussed in a previous chapter. As with the other material we discuss, we need to be clear about what we are claiming about written fictional accounts of work and the workplace. As with visual sources, we claim here that fictional writing helps us understand work on at least two levels. First, any written account of work is a reflection of the age in which it is written. Thus it could tell us something about the writer's attitude to their subject or wider society's views about work and labour. Second, again written fictional accounts offer us a way into the often hidden world of work – workplace cultures, emotional experiences of work among other things. As with other media, this is a huge area, one where the sociologist has to recognise that other disciplines are more skilled in understanding the structure and content of this type of writing. Nonetheless the argument of this book and this chapter is that we can use these resources critically in adding a new dimension to our own interpretation and analysis of work.

In terms of novels we could start by looking at a range of fiction from the eighteenth, nineteenth and twentieth centuries. It is important that when examining them we take care to read them carefully and not simply plunder them in a utilitarian way for 'facts' about work. A more subtle and intelligent approach is required whereby we might uncover deeper meanings about the cultural significance of work. Take *Robinson Crusoe*, the famous novel recording the adventures of a shipwrecked mariner. Superficially the book contains descriptions of various types of labour but literary theorists see a deeper set of meanings contained in the book whereby it acts an encapsulation of a putative Protestant work ethic. Thus, Danon (1985) argues that *Robinson Crusoe* is both reflective of, and in turn helps construct a powerful ideological attitude to work among readers. A strong moral narrative about work runs through many nineteenth-century novels. We could look at Dickens' novels. Dickens' writing often portrays workplaces and workers as well as signalling important contemporary social values about work. Running through many of his works are stock characters who act almost as ideal types which sociologists would use. Thus we can see hard work and industry in some characters while other are lazy and wasteful. This reflects the type of ideology about work we saw reflected in other types of nineteenth-century art as, for example, Ford Madox Brown's 'Work' discussed above. Novels of this period as well as later can offer us vivid accounts of the contemporary workplace. In a slightly later period, American writer Upton Sinclair (1906) wrote a famous novel about the meatpacking industry in Chicago. Here he describes women working in the sausage-room:

> There was a sort of spout, like the nozzle of a hose, and one of the women would take a long string of 'casing' and put the end over the nozzle and then work the whole thing on, as one works the finger of a tight glove. This string would be twenty or thirty feet long, but the women would have it all on in a jiffy; and when she had several on, she would press a lever, and a stream of sausage meat would be shot out, taking the casting with it as it came. Thus one might stand and see appear, miraculously born from the machine, a wriggling snake of sausage of incredible length. In front was a big pan which caught these creatures, and two more women who seized them as fast as they appeared and twisted them into links. This was for the uninitiated the most perplexing work of all; for all that the

woman had to give was a single turn of the wrist; and in some way she contrived to give it so that instead of an endless chain of sausages, one after another, there grew under her hands a bunch of strings, all dangling from a single centre. It was quite like the feat of a prestidigitator – for the woman worked so fast that the eye could literally not follow her, and there in the midst of motion, and tangle after tangle of sausages appearing in the midst of the mist, however, the visitor would suddenly notice the tense set face, with the two wrinkles graven in the forehead, and the ghastly pallor of the cheeks; and then would suddenly recollect that it was time to go on. The woman did not go on; she stayed right there – hour after hour, day after day, year after year, twisting sausage links and racing with death.

(Sinclair, 2002, first published 1906: 124–5)

In this graphic passage from *The Jungle*, we can draw out a number of things. On one level we get an important and fairly detailed account of the labour of women working in the sausage room. We get a real sense of the speed of the work but also its monotony and not simply for a shift but potentially for a working life. We also get a sense of the tension between those observing the work and those doing it, the sense of guilt that the narrator can move on, the worker cannot. It is interesting to think about this passage from *The Jungle* and the sociological ethnographies of the workplace. In both instances we get what Clifford Geertz (1973) calls 'thick description'. In both we get a sense of what is being made and how this work is organised. We are also invited to reflect of how the workers feel about their work, and to think about how they cope with the endless repetition of their labour. When the reader knows that Upton Sinclair spent time in Chicago on fieldwork making notes about the meatpacking industry, one realises that, in this case at least the boundaries between fiction and academic work are far from straightforward (see Jacobs 2002). Another illustration of this type of writing on the border between fiction and social reportage is that of George Orwell who in various novels and essays reflected on working-class communities and work. In *Down and Out in Paris and London* (1989, first published in 1933), he describes working as a kitchen hand in a Paris hotel. Orwell portrays the noise, pressure and general atmosphere of the kitchen. Unlike Sinclair, Orwell actually did the jobs he describes and so we can gain a slightly different view of such labour.

There are hundreds of novels which we could look at in various ways to think further about the representation of work from Alan Sillitoe's (1990) *Saturday Night, Sunday Morning*, where we get an important insight into worker alienation at a time of full employment, through to Douglas Coupland in *Generation X* describing the McJob as 'A low-pay, low-prestige, low-dignity, low-benefit, no-future job in the service sector. Frequently considered a satisfying career choice by people who have never held one' (Coupland 1991: 6).

There are a number of commentaries on the role of work in fiction which are written by academics working within disciplines other than sociology which are important and useful for us. Laura Hapke (2001), for example, in her *Labor's Text: The Worker in American Fiction*; this is a wide-ranging book looking at the role of the worker in novels from before the American Civil War through to the 1990s. In the book, she covers issues of gender, ethnicity, the role of the trades unions and the civil rights movement. David Meakin's (1976) *Man and Work: Literature and Culture in Industrial Society*, although dating back to the 1970s, is still an excellent and thought-provoking study of the meaning of work in modern society. There are also a series of books and collections reflecting the role of class in work and working-class life on both sides of the Atlantic (see Bradshaw and Ozment 2000; Breton 2005; Coles and Zandy 2007; Denning 1987; Fox 1994; Keating 1971; Kirk 2003).

Before we conclude, we want to briefly touch on poetry as a source for the sociologist of work. Here we may draw parallels with our discussion of song lyrics and the representation of work. Poetry about work and working life like other art forms has a long history. English social historian E.P. Thompson used poetry as well as other evidence in his attempt to reconstruct the cultural milieu of the English working class during the early Industrial Revolution (Thompson 1968). Like other art forms, the types of representation vary enormously and can give rise to some fascinating insights in to work. Here is a short poem by the US poet Jim Daniels (2003: 9) about a cook in a burger bar (Text box 4.1).

TEXT BOX 4.1 'SHORT-ORDER COOK', BY JIM DANIELS

An average joe comes in
And orders thirty cheeseburgers and thirty fries.
I wait for him to pay before I start cooking.
He pays.
He ain't no average joe.
The grill is just big enough for ten rows of three.
I slap the burgers down
Throw two buckets of fries in the deep frier
And they pop pop, spit spit . . .
pssss . . .
The counter girls laugh.
I concentrate.
It is the crucial point –
They are ready for the cheese:
My fingers shake as I tear off slices
Toss them on the burgers/ fries done/dump/
Refill buckets/ burgers ready/ flip into buns/
Beat that melting cheese/ wrap burgers in plastic/

Into paper bags/ fried done/ dump/ fill thirty bags/
Bring them to the counter/ wipe sweat on sleeve
And smile at the counter girls.
I puff my chest out and bellow:
Thirty cheeseburgers! Thirty fries!
I grab a handful of ice, toss it in my mouth
Do a little dance and walk back to the grill.
Pressure, responsibility, success.
Thirty cheeseburgers, thirty fries.

Source: Reproduced with permission of the University of Wisconsin Press

In Daniels' poem, we get a sense of the complexity of meanings and ideas about work. Here he takes what often stands for the most mundane and boring of contemporary work – flipping burgers – and asks us to think about the skill and knowledge that go into to quickly preparing this meal. We get a sense of the speed of the work, the practice of timing, knowing just when to do what. When the task is complete, we get a sense of the pride a worker can take at having achieved this impressive task. It is interesting to note the way Daniels can find values and express them in his art in the most degraded of work which other artists portray as otherwise.

CONCLUSION

In this chapter we have looked at a range of artistic representations of work, labour and organisations. These have ranged from a variety of visual representation – photography, painting, sculpture, through aural examples to the written word. We have also looked in more detail at how sociology has developed visual methods and techniques in carrying out research into work. As we have made it clear throughout this chapter, what we are arguing is that the sociology of work can, if it chooses, consider the artistic representation of work in order to tell a more rounded story of work. As we noted above we are not suggesting that artistic material gives us unproblematic objective evidence. Rather we have argued that it allows us another slightly different vantage point from which to consider work. It allows us an insight into what different societies at different times thought about work. What they considered important and unimportant. It tells us something about what was valued in people's labour, and finally tells us about the presence and meaning of work. Secondly we argued that the representation of work allows us access to subjective understandings of work. It allows us access to meanings and emotions in the workplace which are often difficult to get using conventional sociological methods. What we suggest is that sociology of work needs to examine and use these resources in an open and critical way in order to understand work more fully.

FURTHER READING

Francis Klingender's *Art and the Industrial Revolution* (1947), remains a classic in the field.

More up-to-date and specifically about work and labour is Tim Barringer's *Men at Work* (2005).

For a short overview of work sociology and visual representation, see Tim Strangleman's (2004a) 'Ways of (not) seeing work: the visual as a blind spot in WES', *Work, Employment and Society*, 18(1): 179–92.

In terms of literary representations of work, Bradshaw and Ozment's *The Voice of Toil: 19th-Century British Writing about Work* (2000) is a very large and comprehensive collection.

WEB SOURCES

The web offers those interested in visual examples of work an amazing array of material and more is being added to it all the time. Using the search engine Google in its image mode is a good place to start. There are numerous archives to take a look at here are some:

http://www.amber-online.com
http://www.lostlabor.com
http://www.californiahistoricalsociety.org/exhibits/atwork/index.html
http://www.unionhistory.info/index.php

STUDENT PROJECTS AND ESSAY QUESTIONS

1   Choose a picture of some aspect of work. Start by describing what you see. Then think more deeply about what the image tells you about the nature of work, the production of the image and the intended audience for the image.
2   What does the visual or another form of cultural representation add to our sociological understanding of work?
3   Select a novel or passage from a piece of fiction which features work in some form. Think about the ways in which work is described and the role it plays in the wider novel.
4   Using a camera, go out around your community/locality and photograph a public form of art which reflects on work.

Part II

Work and Social Change

Work and Industrial Society

▌ OVERVIEW

This chapter will:

- Take the reader through the growth of industrial society from its feudal origins.
- Look at questions of tradition, modernity and problems of social order related to industrialisation.
- Explore the birth of the factory system and the rise of Fordism.
- Ask what the moves towards industrial society meant for the organisation of work, and for the experiences of different groups of workers.

▌ INTRODUCTION

In this chapter we look at how feudal societies became industrialised and at the implications of the moves towards industrialism for the organisation and experience of work. We show that the growth of industrial society stimulated discussions – and fears – as to what these developments meant for the quality of work and for workers' lives. In particular, we look at the growth of the factory to identify a range of fundamental concerns for the sociology of work: concerns to do with discipline, control and resistance; the labour process; rationality and technological efficiencies; and alienation. Finally, we problematise the emphasis on class divisions in the early approaches to industrial society and show that, while class divisions are fundamental, incorporating the social divisions of gender and 'race' is vital too if we want to understand changes – and continuities – in the organisation and experience of work in modernity.

THE SOCIOLOGICAL MISSION

Since the birth of the discipline, sociologists have been absorbed with understanding the organisation of the prevailing form of production in a society, with the techniques that characterise it, and with the living and working experiences of workers within it. It is no coincidence that sociology emerged in Europe during the Industrial Revolution when feudalism and the agrarian mode of production were being replaced, to various extents and at different speeds, by industrial capitalism. Sociologists, then and since, have explored the momentous implications of these changes for work at its macro, meso and micro levels. The Industrial Revolution marked historic societal changes in how and where work was carried out, and by whom, with crucial differences emerging (or shifting) according to a number of social divisions including class, gender, and 'race'. Developments in the dominant mode of production towards industrialism also occurred in conjunction with a growth in urbanised living, with changes in how and where workers lived their daily lives. The first sociologists were living in rapidly changing times, and they raised questions about the origins of the emergence of industrial society; about the implications of the changes for the societal structure and for people's everyday lives; and about the prospects for further change. In effect, the early sociologists were inspired by three main topics: (1) why were the changes occurring at this point in time and what had preceded them?; (2) did the changes represent progress towards more harmonious egalitarian societal structures, or not?; and (3) would change continue to occur and, if so, in what way? These issues of progress, change and continuity have always been fundamental to sociology, and work has featured one way or another in most of the early sociological writing on these issues. In the next section, we ask how the three founders of sociology understood industrial work.

FOUNDATIONS

Generally regarded as the most optimistic of the three founders, Emile Durkheim believed that a more harmonious society was in the process of being created as a result of the specialisation of labour in industrial society. Durkheim stressed progress in his work. He saw the increasingly specialised division of labour as more efficient and as one of the most important aspects of modernity that would lead to an organic social solidarity based on inter-dependence. Durkheim noted that, at the time of writing, an 'abnormal' forced division of labour was occurring, and this was producing tension and conflict in society. But he felt that this situation of *anomie* or lack of attach-ment could be solved in industrial society, the solution being to promote occupational groups that could mediate between the needs of the state and the individual.

For Max Weber, essential to the newly industrialised and capitalist society was a growth in bureaucratic organisations. He looked to increasing levels of rationality in the workplace, and across society more generally, and identified therein the possibilities of more efficient production processes. In his analysis of bureaucracy, Weber identified an ideal typical, rationally operating, highly efficient modern organisation. Although some aspects of it concerned him, not least the real possibilities of an iron cage of bureau-cracy that would stifle individuality and creativity, Weber's ideal type of bureaucracy was fair and meritocratic. As discussed in Chapter 2, however, Weber is often viewed as the most pessimistic of these founding fathers because of his fear that industrial capitalist society could become dehumanised and soul-less.

Karl Marx's work on industrial society focused on changes in the owner-ship and control of the means of production. Like Weber, he stressed the development of industrial capitalism as opposed to the focus on industrial society that had been adopted by Durkheim. One of Marx's main concerns was with the development of the factory system under industrial capitalism, in particular, its potential as a new means of controlling work and workers. His writings and those of Frederick Engels, his friend and collaborator, were influenced greatly by time spent in Manchester studying the lives of the workers in the textile mill that Engels owned. Because of the nature of capitalism, Marx argued that conditions for these people would become in-creasingly impoverished. Industrialism eroded both the physical conditions people enjoyed, alongside the nature of the work that they did. Engels' writing, especially *The Condition of the Working Class in England* of 1845, is full of powerful descriptions of the problems faced by workers under indus-trialisation (see Text box 5.1). In Marxian thought, the development of the factory and modern work brought into existence a truly modern working class, a developed proletariat. It is only with the creation of this body of workers that relies solely on paid employment that industrial capitalist society becomes fully evolved. It is the dialectic process of history that modern industry creates this class of person and, in turn, this class becomes the grave-diggers of the capitalist system.

TEXT BOX 5.1 ENGELS

The supervision of machinery, the joining of broken threads, is no activity which claims the operative's thinking powers, yet it is a sort which prevents him (*sic*) from occupying his mind with other things. We have seen, too, that this work affords the muscles no opportunity for physical activity. Thus it is, properly speaking, not work, but tedium, the most deadening, wearing process conceivable. The operative is condemned to let his physical and mental powers decay in this utter monotony, it is his mission to be bored every day and all day long from his eighth year.

(Engels, *The Condition of the Working Class in England*, 1845, quoted in Thomas 1999: 398)

For the founding fathers, the changes in work that were occurring during the Industrial Revolution were fundamental to the shaping of society. With Durkheim focusing on industrial society and the others on industrial capitalism, these writers raised questions concerning progress towards a more equal societal division of labour and towards improved working and living conditions for the workers; versus the potential for more and deepening inequalities as a result of the industrial changes they were witnessing. In this chapter, we look at the impact of these issues on how sociology understands work in industrial societies.

The growth of industrial society

In the UK, the classical period of industrialisation was between 1760 and 1830, with a maturing of the system thereafter. Before considering industrialisation, however, we need to first understand what was being eroded by its arrival. We argue that the Industrial Revolution has to be understood in terms of technological developments, but also and importantly through its cultural and social significance too. Industrialisation changed many aspects of people's lives profoundly, and it is important to also recognise the way that this change was contested.

The English historian E. P. Thompson wrote widely about the industrialising period and about the experiences and attitudes of those ordinary people whose lives were being radically altered. In his classic *The Making of the English Working Class* (1968), Thompson discusses how, in the pre-industrial economy, work patterns were set by the natural order of the seasons – harvest and planting time, animal husbandry, daylight hours and tides. While work was subject to control (see later), it was possible for workers to exercise more autonomy over how they worked. Such work patterns were themselves embedded in specific social patterns and hierarchies that were seen as more intelligible and humane. For example, in cloth production merchants would often operate a 'putting out' system whereby raw materials were distributed to sets of workers (often families) who would work on a batch system returning the finished product after a certain period. In this period, workers would often work intensively at certain periods and take time off at others.

In looking at the pre-industrial period, however, it is important not to idealise it as a lost golden age. Life for the majority of workers consisted of hard labour in agriculture. What is interesting is the way the pre-industrial world is often looked back upon by those writing about industrialisation. David Meakin (1976) talks about the prevalence of novelists writing in the nineteenth century about shifts in the economy, particularly the loss of rural agricultural work and the rise of industrial and urban forms of employment. Meakin describes this as nostalgia for permanence at work whereby the old stabilities of the past are destroyed or at least under threat. Charles Dickens wrote extensively about the nature of industrial Victorian work, here is his description of Coketown from *Hard Times*:

> It was a town of red brick, or of brick that would have been red if the smoke and ashes had allowed it; but as matters stood it was a town of machinery and tall chimneys, out of which interminable serpents of smoke trailed themselves for ever and ever, and never got uncoiled. It had a black canal in it, and a river that ran purple with ill-smelling dye, and vast piles of building full of windows where the piston of the steam-engine worked monotonously up and down, like the head of an elephant in a state of melancholy madness.
>
> (Dickens, 1854, quoted in Jennings 1985: 273)

There was a fear and wonder, then, both of industrialisation and of the loss of what it was displacing.

In Britain, the so-called 'Industrial Revolution' that was driving this industrialisation was concentrated initially in certain sectors of the economy and in specific regions. The first factories began as large-scale workshops outside London in, for example, the Black Country, Lancashire, the East Midlands and Yorkshire, boosted by cotton production, the mechanisation of the textile industry and the steam engine (see Darley 2003). Manchester, as the centre of the cotton industry in Britain, is often described as the first industrial city of the world. As we have seen, sociology very much emerged out of a concern with the type of society being created in this ferment. The founding fathers were worried about how social order was possible in urban industrial towns and cities, and a whole set of issues were debated around the human cost of industrialisation (see Chapter 2). A core concern that we examine next was the importance of technological developments for the organisation and experience of industrial work.

Technology and work

Technological change was fundamental to the development of industrial societies. It was to become a mainstay in sociological debates over production techniques, control and deskilling, as well as over worker morale and alienation. Sociologists of work have asked, and continue to ask, whether technological developments bring progress to society with improvements in what work is carried out, how and by whom. Questions include whether technology has assisted by minimising hazardous work, with machines replacing humans on the most dangerous and disagreeable tasks, or whether developments in technology have actually created problems by reducing the amount of paid work available and damaging the conditions under which the remaining work is carried out.

The development of technology was, for Marx, fraught with risks for workers. Technology was creating such complex machinery that workers were becoming mere machine-minders and, as such, they were easily replaceable (see Text box 5.2 for a critique).

TEXT BOX 5.2 TECHNOLOGY AS A DESTROYER OF JOBS?

For Raphael Samuel (1977), far from abolishing manual labour, skilled or otherwise, the factory system and greater use of technology actually increased the demand for labour. Increasing production in one section of a trade made greater demands on another. The textile and coal industries are good examples. In the case of the coal industry, demand for steam coal from newly built factories expanded the need for coal miners to hew the coal. While steam engines allowed mines to be sunk to ever greater depths, the labour at the bottom was as manual as ever, carried out with pick and shovel. We see an industrialising world where new technology brings about a new and expanded need for hand manual labour of a wide variety of sorts.

For many other economic historians and perhaps sociologists, the rise of industrialism is far less problematic: the success of industrial production was due to technical superiority and efficiency, as epitomised within the factory system. It was the application of new technology to the labour process, in particular, steam power, that made production more efficient. The factory's success lay in its ability to substitute machinery for skilled labour. Machinery which could then be operated by semi- and unskilled labour: labour that you could pay less and that was more easily substituted. Put simply, the Industrial Revolution = technology + division of labour.

Clearly, industrialisation was processual rather than one big event. Marx himself recognised three distinct stages of change (see Text box 5.3), that are both chronologically and analytically distinct. Samuel's (1977) 'Workshop of the World' suggests an even more complex and contradictory process of industrialisation and the rise of the factory. He suggests that the process towards industrialisation and mechanisation was a case of combined and uneven development, with large variation in the application of technology across region, industry, sector and trade.

TEXT BOX 5.3 MARX'S STAGES OF CAPITALIST DEVELOPMENT

1 *The Handicraft Stage* – petty commodity production, chrysalis from which later stages developed.
2 *Capitalist Manufacture* – concentration of artisan and handicraft production under single capitalist, systematic extension of the division of labour.
3 *Modern Industry* – machine tools and the factory system.

(Capital, vol. I)

While it would be a mistake to see the rise of the factory as a site of production as sweeping all before it, it is equally important to recognise that the factory did bring about a change to the culture of work and, in particular, the discipline of work. Indeed, Marglin (1980) has argued that the importance of the factory is not necessarily to be found in its use of technology but in its ability to exercise centralised control over its workforce, one that was increasingly dependent on wage labour in order to survive, and we turn to control in the next section.

Technology, control and resistance

Moves to industrialisation saw work become subject to far greater levels of rationalisation and control, facilitated by developments in technology. An early and important aspect of this was the shift to clock time, identified by E. P. Thompson (and see Chapter 9 for a fuller discussion). With greater investment in machinery, a return can only be made if this capital is kept busy for as long a period as possible. Boilers had to be kept fired up, steam had to be available. A steady stream of raw materials had to be fed into the factory and the finished product taken to markets quickly. In order to ensure that this happened, employers needed to make sure that they had adequate numbers of workers to operate the new machines which in turn required greater levels of discipline. What employers could not tolerate was a workforce that could choose whether or not it wanted to work.

The emergence of new forms of control of work was central to early accounts of industrial work. Indeed, a core part of Marxist analysis of the new factories was that, as the pace of industrialisation quickened, capitalists looked for new and more efficient ways to establish control over work and workers. The factory became a site of discipline. Marglin quotes Landes: 'The essence of the factory is discipline – the opportunity it affords for the direction of and co-ordination of labour' (Marglin 1980: 238).

Not surprisingly, there was contestation over the new form of industrialised work (see Text box 5.4). E. P. Thompson discusses how industrialisation and the increasingly rationalised economy run on a capitalist logic were seen as an alien imposition by workers, or disruption to an established moral order. In response, to begin with, many workers simply refused to work on machines. At an extreme, the Luddites' campaigns against machines speeding up the pace of work and threatening jobs involved destroying the machinery. Similarly, in France, the saboteurs used their wooden shoes, or *sabots*, to damage machines. Often too, new factories would experience high levels of labour turnover as workers left employment rather than subject themselves to this new industrial discipline. Another documented strategy employed was to restrict management access to the workers' knowledge of the labour process. Goodrich gives an example of such a form of resistance in Text box 5.5.

TEXT BOX 5.4 CONTEMPORARY OBSERVERS DESCRIBED THEIR HORROR AT THE NEW TYPE OF WORK

Whilst the engine runs the people must work – men, women, and children are yoked together with iron and steam. The animal machine – breakable in the best case, subject to a thousand sources of suffering – is chained fast to the iron machine, which knows no suffering and no weariness.

(James Kay-Shuttleworth, 1832, quoted in Jennings 1985: 185)

Overman: 'I never saw him work.'

Magistrate: 'But isn't it your duty under the Mines Act to visit each working place twice a day?'

'Yes.'

'Don't you do it?'

'Yes.'

'Then why didn't you ever see him work?'

'They always stop work when they see an overman coming, and sit down
and wait till he's gone . . . they won't let anybody watch them.'

(1975: 137–8)

Finally, workers also contested change by struggling to improve wages,
reduce working hours and protect their skills, and so the early trades
unions were formed. Work communities also developed distinctive cultures around particular industries and trades, which we discuss at greater
length in Chapter 12 (see also Biernacki 1995; Joyce 1980, 1987;
Roberts 1993).

These issues of control – and resistance to that control – remain core to
the sociology of work, and we return to discuss them in depth in Chapter
8. They are also central to the study of the management of the labour process that we move onto in the next section on later developments in the study
of industrial work where we consider Taylorism and Fordism.

LATER DEVELOPMENTS

Taylorism and Fordism

Frederick Winslow 'Speedy' Taylor (1856–1915) is very important to the
sociology of work because of his contribution to the notion of 'scientific
management', his development of a form of control that rationalised the
work carried out by the workers to control it and manage it to eliminate
inefficiencies.

TEXT BOX 5.6 SCIENTIFIC MANAGEMENT

According to Braverman:

> 'Scientific management' so called is an attempt to apply the methods of science to the rapidly increasingly complex problems of the control of labour in rapidly growing capitalist enterprises. It lacks the characteristics of a true science because it assumptions reflect nothing more than the outlook of the capitalist with regard to the conditions of production.
>
> (1974: 86)

As we saw in Chapter 2, Taylor's ideas were shaped by his time on the factory floor where he saw the culture of the workplace and the resistance exerted by the workers. He noted in particular the practice of restrictive output, which he calls soldiering, the deliberate restriction of output by workers below the level of machine capacity and their physical ability. Taylor believed that workers had too much say in how work was carried out. This was because management had an imperfect understanding of the actual labour process – the way in which work was carried out in detail. As a solution, Taylor suggested the following model of 'scientific management':

1 The dissociation of the labour process from the skills of the workers. Collecting this in the hands of management.
2 The separation of conception and execution.
3 The use of this monopoly over knowledge to control each step of the labour process and its execution.

Put simply, if you knew as much or more than the workers, you could control where, when and how the work was to be carried out. Taylor carried out thousands of 'time and motion' experiments to find the best way of carrying out jobs – timing, placing of tools, distances travelled, the nature of the material being worked on, and so on.

The most influential application of this kind of scientific management was in Fordism, a term derived from the production techniques developed by Henry Ford in his car plant in Detroit. Using Taylorism, all the tasks that went into building a Ford car were fragmented and simplified to increase the speed at which they could be carried out. A result of this simplification process was the reduction in skills required by car workers to perform their jobs. Originally the Model T Ford car, launched in 1908, was put together by a small number of workers. After the Model T group of assemblers was introduced, the time formally needed to make the car was reduced to one tenth. By 1925, an organisation had been created which produced almost as many cars in a single day as had been produced in the early days of Model T production in an entire year. This featured a new labour organisation called a production line, with control by management over the speed of the line and what sort of work was carried out on it.

TEXT BOX 5.7 FORDISM

The earliest attempts to mass-produce interchangeable parts in the USA occurred in the firearms industry, in the sewing machine industry, and in the production of agricultural machinery and bicycles. But it was Fordism that became synonymous with Taylorism, assembly lines, low cost production, and the deskilling of jobs.

Features of Fordism:

1 capital-intensive, large-scale plant;
2 an inflexible production process – the production line;
3 rigid hierarchy and bureaucratic management structure;
4 use of semi-skilled labour performing repetitive rationalised tasks – scientific management;
5 tendency to strong unionisation.

Ford's system, though highly influential, did produce a number of contradictions. For the workers themselves, they faced such monotonous and highly controlled work that strikes were common and labour turnover was massive (fully 380 per cent in 1913). Every time the company wanted to add 100 workers to its factory personnel, it was necessary to hire 963. Ford's answer to his worker problems was to boost wages: the $5 day was introduced. But Fordism faced other problems too including fluctuating demand and shifting tastes, to which the inflexible production process simply could not adapt quickly enough. Writers began to talk about the crisis with Fordism and the developments of post-Fordist alternatives, which we explore in the next chapter. We proceed in this chapter to consider how sociologists tried to theorise the workers' experiences as industrialism grew.

Alienation

Alienation is one of the most important concepts of industrial sociology, emerging from Marxist accounts of work undertaken under industrial society and evidenced especially in factory work. We saw in Chapter 2 that labour is the heart of humanity for Marx, and that through work we create the human world. But under industrial capitalism, workers had to sell their labour power to survive. They had no control over their labour, nor the products that they were making, nor the methods they were using. Workers were alienated along four dimensions: from other workers; from the product; from the labour process; and ultimately from themselves since their potential for self-realisation through work is lost. A concern of industrial sociology was whether the problem of alienation at work could be resolved.

In his (1964) *Alienation and Freedom: The Factory Worker and His Industry*, Robert Blauner, an ex-factory worker, suggested that worker alienation could be solved via the use of technology. He believed that technological development had meant that machines could be built to replace the intelligence and skill of workers, leaving them with no control or power and thus alienated at work. But work is not homogenous, he suggested, since there are different levels of alienation and these depend, in part, on the different technologies in use. Comparing craft, machine tending, assembly line and continuous process industrial technologies in printing, textiles, car manufacturing and chemical work respectively, Blauner concluded that technology could be used to increase the content of jobs and increase workers' control and responsibilities.

In a slightly earlier publication, *Industrialism and Industrial Man*, Kerr and his colleagues (1960) provided a similarly positive interpretation of industrial work and of technology. For Kerr *et al.*, technology demands skilled workers and so it causes a growth in professional and technical jobs. Their 'logic of industrialism' was that industrial growth creates certain types of problem, and there is a limited range of ways in which societies can respond to these, hence we see convergence across industrial societies. Societies become characterised by urbanism, a specialised division of labour, a meritocratic class structure, mobility, mass education, bureaucratic organisations, welfare systems and parliamentary democracies.

A decade on from Kerr *et al.* and Blauner, Harry Braverman, another ex-industrial worker, offered a very different interpretation of the experiences of industrial workers. Staying close to the Marxist notion of alienation, his (1974) *Labor and Monopoly Capitalism: The Degradation of Work in the Twentieth Century* re-invigorated debates around alienation and worker deskilling (see Text box 5.8 on Adam Smith), and remains highly influential today. For Braverman, skill is fundamental – it provides power and control over work. When work is organised around the skill of the workers, then management have to accept the workers' input into how that work is carried out. Under capitalism, however, management have designed the labour process to reduce workers' skills and take decision-making away from the work floor. For Braverman, this arrangement is the foundation of work in a capitalist system and so any attempts to improve work conditions (e.g. via using new technologies as Blauner suggested) are merely cosmetic. Indeed, they are actually manipulative since they aim to control the workers even further by reducing their job dissatisfaction and thus improving their productivity.

TEXT BOX 5.8 DESKILLING

In his *Wealth of Nations* (1776), Adam Smith describes the extreme division of labour in contemporary pin production. Smith saw this as progress on one hand, but he also recognised the important effect it had on the workers themselves:

The man whose whole life is spent in performing a few simple operations, of which the effects too are, perhaps, always the same, or very nearly the same, has no occasion to exert his understanding, or to exercise his invention in finding out expedients for removing difficulties which never occur. He naturally loses, therefore, the habit of such exertion, and generally becomes as stupid and ignorant as it is possible for a human creature to become . . . but in every improved and civilised society this is the state into which the labouring poor, that is, the great body of the people, must necessarily fall, unless government takes some pains to prevent it.

(Adam Smith, 1776, quoted in Thomas 1999: 512–13)

CONTEMPORARY ISSUES AND FUTURE TRENDS

Moving beyond class divisions: gender

Much of the early sociological writing on industrial work was concerned with the implications of changes in work for structures and processes of class, and in particular for the lives of men employed in the new factories and mines. But it is impossible to understand the changes that occurred during industrialisation without incorporating the other major social divisions that we focus upon in the book: gender and 'race'.

If we begin with gender, a fundamental topic for sociologists of work is how and why work is divided by gender. Let us take an arrangement of work in which men dominate paid work in the labour market and women dominate unpaid work in the home as an example. We know that this is a familiar feature of current industrial societies but sociologists have asked when, how and why did this arrangement develop? Is there any variation in its prevalence, across societies, regions, classes and, if so, why? We look at these core questions in the sociology of work and gender in more depth in Chapter 7, but here we are interested more specifically in the impact of industrialisation on the gendering of work.

The consequences of industrialisation for the work typically performed by women and men have been understood by sociologists in a number of ways over the years. For Harriet Bradley (1989), interpretations of the consequences of industrialisation depend to a large extent on how the economic and social status of women and men was seen before industrial capitalism developed. How earlier societies are viewed shapes whether industrial capitalism is seen to have attacked the more equal relations that had existed previously between women and men, or whether industrial capitalism provided more opportunities for gender equality. And how earlier societies are viewed shapes whether the emphasis is on change or continuity in gender relations.

One familiar interpretation of the impact of industrialisation on the sexual division of work is that the 'unit of production' in pre-industrial times and in the first stages of industrialism was the private sphere of the family. Family members: women, men, and children, worked alongside each other and, from some accounts, in largely non-gendered ways. With the expansion of industrialisation and large-scale production, work was necessarily moved outside the 'private sphere' of the home into the 'public sphere': factories, mills and mines. In this interpretation, public work became men's work since women had to remain home to care for young children. This so-called separation of the private and public spheres is fundamental to the sociology of gender and work (and see the quotation by Carol Pateman on its importance for feminism). It meant that those tasks recognised as productive work now only took place outside the home by adult men, with women (and children) remaining in the home performing domestic tasks and reproduction. The public/private split resulted in a diversification of work roles within the family, with significant age and gender differences emerging: 'The dichotomy between the private and the public is central to almost two centuries of feminist writing and political struggle; it is, ultimately, what the feminist movement is about' (Pateman 1983: 281).

This account of the separation of public/private spheres is problematic in a number of respects. First, it is implicitly essentialist, building on a belief that natural differences between women and men inevitably meant that it was men who took on the breadwinner role and women who remained as carers in the home. Many sociologists have offered a critique of this picture of biological inevitability (see Bradley (1989) for a useful discussion). On the one hand, as Chris Middleton (1979, 1988) argues, it seems evident that gender differences in work roles had preceded the Industrial Revolution since, although families worked together, fathers/husbands often supervised the work of the family. On the other hand, the naturalness inherent in the relegation of women to the private sphere and to domestic work is questionable because, in actuality, women and children had entered factory work before men, often because the latter were reluctant to give up the independence that working on the land offered them. Even though women and children were the first factory and mine workers, a series of legislative Acts restricted their employment, limiting the hours that they could work and eventually excluding them from some forms of work altogether. As an example, in agriculture, women, men and children had worked together in work groups. These were family based teams which were derived from pre-industrial teams. The 1867 Agriculture Act stopped women and children from working in gangs with men.

Such restrictive legislation has been interpreted in different ways by sociologists and historians. One conventional interpretation of the formal restrictions of the paid work of women and children is that they were protective measures to protect vulnerable groups from heavy and dangerous work, with Victorian ideas of femininity drawn upon to emphasise women's weaknesses (physically, mentally and emotionally). One immediate problem with this interpretation is that not all groups of women were seen to be in equal need of protection. The notion of an ideal-typical feminine woman in need of the protection offered by a stronger masculine man has always been classed, and 'racialised' (see Chapter 2).

An alternative interpretation proposed by most feminist sociological analyses of work, such as those by Harriet Bradley (1989) and Sylvia Walby (1986), is that the restrictive legislation was patriarchal, aiming to promote a gender division of labour that advantaged men in general and protected the work opportunities of working-class men in particular.[1] The concurrent campaign for a family wage for working men at the time (Land 1980) – a wage large enough to support a wife and children – that was led by working-class male trade unions has been similarly critiqued by Michelle Barrett and Mary MacIntosh (1980) for reinforcing the male breadwinner model and the economic dependence of women on men. At this time, middle-class notions of respectable wives were very much that women had no paid jobs, and this idea of a dependent wife became to be seen as a sign for the working class too that the family was not pauperised: the man could afford to support them (see Irwin 2003).

Sociologists who are interested in gender and work have also been concerned with the early establishment of sex-typed sectors of the labour market and the ramifications of these for the working lives of women and men. Changes in the UK economy at the end of the nineteenth century saw a rapid growth in the number of shops, banks, insurance companies, postal agencies and elementary schools, and a correspondingly rapid increase in the employment of educated women. Louise Tilly and Joan Scott's (1989: 157) study shows that between 1861 and 1911 the number of female clerks rose by 400 per cent and by 1914 women accounted for 75 per cent of elementary school teachers. The reasons why industries or occupations become dominated by women at certain time periods and the impact that such 'feminisation' has on conditions of employment continue to fascinate sociologists.

Although we have little space to cover this topic here, it is important to note that industrialisation was also associated with changes in the age of a worker. Rather than continue to work alongside their parents as the Industrial Revolution matured, Zelizer (1985) shows how children were excluded from various types of work in factories, pits and mills. They became more dependent, and for more years, with adulthood postponed. In effect a new type of childhood was being constructed, with young children being schooled rather than worked (compulsory education was introduced in 1876 for children aged 5–10). The sociology of childhood is a fascinating area of the discipline that is beginning to impact the sociology of work.

Moving beyond class divisions: 'race'

The development of industrial society, as well as being gendered and having ramifications for workers of different ages, was linked inextricably to inequalities between nations and 'races'. Most agree that Britain was the first industrialised nation of the world, with its Industrial Revolution occurring in the late eighteenth century. We noted earlier too that Manchester was the centre of the cotton industry in Britain and the first industrial city of the world. These two statements cannot be understood without recognising Britain's role in the slave trade.

Slavery has a centuries-old history, in Britain and worldwide. The ancient Greeks and Romans kept the slaves that they had won when conquering countries, for example, and Eltis (2003: 58) discusses how slavery and serfdom were part of early medieval England, with 9 per cent of the population reported to be slaves/serfs in 1086. But what we are going to consider here is the British role in the Atlantic slave trade of the seventeenth and eighteenth centuries and its relationship to the growth of industrial work in Britain. Steve Fenton (2003) and James Walvin (2000), a sociologist and a historian of 'race' and ethnicity respectively, show how Britain dominated the slave trade in the eighteenth century, most notably in a trading triangle in which Black slaves were captured or purchased in Africa; transported to the Caribbean and the Americas to work on plantations; and then cotton, sugar, rice and tobacco were then sent to be processed in the mills and factories in Britain that we have been discussing in this chapter. Other countries in Europe, notably Spain, Portugal and the Netherlands, all played key roles in the slave trade but Britain took over as the dominant force in the Atlantic trade by the late 1600s. The majority of black Africans that Britain shipped over the Atlantic worked initially on sugar plantations but slavery began to flourish in both tobacco and cotton production too.

The study of slavery is vital for the sociology of industrial work as it shows how the global movement of workers and commodities was fundamental to the development of the first industrial regions of Britain. The movement of

African slaves to the Americas; the movement of cotton, sugar, and tobacco from the Americas to Britain; and the movement of food, clothing, tools, coal, metals, and so on from Britain to the American plantations, are all essential to understanding industrialisation. A key element in these global chains was British shipping. The necessary growth in the shipping needed to transport slaves and commodities boosted the growth of British industrial cities like Bristol, London and Liverpool, with enormous quaysides and warehouses developing, that called for armies of dockside labour. The profits and the expertise gained by those working in the slave trade also boosted the cities' local economies, with sugar refineries growing up around these cities; tobacco industries around Glasgow; and a cotton industry emerging around Manchester. The demands for bulk products to be shipped out to the plantations: tools, domestic goods, clothes, and chains, also boosted the development of modernised processes of mass production and the bulk selling of commodities that we discussed earlier under Fordism.

Slavery is fascinating for our study of industrial labour processes too. Walvin's fascinating accounts show how, in many ways, the slave plantation was a precursor of the factory system. The plantation was a system designed for the most efficient production of commodities as profitably as possible. It was based on cheap labour, organised in a proto-industrial manner. 'Some of the enslaved labour force – at least in sugar production – worked in "factories" long before the introduction of initial factories in Britain itself' (Walvin 2000: 157). As an example, the large gang system popular in the sugar plantations displayed Taylorist characteristics: three gangs of workers were in operation, all carrying out different tasks. At harvesting time for example, the first gang of strongest workers would cut the cane, the second gang of weaker workers followed the first gang and cleared the fields, while the third gang of the old and very young provided drinks for the first and second gangs and carried out other support tasks (Walvin 1993). It is interesting to note too how different labour processes were developed for different commodities. Heuman and Walvin (2003) discuss how in rice production, for example, a task system was in use, in which slaves were given a task or target that, when finished, meant their work was complete for that time period. For the stronger slaves, this meant valuable opportunities for rest and some autonomy over their work. This 'perk' was less attractive for the weaker slaves since they struggled to meet the targets. In tobacco production, in contrast, small gangs of slaves were used that could be monitored more closely. The strongest slave set the pace and the rest had to keep up.

Slavery also allows us to explore gender alongside 'race' divisions in work. Female slaves were as vital a part of the slave system as male, and their roles were more diverse. Many women worked alongside men in the fields; others worked in the masters' homes cleaning, cooking, washing and as personal maids; others nursed the babies of the home and brought up the older children. Female slaves also reared their own children, a profitable way for the slave owner to gain new slaves. And while household slaves were seen, by some accounts, to be the élite of slaves since they were not out doing back-breaking work in the fields, women working in the home of the slave owners as nannies, maids and domestic workers faced regular domestic and sexual exploitation at the hands of the owning family and their friends. Acts of mistreatment by the wife of the slave owner and by children were common, and female slaves faced the threat of sexual violence from older male children as well as the male head of the household. Being based within or near the owners also intensified the levels of emotional labour (see Chapter 12) expected from slaves, when owners expected displays of affection/ 'love' towards their family, and punished its absence.

Two of the issues central to the study of the emergence of industrial work – control and resistance – are perfectly represented in the study of slavery. The threat of resistance was fundamental to the design of the slavery system, and so mechanisms to deal with it were fundamental too. The need for security was paramount in the design of the slavery process from the first capture of slaves to their transport to the Americas. The plantation system itself, where their work was carried out, had in-built mechanisms to control work and to prevent, reduce and punish resistance to that control.

> The plantation had been first brought to a peak of modern perfection, shaped into an efficient tool of management and control, in the slave colonies of the Americas. It was instrumental in rendering work on tropical staples more efficient and profitable, and also in the subjugation and control of millions of imported Africans . . . The plantation continued the process first begun on the slave ships of hammering millions of African slaves into a disciplined submission.
>
> (Walvin 2000: 62–3)

In some ways, like Taylor's views on workers, slave owners viewed slaves as fundamentally in need of control. As in the factory, a daily weapon to regulate slaves was the exhausting long work day, but incentives such as promotions and time off for slaves were sometimes offered for good work and good behaviour too. Slave owners also employed gang leaders who routinely used whips and sticks to control the pace of work and to maintain discipline. Whipping was so common that very few slaves managed to avoid being whipped, and flogging was so extreme that it often left life-long scars. Indeed, there were actually manuals for slave managers, advising that punishment for acts of transgression had two purposes: to prevent the offender re-committing and to display to other slaves what punishment they would face if they similarly offended.

> The general system of flogging is to give them a certain number of stripes with a long whip, which indicates a dreadful laceration, or a dreadful

contusion; and then they follow up that by severe flogging with ebony switches, the ebony being a very strong wiry plant, with small leaves, like a myrtle leaf, and under every leaf a very sharp tough thorn, and then after that they rub them with brine.

(Sheridan, 1985, quoted in Walvin 1993: 239)

Like worker resistance, slaves' methods of resistance to the extremes of their lives are well documented, from their feigning of incompetence and ignorance to their running away and, less commonly given the systems of control in place, carrying out acts of destruction and outright revolt. The rapid and appallingly violent responses to slave resistance by the owners, and others in white society, are equally well documented. Growing horror at this often barbaric treatment of slaves, and the very ownership of slaves in the first place, led to abolitionist campaigns to put an end to slavery.

The slave trade existed for well over three centuries but, once it was abolished (in 1833 in Britain), this did not mean the end of unfree labour. Other forms such as indentured labour and bondage that had long existed alongside slavery began to grow as slavery came under criticism, and historians and sociologists have explored this expansion. They have shown too how the plantation system did not actually end as it was seen to be too useful an economic tool to lose and, in many cases, slaves were replaced by indentured workers from countries like India and China.

The ramifications of Britain's involvement in slavery are extensive with its legacy still apparent today. It feeds into our sociological understanding of work in many ways that we discuss in Chapter 7. Incorporating a discussion of slavery in the sociology of work is vital since it expands our understanding of what work is, and why workers do it. What distinguishes slavery from other forms of unfree labour is the property relationship. Slaves are things: commodities to be sold, bartered, bequeathed and inherited (Walvin 2000: 166). That slaves were seen as property/things rather than as workers/humans is encapsulated in the following account by sociologists John Solomos and Les Back (1996: 40). They discuss how in 1781, the captain of the slave ship *Zong* jettisoned 131 slaves because the ship was low on drinking water. A court case and investigation followed. The captain had claimed for insurance for loss of his 'cargo'. The murder of the slaves was not an issue. The belief in slaves as non-people also brings us to the close links between British capitalist economic expansion and the emergence of racism. In the white European image of black African peoples, the suitability of black people for the heavy burden of slave work was seen as natural, as fitting to the inferiorities of their 'race'. Such essentialist racist attitudes, while less extreme in many ways today, still persist. We come back to them in Chapter 7 when we look in more depth at 'racial' divisions and work.

New technologies

We saw earlier that the relationship between technology and work has been fundamental to shaping the sociology of work. Key questions raised include how it links to the skill of workers, to issues of control over work, and the ramifications of technology for workers' lives. Most of these debates were based first on factory work and usually on male manual workers. More recently, however, sociologists like Cynthia Cockburn have broadened the study to look at different types of workplace, as well as exploring different groups of workers there. In examining computerisation in goods handling, for example, she found that enskilling opportunities were offered by new technology, but these were gendered with women seen to be unsuitable for the most technological of jobs (Cockburn 1985).

Further developments in technologies – in information and clean technologies – have helped widen these debates and bring further areas of the labour market under the sociological gaze. In Rosemary Crompton and Gareth Jones' (1984) *White-collar Proletariat: Deskilling and Gender in Clerical Work*, for example, they took familiar questions about the impact of technology on skill and work, and applied them to white-collar clerical employment. They asked whether new technologies in word processing were deskilling clerical jobs, converting middle-class to proletarianised work. Or were the technologies upgrading what had previously been low-skilled manual positions by increasing the skills associated with them? As did Cockburn, Crompton and Jones concluded that technology impacted in diverse ways, with different ramifications for the deskilling or enskilling of workers who are female or male.

Questions about the impact of technology on work have also emerged in the study of work located within the home too, in both its paid and unpaid forms. In terms of unpaid domestic work, sociologists have asked whether technology in the form of new household appliances like washing machines, dish-washers and microwaves has made housework easier, reducing the time taken on laborious basic tasks like cleaning clothes, thus freeing time for more rewarding activities like playing with children or more creative cooking. Has technology reduced women's alienation from unpaid work in the home? While these are relatively recent debates in sociology inspired by second-wave feminism, it is interesting to see that the impact of technology on house-wifery has a rather longer history. The story of the design of the first mass-produced fitted kitchens is revealing here because it takes us back to our earlier discussion of Taylorism and Fordism. Architect Margarete Schütte-Lihotzky designed the so-called 'Frankfurt kitchen' in 1926. Schütte-Lihotzky had been inspired by Christine Frederick's (1913) *The New Housekeeping* in which Frederick explains that she had recorded how housewives moved within the kitchen to consider the most efficient ways to work in the home. Schütte-Lihotzky used Taylorist time and motion studies to try to design the most efficient kitchen workplace for women, that could be mass-produced and sold at low cost like Ford cars. The Frankfurt kitchen that resulted incorporated such innovative labour-saving devices as a fold-down ironing board for storage, and time efficiencies, as well as food storage jars with pouring spouts so lids did not have to be removed and replaced. Despite its innovations, the kitchen faced some of the same problems as the Model T Ford, including not providing enough flexibility to cater to changing requirements.

Sociologists have also been interested in the outcomes of technologies on home-working, whereby paid work is undertaken within the home. Home-working has a long history, marked by distinct gender, class and 'race' dimensions, with plenty of historical evidence from Miriam Glucksmann (2000) of working-class women 'taking in' washing and ironing in the late nineteenth and early twentieth centuries, as well as more recent examples from Annie Phizacklea and Carol Wolkowitz (1995) of South-Asian women in 1970 and 1980s Britain performing outsourced work in their homes such as packing and sewing. But the study of home-working has been broadened more recently by studies such as those of Alan Felstead *et al.* (2005) looking at the impact of micro-technologies on the ability of higher educated workers to work from home. Such studies continue to ask if new technology has provided more time autonomy or has it meant there is no escape from work demands for workers with home e-mails, faxes and telephones?

Globalisation and industrial work

The previous discussions of slavery and of technology both lead us to the key issue of globalisation and work. We look to globalisation more fully in the next chapter but here it is important to note how global the organisation of industrial work has long been. Globalisation is a problematic and debated term, as we will see, but it is useful to consider how globalisation and the international division of labour were central to the industrialisation process that we have considered in this chapter. The economic geographer Peter Dicken (1998) shows usefully just how early moves were to a 'world economy', preceding many of the developments we have been discussing here and facilitating them. The expansion of long distance trade in the 1400s and 1600s, for example, primarily for luxury items like spices and fine cloth, preceded the nineteenth-century growth of global production in which Britain as a maritime industrialising country dominated. Initially, then, as we know, Britain was the global leader in world production. Even by 1939–45, 71 per cent of world manufacturing was still carried out in just four countries (Dicken 1998: 21). A combination of the destruction of many of the early industrialised countries' industrial bases during the Second World War, and a growth in technology, saw the highest increases in production export growth rates in East and South-East Asian countries (like South Korea, Taiwan, Hong Kong and Malaysia). The result is a far more complex international division of labour, in terms of where products are made and traded, as well as where the workers come from – and travel to – for work.

As we see in the next chapter too, talking about a contemporary world economy now takes us beyond a focus only on production and manufacturing and on to include service work too. As one example, as Julia O'Connell Davidson (2005) shows, the global inequalities at the heart of the world economy have acted as triggers for non-manufacturing labour migration, including in a global sex trade.

CONCLUSION

In this chapter, we have examined how sociologists have understood the organisation and experience of work in industrialising societies. We showed that the societal ferment characterising the growth of industrial society stimulated early sociological discussion over what these developments meant for work and for workers' lives. Part of the sociological project has been to raise questions on change – and continuity – in work, and we stressed that evaluations of these issues invariably involve comparison with some previous states of affairs. While many studies and theories have incorporated some form of nostalgia for what has gone before, for what has been 'lost', this has not prevented the sociology of work from drawing on historical evidence to identify important continuities in how work is carried out and experienced, as well as considering elements of progress in changes. Finally, as well as asking where any changes have emerged from, and how, sociologists have long asked too: what comes next? Accordingly, in the following chapter, we move on to discuss whether we have witnessed the decline of industrial society and seen its replacement by post-industrial alternatives. What are the consequences of post-industrial developments for how we understand work in contemporary society?

NOTE

1 Jane Humphries (1977, 1981) suggested instead that removing women and children from employment was not a good move for working-class men as it meant eliminating family income sources that were essential for the physical survival of the working-class family.

FURTHER READING

E. P. Thompson's 'Time, work-discipline and industrial capitalism' (1967) remains a classic text for research into time and the control of work.

Frederick Engels' *The Condition of the Working-class in England* (1845) details the experiences of workers in the nineteenth century.

Harriet Bradley's *Men's Work, Women's Work* (1989) provides a historical, sociological account of the construction of gendered work.

Louise Tilly and Joan Scott's *Women, Work and Family* (1989) offers a historical and comparative analysis of women's working lives.

James Walvin's *Making the Black Atlantic: Britain and the Black Diaspora* (2000) offers a fascinating historian's account of Britain and the slave trade.

STUDENT PROJECTS AND ESSAY QUESTIONS

1 Why is control so fundamental to the study of work in industrial societies?

2 How useful is it to make direct comparisons between the factory and the plantation systems of work organisation?

3 Consider the role of technology in work. Have developments in technologies meant progress in the conditions of work? Has technology minimised hazardous work or has it damaged the conditions under which work is carried out?

4 Can you think of any contemporary workplaces where the impact of Taylorism remains apparent? Consider the type of workers employed there, and the ramifications of Taylorism for their everyday working lives.

Work and Post-industrial Society

OVERVIEW

This chapter asks:

- Why and how have sociologists been interested in the issue of post-industrial society?
- How have they theorised trends in mature industrial societies?
- What is the relationship between ideas of post-industrial societies and globalisation?
- Are we witnessing a profound shift in the nature of work or continuity in capitalist development?

INTRODUCTION

This chapter looks at the way capitalist societies mature, and examines the profound changes they have undergone since the 1970s. In particular, we explore the ideas of deindustrialisation and globalisation that have emerged, as a way of explaining some of these wider trends. While deindustrialisation, the loss of large amounts of traditional heavy industry, is usually associated with the Western developed economies, the causes of these trends have their roots in the rise of the global economy and increased international competition. This chapter looks at the consequences of these losses in Western Europe and the USA and the parallel gains in other parts of the developing world. We shall also examine some of the claims about the new society emerging out of these struggles and ask what this means for work and workers across the globe. We are particularly interested in the way these shifts in the global economy have repercussions for different social groups – benefiting some while marginalising others still further.

THE SOCIOLOGICAL MISSION

The changing nature of post-industrial society is of course central to industrial sociology and it could be argued that what we are seeing with current global shifts in the economy is simply a continuation of what was first observed in the mid-nineteenth century. As sociologists it is important that we continue to employ the sociological imagination in the study of these new developments. As in previous chapters we want the reader to get a sense of the power of sociology in being able to analyse the huge changes on a number of levels. It is obviously crucial to study work and post-industrial society at the global level but, equally, good sociology is also about interrogating the changing nature of work at the micro level. What is different about this type of work? Who is doing it? How are they controlled? Sociologists also need to be engaged in this area because of their ability to guard against some of the more simplistic interpretations of modern work.

FOUNDATIONS

Of all the classical theorists of sociology it is perhaps Marx who had most to say about a post-industrial society and a globalised world. He saw capitalism as a revolutionary system which expanded in a series of economic cycles. It was a dynamic system which constantly sought new and cheaper sources of raw materials, labour and new markets in which to sell the goods that were produced. This meant that in capitalist society nothing was ever stable, that change was part of the very nature of the system that both created and destroyed traditions, communities and industries. Marx developed a theory of cycles in capitalisms and the fact that movement, interconnectedness and exploitation on a regional, national and global level were part of this process. He was also interested in the idea of the impersonality of capitalism in that it was a system wherein there was little or no scope for morality – what happened in the wake of industrial development was no concern to that system. Capital was no respecter of tradition, hierarchy or the borders of a nation-state. Marx also saw the potential within capital to spread across the globe as it exploited new markets. Indeed, Marx thought that the real transformation from capitalism could only occur in its mature phase when there was a developed proletariat in a number of countries. It was the dynamism of capitalist development that created the seeds of its own destruction. Here is a famous quote from Marx written in the mid-nineteenth century:

> Constant revolutionizing of production, uninterrupted disturbance of all social relations, everlasting uncertainty and agitation, distinguish the bourgeois epoch from all earlier times. All fixed, fast-frozen relationships, with their train of venerable ideas and opinions, are swept away, all new-formed ones become obsolete before they can ossify. All that is solid melts into air.
>
> (Marx, quoted in Berman 1982: 95)

Marx believed capitalism would eventually be replaced by socialism and communism and in this sense he had an idea of a post-industrial society. There would still be a need for industry in such a society but it would be organised on a different basis.

For our other two theorists, Durkheim and Weber, the analysis of post-industrial society is less obvious. They were theorists of industrial society and were concerned with the problems that were inherent within it. Industrial society, however imperfect, represented the highest achievement of human history. To imagine a society without industry would be one that was regressing rather than progressing. Both can be seen to address issues of globalisation in terms of ideas of the division of labour and the process of rationalisation. It is clear in Durkheim's thinking that the logic of the division of labour within nations can be expanded to consider the relationships between nations. Equally, Weber was always interested in how capitalism was a system that developed beyond the nation-state and that a greater division of labour between countries was part of a wider process of rationalisation in the modern world.

LATER DEVELOPMENTS

In the last chapter we examined the growth and development of industrial societies. The highpoint of this process in the West was after the Second World War where a combination of high levels of employment, growing affluence and a booming economy has been described as a 'Golden Age' for a select part of the world's (often male) working population. In many of the industrial societies at this time, government policy aimed at ensuring full male employment by state intervention in the economy and industry. This was an era that is often referred to as the Fordist welfare state where such full employment paid for high levels of social security. By the late 1960s and 1970s, this Fordist welfare state was beginning to experience problems such as inflation and rising levels of unemployment. Part of the problem was with the efficiency and competitiveness of traditional industries in the West which had been the bedrock of economic success since the Industrial Revolution. A growing threat was posed by the newly industrialising countries of the Far East and South America which enjoyed far lower wage costs. At the same time it was suggested by some commentators that these trends were the natural process of capitalist development and that what was being experienced were the first signs of a new post-industrial society.

The post-industrial society?

It helps us in our discussion of this phrase if we define it:

TEXT BOX 6.1 POST-INDUSTRIAL SOCIETY

Post-industrial society refers to a society with decreasing dependence on manufacturing industry and a greater reliance on service sector employment, especially associated with information technology. This transition is often seen as a natural development of the capitalist process and part of a stage of capitalism.

The post-industrial 'thesis' is that, as developed societies mature, they invest in jobs in services and especially information technology. This kind of society moves away from older forms of industry, such as coal, iron, steel and manufacturing, and instead concentrates on sectors which require a more educated workforce trained to much higher levels. Daniel Bell (1973) was one of the first academics to argue for the idea of the post-industrial society. In his famous book, *The Coming of the Post-Industrial Society*, he argued that Western industrial nations, especially the USA, were increasingly moving away from manufacturing industry and shifting into the service sector. There was a growth in service work and white-collar jobs with an associated decline in blue-collar manual ones. These new jobs required workers to be educated to a much higher standard. It was also suggested that these jobs were increasingly being defined by their use of information technology. We can see that the attraction of this analysis was that the loss of manufacturing employment in the West was not necessarily something to be worried about; rather, it could be interpreted as a positive restructuring of capitalism with the elimination of low skilled tasks that required large numbers of workers. This would leave the Western countries to concentrate on high skilled knowledge work. This process was, in Joseph Schumpeter's (1942) phrase, 'creative destruction', in that it released resources for investment elsewhere. Bell later talked of an 'information society' rather than a post-industrial society but his thesis has undergone sustained criticism since it was first published (see Kumar 1978, 2005; Webster 1995). Bell was criticised for the highly selective way in which he believed the new jobs created would be highly skilled.

Commentators have pointed to the way a great deal of service sector employment is at best semi-skilled and is often routine and lacked autonomy. The post-industrial thesis was accused of emphasising attractive service work at the expense of more mundane examples (Bradley *et al.* 2000). There is a further criticism that Bell is guilty of projecting a simplistic evolutionary schema onto industrial society where older types of employment are shed as part of a natural process.

TEXT BOX 6.2 FEATURES OF THE POST-INDUSTRIAL SOCIETY

- Shift from manufacturing to service economy.
- Greater use of new technology, especially information technology.
- Increased emphasis on 'knowledge'.
- Need for higher skilled and educated workers.

Post-Fordism and flexible workers

One of the key aspects of the post-industrial society is the supposed shift from Fordist production to post-Fordism. In the 1980s, theorists attempted to understand what was happening in the economy and in workplaces in the wake of capitalist restructuring (see Amin 1994; Harvey 1989). In particular, academics were interested in how companies were changing, how they managed production and their workforces in an era of increased competition. Some management theorists and politicians suggested that organisations were, and should increasingly become, flexible by adopting a range of strategies that allowed them to respond quickly to changing market conditions (see Beale 1994; Harvey 1989). Text box 6.3 shows some of the differences between these two eras.

TEXT BOX 6.3 DIFFERENCES BETWEEN FORDIST AND POST-FORDIST PRODUCTION

Fordist production (based on economies of scale)	Post-Fordist production (based on economies of scope)
Mass production/homogenised goods	Small batch production
Uniformity and standardisation	Flexible small batch/variety of product types
Large buffer stocks	No stocks
Resource-driven	Demand-driven
Deskilled labour	Up-skilled labour, knowledge workers

In *The Condition of Postmodernity*, David Harvey (1989) argued that we were perhaps witnessing the period of *flexible* rather than *Fordist* accumulation. Flexible accumulation is defined as:

- directly confronts the rigidities of Fordism;
- flexibility in terms of labour process, labour markets, products and patterns of consumption.

Put simply, the world was now a far more fragmentary place and consumers would no longer accept undifferentiated products – remember the often cited quote from Henry Ford about the colour of his cars – 'any colour as long as it's black'. Production could no longer be based on long production runs of standardised products, and with subsequent economies of scale. Flexible accumulation is based on the understanding that many of the features of Fordism are no longer sufficient for success in the new changed, global economy. If firms are to survive, they have to respond quickly to change in the market.

Flexibility – the firm and worker

In the 1980s, there was a great deal of interest in the phrase 'flexibility' in terms of the firm or organisation and the work that went on in it. We have to be careful here about the gap between the rhetoric and reality of the situation. Harriet Bradley *et al.* (2000) talk about a series of 'myths at work' which sprang up in the 1980s on issues of flexibility and skill, among others, which lacked an adequate evidence base. For our purposes we need to see that during the 1980s and 1990s flexibility becomes an ideologically loaded concept. Successive neo-liberal administrations trumpeted the need for flexibility in the labour market, the firm and in terms of work. The idea was to break with the past and the restrictive practices that were seen as part of the British disease – low productivity and low quality. Rhetorically at least, flexibility is difficult to argue against. Compare the set of meanings which surround the term (Text box 6.4).

TEXT BOX 6.4 FLEXIBILITY AND INFLEXIBILITY

Flexible = versatile, quick thinking, ready for anything.
Inflexible = hide-bound, bureaucratic, resistant to change.

From 1979 onwards, the Conservative governments in the UK set about trying to create and promote the notion of flexibility in the economy in terms of organisations, work practices and workers. Let us take a look at this notion of flexibility at different levels, first, the flexible firm:

Flexibility can be considered along several dimensions:

- *functional flexibility* – breaking down of demarcation barriers;
- *numerical flexibility* – number of people/out-sourcing/increasing the supply of labour;
- *temporal flexibility* – flexibility of labour time – day/week/year.

There were, therefore, several aspects of the notion of flexibility. In the 1980s Atkinson attempted to model the idealised model of the flexible firm (Figure 6.1).

At its simplest was the idea that in order for the firm to compete effectively and to supply changing consumer demand, companies had to change. Rather than the large core workforces, of Fordist organisations, what was now needed was a smaller core of workers and a so-called periphery of workers doing various tasks (Text box 6.5).

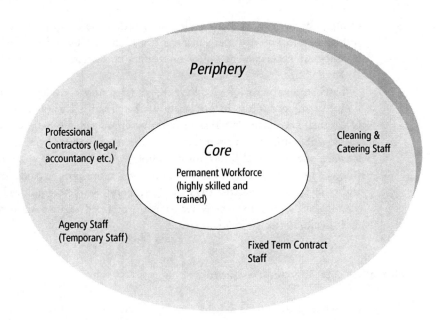

Figure 6.1 The Flexible Firm

TEXT BOX 6.5 CORE AND PERIPHERAL WORKERS

Core	Full-time, permanent staff, central to long-term future of the firm, good conditions and future prospects – functionally flexible, multi-skilled
Peripheral	Full-time and part-time, low/unskilled, lower levels of security and prospects – numerically flexible

This model helps us visualise some of the transitions in the economy but it, and the concept of flexibility more generally, are not without their critics. During the late 1980s and early 1990s, there was a great deal of research in the sociology of work about the extent and nature of flexible firms and work-forces. Almost entirely these writers question the extent to which the concept of flexibility was an empirical reality (Bradley *et al.* 2000; Harvey 1989; Pollert 1988). It was suggested that there was confusion about what the flexible firm is supposed to be, was it an 'Is', a description of reality, or an 'Ought' a target to be aimed at? Second, flexibility was seen as being a better description of the UK labour market rather than one firm, with evidence to suggest that the wider labour market was becoming more segmented than in the past. Sociologist Anna Pollert argued that there had been no dramatic shift in employers' attitudes since the 1960s and 1970s and that neither was it deliberate management policy to create a core related to a periphery (see Pollert 1988).

Later studies by sociologists have suggested a more complex notion of flexibility in the economy. In her study of the privatised water industry, Julia O'Connell Davidson (1993) suggested that employers did make use of a core and peripheral labour market but noted the result was far from the straightforward one described by Atkinson. Rather, what she found was a company whose core directly employed workforce was more poorly paid, less secure and enjoyed fewer benefits than the 'peripheral' workers employed by contractors. She argued that the water company retained a core workforce to give itself flexibility in the marketplace.

Flexibility and the quality of work

But what of the micro detailed quality of the work in this new era of post-Fordism and flexibility? Some of the proponents of the change argue that this is a qualitatively distinct transition and that flexibility heralds a whole series of improvements to the nature of work. If we think back to the previous chapter on industrial society we saw the way in which work under Fordism was seen as alienating and degrading. For some work in this new era can potentially be enriching and stimulating (Text box 6.6).

TEXT BOX 6.6 DIFFERENCES BETWEEN FORDIST AND POST-FORDIST LABOUR RÉGIMES

Fordist Labour	Post-Fordist Labour
Single task performance by worker	Multiple tasks
Payment by rate	Personal payment
High degree of job specialisation	Elimination of job demarcation
No/little on-the-job training/learning	Long on-the-job training/learning

So work would seem to be potentially more rounded and fulfilling, companies train, educate and make use of their staff's discretion – very different from the situation under Taylorist work regimes with the separation of conception and execution. But we have to be very careful here, if we actually explore accounts on the shop floor at times we get a very different picture of work. As long ago as the 1970s, employers used notions of 'job enrichment' – or rotation of tasks to keep workers interested, or stave off boredom. But as Nichols and Beynon reported at the time, the reaction of a worker at a chemical plant was: 'You move from one boring, dirty, monotonous job to another boring, dirty, monotonous job. And somehow you're supposed to come out all "enriched". But I never feel "enriched" – I just feel knackered' (1977: 16).

In subsequent accounts of some of the new factories, or of old ones that had gone over to these new methods, there is equally a mismatch between the management rhetoric about work conditions and the reality workers face on a daily basis. When sociologists researched working conditions in supposedly post-Fordist workplaces they often revealed a different story. Good examples of this, both from the automotive industry can be seen in *The Nissan Enigma*, Garrahan and Stewart's (1992) study of the newly opened Nissan car plant in Washington in the north-east of England, and an American example from Laurie Graham (1995) *On the Line at Subaru-Isuzu*. In both books, workers speak of very similar conditions that other Fordist production plants were defined by. Work is hard, physically and mentally demanding, repetitive, and there are often increased line speeds. Perhaps the difference is that there is a sense in which workers are expected to conform in the contemporary workplace in a way Fordist workers were not. Thus rather than being a new form of work, post-Fordist management techniques could be seen as an intensified version of Fordism. We will explore this issue more in Chapter 12. Equally, flexibility could be seen as a way of cutting jobs by making a smaller workforce work harder.

Here we need to use an analysis which combines detailed studies within the workplace with a theoretical understanding of the context in which work is performed. Many of the reforms introduced in the 1980s and 1990s occurred against the background of high levels of unemployment which acted as a powerful disciplinary device.

The deindustrialisation of society

Less than a decade after the publication of *The Coming of the Post Industrial Society*, the process of industrial change in the West was becoming clearer and its portrayal and analysis were becoming more pessimistic than that given in Bell's account. Some commentators suggested that the industrial societies were experiencing deindustrialisation.

TEXT BOX 6.7 DEINDUSTRIALISATION

According to Jary and Jary, deindustrialisation is: 'The process in which a previously industrialised or industrialising economy or society, or region reverts partly or wholly to a pre-industrialised form' (1991: 149).

In the early 1980s, two US economists Barry Bluestone and Bennett Harrison (1982) wrote *The Deindustrialisation of America*, which plots the systematic disinvestment by US corporations in their domestic industry while redirecting capital to overseas investment. Domestic industry was being used as 'cow' plants with older factories 'milked' for profit while being run into the ground before subsequent closure. *The Deindustrialisation of America* was an influential book as it studied both the macro trends in US corporate strategy but also highlighted the effect of these decisions on the communities in which the older domestic plants were based. Plant closures had a devastating effect on local economies, communities, families and individuals. Many towns had grown up around single industries or had effectively been created as company towns dominated by a single employer. When these employers went, places had literally no purpose (see Doukas (2003); Luxton and Corman (2001); Dudley (1994); Fine (2004). Even where there were alternative sources of employment, communities suffered greatly from the 'ripple effect' caused by closure on other businesses which were reliant on income from the workers employed in heavy industry (see Chapter 11 for more on unemployment).

When we look at deindustrialisation as sociologists it is important to look beyond the statistics of industrial change, what Jeff Cowie and Joseph Heathcott (2003) term the 'body count' of manufacturing jobs. The problems associated with closure are not simply the presence or absence of a job. As we have seen and will see later in this book, people's identity has often been bound up with their work and working life and as sociologists we try to understand what these economic shifts mean for communities and individual workers.

Deindustrialisation was not a trend which happened in the United States in isolation. Rather, deindustrialisation was an experience shared across the Western industrial economies in the 1980s, and in Eastern Europe and Japan in 1990s. This change was felt particularly in traditional industries and sectors like coal, iron, steel, shipbuilding, or engineering. In the USA, between 32 million and 38 million jobs were lost during the 1970s (Cowie and Heathcott 2003: ix) while in Britain over 4 million manufacturing jobs were lost during the period 1971–95; employment in this sector fell from 7,890,000 to 3,845,000 (Noon and Blyton 2002: 34).

All of the developed economies had seen their heavy industry subject to upheaval and change, and while some have been more successful than others at mitigating the effects of this process, deindustrialisation has often been devastating. Plant closures and lay-offs meant that some workers would never have a job again. Many men in their fifties or even their forties were resigned to a life on unemployment or invalidity benefit. In some instances, closure has meant a mass outward migration of workers who seek new jobs elsewhere. This approach has been more noticeable in the USA where large numbers of workers and whole families have relocated from the so-called 'Rust Belt' states of the North and Mid-West of the country to the 'Sun Belt' in the South and West (Maharidge 1986). In Europe, while there has been some out-migration from former industrial areas, mass movement has been less apparent. In many ways, this reflects a variety of cultural, social and economic reasons which sociologists have attempted to explore and explain. One of the main differences between the USA and other countries is the less developed welfare state there. Some argue that this forces people to move to work rather than wait for work to come to them. Those who do stay in deindustrialised communities often face a bleak future. A variety of social problems follow in the wake of closure including family breakdown, long-term unemployment and drug and alcohol abuse.

It is interesting the way the loss of industrial work has allowed a new perspective to be drawn on older types of industrial employment. Many commentators on deindustrialisation have been quick to point to the dangers of lamenting uncritically the loss of these jobs. As Cowie and Heathcott (2003) point out in their important essay on deindustrialisation, we have to be careful of 'smokestack nostalgia' or 'a creeping industrial nostalgia'. They note that many of the jobs lost over the previous three decades were hard, dirty, and routine and often the industries themselves polluted the very communities they helped created. Cowie and Heathcott refer to Ruth Milkman's (1997) writing where she notes the reluctance on the part of the unemployed autoworkers she interviewed to return to their former work. We will talk more about the problems of unemployment in a later chapter.

Another issue that we need to be aware of is that the term 'deindustrialisation' alongside post-industrial can be misleading. To read some commentators you would be led to believe that all manufacturing and heavy industry has been lost. Cowie and Heathcott point to the fact that while many jobs in the older industrial sectors have indeed been lost, new ones have been created. In the UK, there has been a fall, but not complete eradication of manufacturing jobs – in 1971, 7,890,000 were employed in the sector down to 3,932,000 in 2000. At the same time, service sector employment grew from 11,388,000 to 18,631,000 over the same period (Noon and Blyton 2002: 34).

What is clear from the writing about deindustrialisation is that it is a complex process where sociologists and others need to address a number of factors and a variety of perspectives. The contradictory nature of the evidence on industrial change is interesting and not a problem to be solved by reducing it to an either/or answer. To understand more fully what is going on in the contemporary economy, we need to address the issue of globalisation. But before that, we want to highlight the gendering of the processes discussed so far.

Feminisation of paid work: a female takeover?

The two main developments we have been examining in this chapter so far – the long-term decline in manufacturing bases in developed countries and new job creation in service sector work – are both strongly gendered. The decline in manufacturing has signalled redundancy and unemployment in Western economies for men, in large part. The growth of service sector work has created job opportunities that have been taken up far more by women. Indeed, for theorist Gøsta Esping-Anderson (1990), one of the key features of 'post-industrial economies' is their increasing feminisation: a substantial growth in women's share of the labour market due to a rise in women's participation and/or a fall in men's.

The idea of a feminisation of paid work has become widespread. It has been prevalent in some rather cataclysmic media accounts – many of which proclaimed men's imminent superfluity in all areas of life, others that feminism has imposed an impossible double burden of work on women. Such media reportage reflects what Susan Faludi (1991) termed a 'backlash' against feminism and its actually quite slight gains for women. In more optimistic and rather less melodramatic interpretations of a feminisation of paid work, feminisation has been seen as a route to equality between women and men in the labour market and a necessary precursor for gender equality of unpaid work in the home. In some pessimistic interpretations, it is a route to the downgrading of the job market. As is hopefully clear, then, there have been a range of evaluations of the feminisation of paid work. However, it is useful to go back to reconsider the extent to which the labour market has indeed been feminised. The actual outcome of the developments discussed in this chapter has not been that women have taken over men's jobs from them and now dominate in paid work. The labour market as a whole has not been feminised, the feminisation that has occurred 'implies increasing numerical dominance of women in low-ranked jobs' (Bradley et al. 2000: 91).

The actual form that feminisation has taken has raised a number of key concerns for work sociologists. Some elements of the cataclysmic accounts mentioned above do emerge here. For example, feminisation has not meant women substituting for/expelling men from secure well-paying jobs but instead the growth of low-paying jobs often in low status part-time employment (Hakim 1993). There have been fears among sociologists of work that an influx of women workers 'willing' to accept low pay will serve to pull down wages and job conditions across the labour market as a whole by reducing the bargaining strength of labour. A second interest for sociology has been with the implications of the mass loss of male jobs, in particular in certain de-/post-industrialising regions, and its repercussions: for household incomes, for men's sources of identity, for men's masculinities and for relationships between men and their families.

Third, since women have entered 'women's jobs' in service sector work like retail, catering and personnel services, on the whole, and not displaced or replaced men from traditional male jobs in manufacturing, are these de-/post-industrial developments serving to intensify rather than challenge ideas about what is gender-appropriate work? Linked to this, relatively few men have entered the expanding feminised work sectors, aside from young entrants to the labour market and older men approaching retirement. This is not least because the jobs pay so poorly but also because the men themselves – and employers – do not see male workers as 'right' for the new work. Some fascinating studies of men who do work in feminised occupations have been carried out. In Simon Cross and Barbara Bagihole's (2002) small study, for example, the men they interviewed worked to actively maintain their traditional male selves, with many even concealing the details of their job from friends and strangers. A 24-year-old cleaner in a hospital who was previously a car mechanic said: 'Well, my friends don't know what I do even now. They think I'm a porter' (2002: 215).

Finally, sociologists such as Judy Wajcman (1998) have highlighted that the increased entry of women into the labour market has not been associated with feminising or 'softening' the workings of capitalism, even when women workers make it to high-level management positions. For Stephen Whitehead (2002), even though women have been moving more into paid work, the capitalist system retains values that are associated with dominant discourses of masculinity. Masculine values still pervade organisational cultures, locating femininity – and those who are feminine – as 'other' and marginal to much paid work.

We look more explicitly at gender and other social divisions in work in a later chapter but it is useful to remind ourselves here that large scale societal developments – such as post-industrialisation or deindustrialisation – are invariably gendered, as well as classed and 'raced'. We come back to this point after discussing globalisation, next.

CONTEMPORARY ISSUES AND FUTURE TRENDS

In many ways, much of what we have discussed in this chapter is of contemporary relevance and it would seem that these issues will continue to exercise sociologists. In this section we want to look more closely about what is being made of these trends and how this analysis may develop in the future.

Globalisation

While the trends and issues that the label globalisation encapsulates may not be novel, the phrase itself is relatively new (Held *et al.* 1999; Waters 1995). Essentially it has come to summarise a whole series of aspects of modern society such as the idea that we increasingly live in a world which is interlinked.

TEXT BOX 6.8 GLOBALISATION

Globalisation is a multifaceted process in which the world is becoming more and more interconnected and communication is becoming instantaneous.

Like post-industrial society, globalisation has a variety of aspects to it. So, for our purposes in this book we can think of it in terms of:

- the globalisation of work, the economy and trade;
- the transformation of spatial arrangements and organisation of social relations;
- the increasing extent, intensity, velocity and impact of global social relations and transactions;
- the creation of the 'Network Society';
- the changed relationship between 'Global' and 'Local'.

Critics of the novelty of debates about globalisation would argue that all these ideas are part of a continuity within capitalism, but there is a widespread belief that the contemporary world is experiencing a speeding up and intensification of these processes. What modern information technology, especially the Internet, has allowed is the greater coordination of production processes and information flows. This allows for genuine global production and distribution on a scale that has not been seen before. Capital can now search the world for cheaper raw materials and especially lower waged labour in very different ways than it did just a decade or two ago (see Taylor and Bain 2005). One of the problems with globalisation is that discussion of its meanings and effects is often carried out in quite an abstract way (see Bradley *et al.* 2000). In this book we have constantly stressed that we need to combine a theoretical approach with a more detailed empirical account of what is happening on the ground. The crucial thing is to hold these two elements in tension.

So how does globalisation manifest itself on the ground at a local level? Well, for a start, in the Western industrialised economies, globalisation is one of the main factors cited in explanations of deindustrialisation. Since the 1970s, or even before this, trans-national corporations (TNCs) and multinational corporations (MNCs) have shifted production, and increasingly other services to other parts of the global where the various factors of production are lower. But this is a complex story and here is where it is important to look at case studies of industrial change. So when companies make decisions about where to locate, they are constantly calculating a range of factors. Often the search for cheaper labour does not mean that companies will always go to the other end of the earth.

Jeff Cowie (1999) in his book *Capital Moves* tells the story of one company, Radio Corporation of America's (RCA) search for cheaper labour. Over a 70-year period RCA moved production from New Jersey in the north-east of the United States through plants in Bloomington Indiana, Memphis Tennessee, before finally building a fourth new factory across the US Mexican border in Ciudad Juárez. At each stage, RCA were looking for a cheap compliant workforce but they also had to ensure that the products that these plants made, mostly television sets, could be easily transported to the core market which continued to be the USA (Figure 6.2).

The company also had to calculate strategy on the basis of their capital investment. So it was not the case that the company could move anywhere at any time, rather, Cowie argues that RCA made decisions at key moments about whether to reinvest in existing plants or to search for newer cheaper locations. The plant in Mexico, for instance, was not the cheapest option in terms of the cost of production but when transport and other costs were factored in, it made sense for the company to draw on relatively cheap and pliant labour, while enjoying relatively low and predictable transport costs.

This use of what economists and geographers refer to as peripheral labour markets is common across the world. Essentially it means that capital can take advantage of cheaper production and other costs near to the core markets. This could mean that businesses settle in cheaper parts of cities, regions or countries, or increasingly work is dispersed across national borders and differences between continental regions are exploited. So, for example, Cowie's study highlights regional differences *within* the United States as well as national differences *between* the USA and Mexico and more widely Central and South America. In Europe, we can see these differences between high and low cost areas replicated. In the UK, for example, there are wide differences between London and the south-east region and parts of the older industrial Midlands, and the North of England and Scotland. On a wider European scale, capital has increasingly made use of these inequalities by locating business in poorer parts of the continent in Eastern and Southern Europe.

Theo Nichols and Surhan Cam (2005) in their book, *Labour in a Global World*, look at the production of what are known as white goods – refrigerators and washing machines – and examine the way companies make use of

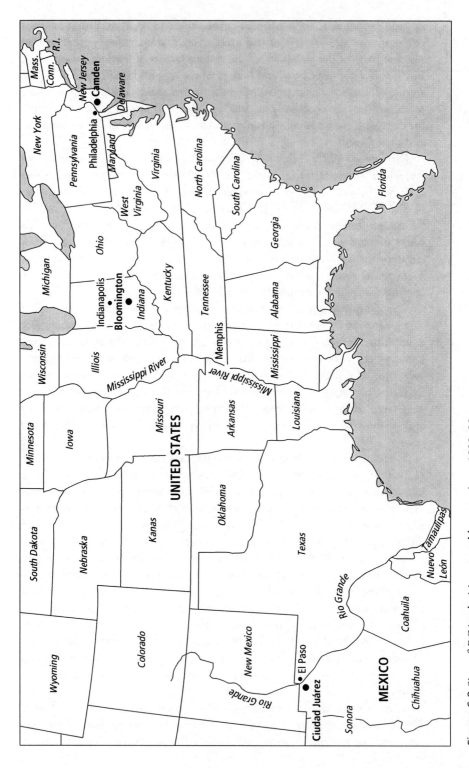

Figure 6.2 Sites of RCA television assembly operations, 1929–98
Source: Cowie (1999), reproduced with permission of Cornell University Press.

cheaper labour costs across the globe. One of the most important areas for supplying the European market is Turkey. As was the case in the example of RCA, companies locate production on the basis of a series of calculations including labour costs, transport links, type of commodity being traded and the nature of the state where production is being located. In each of these examples, capital can avoid, or at least reduce, their costs by locating where wages are lower and conditions of service and tax régimes are more attractive. In her widely acclaimed book, *No Logo*, journalist Naomi Klein (2000) gives many illustrations of the shifting of production away from the industrialised countries of the West in a bid to drive down wages. This process is increasingly marked by large multinational companies who own famous brands, in turn subcontracting the manufacture of products to other companies.

Often, however, when we talk about globalisation, the more dramatic examples are cited. Rather than production being located across borders or within regions of nation-states, globalisation is often taken to mean the relocation of industry and services in parts of the world, far away from Western Europe and North America. In the 1960s and 1970s, Japan was looked upon as a growing competitor to the West, but by the 1980s and 1990s, other parts of Asia such as Hong Kong, Taiwan, Singapore, South Korea, Malaysia, Indonesia and increasingly China were seen as the place where manufacturing was being located. Here employees often work long hours and receive a fraction of the pay and conditions their Western counterparts enjoy, or had previously enjoyed. Here Isabel Hilton graphically portrays the calculation to be made:

> The best thing that China had to offer the foreign investor was cheap, attentive and disciplined producers. The difference in wages between China and the old industrialised world was huge: a worker in Britain earning, say £1,200 a month could be substituted by a Chinese worker earning the equivalent of £30 a month. The reduction in price offered a startling competitive advantage in the international market, even when transport costs were taken into consideration. China also offered tax concessions, a fairly stable political environment, an apparently inexhaustible supply of workers and local officials who were happy to waive the rules in favour of profits.
>
> (Hilton 2005: 39)

Some of the complexity involved in debates on globalisation can be seen in the case of China. While much of the production opening up in the country is attracted from the West because of absolute wage level differentials, work is also migrating to China from states such as Hong Kong. Hilton goes on in her piece to say that by 2002 nearly 60,000 factories had moved from Hong Kong to Guangdong Province, where they employed 11 million people (Hilton 2005: 39). At the same time, while China is experiencing massive growth in certain sectors it is also experiencing deindustrialisation in some of its older industrial regions where state industries are no longer competitive.

This issue of the globalisation of production and the speeding up of capital flows and industrial change is putting tremendous pressure on other parts of the industrialising world. In *Dragons in Distress* (1990), Walden Bello and Stephanie Rosenfeld look at the experience of the so-called 'miracle economies' of South-East Asia such as Singapore, Taiwan, South Korea and Hong Kong. These economies have been, or at least were held up as, miracles because of their success in evolving into modern industrial societies in a matter of decades. But Bello and Rosenfeld tell a more complex story about their development. They point to the series of huge contradictions which each state now faces. Essentially what each of these countries has done is compress a process of industrialisation into several decades where as in the West this process took place over a century or more. The result is a series of problems, social, political and environmental. These countries often have authoritarian régimes and primitive labour conditions. Often broader reasons for the development of these economies are ignored. In the case of South-East Asia, what is often forgotten is that the Korean, Vietnam and the Cold Wars all helped to stimulate industrial development. The miracle economies also face the growing problem of competition from their large regional competitor China, where wages costs are even lower than their own.

Global migration of workers

Globalisation becomes even more complex when we look at the rise in migration of workers from poorer regions of the world to the richer parts. This is a complex and multi-dimensional process. What drives migrants to leave their homes are enormous differences between wages in different parts of the world so that, even allowing for higher living costs, migrants can work in more developed regions and still send back money to support families at home. Often flows of migrants follow patterns of established networks, with people going to countries and regions where there is an already established expatriate community. However, there are a series of problems for migrants when they arrive in the host economies. Often migrant labour is associated with the bottom end of the labour market with workers recruited to work in the service sector or in agriculture. It is precisely these sectors where workers are most vulnerable with little in the way of trade union presence or state regulation. This makes migrants especially vulnerable to exploitation and dangerous working practices. Steve Fenton (2003) argues that migrant workers are the most open to exploitation, with undocumented migrants facing 'super-exploitation' in contemporary societies (Text box 6.9).

TEXT BOX 6.9 ILLEGAL CHINESE IMMIGRANT WORKERS

On the evening of the 5th February 2004, a gang of Chinese illegal immigrant workers set to work harvesting cockles in Morecambe Bay in the North-West of England. The group had travelled across the world from the Fujian province of Southern China. Each had paid £13,600 to people smugglers to reach the UK from their homes. That night 23 members of the inexperienced group died in the Bay when they were cut off and drowned by the incoming tides. The youngest person was just 18 and the oldest 45. Each had come to the UK to earn money to send back to families at home. The story exposed various aspects of globalisation, the system of people trafficking, the lax labour laws in the UK, and the power of gang masters who are able to exploit vulnerable workers who were working outside the law.

(*Guardian*, 25 March 2006)

In the USA, thousands of Mexicans cross the border every year to work in low-paid jobs in the rich North. They often risk their lives in order to get to the USA where they take up the jobs that employers find difficult to fill with indigenous labour (Ellingwood 2004). In his collection of oral histories of Mexican migrant workers, Daniel Rothenberg reflects on the hard life of those like Lucy Quintaunilla who was born in Mexico but spent her life travelling between border towns in the USA and the land of her birth. She talks in this passage about the reception of migrant workers in the USA:

A lot of Americans look down on us. They see Mexicans as beneath them. They think that we're uneducated or that we steal. They think we've come here to take things from them. It isn't like that. You don't travel the way that a migrant travels, wandering from one place to another, coming here from so far away, without a good reason. We've come here to work. All of us work in *la labor*. We come here because we want to earn money to buy things – a sofa, a refrigerator, a stove – to fix up the houses we've left back in Texas or Mexico.

(Quoted in Rothenberg 1998: 183)

Migration: gender, class, nationality and 'race'

In many countries, women now represent the majority of migrant workers. Two-thirds of all Filipina migrant workers today are female, for example (Sassen 2002). In the past, women migrants were largely viewed as migrating to re-unite families: to join up with male partners who had already arrived in another country and obtained work there. But the extent and new forms of female migration have awakened interest in the gender and racialised nature of these global movements, in addition to their clear class and national dimensions, that we discuss briefly here.

We saw earlier that many MNCs operate in so-called export processing or free trade zones, where rights of workers have been restricted by governments to attract investment. But it is impossible to understand the division of labour in these MNCs without resource to issues of class, 'race', gender, and age too. For Annie Phizacklea (2003), it is young minority ethnic women workers who are at the bottom level of multinational corporations in the global market. In Klein's *No Logo*, she details the deplorable working and living experiences of young women workers in the Philippines and other free-trade-zones who migrated from severely disadvantaged areas to make clothes for, among other firms, Gap and Nike. Klein found that the free-trade zone employers expressly prefer to employ young migrant women who are far from home and have not finished their schooling because they are 'scared and uneducated about their rights' (Klein 2000: 221).

Issues of gender, class, 'race' and age all emerge too in studies of those who migrate into domestic work. The migration of domestic workers has fed into influential discussions of 'global care chains' and a globalisation of the commodification of caring. Such debates are welcome because they are taking us beyond the over-focus on manufacturing that has dominated the debates and empirical studies of globalised work so far. A core interest is in the work of migrant women. The domestic work that these migrant women provide has been analysed in terms of its releasing other women – women in high-class positions and often of different ethnicities and nationalities – from domestic tasks and child-care (Acker 2004). In sociologist Bridget Anderson's (2000) *Doing the Dirty Work?: The Global Politics of Domestic Labour*, she explores the importance of nationality, race and colour, as well as gender, class and age, in the domestic employment relationship. Anderson shows that employment agencies and employers look specifically to employ women from certain countries for the perceived benefits of their 'race': 'preferences often reflect racial hierarchies that rank women by precise shades of skin colour' (Anderson 2002: 108). Anderson's work is influential because she has also added a more nuanced interpretation to theorising around the employment of domestic workers. In particular, she has queried the over-focus on work substitution: that migrant workers simply substitute for the work the female employer would be doing in any case. She has argued instead that domestic workers perform tasks that no-one would do, given the choice, and so rather than providing essential work tasks they are also facilitating the high-status life styles of the employers and their families. The right type (colour) of migrant worker is vital for this.

An emerging issue for sociologists who study migrant domestic workers is the impact upon women's own domestic and caring responsibilities when they move away for work. Many of the migrant women who are employed as nannies, for example, have their own dependent children who remain at home, usually in the care of their relatives and older siblings. Rhacel Salaza Perreñas (2002) has examined the emotional impact on mothers and on their children when the women have migrated hundreds of miles away for work, and are caring for other people's young children.

We end this section on migration and social divisions with the issue of the forced migration of workers. It is vital to do this because it highlights how many contemporary debates over migration across the globe approach migration as voluntary: as an economic choice made by the migrant workers. But migration is a complex concept and Stephen Castles (2003) has shown that the boundary between voluntary and forced migration, while never very clear, is becoming increasingly blurred under globalisation. Accordingly, sociological accounts now consider how constrained migration choices can be, given the lack of opportunities for paid work in the home areas of the migrants. We know of course that totally forced migration marks the history of many societies, with a documented 15–20 million people transferred as slaves from Africa to the New World from the seventeenth to the nineteenth centuries (Fenton 2003: 118), but it is important to note that forced migration has not disappeared, as studies into trafficking of workers are showing. Saskia Sassen (2002: 267) has defined trafficking as 'the forced recruitment and transportation of people for work'. In her contribution to the book *Global Woman* by Barbara Ehrenreich and Arlie Russell Hochschild, Sassen discusses the trafficking of women and children to work in the sex industry, alongside other more 'voluntary' female migration such as being a mail-order bride. An important contribution from her discussion is that the sex industry, and the trafficking that maintains it, play a large part in government-promoted, economically driven, globally orientated tourist industries in many developing countries.

A new capitalism?

In the past decade some analysts of work and employment including some sociologists have suggested that capitalism has changed its nature and that we are entering a new stage in its development. In many ways we could see this as a continuity of the debates around the post-industrial society that Daniel Bell discussed in 1973. However, rather than the benign reading which Bell proposed, writers now interpret change in a far more pessimistic way. Where Bell wrote positively about information technology and knowledge work transforming capitalism, what we now find are a series of writers talking variously about the 'end of work', the 'new capitalism', or indeed the 'brave new world of work' in a negative sense. What all of these have in common is a sense that capitalism in its latest guise has changed qualitatively and quantitatively. Capitalism now has speeded up and with the aid of information technology and global communications, it can act in a way it hitherto had not been able to.

At the forefront of this writing was the US journalist Jeremy Rifkin's (1995) *The End of Work* where he suggests that work, as we have known it, is under pressure on two fronts. First, from the rapid introduction of new technology that is abolishing jobs at an ever-quicker rate. Second, the greater impact of global market forces, unrestricted by regulation from the nation-state. Rifkin's book was important in tapping into popular concerns about the changing nature of work in Western industrial societies. Arguably, his audience was not a blue-collar one which had been experiencing deindustrialisation and downsizing since the 1970s but a white-collar one. It was these people who had seen huge changes in their organisations in the late 1980s and into the 1990s (see, for example, Fraser 2001).

In a series of later books by academics this theme was picked up and what followed was a series of interventions about the social consequences of what jobs in this new economy would mean for individuals, their families, communities and wider society. Underpinning almost all of these books was a concern with the instability that was perceived to be a general feature of this new era. In particular, there is a great concern with the loss of the 'job for life', or at least the idea that this may be something a proportion of the workforce could look forward to. In his book, *Work, Consumerism and the New Poor*, Zygmunt Bauman writes that work was once the main orientation point in a person's life but says:

A steady, durable and continuous, logically coherent and tightly-structured working career is, however, no longer a widely available option. Only in relatively rare cases can a permanent identity be defined, let alone secured, through the job performed.

(1998: 27)

Bauman believes we have witnessed a shift from a modern to a post-modern society, and that work which used to be a collective experience is now highly individualised. Bauman goes on to argue that while work recedes in importance in people's life, identity is now derived from what people consume. Therefore consumption has marginalised work-based meaning, with identity largely or solely derived from what *individual* consumers want (see Ransome 2005). This theme of disorder in people's work life is a popular one with other writers. For Beck in *The Brave New World of Work*, the ' "job for life" has disappeared' and 'Paid employment is becoming precarious; the foundations of the social-welfare state are collapsing; normal life-stories are breaking up into fragments' (Beck 2000: 3). Beck argues that the West is suffering what he describes as a 'Brazilianisation' in terms of work and social welfare, by which he means a rapid erosion in the once good conditions of work and the welfare state. The impact of globalisation means that such conditions are unsustainable as they can no longer be paid for if industry or services are to be competitive.

American sociologist Richard Sennett has spent much of his career exploring the changing nature of industrial culture. In *The Corrosion of Character* (1998), he explores what he labels the 'new capitalism'. This is the speeding up of capital flows, the shorter time horizons which corporations now work to and the effect all this has on workers and communities. He suggests here and in later books that the insecurity felt by many people has profound implications for moral identity. Basically, the discipline this new capitalism demands is corrosive of both individual and collective identity in that it forces people to adopt increasingly superficial relationships with others and, as part of that, people are rewarded for moving jobs on a regular basis.

While much of this writing is negative, there are some who find positive signs in the current nature of capitalism. Essentially we could see this interpretation as a neo-Marxist projection about the collapse of capitalism. Authors such as Ulrich Beck, André Gorz and Zygmunt Bauman have suggested that we have reached a stage within capitalist development that it has become obvious that it must be transcended and replaced by a more humane and ethical system. Gorz (1999), for example, in his recent writing talks of 'reclaiming work' so that people can do rewarding and socially necessary work rather than alienating boring repetitive labour. Ulrich Beck (2000) goes further to suggest that such a transition could see the birth of a 'second modernity'. There are a number of problems with these ideas which have been lumped together here. Perhaps the greatest weakness is the lack of empirical research upon which these sweeping generalisations are based. The authors here take a very pessimistic line with the only positive note being an appeal to a utopian future. We will come back to some of these ideas later on in the book, especially on questions of identity. Another interpretation of the type of society we are now living in is provided by American sociologist George Ritzer, outlined in his book *The McDonaldization of Society* which we discussed earlier in Chapter 2.

Where next with globalisation?

It is important to realise that the accounts of capitalism and contemporary society are useful if we recognise their limitations. The theories of the speeding up of capitalism and processes of globalisation are important but we have to recognise that they are macro theorisations and caricatures and not empirical descriptions of actually existing reality. But this begs a question about how we think about and research a global society, recognising the need for both an empirical and theoretical understanding. What we want to suggest here is an approach which develops from the best traditions of the sociology of work, namely, one that is always a combination of theory and empirical research which applies sociological concepts and methods to actual workplaces.

Harper and Lawson come to a similar conclusion in their collection, *The Cultural Study of Work* (2003). In their Introduction, they call for 'an intimate study of work in a global context' (ibid.: xvii). In many ways this is reflected in some of the accounts that are being published within the field. We could, for example, look at Michael Burawoy *et al.*'s (2000) *Global Ethnography*, which looks at work, among other issues, in a global context. Contributors to the volume look at trans-national migrant labour, high tech software developers and shipyard workers among others. Another aspect of this growing internationalisation of the study of work can be seen in the study of service sector work at the bottom of the labour market. The collection by Ehrenreich and Hochschild (2002) is a good example of this. One of the important aspects of this collection is the decentring of the study so that the viewpoint of the workers themselves is taken seriously. This helps the reader to transcend the traditional approach which places work in the West, often carried out by men, as the norm against which others are measured.

Perhaps one of the richest examples of this qualitative approach can be found in French sociologist Pierre Bourdieu *et al.*'s (1999) *The Weight of the World* which is a wonderful example of careful and critical ethnographic interviewing, placing individuals' detailed account into a wider story of industrial change and global shifts. While these are edited collections, there is much useful research being published that helps us to understand the experience of global change in a particular place.

One of the most encouraging developments within the literature on globalisation has been the attempt to understand the ways in which people respond to such pressure. As in any good sociology, we have to look for the contradictions and ambiguities in what is happening rather than see globalisation as an unstoppable and wholly negative process. What often happens in the more abstract accounts of globalisation is that the role of agency is ignored or downplayed. Beck (2000), for example, talks of capital being global and labour as tied to the local. When we look in more detail we can always see examples which illustrate that workers can exercise power and that often this is done by the most marginal and supposedly powerless in our society. Jane Wills has studied a grassroots movement in East London which mobilises workers around the idea of the living wage, rather than simply the minimum wage (Holgate and Wills 2007; Wills 2004). The important thing about this group is its ethnic diversity and the fact that these workers are cleaners, a combination which often makes them the most vulnerable.

Finally, it is important that we recognise the continued existence of a range of very poor work conditions which are integrally linked to the global economy. These range from low subsistence pay, indentured labour, down to the widespread existence of slavery. It is important that we do not see these types of work in isolation but make the connections between developed, developing and underdeveloped countries (see Bales 1999; Ross 2004).

CONCLUSION

In this chapter we have examined what sociologists and other commentators have made of contemporary society. What some have suggested is that we have experienced a transition from industrial to post-industrial society. This is based on an understanding of the impact of globalisation and the consequential restructuring of paid work. As part of this process we looked at the ideas of deindustrialisation and changing nature of the work. In trying to make sense of what is happening to work and industrial society in the contemporary world, it is crucial that we place contemporary developments in an historical context. We must always be alert to the historical continuities as well as changes. So the serious sociologist must always ask: what is novel about the world we live in?; what is novel about what is being suggested about work in modern societies?; what is really changing?; what is the experience of work like for people? As part of this process, we always need to be cautious about academics and more popular commentators who make sweeping statements about the world of work and globalisation which are often based on little or no research. Equally, we need to place detailed studies of work in a larger context and we have suggested here that we need a sociology of work which examines how the global impacts on the local and the local on the global.

FURTHER READING

David Harvey's *The Condition of Post Modernity* (1989) is a classic statement on the shift in late modernity from classical Fordism.

Jeff Cowie's *Capital Moves* (1999) is a great way of seeing industrial transition over the course of the twentieth century.

Barbara Ehrenreich and Arlie Russell Hochschild's *Global Women: Nannies, Maids and Sex Workers in the New Economy* (2002) is an edited collection on the experiences of women workers globally.

Pierre Bourdieu *et al.*'s *The Weight of the World* (1999) is an excellent example of sociology's ability to marry the global with the local.

Paul Ransome's *Work, Consumption and Culture: Affluence and Social Change in the Twenty-First Century* (2005) gives a good overview of the challenge of consumption with regard to work sociology.

WEB SOURCE

The ILO: http://www.ilo.org/global/lang—en/index.htm

STUDENT PROJECTS AND ESSAY QUESTIONS

1   What is new about the nature of work in the global economy?
2   Are we living in a post-industrial world?
3   How might globalisation reduce or intensify social divisions?
4   Are we witnessing an end of work? What would that mean?

Part III
Understanding Work

Divisions and Work

▌ OVERVIEW

This chapter will:

- Showcase the centrality of inequalities to the sociology of work.
- Examine how sociology has theorised and studied a variety of social divisions over time.
- Discuss how social divisions are fundamental to any understanding of how work is organised and experienced.

▌ INTRODUCTION

We devote this chapter to discussing inequalities in work, showing that social divisions are vital to any understanding of how work is structured and experienced. The chapter will examine how sociologists view social inequalities more broadly as well as discussing more specifically how inequalities in work have been approached. We will see that a range of examples of social divisions, such as class, gender and 'race', have been theorised and studied by sociologists in various ways over the years, in isolation and in combination with other divisions. The chapter will show that such divisions made it onto the agenda of work sociology at different times, for different reasons, and that they have received varying degrees of coverage. The main purpose of the chapter, however, is to underline just how fundamental inequality has been to theories about work and to studies of work. We conclude by stressing that the sociological aim is to explore the complex interpenetration of different forms of inequality. We hope to show readers just how vital an understanding of these interconnecting social divisions is when examining work and workers' lives.

THE SOCIOLOGICAL MISSION

Researching and theorising inequalities in work are core to the sociology of work. Three fundamental questions have concerned the discipline: (1) what are the sources of inequalities?; (2) how are inequalities in work experienced?; and (3) can inequalities in work be eradicated? (and, if yes, how?). These questions reflect sociology's fascination with the distribution of societal resources, and with structures of power and (dis)advantage. This fascination has inspired a substantial body of writings on developments in work and their links to a range of social inequalities, but in particular those of class, gender and 'race'. Sociologists have asked, for example, whether class divisions in the workplace are deepening or blurring; whether gender is still a key indicator of inequalities in housework and other forms of work; and whether 'racial' disadvantage in work has been diluted. What links the sociological interest in these three, and indeed other, sources of inequality is the belief that class, gender and 'race' are socially constructed and not the result of innate differences between groups. As sociologists, we critique so-called essentialist assumptions about inherent differences and we ask instead about how and why social divisions are created. In work sociology, we ask about trends in the patterning of social inequalities, and about how inequalities in work are experienced. By asking these and many other questions around social divisions in work, sociologists try to understand who faces what kinds of dis/advantage in work, whether these (dis)advantages are stable across time and place, and why.

FOUNDATIONS

The study of work inequalities draws upon and feeds into much broader sociological debates over the origins of difference and over the prospects for achieving equality. While sociologists over the years have agreed that we live in societies in which certain types of people fare better in many ways than others, with stark differences existing in people's life outcomes, there has been some disagreement about the causes of these differences. If we look first at the three founding fathers, we can see variation in their approaches that were to impact on later developments in sociology, with Durkheim inspiring debates over meritocracy, Marx stimulating studies that focus on class inequalities under capitalism, and Weber's ideas encouraging attempts to develop multidimensional accounts of social stratification.

Beginning with Durkheim, a crucial question for sociology has been whether we live in a meritocratic society where your position in life is based on your merit: on your innate abilities and on how hard you work. In an ideal society, for Durkheim, the division of labour would indeed be merito-cratic: people would find a niche that best suited their abilities and qualifications. But the way society was organised at the time of his writing was not ideal, Durkheim felt, because there was a forced division of labour. Social inequality meant that people were being forced into the wrong positions, causing tension and conflict within society. His solution to this conflict, as we discuss in Chapter 2, was the promotion of professional work groups that would mediate between the state and the individual, and help establish a new moral order.

The Marxian approach to inequalities in society focused on class and the production relationship. Marx believed that ownership of the means of pro-duction was the means of exploitation of the proletariat by the bourgeoisie. The working class were the revolutionary class who would ultimately lead society to a more equal future where there was communal ownership of the means of production. Marx believed that central to this revolutionary pro-cess was the transformation of the nature of work, since its degradation and dehumanisation would lead to increased alienation of the workers and this would lead to a class struggle and ultimately to revolution. We should also remember Engels' (1884) *The Origin of the Family, Private Property and the State* here because it was to influence writings on the sociology of gender and work, since it explored changes in societies from matriarchies towards patri-archies as a result of the development of private property and men's wish to pass property on to their biological offspring.

The core of Weber's approach to societal inequality lay in his emphasis on the complexity of stratification: that it is multidimensional, cross-cutting and not just about economics and class. As well as class, which he thought was very important; Weber identified two other dimensions of stratification: status and party. Status refers to social esteem and, while it is often linked to class, status is not determined by it because non-market factors such as life-style, consumption patterns and education shape status too. Parties in the Weberian sense are groups which come together to acquire power, and again these groups are not necessarily class-based.

LATER DEVELOPMENTS

The ways in which sociology has explored inequalities at work are many and varied. Early work sociologists very much followed in the footsteps of three founding fathers, with studies and theories inspired by differences in their ideas but nevertheless still united in the concern with the work inequalities that were emerging from the capitalist mode of production. We will discuss the importance of this classic heritage here, and then move on in the next section to address more contemporary debates that both build on and offer critiques of this foundation.

Differences or divisions in work?

The belief in a meritocracy in Durkheim's ideal division of labour was to re-emerge in twentieth-century *Functionalist* sociology, as we saw in Chapter 2. Dominant in the 1950s, this school of thought argued that societal stratification arises out of the distribution of natural abilities. It took this one step further, however, by arguing that stratification is necessary for the survival and smooth functioning of a society. For theorists Kingsley Davis and Wilbert Moore (1953), some positions in society are functionally more important than others, but only a select amount of people have the natural talent to fill these positions. The talented need to be trained to turn their ability into skill and since this period of training necessarily involves sacrifices in terms of time commitment and wages reduction, the end rewards must be sufficient to ensure that the sacrifices will be made. A society thus needs a system of unequal rewards to ensure that the most important positions are filled.

TEXT BOX 7.1 HUMAN CAPITAL THEORY

One of the earliest economics theories to feed into debates over differences in work was human capital theory. The orthodox economics tradition that in which it arose emphasised rational explanations for differences in paid work: employers must select workers from a pool of available people, and they rationally select the best workers for the job on the basis of the workers' human capital; their education, qualifications and skills.

The natural, functional explanation of stratification has been roundly criticised (see Tumin 1953, for a critique of Davis and Moore, for example), and it would be fair to say that a more critical approach has dominated the bulk of sociology's history (but see Text box 7.1 on human capital theory for the profound influence of meritocratic ideas on economic theory). In this critical approach, the sociological concern is with divisions between groups rather than differences between individuals. That is, sociology sees that society is not just made up of many individuals who succeed – or not – according to differences in their own natural talent and hard work. Instead, divisions exist that advantage some groups at the expense of others within a hierarchy of equality. Importantly, these divisions are socially constructed not natural. Since they are not natural, neither are they fixed and permanent, and so they can and indeed do vary over time and from place to place. This is as true of the social division of class as it is of gender or 'race' (see Text box 7.2). We proceed in this chapter by focusing on the developments in work sociology that focused upon class inequalities.

TEXT BOX 7.2 CORE CHARACTERISTICS OF A SOCIAL DIVISION

- Social divisions are persisting, supported by dominant cultural beliefs.
- Members of different categories of a social division face unequal opportunities in life.
- Membership of a category of social division tends to result in shared social identity.
- Social divisions are socially constructed.

(Payne 2006)

Work and class divisions

Questions for sociologists of work have been sparked over the years by changes in societies' socio-economic structures. Mike Savage, writing ostensibly about class and British sociology wrote of '[the] remarkable wave of sociologically informed studies of work and employment that claimed to represent a bright new future for social scientific research' (2000a: 25). He suggested that the period 1955–75 represented a 'golden age of British occupational and industrial sociology' with researchers fascinated by industrial modernisation and class cultures (ibid.: 25). Important studies included Norman Dennis *et al.*'s (1956) *Coal is Our Life*; Richard Brown and Peter Brannen's (1970) research on class and status differentiation among shipyard workers; Huw Beynon's (1973) *Working for Ford*; and John Eldridge's (1968) analysis of industrial disputes and status hierarchy. Arguably the most prominent study emerged from the growing prosperity and rising wage levels that were occurring for certain sections of the male manufacturing workforce during the 1950s and 1960s. The so-called embourgeoisement thesis was proposing that these previously working-class men were actually becoming middle class in their working and leisure lives. In the mid-1960s, John Goldthorpe and colleagues set out to test whether the embourgeoisement thesis could be supported empirically in Britain. In their seminal 'Affluent Worker' series of publications (Goldthorpe *et al.* 1968a, 1968b, 1969), the team displayed a mass of evidence from their combined qualitative and quantitative research into car manufacturing workers employed in the then new town of Luton in south-east England. Based on these findings, the researchers concluded that embourgeoisement was not in fact occurring in Luton. Yes, the men in their sample were earning higher wages than they had previously, Goldthorpe *et al.* argued, but they were not becoming middle class in other aspects of their jobs: they were still working very long hours, their work was labour intensive and monotonous, and the car workers still had very different career paths to middle-class workers. Importantly too, the men didn't feel that they were middle class nor did they socialise with middle-class people outside work, spending their leisure time instead with their families. Goldthorpe *et al.* did suggest that the car workers represented a new type of working class – instrumental workers who saw their work purely as a means to earn wages, who saw trade unions as a means of protection rather than for worker solidarity, and who had domestically-based leisure time rather than spending time with other working-class men. Goldthorpe and his colleagues' work helped stimulate a concern with changing patterns of class identification around work groups, occupations and community (see Bulmer 1975; Lockwood 1975; Salaman 1974).

This sociological interest in the relationship between work and class also needs to be placed in the context of a wider upswing of attention paid to the subject by historians and others. During the 1950s and especially the 1960s, social historians such as E. P. Thompson, Eric Hobsbawm and Raphael Samuel examined the interrelationship between class and work, particularly within the British context. Their work drew upon and was subsequently drawn on by sociology (see Thompson 1968, 1991; Hobsbawm 1964, 1984; Samuel 1977).

While the above focus in sociology was often on the boundaries between the working class and the middle class, changes in the socio-economic structure of Britain were also to stimulate research at the other boundary of the working class: was the working class becoming so diverse that an 'underclass' was being created below the main class body? Unfortunately, as we discuss in Chapter 11 on unemployment, underclass debates were influenced in the 1980s by the polemical work of Charles Murray, a right-wing commentator who whipped up a moral panic around a supposed deprived and depraved stratum of 'underclass' society, characterised by lone mother families in which the lack of a male breadwinner role model was resulting in children growing up out of control and with no work commitment (see Kirk Mann 1991, for a critique).

Changes to the socio-economic structure over time shaped the study of more middle-class occupations too. One significant example is the proletarianisation thesis, in which certain middle-class occupations were said to have downgraded so much that they had more in common with occupations typically defined as working-class. An interesting occupation focused upon in proletarianisation debates has been clerical work. A 1958 classic study, *The Black Coated Worker* by David Lockwood, explored clerical workers in Britain, asking whether the differences between white-collar and blue-collar work had reduced, whether offices had become like large factory floors, and whether differentials in educational levels, pay and career prospects between clerical workers and manual workers were disappearing. More recently, researchers stimulated by issues of control in the workplace have been suggesting again that some white-collar workers have lost much of their previous 'middle-class' autonomy in the workplace as a result of the impact of computer technologies on their working lives. The impact of IT on call centre workers, for example, has resulted in a wealth of studies that we will come back to in the next chapter on control and work.

Another key link between the sociologies of class and of (paid) work was to be in the development of so-called class schemas, by which class writers debated the best ways to 'measure' people's class positions. Neo-Weberians (like John Goldthorpe; see Goldthorpe and Hope 1974) and neo-Marxists (like Erik Olin Wright, 1985) formulated occupation-based and employment status-based categories of measurement of class that remain highly influential today, particularly but not only in quantitative research studies including into patterns of social mobility. However, that employment position might signify class position, especially when the class position of the family was often based on the employment of the male 'head of household', was to be hotly debated in sociology (Charles 1990; Prandy and Blackburn 1997; Roberts, H. 1993).

Finally, one of the most important ways in which class was placed on the sociology of work agenda during the 1970s is by the publication and subsequent discussion of Harry Braverman's (1974) *Labor and Monopoly Capital.* Braverman's book, as we have seen and will see elsewhere in this book, was to play a crucial role in stimulating debate on the labour process and, as part of that, stressing the fundamental structural inequalities within capitalism, especially in terms of class.

Moving beyond class: work and other social divisions

The (over-)focus on class divisions that marked the bulk of early sociological writing on work was to be re-evaluated, with the impetus for the re-evaluation coming from some quite diverse sources. On the one hand, in the 1970s, class theorists themselves began to question how useful the concept of class was as an indicator of changing social inequalities, not least in the light of developments in the socio-economic structure discussed above such as proletarianisation and embourgeoisement that were impacting on working-class and middle-class occupations.

At the same time, the centrality of class began to be critiqued soundly by writers who stressed instead the significance of non-class-based divisions as sources of persistent inequality in society. With the expansion of new social movements uniting along issues such as gender, 'race', disability, ecology, age, and so on, the usefulness of a class-only approach to social inequalities came under attack. This was less from an interest in its fragmentation and more from the alternative important possibilities that other divisions offered for sociological analysis. The new social movements have had a significant impact on many academic disciplines, not just sociology. As feminist writer Dale Spender (1981) has argued, this impact included placing on the agenda the topics a discipline should actually be studying, how academics should be carrying out research, and which academic voices dominate disciplines with what consequences. The first social movement to really influence the sociology of work was second-wave feminism, and so we turn here to a review of the sociological study of gender inequalities in work.

Work and gender divisions

At the heart of the sociological approach to gender is the conviction that women and men are not just in different positions in society but rather that inequalities exist between them. Since gender is a social division, the sociological approach pioneered by sociologists like Ann Oakley (1972) in Britain and Christine Delphy in France (1977) is that gender inequalities are structurally determined, not natural outcomes. While by sex we are indeed referring to biological differences between women and men, by gender we are interested in how – as US sociologists Candace West and Don Zimmerman (1987) put it – we learn to 'do' our gender roles. Not only is gender socially constructed, but its construction reflects power imbalances between men as a group and women as a group. The idea of hierarchy is thus core to the concept (see Text box 7.2 from Payne), with its categories of masculine and feminine reflecting hierarchical notions of strength/domination and weakness/subordination respectively.

Work sociologists have asked a range of questions concerning gender inequalities, summarised here as: how is work gendered?, why is work gendered in this way?, and what are the implications of this gendering? They have asked whether the gendering of work is unchanged over time and across different societies, and if so, why. If not, why not? They have asked how the gendering came about, and when. And they have asked about the implications of the gendering of work – for women, men, families, and public policy. The sociological response to these and indeed many more questions around gender and work has introduced a whole range of concepts into the sociological lexicon. A small selection includes patriarchy, gender régimes, feminisation, housework, gender wage gaps, and male breadwinning. We cannot cover even a small fraction of the influential debates on gender and work in detail here (but see Further Reading for guidance on useful sources), although many will appear in other places throughout the book. What we try to do instead is stress, using pioneering examples, how sociologists have studied gender inequalities in work in diverse and innovative ways and how they have theorised them. We hope to show that the inclusion of gender into sociological work debates has, despite its relative lateness in the history of the discipline, helped to revitalise the subject area.

Studying gender inequalities and work

It is well recognised that women were largely invisible as the subject of sociological research before the 1970s and many sociological theories, concepts and studies have been justifiably criticised or ignoring women in their focus purely on men. The 1970s brought a strong feminist call for women's lives and experiences to be documented. Historically there have been three typical responses to feminist demands for inclusion and the sociological reaction fits well into these: (1) ignore the call and carry on as before; (2) include women in the mainstream but do not question its basic assumptions; (3) include women and transform the mainstream. For (1), some areas of work sociology remained more heavily male-dominated, retaining a focus on mainstream concepts and approaches. Industrial sociology is perhaps the most obvious example here with many writers continuing to study male-dominated employment sectors only. Since we draw on this work throughout the book, we focus here on (2) and (3).

Studying women's paid work

The second response – in which women were included in projects that were concerned with mainstream interests – has produced a wealth of informative accounts of the gendering of paid work. Though these adopted mainstream interests, commonly in paid work, this has resulted in a number of fascinating studies of women's experiences of employment. From these accounts, we can trace the growth of female employment in Britain right from the Industrial Revolution, through the post-war growth in women's part-time service sector jobs, and see the emergence of influential debates over gender wage gaps, the feminisation of occupations and the alleged female take-over of the contemporary labour market.

Women's entry into paid jobs has long been of interest to sociology. The Industrial Revolution was associated with restricting most women to work carried out largely within the private sphere and, in Chapter 5, we highlighted debates on the separation of public/private sectors and subsequent campaigns for a family wage for male workers. Sociologists have been interested in the growth in the employment of women, in which jobs women have entered, when and why. The sex-typing of jobs has a long history in Britain, with Sylvia Walby (1986) and Harriet Bradley (1989) showing that 'women's jobs' and 'men's jobs' were already evident in the 1800s. This gendering of work was seen to be natural, arising from biological differences between women and men. In the twentieth century, however, the two world wars offered a direct challenge to such assumptions about women's and men's natural capacities for work. The wars, for some, heralded the seeds of economic liberation for women. Indeed, perhaps the most prevalent popular interpretation of the impact of war on gendered work is that since most men of working age were overseas, women were substituted to do their work in factories and on the land, and it was seen by everyone that women could indeed do what had previously been seen as 'men's work'. For historians like Gail Braybon (1982; Braybon and Summerfield 1987) and for sociologist Sylvia Walby (1986), however, this emancipatory story fails to take into account the significance of employer and trade union resistance to women substituting for male workers. Even when economic demand for workers was intense and was actually seen to be holding up the war effort, in each of the wars, settlements had to be reached between state, employer and unions – asserting the temporary nature of women's contracts – before employers and unions would allow their entry: 'We, as an organization are opposed to the introduction of women as a general principle' (Jack Tanner, President of the Amalgamated Engineering Union, 1940, quoted in Walby 1986: 1).

In a post-war context of further employer and union resistance – and developing debates over maternal deprivation and the alleged need for mothers to stay full-time with their babies – still women continued to enter paid jobs, as Viola Klein's (1965) study of married women workers demonstrated. But research showed that the form of women's paid work was very significant when compared with that of men: it was largely low level, low status and low waged, and in Britain was increasingly becoming over-concentrated in part-time service sector posts. Decades of in-depth research have demonstrated the persistence of this gendered patterning of employment in Britain. Women and men are largely segregated into different job sectors. Catherine Hakim's (1979) influential government report showed that women were mostly working in different kinds of jobs than men (she called this horizontal gender segregation) and at lower levels (she termed this vertical segregation).

The particularities of women's experiences of paid work inspired a series of fascinating studies by sociologists in the 1970s and 1980s. Research into female factory workers, for example, began to fill the void in sociology created by such influential studies as Beynon's *Working for Ford* (1973) that only examined men (such as Pollert's (1981) *Girls, Wives, Factory Lives* and Glucksmann/Cavendish (1982) *Women on the Line*). These projects were replicating mainstream interests in paid factory work, but they did ask new and important questions around the gendering of work. Rosemary Crompton and Gareth Jones' (1984) *The White-collar Proletariat: Deskilling and Gender in Clerical Work* looked to the mainstream debate over the proletarianisation of clerical work (see David Lockwood earlier), but in doing so they highlighted the crucial importance of gender in deskilling. They found that, unlike their male peers, female clerical workers had not been seen as middle-class workers. They were viewed as semi-skilled, they were not highly trained and did not have higher qualifications, and their pay was about equal to that of manual workers. The promotion chances of female and male clerical workers were substantially different too and so, in the very same profession, women and men were in quite different career situations. Bringing women into the analysis showed how male-centric the proletarianisation debate had been.

Studying women's unpaid work in the home, and questioning the private/public divide

The UK project celebrated for initiating the third response to the feminist call to include women – including women *and* transforming the sociological mainstream – was Ann Oakley's (1974) *The Sociology of Housework*. Oakley was building on sociological traditions, here the mainstream tradition of studying male factory workers, but in researching housework she began a re-evaluation of what was seen to be a suitable topic for sociological investigation. Until the 1970s, the bulk of studies and theories in the sociology of work had been concerned with the paid work that was carried out in the public sphere by men. In Oakley's PhD research, she interviewed 'full-time housewives' about their working lives. Asking similar questions of the women that were being asked of male factory workers in other studies at the time, Oakley showed that the female housewives reported similar discontents to male manual workers, expressing dissatisfaction with the monotony of their routine work and with long tiring weeks. Indeed, women's weeks were even longer than male factory workers at 77 hours on average. She also identified class differences among the women, with the working conditions of the middle-class housewives improved substantially by their access to hot water and their own washing machines and vacuum cleaners.

We examine the organisation of domestic work in more detail in Chapter 10 on domestic work, but here it is useful to flag up that a range of classic sociological studies – identified as feminist and not – were subsequently to approach work in a much more holistic way than in the previous over-focus on paid employment. Ray Pahl's ([1979] 1984) ethnography and survey of the working lives of women and men on the Isle of Sheppey, in Kent, for example, looked at the household organisation of paid work, unemployment, domestic work and informal work. Pahl's work was useful in revealing empirically the limitations of the assumed separation of work in the public from the private sphere. Janet Finch's (1983) *Married to the Job: Wives' Incorporation in Men's Work* examined women's involvement in their husbands' paid work, showing how work carried out in the public sphere is linked inextricably to that in the home. This acceptance of the linkages between public and private work also influenced the government-funded (1980) Women and Employment Survey. The main results were published in Jean Martin and Ceridwen Roberts' (1984) *Women and Employment: A Lifetime Perspective* and, although entitled 'employment', the report also explored women's unpaid work in the home as well as their attitudes to the gender division of labour:

> Women's employment cannot be studied separately from the unpaid work most women do at home, in their roles as wives and mothers, running a house and looking after a husband, children and sometimes sick or elderly dependants.
>
> (Martin and Roberts 1984: 96)

By the 1980s, then, the sociology of work had drawn attention to women's dominance of unpaid work in the home, and to men's domination of paid work and of high-level, well-paid jobs in particular. Sociology had also begun to question the alleged distinct separation of the private from and public spheres of work. How did sociologists try to explain these gendered work inequalities?

Theorising gender inequalities and work

Attempts to explain gender differences in work began by drawing on and adapting existing theories of work, but these gave way over the years to re-evaluations. One group of economic theories that were influential on the sociology of the gendering of work took as their focus the structuring of the labour market, interested as they were in employers' demands for different types of workers – some core, some more peripheral to the companies' needs. Drawing on Marxian ideas, a 'segmented labour markets' approach within economics by Christine Craig, Jill Rubery, Roger Tarling and Frank Wilkinson (1982) offered a radical rejoinder to 'rational' economic accounts of internal labour markets in which employers were seen to be just trying to keep prized 'core' workers close. Their Marxist-influenced analysis saw instead that employers were attempting to divide the labour market into segments as a part of a divide and rule process. In sociology, influential writer Harry Braverman (1974) had argued earlier that by making use of already existent divisions such as gender (or 'race'), employers segmented the labour force, keeping wages differentiated and reducing overall worker solidarity.

Another Marxist idea adapted to examine gender divisions in work was the reserve army of labour thesis. As we see in Chapters 2 and 11, here capitalism is seen to need labour that it can draw on in times of boom and lay-off in slumps. When demand for labour uses up the traditional supply, reserves have to be pulled into the labour market. Veronica Beechey (1977) brought gender into this theory, arguing that married women provide a flexible and disposable reserve army since the home is their first priority and employment is secondary. This theory suffered some critique when women were not the first to be laid off in times of economic trouble in the 1980s and when it was noted that women had never really replaced men in their jobs in the 1970s since women had been entering newly created women's jobs in the service sector.

As seen in Chapter 2, for feminist theorist Sylvia Walby (1986), problems with such accounts included their presumptions about gender differences, and the over-domination of class. For Walby, and for Heidi Hartmann (1979) too, gender stands apart from class as an independent source of inequality. Theories of class and of gender inequalities are needed since one without the other cannot explain how work is patterned, but these need to be inter-linked. In the so-called dual systems approach that is associated with the early work of these two writers, structures of gender and of class are both examined, patriarchy and capitalism.

A second grouping of influential early economic theories examined the characteristics of people 'supplying' their labour to the market to account for gender differences in work. One of the most influential accounts came from economics: human capital theory. Rooted in an orthodox economics tradition that emphasised rational explanations, the human capital explanation of gendered work was based on the idea that employers must select workers from a pool of available people, and they rationally select the best workers for the job on the basis of the workers' human capital. Women accumulate less human capital than men because of caring responsibilities (Mincer and Polacheck 1974). For economist Gary Becker (1985) similarly, families share work by making the rational calculation that it is more efficient for women and men to specialise and to accumulate different types of capital; women in the home and men in the labour market. A main early critique of such ideas was that they failed to explain gender-typing and instead assumed natural divisions between women and men.

The critique of only demand or supply explanations for the gender division of work leads us towards more structural explanations that we explore in the contemporary section.

Work and 'racial' divisions

The interest in 'race' as a social division emerged in the 1950s in Britain, reflecting both the impact of post-war immigration to Europe and the decolonialisation of the British Empire. But it was not until the 1960s and 1970s that research into black and other minority ethnic people began to influence work sociology in Britain. In parallel moves to the impact of feminism on sociology, the black rights movement was important in stimulating critiques of mainstream sociological theorising and research and in inspiring new research questions about workers' lives and the structuring of work. However, it is fair to say that the impact of black and minority ethnic rights movements on the sociology of work in Britain has been less significant than the impact of feminism has been. Many influential sociological theories and studies do have 'race' and ethnicity at their heart of course and so, while noting the limitations of the sociology of work in this area, what we hope to do is to showcase the influential sociological studies and debates into 'racial' inequalities in work that were produced, and in contemporary developments we consider the future for the sociology of 'race' and work.

The sociology of 'race' has some clear parallels to developments in the study of gender/sex in that sociologists are concerned with deconstructing essentialist arguments in which inequalities in society are explained by reference to natural differences, here between 'racial' groups. Michael Banton (1967) discussed how the development of the term 'race' in the 1900s reflected white beliefs at the time that physical attributes such as white skin and European features were advanced/superior while Asian or African features were inferior. It is part of the sociological project to deconstruct biological determinism since our interest is with socially constructed disadvantage and advantage. For sociology, 'racial' inequalities in society are not biologically but socially determined (Fenton 2003; Pilkington 2003). Indeed, many sociologists in Britain are wary about talking about 'racial' inequalities and about being seen to use the term 'race' uncritically, hence the apostrophes enclosing the word in many texts including this one.

Studying 'racial' inequalities and work

If we adapt the approach taken within the gender section, we can see that sociology has responded in three ways to the issue of 'race': (1) ignore it; (2) incorporate black and minority ethnic groups into mainstream accounts; and (3) re-evaluate mainstream understandings. We will see that sociology – and the sociology of work – developed over the years from an initial focus on immigrants, adopting mainstream theories to explain their experiences, and on to more awareness of imperialism and structural disadvantage within an emergent sociology of racism.

Any understanding of 'race' and work in Britain needs a historical aware-ness. The story of 'racial' disadvantage is strongly linked to the history of empire that reinforced white paternalism and the white belief in certain non-British 'races' as inferior. A classic account of migrants in Britain by Sheila Allen (1971: 14) argued: 'the complexities of British social structure are over-laid by the long history of overseas empire'. Accordingly, and as we saw in Chapter 2, an understanding of empire is crucial to the sociology of work. The twentieth-century history of the sociology of 'race' and work in Britain is also highly pertinent, in particular its clear flashpoints around migration to ease the labour shortage that followed the end of the Second World War; and the later attention to racial discrimination in the labour market.

Much of the early sociology of 'race' was concerned with migrant workers. Documented migration clearly identifies the vast extent of forced migration in the seventeenth and nineteenth centuries, with a staggering 15–20 million people transferred for slave work from Africa to the New World during these years (Fenton 2003: 118). Over time, migration became more globalised, with more countries involved in sending and receiving migrants. Over time too, the bulk of economic migration changed from being from field work to plantation economies; from peasant to industrial economies; to the twen-tieth century where it became predominantly from labouring and services to rich economies. This latter type of economic migration appears in many places in this book since migrant workers have emerged as the most open to exploitation, with undocumented migrants facing what Steve Fenton (2003) terms 'super-exploitation' in contemporary societies.

In the UK, after the Second World War, aided immigration brought in migrants to regions where demand for workers was outstripping the 'tradi-tional', that is white, supply. Facilitated by the 1948 Nationality Act that granted citizenship and hence the right to live and work in Britain to members of British colonies and ex-colonies, as well as by active recruitment of workers abroad by British firms, migrants began to arrive from the Caribbean, India, Pakistan, Bangladesh and Sri Lanka. Since the immigration was largely to areas where there were job vacancies at the time, striking regional concen-trations of minority ethnic groups developed, with immigrants settling in manufacturing areas of the south-east and Midlands, for example, and in northern cities with available textile work. These residential patterns persist today. Although the numbers of immigrants of colour were very small initially (just under 500 immigrants from Jamaica were aboard the ship *The Empire Windrush* in 1948, for example), and certainly very small in propor-tion to white immigration from eastern Europe, it was black immigrants who became the focus of most academic and policy concern. Some of the most influential British sociological studies of migrants, that feed into debates about though were not solely concerned with work, were carried out in Birmingham by John Rex: his (1973) *Race, Colonialism and the City*; work with colleague Sally Tomlinson (1979) *Colonial Immigrants in a British City:*

A Class Analysis; and that with Robert Moore (1967) *Race, Community and Conflict: A Study of Sparkbrook.*

Peter Braham *et al.*'s (1981) influential edited collection, *Discrimination and Disadvantage in Employment: The Experience of Black Workers*, looked specifically at 'race' and work. In it we can see some of the core themes for sociologists throughout the 1970s and 1980s. It explored the role of immigrant labour; ethnic minorities' experiences in the labour market; black workers and trade unions; equal opportunities in employment and unemployment; and it pulled together the work of writers like Shelia Allen, Robin Blackburn and Michael Mann, Stephen Castles and Godula Kosack, Theo Nichols and Huw Beynon, and Ambalavaner Sivanandan, as well as research from policy-makers.

Looking at just one of these themes, the study of trade unions saw socio-logical interest in the representation of minority ethnic workers by the white dominated trade unions, and in industrial disputes dominated by minority ethnic workers. In Brooks' (1975) study *Race and Labour in London Transport*, a section in Braham's collection, white workers voiced opposition to the recruitment of 'colonial immigrants', with the colour of the workers seen as a real problem, particularly for supervisory roles. Writers like John Rex and Sally Tomlinson (1979), Paul Gilroy (in CCCS 1982), and Ambalavaner Sivanandan (1982) all identified a lack of support for minor-ity workers from the white unions, with some suggesting that an effect of racism among trade unions was that white workers saw their interests lying more closely with white employers rather than with their black co-workers (Satnam Virdee 2000 provides a useful analysis).

Theorising 'racial' inequalities and work

Sociological theories of 'racial' inequalities that fed into a work sociology were to develop over the years from an initial focus on newly arriving 'different' immi-grants and their relationship with the 'host' nation, to more awareness of impe-rialism and structural disadvantage within an emergent sociology of racism. In the first approach, as exemplified by Sheila Patterson's (1963) *Dark Strangers: A Sociology Study of the Absorption of a Recent West Indian Migrant Group in Brixton, South London*, the emphasis was on the possibility of harmonious host–immigrant race relations that very much stressed the need for immigrants to adapt to the host society. This approach gave way to one that highlighted the structurally disadvantaged situation of black and other minority ethnic groups. Theory also developed away from a concern with immigrants *per se*, not least since the proportion of people from minority ethnic groups living in Britain who were born in Britain expanded, and towards issues of 'race' and racism.

After the early host–immigrant focus, more critical theoretical approaches developed in the 1960s and 1970s. Marxist and Weberian theories of class divisions were adapted, and debates were heavily influenced in Britain by the writings of neo-Marxists like Robert Miles (1982), Stuart Hall (Hall *et al.* 1979), Stephen Castles (with Kosack 1973); and neo-Weberians like Frank Parkin (1979) and John Rex (above). The neo-Marxists largely examined ethnic disadvantage as a form of economic disadvantage based on the system of production, in which minority groups were seen as a source of cheap labour who could be dismissed in a recession. Neo-Weberian writers drew on a variety of Weber's ideas to inform their analysis of 'race' including his theory of closure and exclusion as well as his multi-faceted development of class, status and party. For neo-Marxists, black workers living in Britain were part of the working class but they were split apart from the white working class in what Miles (1982) called a racialised class fraction. Neo-Weberians John Rex and colleagues (seen earlier), similarly concerned with class explanations, proposed that black workers were a separate, underprivileged or underclass, in a different class position to the white working class. White workers had won rights via working-class movements like the TU movement, but migrant workers were excluded from these. Drawing on Weber's use of status, Rex and colleagues also argued that differential power in the housing market differentiated into separate housing classes the white from the black working class, with the latter overcrowded in multi-occupied homes in predominantly inner-city areas.

After this period of the adaptation of existing class theories to incorporate 'race' issues, sociologists began to develop new approaches and reframe the core questions of concern. A key part of this development was a move away from the domination by class and economics as explanations for 'racial' inequalities. Theories emerging in the 1970s and 1980s argued both that 'race' was distinct as a sociological issue: it was not reducible to class, and that cultural explanations were as vital as economic. Very influential in this was the Centre for Contemporary Cultural Studies (CCCS) at Birmingham University in England where writers like Stuart Hall and Paul Gilroy were working (see CCCS's (1982) *The Empire Strikes Back*, for example). The CCCS writers on 'race', although influenced by Marxism, gave impetus to the birth of a new sociology of racism and boosted research into ethnicity, culture and resistance. As with gender and class theorisation, the influence of writers like Paul Gilroy (1987) was that 'race' and class began to be seen as relatively autonomous features of society.

CONTEMPORARY ISSUES AND FUTURE TRENDS

Class and work

One of the welcome developments in the social sciences in recent years has been the strong revival in the study of social class. After a period when social stratification analysis became relatively marginalised, for a variety of reasons it has reclaimed some of its lost ground in British sociology. The area has seen a host of books producing both new conceptualisations of class coupled with a thorough-going critique of the field (see Bottero 2004; Crompton *et al.* 2000; Devine and Waters 2004; Devine *et al.* 2005; Savage 2000b; Skeggs 2004). For the purposes of our book on work, this renaissance stresses the need to examine class in the context both of the economy and culture, and what has emerged is a more rounded account of class as a lived experience as well as reflecting deep-seated structural inequality. In the USA, there has also been a revival in class analysis among researchers across the social sciences and humanities. One aspect of this is the emerging field of working-class studies which explicitly attempts to focus on class in new ways, in particular on issues of intersectionality between class, gender and 'race' (see later). Much of the impetus for this field of working-class studies comes from a deep-seated reflection on the meaning and significance of class, often associated with male working-class occupations in the wake of major waves of deindustrialisation and economic restructuring. What a number of books and articles coming out of this tradition do is reflect upon work in the wake of these changes, as well as rethinking the nature of working-class community in the past. It is important to note that alongside this commitment to intersectionality is also the interdisciplinary nature of the field which has implications for the sociology of work, namely the possibility of borrowing theories, methods and approaches (see Russo and Linkon 2005).

Gender and work

Contemporary developments in the sub-discipline of gender and work have been: (1) towards recognition of the importance of differences among women; and (2) away from focusing purely on women as the gendered group and on to studying the work of men through a gendered lens too.

A succinct critique of the second-wave feminist approach to studying only women is to ask: when we say 'women' or 'men', does it apply equally to the experiences of all women or men? US black feminist bell hooks questioned the feminist call for equal rights with men: 'since men are not equal in white, supremacist, capitalist patriarchal class structures, which men do women want to be equal to?' (hooks 2000: 19). Examining only what unites women and separates them from men passes over major, significant divisions, such as 'race' and class, that have ramifications for understanding the experiences of different groups of women and men in society. It is vital then to examine other social divisions, in addition to gender, to better understand women's working lives. Sociologists of gender and work in Britain such as Harriet Bradley, Irene Bruegel, Rosemary Crompton, Miriam Glucksmann, Lydia Morris and Sylvia Walby, to name only a few, have provided a wealth of evidence pointing to the persistence of class divisions that impact on women's experiences of work and employment. And, as we will see in the next section, 'racial' diversity in work among women has been shown too.

Inspired by the growing recognition of heterogeneity within women's working lives, a recent, influential – if controversial – account of gender differences in work is Catherine Hakim's 'preference theory' (1996, 1998, 2000, 2003). Hakim's argument is that work–life preferences among women are heterogeneous, and that women – far more so than men – are able to act out these differing preferences, and this accounts for more diversity in women's patterns of engagement with the labour market than is true for me. Reflecting earlier 'supply-based' theories of gendered work patterns, preferences and choices are the most important forces shaping women's lives for Hakim, including their labour market behaviour. Women in the UK face a genuine choice between the home and the labour market, she suggests. What is controversial in this argument is not that preferences inform behaviour but that they potentially over-ride the influences of demographic, social, economic and institutional factors. A range of critics have emphasised instead the effects of gender inequalities on women's work–life preferences, stressing the constraints that are exerted on both the formation and enactment of preferences (Breugel 1996; Crompton 2002; Ginn *et al.* 1996; McRae 2003, Warren and Walters 1998).

The welcome recognition of heterogeneity in women's working lives has been boosted too by cross-national research and theorising of gender and work. Cross-national empirical comparisons of gendered work have helped sociologists to question what may seem ordinary in one country but may well be uncommon in another. As a result, more sociological questions can be generated about the forms of gendered work and about whether different, better forms of the gendered division of labour are possible. Comparative studies of women's work have affirmed the universality of gendered work roles and of the male domination of paid work, but they have revealed differences in the strength of 'male breadwinning/female caring' in different societies, with debate about how we use these terms too (Crompton 1999; Ungerson 1983, 2002; Warren 2007). Jill Rubery *et al.'s* (1999) *Women's Employment in Europe* provided detailed comparative information, derived from quantitative data, on women's employment patterns in all countries in the EU. Using a quantitative approach too, Warren's (2001) research into female part-time employment showed that working part-time is not the only or usual way that women with caring responsibilities combine home and work in Europe. Rather, extensive female part-time employment only emerges under specific societal conditions. Drawing on qualitative and quantitative comparative case studies, Rosemary Crompton's extensive research has identified variation and similarities in the gendering of certain occupations (like pharmacy, medicine, accountancy) in different countries (see Gornick and Meyers' (2003) cross-national review of working families that focuses on gender too).

How has such cross-national variety, alongside persistent gender in-equalities in work, been explained? We saw earlier that economic models of supply or demand were each deemed too one-sided to explain the gendering of work. In sociology, more structural explanations were developed. The concept of patriarchy, for example, was used initially to create a concept of universal gender inequality, but questions were raised over its ability to capture substantial diversity in women's experiences. New theoretical approaches have been developed by early writers on patriarchy like Sylvia Walby and other sociologists to try to explain variations in gender equality in work roles in different societies. A range of approaches have looked to identify how a range of key institutions (such as family relations, the labour market, gender culture), come together in different ways in diverse societies to shape a societal gender regime.

Social policy theorist Jane Lewis' (1992) identification of cross-national differences in the strength of 'the male breadwinner model' is one such example, as is German sociologist Birgit Pfau-Effinger's (1998) 'gender arrangements' approach, Swedish feminist historian Yvonne Hirdmann's (1998) 'gender contract and gender order' analysis; and Australian Raewyn (previously Robert) Connell's (1987, 2002) development of the concepts of 'gender orders and gender régimes'. Central to these approaches is that societal gender arrangements (orders, régimes, models, contracts, and so on) vary, be it over time, place, region. The work of geographer Simon Duncan, joint with a range of colleagues, on 'gendered moral rationalities' has also stimulated influential debates over how people make decisions about their working and caring in these differing contexts (see Text box 7.3).

TEXT BOX 7.3 GENDERED MORAL RATIONALITIES

According to Duncan *et al.*:

> Evidence about how people make family decisions – including how parenting might be combined with paid work, and how children should be cared for – shows that people do not act in . . . individual-istic, economically rational way. Rather, they take such decisions with reference to moral and socially negotiated views about what behaviour is right and proper, and this varies between particular social groups, neighbourhoods and welfare states.
>
> (2004: 256)

Recognising heterogeneity in women's working lives – within and between societies – is now common in the sociology of work. Alongside this improvement in the discipline has been an emerging interest in men's experiences. This is not to forget, of course, that much of early work sociology invariably focused on men, and that many sociologists still do. What is new in the approach we are highlighting here is that men, and not just women, are looked at through a gendered lens. Interest in men's work was re-awakened by the impact of extensive unemployment on men's working lives, as we discuss in Chapters 6 and 11. With the security of the male breadwinner role under attack for many men, in particular working-class men living in deindustrialising regions in which there is an alleged female takeover of the labour market, what were the implications for men's working lives and their sources of identity formation?

The male research agenda was boosted too by a growing theoretical attention to men and masculinity within gender studies, in which Connell's writings on gender again – and here the concept of hegemonic masculinity – have been particularly influential. The crux of Connell's (2000, 2002) use of gender is that, as well as capturing inequalities between women and men, the concept should also be able to include patterns of difference among women, and among men. Focusing largely on men in her work, Connell stresses, first, that different masculinities exist (for example, violent and non-violent masculinities) but, second, that the cultural ideal of masculinity – hegemonic masculinity as characterised by such traits as physical strength – is actually unattainable to many men. Hegemonic masculinity is not constructed only in relation to women but to 'subordinated masculinities' too, and a key feature is that it is heterosexual. Therefore, a crucial form of subordinated masculinity is homosexuality. Crucially, then, although men in general benefit from inequalities of gender, many men do pay a considerable gendered price. 'Boys and men who depart from dominant definitions of masculinity because they are gay, effeminate or simply wimpish are often subject to verbal abuse and discrimination, and are sometimes the targets of violence' (2002: 6). How have these theories of masculinities fed into work sociology?

An important recent theme in the sociology of work has been the impact of job loss on men's masculinity. In a society with a work ethic, the value of having a job and of bringing in income is important. We see in Chapter 11 that unemployment is materially distressing. But for men, the ideology of the male-breadwinner means that if they are not the worker and earner of the home, these are critical implications for men's sources of identity formation. Nickie Charles and Emma James' (2005) study of men in former mining communities in South Wales is revealing here, and we come back to it in Chapter 11 on unemployment. John Goodwin's (2002) research into unemployed young men in Dublin drew directly on Connell's notion of hegemonic masculinity to consider whether being unemployed was also a 'subordinated masculinity'.

A second influential theme for men and work is the study of gendered work cultures. In 1985, Cynthia Cockburn argued, 'the hegemonic ideology of masculism involves a definition of men and women as different, contrasted, complementary and unequal, It is powerful and it deforms both men and women' (1985: 85).

More recently, building on developments in theories of masculinity, Stephen Whitehead (2002, 2006) has argued that despite the fact that women are moving into paid work, the capitalist system itself retains values that are associated with dominant discourses of masculinity. Masculine values still pervade organisational cultures and locate femininity as 'other' and marginal. Using David Morgan's discussion of the 'ideal type' of worker (someone who is instrumental, unemotional or hides emotions, objective, dominant, active, competitive, logical, skilled, direct, worldly, makes decisions easily, acts as a leader, ambitious, etc.), Stephen Whitehead suggests that these attributes reflect dominant notions of masculinity, and their performance enables men (and women too) to remain in work and progress, but not all men are able to/or want to work within such a masculinist culture.

The ideas have emerged clearly within much more nuanced accounts of gender than was seen in early studies of women versus men, or indeed just of women. The more sophisticated understanding of gender featuring in newer sociologies of work also makes links between gender inequalities in work and sexuality, as we discuss in more detail in Chapters 8 on control and 12 on identity, culture and emotion. In the latter chapter, for example, we discuss Arlie Hochschild's argument that certain jobs formally require emotional labour – that people engage in 'the management of feeling to create a publicly observable facial and bodily display' (1983: 8). Developing notions of masculinities/femininities are also stimulating some fascinating sociology. This includes studies on men who work in female dominated occupations and on women in male-dominated professions. In these and other chapters, we hope to show that the sociology of work is no longer concerned only with the production/economic paradigm but is increasingly reflecting the 'cultural turn' of sociology as a discipline too, while reflecting its economic heritage.

'Race' and work

One of the key developments in the sociology of 'race' has been a move away from comparing dichotomies (of white and minority ethnic, for example), and onto recognising the diversity that exists within 'minority ethnic', thus paralleling developments within the sociology of gender that look to divisions within the gender categories.

The most persuasive and large-scale evidence on diversity among minority groups in Britain emerged from the 1994 Fourth National Survey of Ethnic Minorities. The report by Tariq Modood *et al.* (1997) showed important differences among men in their employment patterns, raising questions about differential disadvantage as well as about the potential of divergence between minority ethnic groups over time. Over half of Bangladeshi and Chinese men were working in hotel and catering jobs, for example, while white and West Indian men were more likely to be in manufacturing. Another interesting finding was the high levels of male self-employment among certain Asian groups. Older theories had explained this by reference to the alleged characteristics of these groups – their hard work and enterprise, but more recent non-essentialist explanations have looked to the lack of alternative employment opportunities for the men. Rather than a simple success story of entrepreneurial achievement, studies have revealed too that many self-employed minority ethnic men are working long unsocial hours, in poor conditions for low wages. Self-employment is often a response to racism, as studies by Monder Ram (1992) and Robin Ward and Richard Jenkins (1984) demonstrate, with many Asian businesses marginal in the economy, offering services to an ethnically select set of customers. However, Modood *et al.* (1997) and Metcalf *et al.* (1996) have suggested some self-employment achievements are because certain ethnic groups fare better as self-employees than employees, although again interesting ethnic differences emerge with the Bangladeshi and Pakistani self-employed faring poorly. Sociologist Satnam Virdee advises caution in any interpretation of progress and advancement: the growth of Asian self-employment since the 1970s ought to be 'interpreted as working class accommodation to the ravages wrought by the rise of a neo-liberal modernity and the revival of neo-utilitarian doctrines of the minimalist state over the past thirty years' (Virdee 2006: 610).

The more complex picture Virdee paints is demonstrated well in Virinder Kalra's in-depth study of self-employed male Pakistani workers in Oldham (see Ramji 2005 too). While setting up a take-away business fit under the 'general rubric of the ethnic entrepreneur' (Kalra 2000: 177), taxi driving was seen less positively and taxi-drivers were not viewed as 'business men' in the same sense. An interviewee, Ikram, who entered taxi-driving after being made redundant in 1989, stated:

> Our men have come into taxis because they have no choice. If they could get a better job, they would not do taxis, because at the weekend we still get abused. If you had the choice you would not put your life at risk. Every time some man gets in the car you never know if he has a knife. You have to be very careful.
>
> (Kalra 2000: 183)

For Virdee, the growth of taxi driving was 'not motivated by the prospect of driving in declining urban conurbations for low wages under a constant threat of racist violence from customers' (2006: 611), but by the need for employment in an area in which previous work in the textile industry has been eradicated in economic restructuring.

Another key theme – that emerged in the PSI work and other studies such as those by Richard Berthoud (2000) and Paul Iganski and Geoff Payne (1996), has been the relative occupational success over time of men from some minority groups, but not others. Comparing findings with those of previous studies in 1968 and 1993, Modood *et al.* suggested that men of Bangladeshi, Caribbean and Pakistani origin continued to face severe disadvantage in the labour market, being over-represented in manual jobs or in unemployment, while men from African Asian and Indian backgrounds had made significant gains over time into higher levels of the occupational structure.

The picture of diversity – albeit alongside persistent 'racial' disadvantage – among men is fascinating, but studies reveal even wider differences in work experiences among women from different ethnic groups. To begin with, Modood *et al.* show over 70 per cent of Bangladeshi and Pakistani women were not in paid jobs, but were looking after the home and family full-time, compared with 25 per cent of white, Chinese and African Asian women and one-third of Indian women. African-Caribbean women were most likely to be in paid work than the other groups, and to be working full-time when there. Educational researcher Heidi Mirza's (1992) qualitative study of young women's views of work and motherhood casts some light on these differences since it identified substantial attitudinal variation between young black and white women. Young black women were more likely to stress commitment to full-time employment and a desire for economic independence while fewer of the white women wanted a full-time career after leaving school. The young Black women expected to do paid work – just as their sisters, mothers and aunts had – regardless of whether they had children or not. The interest in diversity between minority ethnic groups, and gender and age differences within a group, is featuring predominantly in influential analysis in sociology. It is seen in Angela Dale and colleagues' (1998; 2002a; 2002b) studies of Bangladeshi and Pakistani women, and similarly in Tracey Reynolds' (2001, 2006) qualitative research into African Caribbean mothers (see also Bhavnani 1994; Bhopal 1998; Bloch 2004).

In recent years in Britain, one of the most influential concepts to emerge from the study of 'race', for public policy as well as academia, has been 'institutional racism'. Coined in 1967 by US black activist Stokely Carmichael (Pilkington 2003: 85), the concept gained widespread renown in the UK when it appeared in the McPherson Report into the police investigation of the murder of black teenager Stephen Lawrence. In brief, racism is institutional when it has become part of the hierarchical structure of society, when it is not random but represents systematic social disadvantage, and when it is present in the patterns of beliefs of a society and its institutions. In sociology, Nirmal Puwar (2001) has examined how institutional racism is perpetuated in organisations through a study of Black senior civil servants in Britain. The civil service has become naturalised for white men, Puwar argues. Drawing on the sociology of the body, she shows that the white male body is the 'somatic norm' in the organisation and, as a result, other bodies that are 'different' stand out, generating disorientation.

In the USA, there is a large and growing literature on 'race' and work which picks up this theme of difference within and between ethnic groups. The volume of this research reflects, in part, the academic make-up in the USA with influential sub-disciplines such as American and African studies. Much of this material is historical in nature but is often informed by sociological ideas. Examples include Bruce Nelson's (2001) *Divided We Stand* about black workers in the steel and port industries; Michael Honey's (1999) *Black Workers Remember,* which is an oral history of the group; and Melinda Chateauvert's (1998) *Marching Together,* a study of female sleeping car porters.

A final but key emerging issue in the study of 'race' concerns ethnic diversity among white groups and the need to problematise whiteness more generally, as seen in work of Richard Dyer (1997), Martin Mac An Ghaill (1999) and Maria Kefalas (2003). These are exciting times for sociologists of work who are interested in 'race' inequalities and it will be fascinating to monitor how sociology deals with the challenges it faces to study 'race' and ethnicity in work more comprehensively.

Other social divisions

There are of course other forms of social division which have an influence of paid and unpaid work, and we want to briefly examine two of these, skill and age.

Skill

Skill has historically been an important division in work and can be seen as being useful for particular sections of the workforce as well as for employers. Unlike class, gender or 'race', skill can be thought of a technical attribute or talent which is learnt or acquired through training or socialisation. Where it becomes a division is in relation to those workers who do not have a skill. Historically groups of skilled workers have often occupied a privileged position in labour markets. Often such workers have sought to ensure closure of their work group by limiting the numbers of those practising the trade – usually through apprenticeship. By limiting the numbers in a trade, work groups can ensure that they can gain greater wages when they come to sell their scarce labour. As we have seen, employers have often tried to replace the type of work carried out by skilled workers by using semi- or unskilled workers instead and by the substitution of technology. Historically skilled workers have tried to enforce labour market closure by grouping together in occupational groups, initially the ancient guilds of the Middle Ages and later into craft trade unions. Therefore, the relatively privileged position skilled workers had in the labour market could be maintained and reproduced economically as well as socially. This situation is made even more complicated by the emergence in the nineteenth century of a so-called labour aristocracy made up of élite craftsmen and other workers who had scarce skills. Some historians have argued that the existence of craft unions and the aristocracy of labour had important implications for class solidarity in that it separated out a key element of the working class (see Hobsbawm 1964, 1984). One element of this debate that we should acknowledge is the way these craft and skill distinctions help to form particular workplace norms, values and identities, the exercise of which help to enact occupational closure over time. We also need to recognise that just as skill acts as a division between the skilled and unskilled, it has also acted as division between skilled workers of differing trades, with industrial relations in some sectors of the economy being marked by demarcation disputes between rival trades over who could legitimately carry out certain types of work (Eldridge 1968). Skill as a division is of course underpinned by other sources of division. Often the most successful groups at claiming skill have been white men, rather than, and often at the expense of, female and/or minority ethnic workers. Cynthia Cockburn's (1983) classic book *Brothers* is a good illustration of male occupational closure in the printing industry.

Age

Our second form of social division that we want to consider here is that of age. Age is important in thinking about divisions at work as it has multiple and differential effects depending on which groups we are looking at. For white male senior executives in financial organisations, for example, there may be many privileges associated with growing older. On the other hand, for many unskilled working-class men and particularly women, life chances diminish with age. Unlike categories of gender or 'race', older age is a category that most of us (hopefully) will go through (and accordingly there have been debates as to how well age fits alongside other social divisions like gender). Age has become an increasingly important topic within discussions of work as it is becoming clearer that it has important implications for the ability of individuals to access work, or even retire from paid work as they choose. In the 1980s and 1990s in the UK, substantial numbers of older male workers exited the labour market at an earlier age. In 1974, over 93 per cent of men in their fifties were in full-time employment, whereas by 2000 this figure had fallen to just 77 per cent (Scales and Scase 2000). However, this statistic, while important, hides a range of experiences as to how workers leave employment (Phillipson and Smith 2005; Vickerstaff *et al.* 2004). While some workers who experience redundancy are happy to end their employed life, for others this is not the case: their 'choice' is shaped by lack of qualification, skill, and commonly in depressed regions, an objective lack of employment. Older workers in such positions have often experienced discrimination when applying for jobs on the grounds of age in that employers often perceive older workers to be less flexible and motivated than younger workers (Loretto *et al.* 2007).

Intersectionality

Our sections on contemporary approaches to social divisions in work have all shown that focusing on only one social division is limited and limiting (and see Bradley 1996; Payne 2006). For British theorist Floya Anthias (Anthias 2001; Anthias and Yuval-Davis 1983), we need to think about social inequalities in a more holistic and multidimensional way. This theoretical call has been heeded in work sociology, with a growing number of studies of work exploring how divisions such as class, gender and 'race' impact. Indeed, we should note how one influential study back in the CCCS's *The Empire Strikes Back* (1982) collection already examined gender, 'race' and class issues. Accepting that women face gendered labour market disadvantage, Prathibar Parmar (1982) argued that women from black and minority groups were experiencing the most restricted range of opportunities. Women of Asian background were least likely to be in employment and, if there, were found concentrated in low skilled jobs or in home-working. Meanwhile, Black women were likely to be in jobs but these were largely in unskilled and low status occupations. More recently, we can point to Brigit Anderson's (2000) study *Doing the Dirty Work?: The Global Politics of Domestic Labour* that would be impossible to discuss under our sections of class, gender or 'race' since it covers all these divisions in its analysis of migrant domestic workers (see Chapter 10).

TEXT BOX 7.4 INTERSECTIONALITY

According to Yuval-Davis:

> Intersectional analysis of social divisions has come to occupy central spaces in both sociological and other analyses of stratification as well as in feminist and other legal, political and policy discourses of international human rights. There has been a gradual recognition of the inadequacy of analysing various social divisions, but especially race and gender, as separate, internally homogeneous, social categories resulting in the marginalization of the specific effects of these, especially on women of colour.
>
> (2006: 206)

CONCLUSION

This chapter has stressed that social divisions are central to the sociology of work. Inequalities within work have been core to the discipline, and social divisions have been the main way that inequalities have been studied and theorised by sociologists. The main social divisions that work sociologists have been concerned with have been class and gender. Divisions of 'race' have been considered too, but less extensively within the British sociology of work than have class and gender. The current state of play in work sociology is that numerous divisions, including those of age, sexuality, disability and more, are being researched. Paying more direct attention to the 'new' as well as the old social divisions, in addition to recognising the complex interpenetration of different forms of inequality, is part of the sociological mission. The sociological approach to inequalities in work is therefore at an exciting juncture.

FURTHER READING

Sylvia Walby's *Patriarchy at Work* (1986) for a review and critique of classic theories of gender inequalities in work, as well as a historical account of gender relations at work.

Rosemary Crompton's *Women and Work in Modern Britain* (1997) and her *Employment and the Family* (2006) are excellent accounts of the gendering of work.

Stephen Small and John Solomos' article 'Race, immigration and politics in Britain: changing policy agendas and conceptual paradigms, 1940s–2000s' (2006) traces changing academic and policy concerns with 'race' in Britain.

Tariq Modood *et al.*'s edited collection *Ethnic Minorities in Britain: Diversity and Disadvantage* (1997) has a very useful chapter on employment that provides extensive, though dated now, information on patterns of employment by ethnic group in Britain.

Harry Braverman's *Labor and Monopoly Capital* (1974) plays a central role in debates on the labour process and on class inequalities within capitalism.

Floya Anthias' 'The concept of "social division" and theorising social stratification: looking at ethnicity and class' (2001) outlines her interpretation of intersectionality.

Wendy Bottero's *Stratification: Social Division and Inequality* (2005) provides a useful discussion of the main social divisions.

WEB SOURCES

Commission for Racial Equality:
http://www.cre.gov.uk

Equal Opportunities Commission:
http://www.eoc.org.uk

European Commission's 'Employment, Social Affairs and Equal Opportunities' division. Site on Gender Equality:
http://europa.eu.int/comm/employment_social/equ_opp/index_en.htm

Women's Unit:
http://www.womenandequalityunit.gov.uk/

STUDENT ESSAYS AND PROJECTS

1   To what extent are social divisions in work natural?
2   Persistent disadvantages in work are faced by large groups in society. Discuss.
3   Using some of the ideas in Chapter 3, think about how social divisions are manifest in representations of work.
4   Take one product or commodity and think about how it is gendered, classed and 'racialised' through its lifespan from design, construction, distribution, retail, consumption and disposal.

Control and Resistance at Work

▌ OVERVIEW

This chapter will ask:

• How and in what ways has work been controlled?
• How have sociologists looked at this issue and theorised control?
• How and in what ways have sociologists examined resistance by workers to management?
• How has sociology broadened its interest in work control beyond paid employment?
• What distinguishes sociologists in this field from other disciplines?

▌ INTRODUCTION

In this chapter we examine how work and employment has been controlled over time. Classical theorists saw the social organisation of labour as the mark of humanity, but the context in which work is carried out varies enormously. Work does not 'just happen' but is organised and controlled by managers, supervisors and by those doing the work. As capitalism developed and organisations grew, it was no longer possible to control work in the same way as it had been in small-scale workplaces and the home. The chapter looks at how sociologists have made sense of management and in doing so how they have theorised the exercise of control and worker resistance to it. Later we go beyond the established focus on the employment relationship and paid work to examine a range of other ways in which work is controlled, such as gender and 'race'.

SOCIOLOGICAL MISSION

Understanding the control of work is central to sociology, and early theorists were interested in how industrial societies differed from those based on feudalism or slavery. Sociology has always tried to understand the underlying structures, patterns and tensions in industrial society, to appreciate how social order is possible. Sociology has also been fascinated with the detail of how work is organised at the point of production, and using a range of techniques, sociologists studied how control, power and resistance is realised in workplaces. But we argue that a focus simply on paid work, and indeed on undifferentiated 'labour' is insufficient. Drawing on a range of sociological literature from different areas of the discipline, we show how issues of gender and 'race' can inform the study of paid and unpaid work.

FOUNDATIONS

Marx saw the role of management and supervision of workers as central to his model of how capitalistic society operated. For Marx, the employment relationship between capital and labour was fundamentally contradictory and therefore conflictual. We can express this simply as, on the one hand, capital wishing to buy as much labour as it needed for as little cost as possible, whereas the worker wants to maximise their income while minimising effort. The wages of the worker were the cost of the employer. In addition, in a capitalist society, workers had no alternative but to work for wages, control therefore was enforced indirectly by material need. While the political economists before him saw the exchange between capital and labour as a neutral market transaction, Marx saw this relationship as an expression of a fundamentally unequal system. To add to the complexity of this relationship was the fact that when employers purchased labour, what they bought was a potential for work. In order to realise labour, there needed to be some level of coordination, and discipline, hence the need for the management of labour. It must be stressed here that this is an abstracted or idealised theoretical understanding of the labour/capital relationship. As we saw in the chapter on theories of work, control over the labour process was essential for the capitalist as labour was the source of surplus value. Basically as greater amounts of fixed capital were employed, a capitalist's ability to realise profit was limited to its use of variable capital, particularly its labour. The problem for capital was that this system brought about conflict and resistance among the industrial workers.

For Emile Durkheim, there was a need for management and supervision within industrial society. In such societies the complexities of technology and the greater size of industrial enterprise meant that hierarchy was an absolute necessity, and management was a natural part of the division of labour. The important point for Durkheim was that such a division was based on meritocracy – the idea that people's position in society was achieved by talent and qualification, not simply tradition or who they knew. Therefore, in modern societies, the position of the managers and, for that matter, the different workers under them was based on objective criteria which would be accepted as rational by all. In such a society, industrial conflict over work and its organisation would be minimised or abolished altogether. Durkheim did not believe that this situation had been reached, on the contrary, he saw modern society as full of conflict because of the imperfect, or forced division of labour. In such a state, conflict was inevitable because of the frustration felt by people at the mismatch of their talents and their opportunities in society.

In his *Professional Ethics and Civic Morals*, Durkheim (1992) argues that work groups of different kinds potentially form the basis of a new moral order in modern societies, ones that enjoyed organic solidarity. Such groups bridged the gap between institutions of the state, on the one hand, and the family, on the other. Durkheim stressed that these morals were those of the group, and not imposed upon them from above: 'A system of morals is always the affair of a group and can operate only if this group protects them by its authority' (1992: 6).

This has implications for how workers within the organisation are governed, and has important consequences for the study of control, and resistance in that Durkheim seems to be suggesting that work groups effectively become self-policing. Further, the imposition of outside authority lacks a legitimacy that is needed for workers to give consent.

For Weber, management and control of labour were an inevitable part of the modern world. Weber saw industrial society as distinguished by greater levels of rationalisation in all branches of life, and work was no exception. This rationalisation led to greater specialisation within the division of labour including management and supervision. Control was also enacted in a variety of other ways, specifically in terms of the structures of the new organisations. With the rise of complex organisations, Weber identified the growth in a specialist group of managers working within a developed bureaucracy. Control was exercised within a hierarchy, again like Durkheim, based on talent and qualification. In the modern world, control was exercised by those who occupied positions of legal rational authority, rather than because of tradition or because they were charismatic leaders (Sennett 1993). Unlike Durkheim, Weber recognised that while conflict may have been managed, it would not disappear.

In addition to concepts such as authority and bureaucracy Weber also saw control being exercised in more subtle ways. He tried to understand the ways in which cultures, norms and values had a very real effect on the way people lived their lives. Indeed, Weber believed that capitalism had emerged in the West because of the combination of historical circumstances, techno-logical innovation with a specific set of cultural values, namely a particular sect of Protestantism which happened to offer the perfect conditions in which capitalism or at least its early stages could flourish. Most importantly for our purpose here is the element of this religious belief, the Protestant work ethic, which acted as a powerful self and social disciplinary mode of control within newly emergent industrial societies (Marshall 1982).

So for each of the classical theorists, control of labour was an issue, and was part of their wider concern with the transition from traditional to modern society. In the work of Marx, Durkheim and Weber we see a set of concerns and questions about control and resistance which in many ways are just as relevant today. The founding fathers offer us a set of analytical tools, which have been developed or changed by later theorists.

LATER DEVELOPMENTS

In looking at how sociological conceptualisations of control and resistance at work have developed, it is important that we do not ignore the ideas of those in other disciplines. Within the fields of economic and social history the nature of industrialisation has been an important point of debate. What many of these historians were interested in was why a working class developed within the British Isles. One of the most important figures here is the Marxist historian E. P. Thompson, who in a series of books and articles wrote about the transition from feudalism to capitalism, and the way ordinary people experienced and resisted the new social order (Thompson 1968, 1991). In his *The Making of the English Working Class* (1968), Thompson examines the experience of change from the point of view of those involved, examining in detail the way the social relations of traditional societies were disturbed by industrialisation. Thompson's work is important as it stresses the role of individual and collective agency in understanding how change occurred. In particular, his writing lays emphasis on the role of culture, custom and ideas in understanding resistance to change. For example, Thompson, in one of his essays 'The Moral Economy of the English Crowd' (1991), examines bread riots and other forms of social protest and argues that these have to be placed in the context of social relations and the norms and values of contemporary community. Often protest occurred when social groups felt marginalised by the effects of industrial change. Thompson (1991) also wrote about the profound change brought about by the adoption of clock time on work (see Chapter 9). Again, the rationalisation inherent within capitalist forms of management was resisted as it was felt to be an alien imposition upon established patterns of work organisation. Nonetheless Thompson recognises the success of capitalist ideology in modifying and transforming working-class values during this period, especially regarding the creation of work disciplines.

Another strand in the debate over industrial change within social and economic history can be seen in discussions of the role of technology. Some historians have argued that the Industrial Revolution was important in that it disciplined and created a new industrial workforce. Key to this transition was the role of technology and the pacing of work by machines housed in factories. Control was achieved by a combination of technology and the discipline of the factory setting where supervision could be more easily enacted. As we saw in the chapter on industrial society, pre- or proto-industrial society was marked by work carried out in domestic settings where a good deal of control could be exercised by the family members themselves, albeit within the context of a patriarchal household (see Bradley 1989). It is also important that the attempt to impose control by technology was met with resistance, sometimes violent. Considerable historical attention has been paid to the practice of machine breaking where workers displaced by new technology destroyed new machinery. Often these groups were named Luddites after Captain Ned Ludd who signed warning letters to employers using new technology, and the term Luddite has often been associated with individuals and groups who resist progress, but others such as Thompson have drawn attention to our need to see such responses not as irrational wrecking but rather as a legitimate action in the context of a particular moral work culture (see Hobsbawm 1964; Reid 1986; Thomis 1970).

Other historians have emphasised that many of the early factory workers in Britain were women and young children rather than men, since men often resisted the new levels of control in the factory setting (Joyce 1980). Finally, historians have also suggested while technology could play an important role in controlling industrial workplaces, it was the concentration of workers into new spaces of work that was crucial. In other words it was the factory that acted as a key technology in enacting control and discipline over workers (Marglin 1980).

In any history of controlling and managing work, F. W. Taylor (1856–1915) is a central character because of his attempt to define and promote what he called 'scientific management' (Kanigel 1997). Taylor began work on his theory of management in the 1880s, and during the 1890s he wrote papers and gave lectures popularising his work. As we saw in Chapter 5, Taylor labelled the deliberate restriction of output by the workforce soldiering. This was the level of output arrived by the norms, values and customs of the workers in a particular shop or factory. Taylor developed a form of control that rationalised the work so that managers rather than workers specified when, where and how tasks were to be carried out.

The problem for management was, how did you control work and make sure you maximised efficiency? You could simply pay workers according to hours they worked. But that did not guarantee they would work hard. You could pay according to a 'piece work' system, one where there are fixed payment depending on output. But the recurring problem is how do you arrive at the system of classification? What was the going rate for a job? What is reasonable? And who decided what is reasonable? What Taylor identified was that workers negotiated what is reasonable on the basis of the power they could exercise over particular tasks. As we saw before, Taylor argued that management had to wrest control of this knowledge over work processes so as to be able to design and specify work tasks themselves.

Taylor and his ideas met considerable resistance from those who were subject to it (Kanigel 1997). His ideas assumed that an objective way of ordering and controlling work processes would be achievable, but rather, as we saw before, the employment relationship is a contested terrain and that for many who study the workplace conflict is legitimate and expected (Littler 1978).

Fordism

The best illustration of scientific management in action is in the case of mass production Fordist assembly lines of the mid-twentieth century. These were based on use of semi-skilled and unskilled labour with jobs designed and closely supervised by management.

As we have seen elsewhere in this book, Braverman (1974) argued that this combination of Taylor's idea alongside Fordist production techniques and technology produced the defining control style of management in late or what he called monopoly capitalism. Perhaps the most important feature of Braverman's work is the way he sees the labour process as developing under this régime. He saw the separation of conception and execution as crucial, and that in an era of monopoly capitalism what was occurring was a sustained process of a deskilling of the workforce as management attempted to gain greater levels of control over work.

There have been many criticisms of Braverman's thesis over the years, and these have focused upon the way he overstates the power of management to effect change and their concentration on deskilling to the exclusion of other aspects of securing surplus value (see Brown 1992; Edwards 1979; Elger 1982; Friedmann 1977; Roberts 1993; Wood 1982). Writers have focused upon detailed case studies of work and have suggested other ways of seeing the idea of control enacted in work.

At its simplest is the idea that in order to survive in a competitive marketplace firms have to produce things and that there is not only one way, or one best way, of doing this. In his book *Contested Terrain*, Richard Edwards (1979) stresses the variability of control and management strategies within work in the twentieth century and develops three models or types of control: Simple/Direct, Technical, and Bureaucratic.

TEXT BOX 8.1 RICHARD EDWARDS' FORMS OF CONTROL

- *Simple/direct control* – Era of small business where founding owner or entrepreneur could exercise a very direct form of control over a workforce. Owners knew how the business was run and had strong expectations of quality and quantity of work to be undertaken. Growth of firm and need for co-ordination make this problematic.
- *Technical control* – More sophisticated in that it embedded conflict within a seemingly objective 'technical' process. Work pace set by machines, workers more easily substituted. Resistance to machine pacing/autonomy in work.
- *Bureaucratic control* – Embedding control in the social structure or social relations of the workplace. Institutionalisation of hierarchical power. Work becomes highly stratified (horizontal and vertical) – impersonal rules – notion of career. Dependent on monopoly position, stability, tight labour markets.

Edwards shows the way there is a continued struggle over work and how it is to be carried out. His work suggests a dialectic relationship between workers and their managers and supervisors, which is dependent on a range of variables in particular workplaces, industries and countries. These factors could be historical, contextual, and they could even be simply chance. Edwards also stresses that it is possible, even probable, that all three of these strategies will be in existence at same time. Importantly, what Edwards' model allows for is a greater sense of the way conflict is structurally inherent in the capitalist system and yet is managed through a variety of approaches across time, place and space.

Braverman has also been attacked for his stress on the separation of conception and execution with a number of writers suggesting that this was neither fully possible nor desirable. Researchers have pointed to the fact that almost every job, however deskilled, will require some conceptual skills particularly in terms of need for tacit knowledge and understanding. Without this, there is a loss of flexibility. Friedmann (1977) suggests that inequalities within capitalism meant that the experience of management control differed within and between sectors, industries and workplaces. Pressures on particular firms and the management régimes within them were felt differently. For example, larger firms competed not on price but sales effort or cost reduction, whereas for smaller firms cost may be the difference between survival and going bust. Friedmann suggested that management strategy was determined by range of factors including relative strength of labour within their undertaking. So you could have two firms making identical products which may have very different control and management strategies at the shop floor because one was highly unionised. Rather than the simple process of deskilling, as Braverman would suggest, Friedmann identified two forms of control over the labour process, both existing throughout the history of capitalism. These were 'direct control' and 'responsible autonomy'.

TEXT BOX 8.2 ANDREW FRIEDMANN'S CONTROL CONTINUUM

- *Direct control* – limits the scope for labour power to vary by coercive threats, close supervision and minimising individual worker responsibility.
  - Expensive, as it requires enhanced monitoring of workers by supervisors; it also is wasteful of human creativity.
- *Responsible autonomy* – attempts to harness the adaptability of labour power by giving workers leeway and encourage them to adapt to changing situations in a manner beneficial to the firm.
  - Based on trust which could be abused, leading to loss of production and loss of overall control.

A theme running through many accounts of control and resistance is that both sides of the employment relationship are involved in a dialectic process, where one control strategy fails because workers adopt new ways of subverting it. Management in turn then adopt another to deal with this novel form of desubordination. Richard Hyman (1987) stressed that in the long term any attempt to fully control work is ultimately contradictory in that capital and labour are in a dynamic and contradictory relationship and that in trying to impose one fixed way of control on the workforce simply creates a new set of contradictions.

Understanding resistance

The role of management in trying to control work is of course only part of the story. To fully understand the workplace we need to look at the role of management *and* labour. If we recognise control strategies as variable and contingent, then we must also see resistance in the same light. It will help if we try to conceptualise different standpoints towards it by work and organisational researchers. Alan Fox (1966) developed a framework for thinking about the analysis of conflict as he wanted to recognise that conflict within industrial organisations had an objective set of causes rather than conflict being seen as irrational action on the part of the workforce. He wanted to map the ways in which theorists of industrial relations approached conflict, labelling them *unitary*, *pluralistic* and *radical* approaches or perspectives.

Those who saw organisations as essentially marked by a common set of interests adopted the unitary perspective. The management are best placed to decide how best to cope with the problems of the firm. Pluralistic perspectives allowed greater scope for conflict within organisations. It recognised that there were legitimate differences between different organisational actors. Ultimately, however, conflict could be ameliorated by negotiation. Radical approaches suggested that the contradictions in capitalist society were so great and deep-seated that they could not be negotiated away or solved. Fox noted that the latter position most accurately reflected modern society and its work patterns. This is a position that most sociologists would hold, but this does not necessarily make them Marxist (see Fox 1985, 2004).

Following on from Fox, it is important that we recognise that although we might see conflict as inherent within capitalist society, we do not run away with the idea that there is always disruption at work. The varieties of forms of resistance within the workplace are infinite – imagined on a continuum, minor forms of resistance could be seen as leaving work early, stealing paper clips, at one end of the spectrum with striking, machine breaking, sabotage at the other. The role of work sociology is therefore, to try to understand how the employment relationship works and in particular how the deep structural inequalities of power are mediated in the workplace. Two points to note here are that:

1   From a Marxist point of view, although capital and labour are in conflict, the way this conflict is mediated and experienced at the point of production is not always, or even usually, overtly conflictual.
2   The absence of overt conflict at a particular workplace is not a positive signal that there is no conflict.

Brown (1988) argued that the employment relationship was best conceived of as a *negotiated order* – one where there was and had to be scope for negotiation over how work is to be done, how much is to be done and by whom. The strength of sociology here is being able to combine in its analysis an appreciation of the deep structural inequalities of the workplace with a detailed, often ethnographic understanding of work interaction. So we have both the broad canvas of capitalism combined with the fine-grained detail of social interaction at the point of production.

Self-control by work groups

We have based much of the preceding discussion on the simple idea that in the employment relationship capital wants as much labour for the smallest possible cost and labour wants to maximise wages for minimum of effort. However, it is important to note the way that workgroups almost always police themselves to some extent with or without supervision. At a very broad level we could say that the work ethic, whether informed by religion or not, is a powerful control mechanism exercised by workers themselves, by work groups or by wider communities. In many modern societies self-identity is bound up with the work one does. Historically skilled trades and occupations, and by extension professions, have taken pride in doing a job well but there are also numerous examples where unskilled workers doing mundane tasks display such attachment to work.

Michael Burawoy (1979) turns round the usual management question 'how can workers be made to work harder?' by posing the question 'why do workers work as hard as they do?' In his classic ethnographic description of a Chicago factory, Burawoy described the intricacies of shop floor relations. The workers at the factory were paid on a bonus system whereby extra pay was given for production over a given amount. He describes the ways in which workers played games so that they could get the bonuses without breaking collective norms on production.

> In 1975 quota restriction was not necessarily a form of restriction of output, because operators regularly turned out more than 140 percent, but turned in only 140 percent, keeping the remainder as a 'kitty' for those operations on which they could not make out. Indeed, operators would 'bust their ass' for entire shifts, when they had a gravy job [an easy task], so as to build up a kitty for the following day(s). Experienced operators on the more sophisticated machines could easily build up a kitty of a week's work. There was always some discrepancy, therefore, between what was registered in the books as what was completed and what was actually completed on the shop floor. Shop management were more concerned with the latter and let the books take care of themselves. Both the 140 percent ceiling and the practice of banking (keeping a kitty) were recognized and accepted by everyone on the shop floor, even if they didn't meet with the approval of higher management.
>
> (Burawoy 1979: 58)

Importantly, it is the work group who are effectively self-policing. Front line managers allowed rules to be flouted providing production levels were maintained.

At a wider level, autonomy and control over work can be exercised by communities themselves. In qualitative accounts of work we can often find examples where control at work is exercised through family and community. Here a mine union official from the north-east of England talked at length about the way in the past social relations in the pit spilled out into extra-workplace situations:

> Young people entering the mining industry were very very quickly brought into an atmosphere of self-discipline, because when they got under-ground, you have to have very good discipline . . . you might have three generations of people working in the mine and the elderly generations, was always very well respected that discipline and respect of yer elders was immediately fostered onto you. So, you got people growing up with respect, for the elderly people. The mining industry itself, formed part of the discipline, that's required in society in general, and I'm not talking about discipline in the sense, where you brutalise people, anything like that, it's a condition of mind, it's how you condition people's minds, as to which way they should be conducting themselves, not only in their work, but in society in general.
>
> (Strangleman 2001: 258–9)

We can see the way occupational identity and community identity, norms and values are produced and reproduced within the context of workplace and community networks. This quote points to the positive aspects of discipline within such a context – the sense in which stability or predictability is valued, acting as a basis for individual realization, enabling identity through the achievement of role.

Trade unions and resistance

One important aspect of control and resistance that we have not touched on yet in this chapter is the role of trade unions, which began to form in the early nineteenth century in the UK and other industrialising countries in Europe, North America and the Australasian nations. They represent groups of workers employed in similar trades, industries or workplaces. Often the first groups of workers to organise would be the most highly skilled, often the best paid and almost always male and white (see Fox 1985; Hobsbawm 1964, 1984). Later on, less skilled men and women began to be organised in to general or industrial unionism. Importantly the origin and subsequent development of the trade unions are often highly specific to the nation-state with differ-ent factors being more important in one tradition than another. So in some parts of Europe, religion is the basis for collective organisation while in others it is politics and in others skill differentiations are the most obvious divide.

For our purposes in this chapter, unions are important because they help us to understand both control and resistance. Trade unions are most obviously associated with the latter, as they offer a collective voice to rival that of employers. Unions therefore try to exert their monopoly power of labour against the employer to try and win concessions – greater levels of pay, better conditions of work or service or shorter working time. The most obvious form of resistance the trade unions provide is through the strike action. However, it is important to acknowledge unions' ability to act as another form of control on a workforce. In many ways what trade unions effectively do is act as a way of solving problems or at least offering the possibility of expressing problems at the workplace. It is possible to see unions as part of the rationalisation and bureaucratisation of organisations and industrial society because disputes are solved by discussion, agreement and work-place law, rather than by violence or oppression. What often occurred in the Western industrial economies after the Second World War was an ever more elaborate system of industrial relations based on formal agreements. The trade unions therefore occupy an interesting place and some sociologists argue that this is a profoundly contradictory one as they are at times revolution-ary in their politics while at others seeking to preserve the capitalist system (Lane 1974).

CONTEMPORARY ISSUES AND FUTURE TRENDS

In the past two decades, there have been important developments in the way sociologists and others conceptualise control and resistance. Some of these shifts represent changes in the economy where new forms of work usher in new forms of management and represent a continuation of dis-cussions of the employment relationship. Others, however, reflect a change in intellectual fashion, especially when we consider the control of unpaid work and the importance of widening out discussions to include gender and 'race'.

New forms of work

As we saw in Chapter 6 in the 1980s and 1990s, there were major shifts in the way work is organised and the way labour is managed. Since the early 1980s, a series of management trends have been adopted including Total Quality Management (TQM), Just In Time (JIT) and Human Resource Management (HRM). These developments separately and in combination represent a major transformation in the way employees are managed and involved in the production and latterly service sectors. Some theorists have claimed that this sort of production marks a distinctive shift from a so-called 'Fordist' production to a 'post-Fordist' production régime.

TEXT BOX 8.3 FORDIST AND POST-FORDIST PRODUCTION RÉGIMES

- Fordism is characterised by a push-through system of production. You make mass standardised/undifferentiated products and then attempt to sell them.
- In post-Fordism the pull-through, build-to-order, product is pulled through the plant by a market signal.

Others see this as an era of flexible, rather than Fordist accumulation (see Harvey 1989; Amin 1994). These new management techniques therefore represent an answer as to the question as to how work is to be controlled in the new economy.

JIT and TQM aim to eliminate waste from the production process – mainly manufacturing – by identifying elements of the production process where there are delays or hold-ups, where products and parts are standing idle. The philosophy behind this so-called 'lean production' it is to eliminate wasted capital that is tied up in parts or product – buying at the last minute only when you need to, and selling immediately, at its most extreme the organisation is effectively selling and building to order.

Essentially, the idea behind TQM is that quality, or fitness for purpose is everyone's responsibility, not just that of the quality department. Quality built in rather than errors inspected out. Both JIT and TQM are seen by their champions as a significant development from Fordist production. Emphasis is placed on quality and being close to customers and the firm and its members are responsive to change in market signals and constantly monitor production. However, others have seen these as more developed forms of Fordism, or Taylorism, rather than empowering the workforce, these systems are a higher form of control, and others go still further suggesting that it is creating self-disciplining workers by enrolling the worker in to the production process, drawing on their tacit skills and knowledge. A series of workplace ethnographies have highlighted the continuities between Fordism and what is supposed to be post-Fordist work (see, for example, Graham 1995).

Importantly, quality management techniques have increasingly been applied outside manufacturing, and are now widely seen in the service sector. In the 1980s and 1990s, a whole series of quality initiatives in the private and public sector were implemented, including in the UK the Citizens Charter, the Patients Charter, the Passengers Charter. In their collection on quality initiatives in the public sector, Kirkpatrick and Lucio (1995) highlighted a range of examples of organisation where management increase control over work often at the expense of the autonomy of professional groups (see also May 1994).

A third and final aspect of new forms of management and control can be seen in Human Resource Management (HRM). HRM can be defined as a more conscious and deliberate attempt on the part of organisations to manage and develop their human resources effectively. HRM is again linked to the supposed changing nature of world markets and organisations themselves. At its most idealistic HRM sees the pushing down of decision-making to the lowest level, cutting layers of management and supervision, harnessing the creativity and knowledge of the workers. There is an explicit assumption of change from Fordist to post-Fordist organisational structures with HRM ensuring that organisational members are able to take greater responsibility. There has been a lot of debate within management circles as to how far HRM represents anything new or if it is just another management buzz phrase.

It is important to grasp that HRM, JIT and TQM are contested concepts inside and outside management circles (see Beale 1994; Elger and Smith 1994; Wilkinson and Willmott 1995). What they have in common is a tendency to individualise the relationship between employer and the employee. This fragmentation leads to a situation where the employee is potentially more vulnerable in terms of control exercised by the organisation, and this leads to a situation where workers internalise disciplinary codes.

Surveillance and the management of self

Common to these new forms of management control has been a greater emphasis on individualisation at work with workers being accountable and responsible for what they do and how they do it. Intellectually many writers and theorists on organisations and work have found the writing of Michael Foucault useful and in particular his writing on the self-disciplining subject (see Burrell 2006; Jermier *et al.* 1994; McKinlay and Starkey 1998). In *Discipline and Punish*, Foucault (1975) draws on the model of the Panoptican, a nineteenth-century penitentiary where the guards could see the prisoners but could not themselves be observed. The intention of this model was that the inmates were rewarded for good behaviour and punished when they broke the rules, so they had to assume that they were always under observation and therefore internalised the need for good behaviour. This idea of self-discipline has been picked up by many working in the field of organisations and work because of the explanatory power the metaphor holds for work control and discipline. While workplaces differ from prisons in important ways, the parallels between the guards as managers and prisoners as workers has proved attractive. So the new forms of management act as surveillance mechanisms whereby workers feel that transgressions will be easily spotted and therefore internalise the need for acting in the way management want.

One example of this is in the surveillance techniques used in contemporary call centres where the interchange between customers and operators is recorded and can be used in the disciplining of workers. Workers do not know when a supervisor is listening to the call live or indeed if the recording will be listened to later on, and therefore are supposed to act in the way they have been trained. Taylor quotes from one of his respondents, a call centre worker: 'I had one really ignorant git on the phone once, I was seething, but I knew she [the supervisor] was listening so I had to contain it' (1998: 95).

Self-control by workers has also been studied in other ways. In a later chapter we will pay closer attention to issues of subjectivity and emotion at work but it is worth spending a little time in this chapter thinking about these ideas in relation to control and resistance. As we have seen, the idea of self-imposed control by workers and work groups is not new. What is being suggested now, and related to the kind of analysis developed above, is the idea that management manipulate norms and values to provoke such self-discipline. An example of this can be seen in Chris Grey's work on trainee accountants who internalise and identify so strongly with their companies that they self-exploit as they see their career, in Grey's (1994) phrase, as a 'projection of the self'. And to go back even further, Savage in his work on the Great Western Railway, rejects the notion of simple discipline being enacted on the workforce but rather:

> They revolved around attempts to motivate and discipline workers by using career ladders to encourage workers to monitor and regulate their own actions. It is this attempt to 'work on the soul', rather than to inflict punitive punishments and fines on workers, which can be seen as the truly 'modern' solution to the problem of labour control.
>
> (Savage 1998: 88)

There are a number of examples in other research of this type of identification and self-discipline including Du Gay's (1996) study of retail workers and Casey's (1995) research on workers involved in the manufacture and use of advanced technology.

Another aspect of new types of control, which engender management of the self, can be seen in the emotional labour literature. Hochschild (1983) developed a framework for thinking about the way organisations try to get workers to manage their feelings in the workplace. This could include the suppression or amplification of feelings in order to elicit responses from others; Taylor (1998) is a good example of this. Hochschild saw this type of emotional labour as being an increasing feature of the contemporary workplace where customer-facing service work became more common. What was new for Hochschild was the extent to which managers went to codify and specify the interaction between worker and customer. Hochschild discussed the detrimental effects of prolonged managing of emotions and suggested that it could damage those engaged on some types of emotional labour. This danger is illustrated by a critical study of Disney theme parks where one female worker who dresses as one of the cartoon characters explains how hard it is for her to step out of character: 'I sometimes find myself smiling at people. They're like, "What are you smiling at me for?" I know they are thinking that, but it's because I still feel I'm constantly this character' (The Project on Disney 1995: 138).

Resistance in the new workplace?

From reading the above, one can get a sense that contemporary management are all-powerful and that they can control work and workers in a way that would have been impossible in the past. Workers seem to be subject to far greater surveillance and detailed scrutiny than ever before. Throughout this book we have been clear that good sociologists always look for the contradictions in any situation and especially in the workplace, and it is vital that we do not lose sight of resistance to these new forms of management and surveillance. We need more detailed sociological accounts of how these new régimes of control are experienced at work. We need a better understanding of the ways people subvert and reinvent workplace practice in the same ways they have always done. In their book *Organizational Misbehaviour*, Ackroyd and Thompson (1999) challenge the idea promoted by many in management science that the contemporary workplace is one devoid of opposition or resistance. They suggest that we need to look beyond the surface situation in the new workplace and in doing so we can see real and enduring tensions at work that have not been swept aside or ameliorated by management changes. Virtually all critical studies of the contemporary workplace will offer examples of such resistance. We want to broaden out our discussion to examine a range of new development drawing on other literatures for the study of control and resistance.

Gender and control in work

One of the welcome developments in the study of control and work in recent years has been the focus on gender inside and outside the realm of paid work. In early feminist analyses of the workplace, attention was directed towards how gender restricted or even prevented women's access to paid work. This was seen to be maintained 'primarily by patriarchal relations in the workplace and in the state, as well as by those in the household' (Walby 1986: 55), although the form and extent of control varied across time and place. Walby developed Frank Parkin's (1974) work on the Weberian notion of closure, whereby social collectivities seek to maximise their resources by restricting access to their membership, to consider patriarchal social closure in which men restrict women's access to resources in work. She identified a range of historical examples of patriarchal closure, grouping them into the non-admittance of women and their expulsion. Practices of non-admittance included to training (like university degrees or apprenticeships) and to certain occupations, as well as restricting the numbers of women allowed entry via quotas. Examples of the ejection of women rather than men included the dismissal of women or a reduction in their rights on marriage, and growing restrictions in the type of work women could do in factories and mines. For Walby, the agents of this control included male-dominated trade unions and organisations and not just employers.

The study of gender and control has also focused on gender relations in work, including the ways in which masculinity and femininity play out here to control women's work. Notions of maleness as powerful and dominant stimulated sociological studies into women's experiences in male-dominated workplaces where old boy networks and male camaraderie have acted as another form of closure against women. Sarah Rutherford (2001) offers a useful analysis of how the long hours culture in the city acts as a means to exclude women workers (see also McDowell 1997).

The topic of control and surveillance, gender and work, is also relevant to the study of domestic work, although it has been less expressly addressed in the bulk of work sociology. But as we see from Oakley's (1974) account, housewives are interesting here because they do not have a boss present all day to monitor their work performance. Nevertheless, the women were working long and hard weeks, seemingly being 'their own boss' and setting their own standards to work to. Of course, these standards reflected strongly gendered norms of what good housewives do, and normative notions of what clean, respectable homes should look like. The women demonstrated this to Oakley by referring to how their own housework was influenced by what their mothers had done (or not done) well, and how their friends cared for their homes.

When domestic work is provided by paid workers, mechanisms of control fit more neatly into the concerns of the mainstream sociology of work. Studies show how domestic workers, often working without formal contracts, can be sacked for not performing to the often very high standards set by the employer (Anderson 2000), and that these standards are monitored rigorously by employers. Reflecting the 'seen and not seen' Panopticon, in Barbara Ehrenreich's (2001) account of her own employment as a 'Maid' that we discuss in Chapter 10 on domestic work, she mentions the threat that hidden surveillance equipment like CCTV and radio 'might be' in use to monitor what work was being carried out when householders were not present.

Control, sexualised and embodied work

The move away from the production or economic paradigm and towards the cultural in studying control has been highly influential in the study of sexualised and embodied work. These are fascinating developments within the sociology of work since it moved on from seeing gender, sex, sexuality and the body as being controlled and expelled from the paid workplace to seeing them as central within organisations. Writers have thus identified how surveillance in work has expanded from the focus on workers' actions and words, towards the surveillance of their attitudes, culture, bodies and even bodily fluids (Deetz 1998).

In 'Hierarchies, Jobs, Bodies', Joan Acker explored the role of gendering and embodiment in labour market segmentation. For Acker, job hierarchies are not gender-neutral, since the ideas of a 'job' or of 'work' are gendered. She talks about the gendering of organisations: discussing how we 'do' gender relations in work. In gendered organisations, she says, distinctions are created between male and female, between masculine and feminine, and these shape advantage and disadvantage, exploitation and control, as well as meaning and identity (Acker 1990: 140). Furthermore, gender is embodied, physically and psychologically. Men's bodies are seen as natural and normal within an organisation, but women's bodies are less appropriate and less fitting.

Another influential early study demonstrating this cultural turn was Rosemary Pringle's (1989) *Secretaries Talk* in which she used the post-structuralist notion of discourse to explore the employer–secretary relationship, showing how discourses of sexuality, power and domination informed controlled work relations. Some of the other early influential studies of the control of sexualised and embodied work were of airline, tourist and secretarial workers, but Hearn and Parkin (2001) argued that there is a sexual dimension to all organisations.

Various writers have identified the ways organisations attempt to manage the employee's image and demeanour. Studies show the way that this type of discipline is often internalised by workers and they become self-monitoring and self-disciplining as a result. Carol Wolkowitz (2006) has recently written an overview of the relationship between the body and work including discussion of control through embodiment. Anne Witz *et al.* (2003), in their essay on aesthetics and work organisations, broke important ground in this area. In their research on the hotel industry they show the way certain image-conscious organisations in the sector put stress on 'stylized workplace performances or aesthetic labour' (ibid.: 34). Just as Hochschild talked of the commodification of emotions at work, so Witz and her colleagues suggest that certain organisations are engaged in 'the mobilization, development and commodification of embodied dispositions' (Witz *et al.* 2003: 37). This is shown in fascinating studies of flight attendants by Arlie Russell Hochschild (1983) and later by Melissa Tyler and Pamela Abbott (1998). The high level of control exerted by management over the bodies of the women workers is astounding. Hochschild first identified that the job involved very high standards of personal grooming, and that the airline company detailed what physical attributes it required in their selection of cabin crew. Tyler's study showed too how weight watching was 'an accepted management strategy' of the female staff. Only female flight attendants (not the male ones and not pilots) were weighed during routine grooming checks. Reaffirming Hochschild's findings, Tyler also found that female applicants were rejected in selection interviews for not looking right: for having blemished skin; being too short; having messy or severe hair; having too short nails; having chubby legs; lacking poise; being slightly pear-shaped; having a 'common' accent. One woman was rejected when the personnel officer concluded that 'her weakness for chocolate might be progressive' (Tyler and Abbott 1998: 442). A key element of the work expected from flight attendants was that they should make customers feel special, and even sexually attractive, flight attendants were expected to perform as sexualised actors, and to be flirtatious with male business class passengers especially. Lisa Adkins (1995) has also shown how sexual work is part of the leisure industry, and that the right appearance and flirting are crucial elements of the work.

It should be apparent that female embodiment leads to some women being excluded from and some included into jobs. It is apparent too that embodiment brings us firmly back to intersectionality – inter-sections between gender, class, 'race' and age – in terms of controlling which 'appropriate' bodies, behaviours and styles are to be employed. Embodied and sexualised work was identified for young working-class women in Mike Filby's study of betting shops (1992), while Nirmal Puwar's study of the Senior Civil Service shows well the 'racial' dimension of having the appropriate body for the job. Puwar embeds her analysis within the notion of the white male body as the 'somatic norm' (2001) When black bodies enter white work spaces, especially senior spaces like the Senior Civil Service, they are seen as contradictory, as 'Space Invaders'. Black bodies in these places represent a dissonance, are out of place, and white people act accordingly. A Black senior Civil Servant told Puwar:

> I've had occasions when I've gone with a member of my staff to meetings, where people haven't known me and its automatically assumed that I'm not [mentions job title], it's the person who's with me. That sort of thing. It's just a perception that people have that the Grade . . . who has come to meet me is going to be a white person.
>
> (Puwar 2001: 660)

The assumption of heterosexuality pervades many of the above accounts of sexualised work places. In her 'Compulsory heterosexuality and lesbian existence' (1980), feminist Adrienne Rich argued that heterosexuality is an institution that women and men are socialised and, if necessary, compelled into. For contemporary researchers of heterosexuality, the institutionalisation of heterosexuality 'encodes and structures' everyday life (Richardson 1996). How the hegemonic nature of heterosexuality shapes and controls the workplace is a growing interest in the study of work. Studies have explored how heterosexuality is assumed in the workplace, shaping the decision to come out or stay in 'the closet' by gay and lesbian workers in the face of potential discrimination and harassment. Studies like James Ward and Diana Winstanley's (2006) research into sexual minorities working as fire-fighters in London have documented the homophobia experienced by those who did come out or were outed in work, including being shunned by colleagues and losing jobs. Of course, not all workplaces are dominated by heterosexual workers, and some organisations, in the media, for example, had the expectation that gay men would 'form a significant part of the employee base' (Ward and Winstanley 2006: 202).

Violence and control in work

Violence in work, in the form of bullying and harassment, has attracted surprisingly little attention within the sociology of work around the themes of control and resistance. Nevertheless some influential studies do exist, with the study of sexual violence in work receiving the most attention, boosted by the wider feminist analysis of male violence against women from the 1970s onwards in Western Europe and the USA. While there are divergences of opinion, the broad feminist approach to male violence is to understand it not as isolated acts by sick or cruel men, but as a systematic phenomenon in which male power is exerted and women are controlled (Dobash *et al.* 2004; Stanko 1988). Sexual violence in work has been seen to take several forms, including sexual harassment, the use of pornography and rape. For Jeff Hearn and Wendy Parkin (2001), organisations are often violent places: they are sites of gendered and sexualised violation.

The empirical sociological studies that exist of sexual violence in work focus on sexual harassment, and most have examined women working in male-dominated workplaces. In Collinson and Collinson's (1996) study of sales manages in the life assurance industry, male 'homosociablity' was identified as a normal part of the job: male camaraderie expressed in joint leisure pursuits and client entertaining after work. These events were invariably highly sexualised. One manager was seen to be especially harassing to the few women sales managers who had been recruited in an attempt to re-introduce women into the male-dominated workplace. When one woman complained to her boss about this colleague's behaviour, her boss explained that 'it is only Dick', that's just what he was like (Collinson and Collinson 1996: 36). His behaviour was normalised and made light of. The woman who complained was seen by the bosses to be a moaner who had problems with men. Another woman's strategy for dealing with the sexualised environment was to give as good as she got, joining in with the men in sexualised banter.

Her behaviour was seen by the bosses to be too aggressive. Both women were dismissed.

In Chapter 7, we show how 'race' is central to the most highly controlled type of work organisation history has known, slavery. We discuss how extreme violence, its reality and its threat, were integral to the slavery system and seen expressly as a technique for controlling workers. More recent sociological studies of race and violence in work are rare in British sociology. This is not because 'racial' violence or the fear of it are unusual. Indeed, the *Fourth Survey of Ethnic Minorities* shows that over 10 per cent of people from all minority groups experienced some form of racial harassment in the 12-month period prior to being interviewed, and the fear of racial harassment was felt by even higher proportions (see Virdee 1995). Unfortunately, the report does not refer specifically to workplace incidents of violence.

Finally, issues of work and violence as control should not be restricted to paid work as they feed into the sociological analysis of work relations within the home too. The study of domestic violence is a whole sub-discipline within sociology, and one that we cannot do justice to here, but the feminist attack on the notion of the home as a 'haven in a heartless world' should influence our understanding of the control of any work carried out within it. We showed earlier that Sylvia Walby argued that patriarchal relations within the household shape women's access to paid work outside the home. They also shape who does what work within it. Accordingly, we ask in the chapter on domestic work, given the inequalities in power and resources which exist between women and men in the home, how freely do women 'choose' to be the main domestic worker, carrying out and organising the bulk of domestic work and caring? For many women, the decision to provide caring and housework, as opposed to or alongside paid work, is one shaped by the threat – or reality – of a partner's physical and not just economic power. Studies of male violence against their partners show that 'triggers' for men beating their wives include their perceptions of their wives' deficient domestic work: his cup of tea being too warm (Pahl 1985); too much grease on his plate; and his dinner not being ready and on the table in time (see Dobash and Dobash 1979; Yllo 1993).

CONCLUSION

This chapter has looked at the way control is exercised on work, both paid and unpaid. As we have seen, the control of work has been a defining topic for the sociology of work since the nineteenth century. What is distinct about a sociological analysis of control is its attempt to understand control both at the macro level of a social system and at mezzo and micro levels of the shop floor and in the home. As in the rest of this book, we argue that we need both a conceptual and theoretical account of control and resistance but also need detailed study of work interaction. What the sociology of work has traditionally been good at is looking at these issues from within the prism of paid, often male employment. In recent years this focus has been expanded to include a range of new theoretical conceptualisations of work discipline and organisation. Often these developments have been led by those working outside the field of work sociology and so their integration into what counts as the mainstream has been less smoothly achieved than it possibly could be. Throughout the book we have argued that we need to integrate an understanding of what goes on in work within a broader view of social activity.

FURTHER READING

Stephen Ackroyd and Paul Thompson's *Organizational Misbehaviour* (1999) is an excellent summary of both historical and current debates about control and resistance.

The edited collection by McKinlay and Starkey, *Foucault, Management and Organizational Theory* (1988) provides a useful set of essays for thinking about the impact of Foucault's ideas on organisational thinkers.

Arlie Russell Hochschild's *The Managed Heart* (1983) remains a classic in thinking about emotional labour and control.

Sylvia Walby's *Patriarchy at Work* (1986) examines gendered strategies of work control.

WEB SOURCES

The Trades Union Congress is the umbrella group for organised labour in the UK:
http://www.tuc.org.uk/

Useful information on trade union struggle can also be found at:
http://www.unionhistory.info/

At an international level, the International Labour Organisation is at:
http://www.ilo.org/global/lang–en/index.htm

STUDENT PROJECTS AND ESSAY QUESTIONS

1   Do you have to be a Marxist to see conflict as inherent in the capitalist system?

2 What do we need to consider when thinking about the differences in the control of paid and unpaid work?

3 Think about your own experience of work. How was work controlled? How was conflict resolved? Was management authority challenged, if so, how?

4 Is Ackroyd and Thompson's notion of *Mis*behaviour the best way to think about worker resistance?

CHAPTER 9

Time and Work

▌ OVERVIEW

This chapter will:

- Examine how sociology has approached work time.
- Show how sociology sees time as a social and political construct rather than as a natural, objective phenomenon.
- Examine the role of time in the manipulation and control of work.
- Identify as a central sociological concern how work time interrelates with other life times like family, leisure and free time.
- Discuss work time as a valuable resource that is differentially distributed according to the main social divisions of class, gender and 'race' that we examine in the book.

▌ INTRODUCTION

This chapter shows how time is fundamental to debates over work in sociology. It discusses how time was rooted firmly in the thoughts on work of classical theorists, and shows that time remains one of the central concepts within the study of work and employment today. The chapter highlights a range of sociological concerns around work time including time, control and resistance in work; and social inequalities in work time. By drawing on a range of theoretical and methodological approaches, the chapter demonstrates how sociology has provided a comprehensive and in-depth analysis of the importance of time for the study of work and workers' lives.

THE SOCIOLOGICAL MISSION

The broad sociological concerns of progress, cohesion, control and resistance are fundamental to the sociology of work time. Part of the mission is to identify and explain changes and continuities in the 'social constructions' of work time over the years and in diverse societies, and to explore how work time connects with other social times. A core aim is to research how workers experience these diverse work temporalities. Sociology is also interested in whether developments in work time have represented progress towards better societal arrangements of work and other times; and in whether workers' lives have improved, perhaps in terms of increases in the control that they can exert over work time, or in terms of less time pressured lives. And to what extent have diverse social groups benefited or been disadvantaged by developments in work time? Fundamental to all these sociological concerns is the belief that time is central to the ways in which societies operate, but that time is not a natural mechanism that synchronises the societal apparatus according to, for example, seconds, minutes, days, weeks, years. Instead, the concept of 'social time' is used by sociologists to stress that time is a social and political construct. The durations of time and its patterns of use depend on socio-cultural traditions, and these traditions permit (or prohibit) certain activities at certain times of the day and night, or during the year, and at certain periods over the life-course. Since time is created, these traditions can vary across societies and within societies over the years. Our concern here lies with work activities and how sociologists use time to understand them.

FOUNDATIONS

The classical founders were struck by the differences between pre-industrial and industrial work time. In pre-industrial societies, the temporal units of the hour and the minute did not exist, and so time was radically different to that which developed afterwards.

In Chapter 2, we saw that Emile Durkheim's interest in the transition of society from feudalism to capitalism was rooted in his concern with social cohesion and in the ways in which the new society would achieve social order, since the old bonds based on similarity that had held together traditional societies were breaking down. In his *The Elementary Forms of Religious Life* (1912), Durkheim argued that social life draws its rhythm from the interchange between religious festivity times when no paid work was carried out (holy days/holidays) and periods of working. Time for Durkheim was a 'collective social category': the same social experiences in a traditional society gave the same perception of time to its members: they shared a common 'temporal consciousness'. In short, time and its use were seen by Durkheim to be determined by the culture and structure of a society, and time helps society cohere, synchronising one phenomenon with another. His interest in time was to influence Pitrim Sorokin (1963) and Robert K. Merton (1984), who went on to argue more explicitly and in greater depth that time, and the way it is divided up, are a social rather than natural convention and so the social sciences need a different concept of time from that employed by the natural sciences. Part of the coordinating function that is performed by social time is to also define what is the 'right time' to carry out societal activities. For example, going back to Durkheim's sacred (religious) and profane (work) activities; the right time for praying and celebrating – but not working – was during religious days and festivals. In Durkheimian thought too, social norms define the right or correct length of time for moving through the life-course (we are expected to achieve certain goals by certain ages; to crawl, walk, talk, for example, and to complete education and to find a job). We are expected, in effect, to live our lives 'on time', but 'on time' is socially constructed, varying from society to society and changing over the years.

While Durkheim was to influence the sociological analysis of how time helps society cohere, including how time differentiates activities like work from prayer, the Marxian perspective was more directly concerned with time and new forms of work control that were emerging under industrial capitalism. For Karl Marx, labour power had become a commodity that was exchanged in the market. Time itself became money since payment for work began to be in terms of 'temporal units' like the hour or the week, rather than in terms of completed tasks. Since labour began to be measured in terms of time, time itself became commodified: it could be bought and sold. In a time–money exchange, wages were paid for a given amount of time during which the capitalist bought the labour power of the worker. In more Marxian language, time became equated with value, and surplus value could be achieved by extricating more time from workers than was required to produce goods that had the value of their wages. In simple terms, since time was money, if employers could extract an increased performance from each worker for each hour worked (without increasing wages), then money could be saved, productivity could increase and profits could be boosted. When workers began to be paid by time, and not by the task or final product, employers wanted mechanisms to ensure that their employees were actually working all the hours that they were being paid for. And so, for Marx, the birth of systems to control work time: to control workers' attendance and punctuality and to regulate their pace of work, all boosted by developments in technology occurs. In Marx's analysis, the machinery invested in by the capitalist represents fixed capital which has to be run for as long as possible each hour, day and week. The new factory owners had to ensure, as far as they could, that they had a reliable constant supply of labour who would operate these new machines. Without such a supply, machines would lie idle, production would be lost and profits would be reduced. A core concern for Marx was how these changes were impacting on workers' everyday lives in the factories and mills. We detailed some of these issues in Chapter 5 on the development of 'Industrial Work' and in Chapter 8 on 'Control at Work' too. In this chapter we will look more specifically at how time was used to synchronise and control work.

Max Weber had predicted that as industrial capitalism developed and became more complex, larger and more intricate bureaucracies would need to emerge to administer rationally the workings of the society. The larger and more complex these organisational bureaucracies became themselves, the greater would be the need for the smooth, rational and logical synchronisation of their activities and their workers. Hence tight temporal coordination would become essential, and highly sophisticated 'temporal schedules' would be worked out. The clock became the new instrument for this coordination of work, and of society more generally. For Weber, it was significant that employers could call on religious beliefs to support their regulation of workers' time use both in and outside the workplace. In his *The Protestant Ethic and the Spirit of Capitalism* (1904), Weber explored the interconnections between the growth of industrial capitalism and the predominance of certain religious beliefs. The bedrock of capitalism, indeed its very spirit, was reflected in Protestantism more generally but it was in Calvinism that work, time and discipline were very closely linked since 'waste of time is thus the first and in principle the deadliest of sins' (Weber 1970: 157).

LATER DEVELOPMENTS

Time discipline and the control of work

In the previous chapter, we saw that employers have drawn upon a range of techniques for controlling work and workers. Time has played a central part in these techniques, with employers attempting to control its various dimensions in work: as identified by time theorist Barbara Adam (1990) as time, timing and tempo.

In pre-industrial ages, hunter-gatherers had short working days since work was carried out to provide only the basic necessities of food and shelter. In his influential exploration of working time in the seventeenth and eighteenth centuries and his examination of the development of industrial work time, E. P. Thompson (1967) identified how pre-industrial patterns of working were irregular. For Thompson, a 'natural' work rhythm dominated in which the seasons, night and day and the tides stood in place of hours, minutes and seconds, and in which workers controlled their own time, only working when they needed. In contrast with modern 'linear time' in which tasks are accomplished in as little time as possible, in the pre-industrial era 'task' time (work was understood in terms of the specific activity) and 'cyclical' time dominated (work was done when it was needed, with events unfolding in an ever-recurring rhythm; Hassard 1989, 2000). Work time was originally constrained only by natural realities, but these 'limiting conditions' began to be altered by the use of technologies of time-keeping and energy production (Epstein and Kalleberg 2001). The development of industrial capitalism became linked closely with the standardisation of time and work, and the establishment of a new temporality of 'clock time'.

Sociologists have drawn attention to how the new clock time that developed during industrialisation operated in synchronising and controlling work very precisely. Theoretically, since clock time was standardised and visible to all, it could provide signals at set intervals for all workers to commence work, to take and complete breaks, and to finish work. Indeed, the sound of klaxons, sirens and hooters that signalled the start and end of factory shifts was to become common in industrial towns, and 'clocking in/on' and 'clocking out/off' entered common parlance. Viewed in this light, time is homogenous, objective, measurable and quantitative. Yet historical studies have shown that although clock time implies exact measurements, employers were able to increase profits by obscuring time and 'stealing' it from their workers. According to E. P. Thompson (1967: 86): 'Clocks at the factories were often put forward in the morning and back at night, and instead of being instruments for the measurement of time, they were used as cloaks for cheating and oppression.' When watches first became available and affordable for the working classes, most workers were afraid to carry them to work as it was common for employers to dismiss such 'troublemakers'. In nineteenth-century Japan, employers' time strategies were apparent too.

> 'There are certain factories where working hours are 12–13 hours, and the clock hand is set back as closing time approaches. In the filatures in Suwa, they hoot both at the beginning and closing times; but at times they refrain from hooting in accordance with agreement. This is because if one filature hoots, the clock hand cannot be set back in the others.
>
> (Kuwata, cited in Ikuko 1997: 248)

Compared to this furtive manipulation of clocks, a more subtle method of using time to control work was via the encouragement of workers' self-surveillance. Studies have shown how bosses attempted to smooth the introduction of clock time by instigating a new time discipline in workers and changing their 'inward notations' of time (Hassard 2000). To do this meant replacing the rhythm of task time that workers had felt was natural with the new clock time, and encouraging the 'naturalness' of this time instead. One strategy employed to facilitate socialisation into the new time discipline was the extension of clock time into schools, to educate future workers. For John Hassard (2000), a rigid temporal discipline of schools was established, with fixed lengths of obligatory attendance and the separation of the day into temporal units dedicated to separate tasks. As legislation ensured that more and more children entered schools, greater numbers were exposed to the discipline of the clock. Nishimoto Ikuko (1997) discusses too how school textbooks introduced in Japan in the 1870s urged children to be 'on time' (and see US anthropologist Bambi B. Schieffelin's (2002: s5) analysis of the introduction by missionaries of 'vocabularies and discourses of marking and keeping European-based time' to help regiment and monitor paid and unpaid labour in the 1970s among the Bosavi people of Papua New Guinea.

Perhaps the most blatant – and well-known – of employer systems to use time as a disciplinary device in the workplace occurred when Frederick Taylor established his scientific management techniques. As we saw in previous chapters, his techniques for controlling and managing work were developed through the analysis of results from so-called 'time and motion' studies. These studies broke down the tasks that workers were performing into their smallest units, fragmenting and simplifying them to increase the speed at which they could be carried out, and so that the time taken for workers to learn the job was reduced. A far faster operation of the assembly line in Ford's car plants resulted, the rhythm of work was altered, the work itself was de-skilled, and these employer time use strategies were closely associated with rising alienation among the workforce.

Work time and worker resistance

A fundamental concern for the sociology of work is worker resistance to mechanisms of control. Work time control is a crucial example here. The St Monday tradition is the most notorious early example of severe worker resistance to employers' work time strategies. Douglas Reid (1976) shows how Monday had been a non-work day for many workshop-based workers in the pre-industrial era. It was traditionally a day of drinking and disorder, with some implications for work on Tuesdays! During industrialisation, however, employers saw the casual Monday as a dangerous tradition that went against the structured working week that they were trying to impose. We saw the importance placed on continuous reliable production in Marx's theory of capitalism and we see at this period a struggle between two very different value systems over the issue of time. Many industries began to remove the

Monday holiday, replacing it with a Saturday half-holiday. These changes were met by widespread resistance from workers. The resistance was most effective in cottage industries and small workshops that were still marked by more informal work rhythms, and the St Monday remained more widespread and for longer here (Russell 2000). But in 1847, the 'Ten Hour Act' formalised the Saturday half-day. An interesting aside here is that employers also promoted football matches on Saturday afternoons to discourage their workers from pouring into pubs after they finished work.

Sociologists have looked back with interest on worker opposition to the new time discipline, and have compared it to the experiences of workers who lose or lack clock time discipline. Marie Jahoda *et al.*'s (1933) classic research examining the effects of unemployment asked what people gain from work. As well as providing a wage and an upper time limit for non-work pursuits, paid work provided temporal order to lives and regular activity. Lacking these, many of the unemployed her team researched were at a loss as to what to do with their free time. We might think that being freed from the tyranny of the work clock would be a liberation, but when the 'freeing' from work time is imposed rather than freely chosen, when people become unemployed – or retire from the labour market at state retirement age as another example – it seems that a number of temporal problems emerge. Ray Pahl has commented on the irony that the time discipline that was 'initially so vigorously resisted, should have become so widely accepted that disorientation and stress follow from the withdrawal from the time disciplines of wage labour' (1984: 44).

Worker defiance in the face of working on Mondays was largely quashed by employers and state legislation, but one form of worker resistance to work time control had a valuable impact and still shapes the way we work today. Workers' unions began to campaign for more control over work time via the establishment of 'normal' working hours, and with compensation for abnormal or 'non-standard' hours. Trade unions in the UK called for '48 hours for 48 weeks for 48 years'; in the US for 'eight hours sleep, eight hours work and eight hours for what we will' (Hewitt 1993; Rule 1994; Russell 2000), and these calls became widespread throughout all developed countries, facilitated by the establishment of international working time ideals. Gerhard Bosch *et al.* (1993) show how in 1935, for example, the ILO proposed a reduction of weekly hours to 40. The 1950s and 1960s saw economic growth and strong workers' movements throughout many capitalist societies and, as a result, working hours fell (see Figure 9.1 on manual workers in Britain). The notion of standard working time became established as a regulatory framework through a combination of legislation and collective agreements, and came to stand at the heart of employment law, the social security system, policies for retirement and pensions, the business culture, transport arrangements and the organisation of family life in many countries.

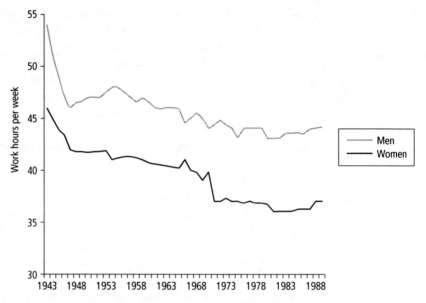

Figure 9.1 Actual working hours of women and men
Note: Evidence only available for full-time manual workers.
Source: Figures from Gershuny (2000), Figure 3.5.

In addition to this large-scale resistance to employer time control, a range of fascinating, classic, largely qualitative sociological studies have identified the smaller-scale, everyday ways in which workers try to 'beat the clock' and make their daily work routines more bearable by creating their own forms of time control. It is pertinent that the bulk of these studies have explored workers employed in manual jobs, since these jobs tend to offer the fewest opportunities for worker time autonomy, and the tasks performed are likely to be more directly clock-controlled. In Roy's (1958) study of factory employees, who were working 12-hour days and 6-day weeks engaged in monotonous machine-operating work, he found that the men had established a 'game of work' or an 'event-based time system' to structure the day. The previously interminable working day was broken up several times by, for example, 'banana time', 'peach time', 'window time' and 'coke time'. Ditton's (1979) study of bakers also saw workers manipulating time in this way, again breaking up what they felt was endless time into more 'digestible fragments'. Strategies were established for 'making' time, 'taking time twice', 'arresting' time, 'negotiating' time and 'avoiding' time. Ruth Cavendish's (1982) participant study of female assembly workers saw time rituals established by the women to make the days and weeks go faster. Working on the factory floor, Ruth Cavendish reports how time dragged much more on certain days than others: Tuesday was particularly slow since it was not a 'special day'. Wednesday was more bearable because bonus points were allocated that would affect pay, it was 'almost Thursday' (pay day) and lunch-time signified that the week was half-way over. Ben Hamper's (1986) *Rivethead: Tales from the Assembly Line* similarly describes his own experiences of time on the assembly line:

> However, my ascension into this new sense of dominance didn't rid me of the age-old plight that came to haunt every screw jockey: what the fuck do you do to kill the clock? There were ways of handling nimwit supervisors or banana sticker rednecks and lopsided rails. But the clock was a whole different mammal altogether. It sucked on you as you awaited the next job. It ridiculed you each time you'd take a peek. The more irritated you became, the slower it moved. The slower it moved, the more you thought. Thinking was very slow death at times. Desperation led me to all the usual dreary tactics used to fight back the clock. Boring excursions like racing to the water fountain and back, chain-smoking, feeding Cheetos to mice, skeet shooting Milk Duds with rubber bands, punting washers into the rafters high above the train depot, spitting contests. Any method was viable just as long as it was able to evaporate one more stubborn minute.
>
> (ibid.: 94–5)

These studies all show manual workers trying to regain some element of control over their work time, albeit within their heavily time-disciplined normal working days and weeks. The qualitative approaches adopted by each study meant that the writers could demonstrate powerfully how time is a subjective state and not just an objective measure of work (see also Roberts 1993).

The decline of normal work time

We know that trade unions have long campaigned, with a great deal of success, for normal or standard work time. As we saw in Chapter 6, however, economic crises and rising levels of unemployment in the 1970s saw employer moves to increase flexibility in the labour market, and part of these moves was towards a new temporal flexibility. Gerhard Bosch *et al.* (1993) show how the 'transparency' of working time in Europe declined, with a reorganisation of the temporal boundaries that marked the working day and week. In contrast to workers spending, say, 9–5 from Monday to Friday in the workplace, staggered hours, compressed working weeks, flexitime, hours-averaging, and part-time contracts proliferated. The restructuring of employment relations after the 1970s led to a questioning of 'what is normal any more about a "normal working day"?' (Harvey 1999: 21).

CONTEMPORARY ISSUES AND FUTURE TRENDS

Work time and social divisions

The focus on the imposition of clock time on workers and the interest in the time discipline of assembly-line workers more broadly have clear and valuable class dimensions. The concern with class inequalities and work time still persists in sociology but gender inequalities have also fed into the sociological examination of work and time, with 'race' and work time a fascinating but still under-explored area.

To begin with, the assumed move from cyclical, natural, task time to linear, clock time, proposed earlier, has been identified as problematic by sociologists who are interested in gender and work time. This case for this change can only be made if 'work-time' is taken to refer to paid work only. In an influential discussion of gender and time, Julia Kristeva (1981) suggested that women's time remains more cyclical than men's. Because this argument has traces of a problematic essentialism (see Chapter 7), Mark Harvey (1999) has argued instead that work time in the home (rather than women's time as such) has a different temporality: it is still structured by tasks rather than hours (Text box 9.1).

TEXT BOX 9.1 TEMPORALITIES

According to Harvey: 'The temporal coordination, squeezing, articulation of work/labour, whether paid or unpaid, formal or informal, establishes diverse regulations and cycles and thereby constitutes particular temporalities' (1999: 22).

'Household temporalities':

1 Have no clear boundaries between working and non-working.
2 Have no fixed ceiling or floor to the amount of time expanded. Household work varies according to need, use and cultural norms.
3 Are structured by the sequencing and synchronisation of different tasks. 'Chronometric' time is a problem since many of these tasks will be performed simultaneously (such as clothes washing and cooking).
4 Are cyclically structured over the lifetime (the care of infants and elderly).
5 Household economics of time vary with the size of the household, and the age and gender of the members (and so can vary over the years).
6 Are highly gendered.

Sociologists of gender and work have also critiqued the class-based campaigns for, and discussions of, a 'standard' working time. For Miriam Glucksmann

(1998), setting 9–5, Monday to Friday as the *optimal* standard week was a markedly gendered decision. Veronica Beechey and Theresa Perkins (1987) had discussed how this union campaign ignored the quite different work time policies that feminists were calling for, such as shorter working days to help employed mothers fit jobs in with school days, and more hours flexibility. Similarly, the union fight for compensation for working 'abnormal' time outside standard hours has been re-analysed by feminist writers. Jill Rubery *et al.* (1999) identified how abnormality was defined in a way that benefited male workers. For example, overtime and weekend work (where men dominated) were compensated but part-time (where women dominated) was not. Sylvia Walby (1988) had argued earlier that because many unions had barred part-time workers from membership, women as the bulk of the part-time workforce were excluded from work time protection.

In summary, then, sociologists of gender and work have questioned how a certain type of work and a particular patterning of work time – namely men's paid work in the public sphere – were taken as standard in the study of work and time. Miriam Glucksmann has pointed to the narrow view of time and work that has resulted, arguing instead that 'many labour activities involve exchanges of time or particular allocations of time use that have no financial dimension' (Glucksmann 1998: 243). Jill Rubery and colleagues (1999: 251) have also shown compellingly that work time is 'a key gender issue', since women and men commonly have quite different patterns of time use, on a daily, weekly and life-time basis (see also Perrons *et al.* 2005).

The importance of gender for the study of work time has been argued convincingly, but when we move on to 'race' and work time, the sociology of work has been rather silent, as of yet. This is disappointing because some of the major areas of interest to sociologists: issues of control in and over work; of long work hours; and of balancing work time and life times (see next section) are likely to be shaped by 'racial' inequalities. As we saw in Chapter 7, for example, slavery is the most blatantly and brutally controlled form of work, and historically slaves' time was fully owned by their masters (Genovese 1989; Harris 1992). In terms of contemporary issues of 'race' and work, some of the longest hours in the contemporary labour market are worked by the self-employed and there are very high levels of self-employment among certain minority ethnic groups in Britain. The extensive research by management researcher Monder Ram (1992) and sociological studies such as those by Robin Ward and Richard Jenkins (1984) have all revealed the long unsocial hours in poor conditions for low wages faced by many self-employed South-Asian men. The hours worked by self-employed Pakistani taxi drivers in Oldham, as revealed in Virinder Kalra's (2000) study, are a telling example. Research has also shown how adult family members and children commonly work alongside the self-employed male when he runs a family shop or a small-scale catering business, adding up the total hours of work carried out (Ram *et al.* 2001). In Anuradha Basu and Eser Altinay's

(2003) *Family and Work in Ethnic Minority Businesses*, for example, the wives of self-employed men were carrying a very large, triple or even quadruple work burden, involving caring, home management, working in the family business and undertaking paid employment to boost family incomes. Annie Phizacklea and Carol Wolkowitz's (1995) *Homeworking Women: Gender, Class and Racism at Work* has also usefully revealed how the three main social divisions that we explore in this book impact on the work time and work conditions of home-workers. Finally, working very long unsocial hours for low wages is a characteristic of the working lives of the migrant domestic workers that we explore in Chapter 10.

Clearly then 'race', alongside gender and class, offers an invaluable route into the sociological examination of inequalities in work and time. It is hoped that more researchers will build upon these studies to enhance an, as yet, underdeveloped sociology of 'race', work and time.

Work time. Life time?

Miriam Glucksmann, above, criticised the overly narrow view of time and work that results when only paid work time is considered. In her development of 'The *total social organization of labour* (TSOL)' that is referred to throughout this book, Glucksmann, like Ray Pahl before her, is at the forefront of writers who stress the need for sociologists of work to incorporate all forms of work in their analyses. The concern is also with extending the study of work to better explore linkages between work and non-work activities. Finding an optimal equilibrium between work and non-work time is a crucial issue in the contemporary work–life articulation debates that are carried out by academics, policy-makers and in the media. Of course, these debates reflect long-standing concerns in sociology, right back to the work of the founding fathers. More recently, influential theorist Norbert Elias (1992) examined the relationship between work time and free time and in particular the role of *loisir*, a time for personal fulfilment; while Barbara Adam (1995) has also talked about better co-ordination of life's 'multiple times'.

So while the relationship between work and the rest of people's lives is not a new interest for sociology, it is one that many sociologists – including ourselves – feel needs to be located more centrally within the sub-discipline of work sociology. The study of time is very useful for helping us move beyond a focus only on paid work. Examining working time means taking into account other aspects of people's lives, and of their time use. Any increase or reduction in working time has implications for the amount and distribution of non-work time, be it family time, and/or free or leisure time. In most societies, dedicating too little time to 'commodified' or waged work can threaten your economic security and that of any dependants. Yet spending too much time on work could damage family and personal life, particularly when work time is at unsocial hours. Elsa Ferri and Kate Smith (1996) show how unsocial hours worked by fathers they interviewed meant the men were less involved in the lives of their families. Research has shown similarly how working long hours in the UK has negative impacts on the opportunities for other types of time use including leisure (Warren 2004). Harriet Presser's research (1995) into shift-workers in the USA reveals how working shifts heralds a host of time-related problems: with workers reporting health problems, but also their detrimental impact on shared family time, on sleeping time with partners, and difficulties experienced in planning social commitments, particularly when shifts rotate.

Just how workers decide how much time they allocate to work, and to other activities, has long been a core concern for researchers outside sociology too. Economists have made a number of attempts to model how and why people dedicate the hours they do to work and other activities, and this has influenced sociological thinking. For example, in what was termed the 'new home economics', workers were seen to be making rational calculations over how best to spend their time so that they had sufficient wages, on the one hand, and sufficient leisure on the other. Notably, the US economist Gary Becker (1985) proposed that such rational choices can explain the increased allocation of time to paid work over the years. This is because more satisfaction is gained by working more hours and by reducing leisure time, and by combining this time package with the goods and services that can be purchased with the higher incomes that result. This rational approach can be, and has been, critiqued, not least by feminist economists who problematise the gendered basis of rational models in mainstream economics more broadly. Yet it also raises the question over how active and free are the choices that we make in the ways we balance our home and working lives, that we discuss in Chapter 10.

Too much or too little work time?

One of the most influential studies shaping the sociology of work/leisure time was Thorstein Veblen's *The Theory of the Leisure Class* published in 1899. In it, Veblen cites the historical distinction between the base and the honourable that we discuss in Chapter 1 where we ask 'What is work?'. For Veblen, dishonour was attached to productive employment. Since labour was associated with 'subjection to a master', leisure was 'ennobling' in the eyes of civilised peoples. The first dominant élite social class thus defined itself through its leisure or the 'non-productive use of time' (Veblen 1963: 46). They pursued 'conspicuous abstention from labour' since 'there are few of the better class who are not possessed of an instinctive repugnance for the vulgar forms of labour' (ibid.: 42). If they can afford it, people will choose to prioritise leisure over work time. And with the greater levels of productivity that result from new technologies, workers will be able to reduce their hours and have more free time. Veblen's prediction of more free time is an interesting one to explore further. Over a century after *The Theory of the Leisure Class* was published, a range of studies suggest, first, we have too much work time, second, women's workloads in particular have increased.

Too much work time?

Some of the most celebrated arguments that suggested we are working too hard and too long in too rushed time-poor societies emerged within the USA. Juliet Schor's (1991) *The Overworked American* refers to the growth in productivity that could herald a new leisure society. With more productivity, a worker can either produce their current output in less time, or remain at work the same number of hours and produce more. The choice is between more free time or more money. For Schor, time was the clear loser since 'by the end of the century Americans will be spending as much time at their jobs as they did during the 1920s' (Schor 1991: 1). A major part of the problem, she suggests, is the growth of a 'long hours culture' that originated among higher level workers such as those on Wall Street but spread throughout other high income occupations and then to the great majority of working Americans, across the income groups, classes and genders. In long hours cultures, devoting surpluses of time is taken to be 'symbols of loyalty and trust, as well as measures of performance and productivity in uncertain "greedy" organizational environments' (Sirianni and Negrey 2000: 67; see also Basso 2003).

Schor's arguments were supported by Arlie Hochschild (1997) in *The Time Bind* where she highlighted the detrimental impact of longer hours in the workplace on family time, and by Jill Andresky Fraser (Text box 9.2) who depicts so graphically the lived reality of the US long hours cultures. These claims were picked up in the UK and Europe too where time poverty, long hours cultures and 'presenteeism' have all been detected (Burchell *et al.* 2002; Garhammer 1998; Purcell *et al.* 1999). In the UK, in particular, working long hours has come to signify status and a commitment to the firm.

TEXT BOX 9.2 THE CONCEPT OF JOB SPILL

According to Jill Andresky Fraser:

> Remember lunch hours? The very term has become an anachronism for many inhabitants of the corporate world. Thirty-nine percent of workers surveyed by the National Restaurant Association report that they were too busy to take a lunch break . . . they just work through it.

In Manhattan, for example, where 'power lunches' have traditionally been a way of life . . . restaurants such as Le Bernardin now offer thirty-minute quickies for working men and women who are too pressed for time to ingest their gourmet meals at a leisurely pace. The latest trend among rising professional? They schedule two or more mini-meals, with one set of business guests arriving at the table as another departs.

(2001: 24–5)

According to *The Wall Street Journal*: 'all kinds of gadgets, from laptops to phones, can now work not just by the pool, but in it'. Among the aquatic-office developments highlighted was a battery-operated cordless telephone complete with water-resistant handset; and a new type of floating lounge chair capable of supporting people who want to combine a swim with work on their laptop computers (ibid.: 80).

Sociologists of work have argued that a significant effect of such a work time culture is the exclusion of workers who are not able and/or willing to give so much time to their paid work. It deters those who have caring respons-ibilities from entering jobs and from advancing when in post, for example. In Sarah Rutherford's (2001) ethnographic study 'Are you going home already?', she proposed that the long hours culture is firmly bound up with specific notions of masculinity, signified readily by the macho culture of the trading floor, and acts as a means of patriarchal closure to exclude women from positions of power. The 'total time commitment' that is expected from many senior executives today (Fagan and Lallement 2000 discuss the UK and France) is also organised around the gendered assumption that senior workers are not involved in domestic work when they (eventually) go home, but rather that 'someone else' performs their domestic duties for them (see Chapter 10).

The evidence for growing time poverty, among high income workers in particular, might seem resounding but a number of studies have queried these work-intensive lives. In the USA, for example, Jerry Jacobs and Kathleen Gerson (1998) suggest that Schor's results actually revealed only small increases in weekly working hours (around 1–2), while John Robinson and Geoffrey Godbey (1997) proposed that people have exaggerated their working hours for 'cachet'. What seems to be true is that this 'time poverty' picture is actually a complex one. Jacobs and Gerson (1998) proposed that the USA does have very high proportions of workers working long hours but, at the same time, there has been an increasing bifurcation of working time, with growth evident in short hours working too. They also highlighted the apparent para-dox that workers' hours are actually shorter but the sense of being overworked has increased, and they suggested that this is a result primarily of demographic shifts rather than genuine changes in working hours. They proposed that there are now proportionally more groups that tend to be over-worked in any case, namely dual-earner couples and single parents. Cynthia Fuchs Epstein and Arne Kalleberg (2001) concluded similarly that a 'time bind' has emerged in the USA but with different roots and a different profile than previously suggested. UK researchers have also questioned the growth of the time squeezed worker. Indeed, Jonathon Gershuny shows that actual paid hours have fallen across the board between the 1850s and the late 1970s (see Figure 9.1), and he and other time use researchers like Oriel Sullivan, suggested only slight increases in all 'working' time (that is, including domestic work) for men and decreases in women's total working time over time. Gershuny also identified significant class divisions between 'work-rich' and 'jobless' households (as did Gregg and Wadsworth 1996).

It seems from quantitative studies that actual work hours have not increased, or not increased much, but qualitative studies are revealing a sense of time squeeze for workers. This is a fascinating paradox, and it is attracting more and diverse types of research. As we saw in Chapter 3, then, comparing results from quantitative and qualitative studies is vital because it helps us to explore quite different aspects of a topic, and in this way we can provide a broader and more nuanced analysis of social phenomena. Some studies have shown usefully that the times of the day when hours are worked, and workers' autonomy over hours, are as important factors as the actual number of hours worked in shaping how workers perceive their time. Epstein and Kalleberg (2001) discussed how night- and shift-workers have qualitatively different family and social lives and are more likely to be subject to physical symptoms caused by tension and stress.

Class, gender and 'race' divisions all affect the degree to which individuals are able to have control over their time or are controlled by others. 'Time sovereignty' is much more of a middle-class prerogative: with studies showing how workers in higher level socio-economic groups are better able to control when and how they work, their working weeks are less likely to be controlled by the clock, with more flexibility over the working day, over breaks and over where the work is carried out. Jane Nolan's (2002) research in the UK demonstrated that if workers have more control over their working time, then time dissatisfaction is much less, job satisfaction is higher, stress levels are lower and workers feel more able to balance their lives, even when the hours worked are very long. The higher up the occupational hierarchy, the more 'time elasticity' is available over the working week, and elasticity is increased yet further since the middle classes are often in the position to 'make' extra time by paying someone else to do domestic work. The ability to 'time appropriately' (Adam 1995) by synchronising leisure, family and work lives is shaped strongly by diversity in access to economic resources. Text box 9.3 reveals some of the ramifications for family life of the long weeks worked away by men in some working-class jobs, as revealed in classic sociological accounts (from Warren 2003).

TEXT BOX 9.3 THE FAMILY TIME OF WORKING-CLASS MEN

McKenna's (1980) study of railway workers highlights a group of train crews who worked such family-unfriendly schedules that the men had become known as the 'double homers'. For better pay rates, they took longer distance train work that entailed lodging away from home for much of the week. Double homers' wives were known as 'railway widows' and the men were 'shadowy figures' in their children's lives.

In Hollowell's (1968) study of long-distance lorry drivers, 'trampers' worked on average four days away from home each week. One lorry driver reported 'There's no home life . . . my boy only sees me two nights a week. I see him on a Saturday but otherwise he's usually in bed when I come home and go away' (Hollowell 1968: 156).

Tunstall's (1962) research into Hull fishermen who worked away from home for three weeks at a time, described the men as 'strangers' to their children.

Women's increased workloads?

In brief, since we examine this topic in more detail in Chapter 10, the core debate here concerns whether, since women – or certain groups of women – have increasingly entered the labour market and increased their paid work time, the hours they spend on housework have fallen correspondingly. On the one hand, it has been argued that women have faced a growing 'time bind'. On the other hand, some writers have suggested that female employers have reduced their housework time while men have taken up some of the slack.

The time spent on housework was predicted to decline with the advancement of technology. Yet Joanne Vanek's (1974) earlier examination of the time women spent on domestic work in the USA found it to be consistent despite new labour-saving devices. The labour per task had fallen but this was counterbalanced by rising standards that meant that tasks had to be carried out more often. In contrast to this account, Jonathon Gershuny and John Robinson (1991) argued that time spent on routine domestic work like cooking and cleaning has decreased markedly over the decades (after controlling for changes in women's patterns of employment and family status. See also Gershuny 2000). For these quantitative researchers, women in the UK and the USA are now doing less housework than women in the past, and men are doing more. We discuss these diverging conclusions more in Chapter 10. There too we examine in more detail the class and 'racial' dimensions to the gendered performance of domestic work. Here, it is useful to note that technology might well have had a divergent impact on the hours spent on domestic work by middle-class and working-class women, reducing those carried out by working-class women as labour-saving devices became more widely available, but increasing those of middle-class women by privatising housework and making the use of domestic servants less common. In a range of publications including *The New Service Economy* with Ian Miles (1983), Gershuny provides a useful analysis of the decline and rise of domestic service, pulling out the class and gender implications.

Work time over the life-course

There is another sense in which we can think about time in relation to work and this is through the concept of the life-course. Sociologists and others are interested in the way time has different meanings and implications through the course of our lives, and there are several aspects to this. We could think of the concept of the career. Traditionally the notion of career which developed in the nineteenth century was associated in Western economies with middle-class, usually white, male employees who could expect a predictable work life trajectory of full employment and gradual promotion. Compare this to the fate of blue-collar workers such as coal miners who might reach the height of their earning powers in their twenties and thirties and then experience loss of earnings as they physically declined. Female workers have in turn experienced a very different working lifetime because of various labour market barriers and the fact that they take a major role in child-care and other caring: thus the female labour force participation profile is quite different to the male, though the gender gap varies between societies (Rubery *et al.* 1999) and within societies by 'race' (see Dale *et al.* 2006, on Britain).

Over the past two decades or more, predictability in work time over the life-course has been called into question by the changing nature of the economy and by other societal trends (see Dikens *et al.* 2003). The whole concept of the working life has been made problematic because of the perceived fragmentary nature of the 'new capitalism' (Sennett 2006). Whereas, in the past, many men would begin their working lives at the age of 14–16, the trend in Western countries is for people to start their first full-time job later, often after further education. At the same time, labour market participation by older male workers at the end of the working life has been made problematic by redundancies, early retirements and the collapse of many staple industries. This clipping of the working life at both ends of the age spectrum means that the older male standard working life of 50 years is made problematic with a 16–65 norm now more often resembling a 22 to early 50s model (Disney and Hawkes 2003). This has important implications for issues such as pensions but also as sociologists we need to be aware of what this does for the age profile at work as well as the social reproduction of the workplace (see Roberts 2006). A related aspect is the experience of work in this new capitalism. Richard Sennett (1998, 2003, 2006) has written a series of books where he tries to explore the effects of the speeding up of capitalism. He argues that the flux and change which are now a feature of a working life mean that a person's time horizon shrinks and that they no longer make long-term commitments to work organisations or to the communities in which they live. The type of worker created by this type of capitalism is one who is constantly calculating their next move in their career. This, Sennett (1998) believes, is creating an increasingly individualised and fragmented society.

Work and time in comparative perspective

Sociologists of work have long drawn usefully on comparisons between differing societies. Recently, the concept of a national 'working-time régime' has been devised as a useful way to carry out cross-national analyses of work time. For Jill Rubery, a management researcher who is very influential in sociology, these refer to the statutory and collectively bargained regulations, as well as norms and practices at the workplace (Rubery *et al.* 1998). Sociologists have been interested in how workers fare under diverse working time régimes. What emerges clearly is that, if we use 'typical' hours as a benchmark to compare societies (Text box 9.4), substantial cross-national differences in working time exist (Table 9.1 and Figure 9.2; see Bosch 2000). The UK and the USA stand out in these comparisons. Working time, abnormal work time, holiday and sickness periods are all regulated firmly in many societies, but the UK and the USA remain significant exceptions. The USA has regional rather than national working time regulations; there are few government work-time initiatives; and worker movements have tended to use any restrictions on working hours to boost pay rather than reduce hours (Roche *et al.* 1996). Hours remain diverse, with very long hours for some groups. In the UK too, a history of weak and uneven regulation of working time has resulted in a wide diversity in the range of hours worked, with very long hours common for men at the top and bottom of the occupational hierarchy in particular. Since workers commonly express preferences for not working very long hours, as Colette Fagan (2001a, 2001b) and other researchers have shown, it is little surprise that the UK and USA are frequently cited in growing debates over 'time poverty'.

TEXT BOX 9.4 WORKING HOURS THRESHOLDS IN EUROPE

In 1998, despite very strong opposition from Britain, the EU Council of Ministers established a common set of hours standards throughout all member states. The maximum working week in Europe now stands at 48 hours including over-time, with a minimum daily rest period of 11 consecutive hours, a daily limit of 8 hours for night workers and a minimum annual holiday entitlement of 4 weeks (Blair *et al.* 2001).

Jonathon Gershuny (1999) also shows how many societies, particularly in what he calls the 'Nice North' of Europe (as opposed to the Wild West of the USA and the UK), are working to reduce work time. A range of studies have been carried out into countries with innovative work time policies, such as France for its 35-hour full-time week (Fagnani and Letablier 2004), Denmark for

Table 9.1 Agreed hours in EU countries, 2001

	Maximum agreed hours	
	Week	*Day*
Austria	40	10
Belgium	39	8
Denmark	48	13
Finland	40	8
France	48	10
Germany	48	8
Greece	48	8
Ireland	48	13
Italy	48	13
Luxembourg	48	10
The Netherlands	48	9
Norway	40	9
Portugal	40	10
Spain	40	9
Sweden	40	8
The UK	48	13

Source: EIRO (2002).

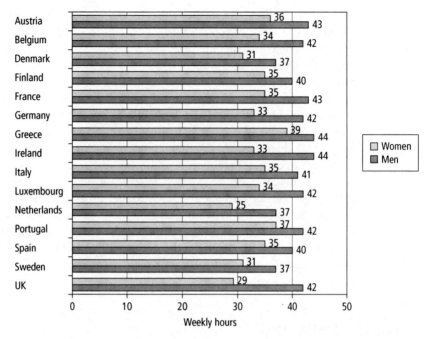

Figure 9.2 Average weekly working hours in EU countries, 1998
Note: Actual hours in main job.
Source: ELFS data derived from Fagan (2001b), Table A1.3.

its 37 full-time hours and controlled part-time work (Warren 2002), and the Netherlands for its promotion of quality part-time employment (Plantenga 2002). They show that demands for new policies of work time are coming from a wide range of sources: trade unions, women's groups and campaigners for children's rights. Accordingly demands for work time reduction and control now include adequate time for caring work, for families, for leisure, and for community and political participation – in addition to having enough (but not too much) paid work time.

CONCLUSION

Time is central to the study of work, from the paid work of the factory or office floors to waged domestic labour and to the unwaged care work that is carried out typically by women in the home. Time shapes the way we organise this work over the day, week, year and even life-time. Yet it is important to remember that the organisation of work time is a social construct that can and has varied over the years and across different societies. As sociologists, we are interested in the whens, hows and whys behind the changes and any continuities in work temporalities. Jacobs and Gerson (2001) have usefully summarised a range of topics that lie at the heart of the sociology of work and time. These include how work and time intersect in the social structuring of the work day and work week; how work time is regulated and how this regulation has been accepted or resisted by workers; how part-time and overtime work impact on workers and society; the effect of new technology on the pace of work; and the 'symbolic meaning' of time in work. As researchers, we are also interested in how best to investigate these topics. It is apparent that the different dimensions to work time are open to being researched using both quantitative and qualitative methods and, indeed, the picture we hold of work time today depends on studies that have employed both. Thus we can read about broad changes in patterns of time use over the years as well as the lived time experiences of workers. We have aimed in this chapter to use work time to showcase the benefits of quantitative and qualitative studies in sociology, the advantages of historical and comparative approaches, and the necessity of interrelated theoretical and empirical approaches to a concept.

FURTHER READING

In the UK, E. P. Thompson's 'Time, work-discipline and industrial capitalism' (various reprints) (1967) remains a classic reading.

Jonathon Gershuny's *Changing Times: Work and Leisure in Postindustrial Society* (2000) presents details of time use across a range of societies.

Keith Grint's edited collection *Work and Society: A Reader* (2000) contains a useful selection on time including John Hassard's theoretical 'Images of time in work and organization'.

In the USA, Cynthia Fuchs Epstein and Arne Kalleberg's article 'Time and the sociology of work' (2001) provides a good review of debates.

Arlie Russell Hochschild's *The Time Bind: When Work Becomes Home and Home Becomes Work* (1997) was a landmark US study showing how longer hours in the workplace impact on family time that had major influence outside the USA too.

WEB SOURCE

European Industrial Relations Online. http://www.eiro.eurofound.ie/. A very useful site with up-to-date, often free to download, quality information on developments in work time in European countries. It has a wealth of excellent links to sites within each country too.

STUDENT PROJECTS AND ESSAY QUESTIONS

1 How, why and with what success did employers instigate a new time discipline in the nineteenth century?
2 How does the 'working time régime' of Britain compare with that of another society? Why?
3 Consider long working hours. Are they a good or bad thing, for what or for whom, and in what ways? How does an understanding of social divisions feed into your answer? If you were a policy-maker, would you seek to curtail work time or not, and why?
4 How useful do you think it is to combine qualitative and quantitative approaches to researching work time? In considering this, reflect on what John Hassard (2000) means by the 'qualitative construction of temporal meanings'.

Domestic Work

▌ OVERVIEW

This chapter will:

- Examine how sociology has approached the main form of work that is carried out within the home: housework or domestic work.
- Look at sociology's initial reluctance to see domestic work as 'proper' work meriting academic attention.
- Consider social inequalities in how domestic work is organised according to the main social divisions identified in the book: class, gender and 'race'.
- Explore the impact of feminist sociological analysis of domestic work on how 'work' is defined and studied.
- Examine the necessary links between the work that is carried out within and outside the home, revisiting debates over the separation of public/private spheres.

▌ INTRODUCTION

In this chapter, we explore how housework is carried out, and by and for whom. We show that the topic of housework or domestic work highlights how sociology approaches work in a number of crucial ways. We argue that although the classical sociologists showed little interest in the division of domestic work, the increased attention it has received over the years has helped advance the discipline. We demonstrate how the study of domestic work has contributed to and provided a valuable critique of what sociologists mean when they discuss 'work'. We show too that, since housework is seen by many as unrewarding and dirty work, the study of who carries it out, for whom and on what terms, is an exceptionally useful tool for exploring social inequalities in work. And we use domestic work to re-problematise the assumed separation of work carried out in the public sphere and the private. Finally, we discuss the ways in which the study of domestic work has contributed to a more sophisticated sociological understanding of how diverse forms of work are inter-related.

THE SOCIOLOGICAL MISSION

The sociological analysis of domestic work is a relatively recent addition to the discipline but we want to show how valuable it has been and how much more it has to contribute. It is fascinating to consider the transformation in the way that sociologists have approached the topic, because initially 'housework' was not part of the sociological mission at all. Domestic work was not seen to be a subject worthy of serious sociological attention, falling as it often does outside the confines of the employment relationship. Instead it was viewed as just something women did naturally as part of being a woman, and so not real work that involved any skill. Since it was seen as natural – not social – it fell outside the boundaries of the academic discipline whose concern was the social construction of work. In marked contrast, the contemporary sociological mission now includes a critique of the dismissal of domestic work in our classical inheritance, and sociology asks important questions about the essentialism inherent in such interpretations of domestic work. The study of domestic work is important to sociology because it feeds into the growing sociological interest in defining 'work' more broadly than merely waged work performed in the labour market. It also allows sociology to critique the alleged separation of private and public spheres during industrialisation, and the analysis of domestic work today has helped writers to reconsider the necessary links between the two spheres. The examination of domestic work is also part of a work sociology that does not see the individual worker as the only 'unit of analysis' of work, but views households as appropriate ways to approach work sociologically too.

FOUNDATIONS

The three founding fathers had very little to say on domestic work. In his 1893 *The Division of Labour*, Durkheim's core focus was the public sphere, but he did develop ideas on the gender division of labour that would influence later sociologies. Durkheim's own ideas were themselves influenced by the work of Auguste Comte who, on gender divisions, had argued that a certain type of family was needed within modern society. It was 'reducible to . . . two orders of relations – namely the subordination of the sexes which institutes the family, and that of the ages, which maintains it' ([1855] 1974: 503). For Comte, 'Sociology will prove that the equality of the sexes . . . is incompatible with all social existence, by showing that each sex has special and permanent functions that it must fulfil in the natural economy of the human family' (quoted in Pedersen 2001: 505). Durkheim also argued for the naturalness or essentialness of a natural 'conjugal family' for civilised society and for different roles for women and men. We know that modern society was, for Durkheim, marked by growing interdependence between individuals and that a specialised division of labour was core to this inter-dependence. In his short discussion of the sexual division of labour (in a section entitled 'Cases where the function of the division of labour is to bring forth groups which would not exist without it'), Durkheim argues for the importance of specialised tasks, based on natural differences between women and men (Lehman 1995). As societies have developed, he asserts, men have evolved and become more social, the products of society, but women have remained primitive and asocial, the products of nature. Among modern people, he says, women and men thus lead completely different existences: women focus on the 'affective functions' and men the 'intellectual functions'.

For Durkheim, the natural sexual division of labour, and the traditional family that results from it, are functional for smooth conjugal relations and for society overall. Many of his ideas were picked up later in the work of Talcott Parsons. Parsons, a core member of the *Functionalist* School, was highly influential in 1950s sociology, but his work fell out of favour later in part but not only because of the growing critique of its essentialism by feminist sociology. Like Durkheim, Parsons (with Bales 1955) was concerned with issues of social order and the individual, suggesting natural differences between women and men led to their different roles within the family: with women's main role an 'expressive' one and men's 'instrumental'.

The Marxian tradition is similar to the Durkheimian one in some ways, as we saw in Chapter 2, because it drew on notions of the natural woman/cultured man dichotomy and focused on work carried out in the public sphere. Marx himself was interested in relations of production, seeing domestic work as reproduction. In *Capital*, Volume II, for example, he explores how a mode of production survives, with domestic labour required to reproduce humans (see Jefferson and King 2001). As discussed in Chapter 2, Frederick Engels offered more to the study of the social construction of gendered work. In his *The Origin of the Family, Private Property and the State* (1884), for example, Engels identified the emergence of women's subordination to men as men sought to establish ways to pass privatised property to their own offspring. He does not pay much attention to domestic work, but does identify it as a problem for women that would be resolved with communism:

> With the passage of the means of production into common property, the individual family ceases to be the economic unit of society. Private house-keeping is transformed into a social industry. The care and education of the children becomes a public matter.
>
> ([1884] 1972: 76)

Meanwhile, Max Weber paid almost no attention to domestic work.

The result of this foundational inheritance is that domestic work has been largely ignored for much of the history of the sociology of work. A classic separation of paid work for men and 'no work' for women was established: public and private spheres – and production and reproduction – were dichotomised. The subject matter for the sociology of work, or industrial sociology as it is sometimes described, is that work is defined by and analysed through the lens of the employment relationship. Given this history, we show how attention to domestic work in the sociology of work has been revolutionary.

LATER DEVELOPMENTS

It is valuable to begin this section by considering what sociologists came to mean by domestic work; by noting that a range of different terminologies have been used; and also by pointing out that different studies explore different aspects of the concept. Some sociological studies talk about housework, others use domestic work, and yet others still domestic labour. Domestic work for sociologists commonly includes the routine domestic jobs that most people commonly call housework: cleaning, ironing, vacuuming, washing the dishes, and so forth. It also includes more skilled tasks like cooking. But domestic work also includes such 'DIY' jobs as painting and decorating, gardening and car maintenance. And it might include caring work like looking after children or dependent relatives. More recently, emotional labour (see Chapter 12) has been identified as a crucial part of what work goes on in the home too. In summary, domestic work is broad and multi-faceted but it was largely ignored in academic debate until recently.

Domestic work as real work?

The first real impact of domestic work on sociology was in the 1970s. One of the first issues raised was whether housework should be seen as 'work'.

Since it is not waged for most who do housework (though see Text box 10.1), housework fell awkwardly outside many of the debates that were taking place in sociology around work at the time. A real issue for feminist sociology in the 1970s was the inadequacy of the most critical of sociological theories, Marxism, for analysing domestic work. We saw above that the Marxist view was that housework fell into the realm of reproduction not production. It was not real work since work produced a commodity and surplus value for capital. Feminists began to raise questions concerning what we mean by productive – and unproductive – labour, about what is a wage and what is it paid for, and about the relationship between housework and class. For many feminists, Marxist theory had overlooked the centrality of housework to any analysis of paid labour, and we come back to the necessary links between these forms of work later in the chapter. Writers identifying as Marxist feminist such as Annette Kuhn and Annemarie Wolpe (1978) argued that while housework was part of the reproductive process of capitalism, it was important for the economy (see Text box 10.1) and ideologically important for capitalism too.

TEXT BOX 10.1 THE INTERNATIONAL WAGES FOR HOUSEWORK CAMPAIGN

This feminist campaign argues that women should be paid a wage for the domestic work that they perform in their own homes, and that the labour costs of domestic work should be included in official statistics.

Housework 'worth' £700bn
    The government statistical service has estimated that if domestic work was paid at the hourly rate of pay for each task (cleaning, ironing, etc.), then it would cost £700 billion a year in the UK.
(The UK 2000 Time Use Survey, released by the Office for National Statistics. BBC News Online (2002). Wednesday, 24 April)

As we saw in Chapter 7, in the UK, Ann Oakley's (1974) *The Sociology of Housework* was very influential for arguing that housework should be seen as work. One of her four characteristics of the housewife role in modern industrialised society (see Text box 10.2) was that housework is viewed as non-work. Indeed, the sociological understanding that housework was not real work meant that Oakley faced serious opposition to her proposal to carry out research into housewives' working lives. Her persistence led to a PhD based on in-depth interviews with a number of housewives about the housework carried out in their homes.

The four characteristics of the housewife role in modern industrialised society are:

1 The housewife role is exclusive to women.
2 Housewives are economically dependent.
3 Housework is seen as non-work rather than economically productive.
4 The housewife role takes priority over other life roles for women.

(Oakley 1974: 1)

Oakley argued that housework is not seen as proper work because of its 'social trivialisation'. She found this trivialisation expressed by the housewives themselves too when they were assessing their own lives. They held very ambivalent feelings about their work, reflecting the downgrading of the role in society that is epitomised by the statement 'I'm *just* a housewife'. For Oakley, 'The admission "I am just a housewife" disclaims any right to feel pride in this status' (ibid.: 4). Nevertheless, at the same time as trivialising it themselves, home-making was central to women's lives. That is, while the women found many of the domestic tasks they were performing dull and monotonous, they identified firmly with the housewife role itself (Oakley's fourth characteristic).

The first of Oakley's characteristics of the housewife role was that it is highly gendered. This marks the dominant concern for sociology that we turn to next.

The gendering of domestic work

Questions have been asked over the extent of the gendering of domestic work and whether this varies, according to time, class, 'race', and place for example. As the quotation from 1881 shows, the gendering of domestic work has a long history: 'Housecleaning is a terror to everyone, and above all to gentlemen, who resent it from beginning to end' (Helen Campbell 1881, quoted in Reeves 2002: 6).

Exploring the history of the gendering of housework bring us firmly back to the issues we discussed in Chapter 5 on industrial work where we showed that separate breadwinner/housewife roles for men and women have not always existed. Historian Catherine Hall's (1980) *The History of the Housewife* shows that prior to industrialisation, when the family had been the unit of production, the wife was often the co-ordinator of household production. It was only in Victorian times that women not taking paid work became a mark of superiority of upper middle-class households: the Victorian ideal was of a full-time housewife who provided a haven for the man from pressure at his work. Sheila Rowbotham's *Women, Resistance and Revolution* (1973) discusses how this male breadwinner/female housewife-carer ideal was spread to the other classes. Its economic implications for the working class were seen in the family wage campaign that argued working-class men needed to be paid enough so that they could support financially their (newly) dependent wives.

In Oakley's (1974) research, women carried out the majority of house-work in heterosexual couples, even if they had full-time jobs: 15 per cent of men 'helped with' housework and 25 per cent with child-care. As women's participation in the labour market continued to grow after the 1970s, so too did the sociological interest in who carries out domestic work and whether there was any increase in men's share to ease women's 'double burden'. A core assumption for the sociology of work became that just because women do more housework than men, this is not inevitable. Indeed, the withdrawal of men from housework appears to be a recent tradition, an outcome of industrialisation and the new association between 'real' work and the public sphere.

A range of studies after Oakley continued to explore the gendering of domestic work. Some suggested a growing equity between women and men in its performance, but others were less optimistic. A classic conjectural publication, David Young and Peter Willmott's *The Symmetrical Family* (1973), proclaimed the emergence of companionship-based relationships between middle-class heterosexual couples in which domestic labour was shared more equally. We return to this ongoing topic of gender and work in the section 'Contemporary issues'. Before that, it is useful to examine briefly the 1980s sociological interest in gender and work in those households where men were unemployed.

The special case offered when men in couples are unemployed repres-ented a type of natural experiment for the study of gender work roles: what happens when a man loses a core element of his breadwinner role? Some fascinating historical examples were drawn upon by Pahl (1988), who reviews evidence from reports at the end of the nineteenth century of localities in which paid work for men had declined and women had taken over the main breadwinner role. He notes how some accounts show clearly the involvement of men in domestic work: 'It is no uncommon sight to find men cleaning and sweeping, caring for the children and even putting them to bed on the evening when the women were engaged in the family washing' (a factory inspector, quoted in Pahl 1988: 59).

In the high unemployment of 1980s Britain, Lorna McKee and Colin Bell (1985) explored whether male unemployment (in Kidderminster) had led to changes in the domestic division of labour. Interviewing 45 couples, they identified how important it was to examine the wives' experiences of the unemployment of their partners too. For the women, the men did not represent an extra pair of hands around the home but presented more work. Conflicts arose over men doing women's domestic jobs and the 'correct' way of doing the work. Furthermore, McKee and Bell noted that women's domestic work grew when their partners lost their jobs since their managerial roles in managing household finances expanded: they faced debts, arrears and bill juggling, hunted down bargains, made more economic meals and planned menus carefully, refused treats to the children, patched clothes, went without themselves, and shopping was more elaborate at a variety of stores, on foot. In Jane Wheelock's *Husbands at Home* (1990), she asked similarly whether the domestic division of labour was becoming more equal in 1980s Wearside, where male unemployment was high. She found a different range of developments: a traditional rigid gender division of labour, a traditional flexible household, sharing families, and exchanged-role families, but the first remained dominant.

Technology and domestic work

Reflecting the interest in the effect of technology on work performance and work relations in the sociology of work more generally at the time, researchers in the 1970s asked a number of questions about the impact of technology on domestic work. First, had domestic work grown easier over time, facilitated by developments in domestic appliances? The time spent on domestic work was predicted to decline with the advancement of technology. Washing machines, hot water on tap, vacuum cleaners and microwave ovens were to liberate households, and women in particular, from domestic drudgery. Yet Joanne Vanek's (1974) examination of the time women spent on domestic work in the USA found it to be consistent over the years despite these labour-saving devices. The labour per domestic task had fallen but this decline was counterbalanced by rising standards that meant that tasks had to be carried out more often (see Chapter 9). In contrast to the annual 'spring clean', for example, standards of cleanliness have meant far more regular and very thorough cleaning. Betty Friedan, the American feminist, suggested famously that housewifery expands to fill the time available!

Christina Hardyment's *From Mangle to Microwave: The Mechanisation of Household Work* (1989) also argued that the amount of domestic work had not been reduced by technology, but also that technology has changed the form that household work takes. That is, the 1960s did see the introduction of new models of appliances like washing machines that were far easier to operate. At the same time, however, new technology had replaced servants in middle-class homes and encouraged private patterns of housekeeping, increasing domestic work for middle-class women. For working-class families, the previous community-based homemaking and specialisation of labour have been replaced by a self-sufficient private lone housewife. Old occupations like the ice man, the chimney sweep and the knife grinder, who had all come to the back door, disappeared, and the work was now confined instead to the private sphere, increasing the domestic work for working-class women.

As elsewhere in the book, then, sociology has identified complexities in the impact of technology on how work is carried out and by whom. While some of the hardest tasks have been eased, the amount of domestic work has not been eradicated.

Linking work in the public and private spheres

One of the most valuable contributions to sociology from the study of domestic work is that it has revealed the extent to which the so-called separation of public and private spheres was indeed artificial. Put simply, gendered work in the home impacts on how women and men work in the labour market, and gendered patterns of work in the labour market impact on what women and men do in the home. At the most basic level, if someone is spending all their time and energy on one sphere, then they have less time and energy available for the other. But the female-dominated work in the home impacts on the labour market in far deeper and broader ways than this.

Sociologists have shown that jobs are arranged around women's assumed domestic responsibilities in numerous ways. Many jobs that women occupy have reflections of domestic activity and are classified as less skilled since women are seen to be doing them naturally: cleaning, child-care, cooking, serving. Furthermore, a wide range of tasks that women undertake in the home contribute to their partners' ability to engage in waged work. Janet Finch's classic *Married to the Job: Wives' Incorporation in Men's Work* (1983) examined women's involvement in their husbands' paid work, showing how work carried out in the public sphere is linked inextricably to that in the home. Ray Pahl's studies of the working lives of women and men on the Isle of Sheppey, Kent, in the 1980s were also influential in revealing the limitations of the assumed separation of public and private sphere work. His main aim was 'to explain the interrelations between forms of work and sources of labour' (1984: 313), and he showed the linked organisation of paid work, unemployment, domestic work and informal work (see Glucksmann 1990). We return to this key issue later in the chapter.

CONTEMPORARY ISSUES AND FUTURE TRENDS

Gender and work

The focus on the gendering of domestic work, and whether we are seeing moves to more equality in its performance among heterosexual couples, has persisted into contemporary sociology. Jonathon Gershuny and a range of colleagues provided some backing for Young and Wilmott's (1973) earlier proposal of growing equity. Drawing on analyses of quantitative data-sets based on time use diaries, they suggested that we are seeing convergence in the time that women and men spend on domestic work in the UK, the USA and Europe as women do less of it and men do more (Gershuny 2000; Sullivan and Gershuny 2001; Sullivan 2000, 2004). To explain these changes, Gershuny *et al.* (1994) suggested that over an extended period of time, the division of domestic work is adapting to changing circumstances. They called this lagged adaptation. In other words, men who are brought up in more equal homes as children and who live as adults with women who demand equality learn to share domestic tasks.

Other studies – from a range of societies – have concluded less optimistically on moves towards more gender equity in domestic work. Women are identified routinely as the dominant doers of housework, even when they are themselves in jobs. Examples include quantitative research by Ragni Hege Kitterød and Silje Vatne Pettersen (2006) on female full-time workers in Norway; Lyn Craig's (2006) study of the impact of children on the work time of parents using the Australian Time Use Survey; and Janeen Baxter's numerous studies on Australia in a cross-national context. Some studies have shown that men still shun the most routine and mundane of domestic jobs like cleaning the toilet in favour of the more intermittent, 'high impact' tasks like decorating. Sociologists have also pointed out that it is important to consider not just who 'does' the domestic work but who takes ultimate responsibility for it too: who identifies what work needs doing, who allocates it and makes sure that the work is completed and to the correct standard. The majority of studies stress that this role still falls to women. Accordingly, in Arlie Russell Hochschild's qualitative research based on analysis of interview and observational data from fifty couples in the USA, published in *The Second Shift*, she talks about the lack of a revolution in gender work roles for men. She cites instead a 'stalled revolution' in which 'women have gone to work, but the workplace, the culture, and most of all, the men, have not adjusted themselves to this new reality' (1989: 235).

Notwithstanding the different interpretations that have emerged from research into change over time in the gendering of domestic work, all studies report that women still dominate housework. Even those writers who have identified changes acknowledge that they have been slow and slight (Sullivan 2004). It is interesting to note here that some of the differences emerging from the studies are likely to be because researchers are using different definitions of housework, and taking different methodological approaches, as Alan Warde and Kevin Hetherington (1993) point out. For example, Sullivan, Gershuny and colleagues (above) analyse time-use diaries focusing on time spent by women and men on core domestic work like cleaning and cooking. Other writers, using interpretive methodologies, have suggested that the actual time spent on domestic tasks does not reflect people's experiences and perceptions of their domestic labour. Hochschild (1997) has proposed that since women's 'first shift' hours have increased in the labour market, their 'second shift' hours on housework *feel* more harried and segmented. And the rushing and stress that women have to do have led to the need for a 'third shift' of emotional labour to manage the negative emotions produced for the women and their families, increasing the amount of domestic work when it is defined more broadly like this.

We have been talking about the gendering of domestic work in this section, and there is now some debate as to whether child-care should be included within its definition. Feminist economist Susan Himmelweit (1995) argued that domestic tasks are 'work' only if they can be delegated to someone else, and since some child-care tasks are relational between parent and child and cannot be delegated, they should not be seen as work (see Gray 2006 too). Accordingly, some studies separate out child-care, and elder-care too, talking about 'domestic work and caring', for example. Of course, a range of tasks defined as child-care can be, and are, delegated to others, and so do come under our remit of 'work' in this book since they are delegated by parents to others, to use Himmelweit's definition. Such delegated tasks include feeding, washing, dressing and playing with children. Sociologists have asked whether such child-care work is as gendered as the other domestic tasks that we have considered so far. A range of studies, quantitative and qualitative, assert the dominance of mothers in the performance of child-care work. Of interest, as we saw above, an assortment of quantitative time use studies, from the UK, the USA, Australia and a variety of other countries, do suggest a growth in the time that fathers spend on child-care and some convergence between mothers and fathers (Bittman 2004; Fisher *et al.* 1999; Gauthier *et al.* 2004; Sayer *et al.* 2004). But other researchers have asked how or if time spent on work also translates into 'responsibility' for child-care, for organising as well as carrying out the work. Quantitative and qualitative studies in the UK by Warren (2003, 2007) report that far more mothers take the 'major responsibility' for child-care in their homes.

The gendering of domestic work is also fascinating because it raises absorbing questions about the relationship between people's attitudes and the work that they do. Men's involvement in caring for their dependent children is a useful example. In study after study, men's desire to be more involved with their children is reported. We are even accustomed to seeing these desires represented in media reportage of politicised fathers' groups demanding rights to access their children. The European survey 'Eurobarometer' shows that, across Europe, child-care is viewed as men's responsibility as well as women's (Fahey and Spéder 2004: 59–60). But there is substantial divergence between the high levels of support for men taking responsibility, and usual child-care practices, even in the most gender equal of societies (Björnberg 1998). Sociologists are asking why.

An interesting case study here is couples in which men have taken over as the main provider of caring and domestic work. So far there has been little research into men who are 'house-husbands', however, in large part because they are so rare, but Berit Brandth and Elin Kvande (1998) studied men in Norway who were taking parental leave to look after their children. The men interviewed were only a very small group (only 3.6 per cent of the sample), and so were atypical of Norwegian fathers, likely to be the 'most family-involved' men. All the men interviewed had good jobs and were high earners, and their female partners were occupationally successful and working full-time. Still, female-dominated housework persisted among these couples. Other than child-care, the men on parental leave did very little domestic work, with most just doing the same domestic tasks that they always had. And even in this context, the female partners were found to be careful not to make too many housework demands on the men. Many of the women were very grateful for the little that the men were doing. Arlie Russell Hochschild has suggested an 'economy of gratitude' to denote women's acceptance – and appreciation – of their partners' far less participation in housework.

This finding raises interesting questions concerning how women and men in couples assess their own and their partner's contributions to housework. Research shows that men commonly estimate that they do more housework than their wives estimate for them (Laurie and Gershuny 2000). Rather than trying to identify which partner is 'right' or 'wrong', sociologists of work are interested in exploring how such perceptions are formed and how they play out in households. It is fascinating too that women and men invariably feel that the way they share domestic work is 'fair'. Sociologists are asking how the feeling of fairness can be maintained in the face of such clear inequalities between women and men (Sullivan 2004).

The persistence of gendered domestic work and the belief still held by many that women are better suited to it, brings us back to ask why. Economists like Gary Becker (1985) argued for natural, rational explanations for gendered work roles (see Chapter 7), that it is more efficient for women and men to specialise in this way. Functionalist sociologists like Talcott Parsons also believed that specialised roles for women and men within the family grew from natural sex differences, and that these roles were functional for the continuity of society. More recently, Catherine Hakim (2000) has argued that most women make different life-style choices to men, reflecting gendered preferences concerning work roles. As Simon Duncan, with colleagues (1999, 2004), has argued, however, people's choices and decisions are not freely formed; they are shaped by gendered moral rationalities: 'moral and socially negotiated views about what behaviour is right and proper' (Duncan and Edwards 1999: 256).

Moving beyond gender

Gender has been the major social division explored in the sociology of domestic work but other divisions including class, 'race' and age are now informing our understanding of who carries out domestic work, and why. The sociological study of domestic work had its firm beginnings in 1970s feminist sociology that aimed to bring women's issues to the forefront. A main development in feminism itself since then has been the move towards intersectionality, as we outlined in Chapter 7. Accordingly, feminist sociology also began to look more to social inequalities among women too, rather than focusing only on comparing women with men. Looking to other social divisions, as well as gender, has augmented our understanding of the division of domestic work in two main ways. It has allowed sociologists to develop a better understanding of the intra-household division of domestic work, and it has facilitated the study of the provisioning of domestic work between households.

The intra-household division of domestic work

We saw earlier that Young and Willmott predicted more gender equality in domestic work among 'symmetrical families'. Their focus was on middle-class heterosexual couples and it is often believed to be middle-class dual-earner couples in which the 'new man' who shares domestic work equally with his partner lodges. But writers have suggested that high-income husbands are least likely to share in housework, especially when they are of much higher occupational status than their partners. The relationship between women and men's relative participation in the labour market and gender equality in who carries out the domestic work is an interesting one. Most research shows the dominance of female caring even when women and men in couples both work full-time in professional jobs (Brannen and Moss 1991), but it seems that women's higher earning power is associated with more equality in domestic work (Leonard 2001; Warren 2003). In economist Susan Harkness's (2005) quantitative analysis of trends in employment, work patterns and unpaid work since the 1970s in Britain, she shows that working mothers take responsibility for the majority of domestic tasks, but that when women earn as much or more than their male partners, more sharing occurs. Such inequalities in the performance of domestic work have been related to the persistence of gendered power imbalances between women and men in the home that, for many feminists, reflect men's patriarchal position within the family. Men's dominance in the home is built, in part, upon their superior economic power as the main if not the only breadwinner. Men who contribute most financially have been shown to retain the main control of a couple's income, taking the major decisions for the family too (see also the older studies by Edgell 1980; Pahl 1989).

When we move on to look at 'race' and the contemporary intra-household division of domestic work, it is useful to first refer readers back to our discussion of slavery in Chapters 5 and 7. Slaves counted as part of their owners' households and so, in this sense, their contribution to the domestic work of the owners' homes falls under our heading of 'intra-household' work. As we discussed then, while some women worked in the fields alongside men, the main role for many women was to clean, cook and wash for their owners as well as act as personal maids for the mistresses. Others were involved mainly in child-care, including acting as wet nurses for the babies of the home. Being based within or near the owners, they were expected to perform more intensive emotional labour since many slave owners expected affection and 'love' from all their slaves but from the house slaves in particular.

If we consider how domestic work is performed within the homes of families from different ethnic backgrounds in contemporary Britain, there is little research to draw upon unfortunately. Even the influential report of the *Fourth Survey of Ethnic Minorities* does not include domestic work. But it does show the proportions of women aged 16–59 who were looking after a house or family full-time. As Figure 10.1 shows, it was the vast majority of Bangladeshi women, and then Pakistani women behind them, but very few Caribbean women (who were mostly in full-time paid work). For

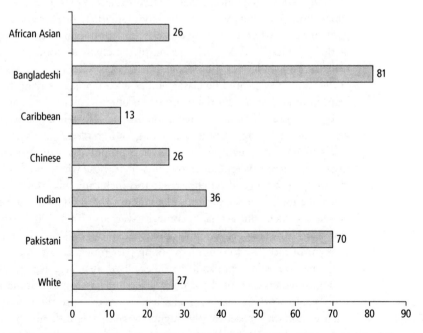

Figure 10.1 Proportion of women aged 16–59 (excluding FT students) in full-time house or family work
Source: Derived from Modood *et al.* (1997), Table 4.1, p. 86.

Bangladeshi and Pakistani women, the older cohorts in particular, caring and domestic work are their primary roles. Brah's (1994) qualitative study adds depth to this glimpse into their lives because it shows too how living in large families and in poverty with few domestic appliances and less access to hot water means very intensive domestic work for the women. The experience of domestic work is far from universal for women from different ethnic groups, even just in Britain.

The inter-household division of domestic work

Class and 'race', alongside gender, are also invaluable in the contemporary sociological analysis of the supply of and demand for domestic work between households. Class divisions here are not a new issue of course since, as Oakley (1974) noted, while the full-time homemaker role was part of the Victorian ideal for women, middle-class housewives did not actually clean, cook, and so on, rather they managed its performance by working-class women. Of course, the intra-/inter-household division of work was complicated since some domestic servants lived in their employers' homes, in servants' quarters. Live-in servants are less common today for middle class families, though they persist among the upper class, but contemporary analyses of class and domestic work still show that middle-class heterosexual couples, particularly those in which both members work in the labour market, often resolve their time-poor and work-heavy lives by outsourcing/contracting out/buying in some of their domestic work. The classing of the chain of domestic provisioning between households is plain. Geographers Nicky Gregson and Michelle Lowe (1994) interviewed middle-class couples who reported paying for domestic help, finding that substantial proportions employed cleaners, nannies and/or gardeners. Judy Wajcman's (1998) managers also relied on paid domestic workers for cleaning, ironing, gardening and child-care as well as buying in meals to 'get by'. Jonathon Gershuny has proposed a 'new service economy' to explain these developments, one in which those who can afford it increasingly rely on a range of purchased services including increasing shop opening times, the use of 'service washes' at laundrettes and mobile cleaning companies, as well as garden contractors. In contrast, Warren's (2003, 2007) research shows that working-class couples rely predominantly on each other, with the woman, in the UK, commonly working part-time at most to ensure she can cover her domestic responsibilities especially if they have dependent children.

The re-emergence of the domestic servant has inspired some fascinating studies into working-class women's lives since they are the workers carrying out the domestic tasks for the higher waged. It is difficult to find reliable figures on how many homes employ domestic workers and how many people undertake domestic work as much of it is informal 'cash in hand' work, but we do know that domestic workers tend to be women with very restricted opportunities for employment. British sociologist Bridget Anderson's *Doing the Dirty Work?* (2000) identifies the gendered and classed as well as 'racial' dimensions of who does dirty work and for whom, and Barbara Ehrenreich makes similar arguments from the USA. Both locate the study of domestic work firmly within an analysis of power relations:

> To make a mess that another person will have to deal with – the dropped socks, the toothpaste sprayed on the bathroom mirror, the dirty dishes left from a late-night snack – is to exert domination in one of its more silent and intimate forms. One person's arrogance – or indifference, or hurry – becomes another person's occasion for toil.
>
> (Ehrenreich 2002: 88)

As we saw in Chapter 7, Anderson has also argued persuasively that domestic workers are not just carrying out the work that the (woman of the) household would be doing in any case. Reflecting their lack of power and authority, and that households use domestic workers to create a certain life-style, the workers routinely perform tasks that no-one would do, given the choice.

Barbara Ehrenreich spent a short time working for 'The Maids' cleaning service. Her work experiences here, though only lasting three weeks, are fascinating because they also show how cleaning services are transforming the home into a 'fully capitalist style workplace' (2002: 96) for domestic workers. As she describes her typical working day, Ehrenreich points out the remarkable similarities between her job cleaning private homes and factory work including its restricted breaks, intensive work days and even the threat of CCTV or tape recorder surveillance:

> But what makes the work most factory-like is the intense Taylorization imposed by the companies . . . In the Maids' 'healthy-touch' system . . . all cleaning is divided into four task areas – dusting, vacuuming, kitchens and bathrooms – which are in turn divided among the team members. For each task area other than vacuuming, there is a bucket containing rags and the appropriate cleaning fluids, so the biggest decision an employee has to make is which fluid and scrubbing instrument . . . to deploy on which kind of surface; almost everything else has been choreographed in advance. When vacuuming, you begin with the master bedroom; when dusting, with the first room off the kitchen, then you move through the rooms going left to right. When entering each room, you proceed from left to right and top to bottom, and the same with each surface – left to right and top to bottom. Deviations are subject to rebuke, as I discovered when a team leader caught me moving my arm from right to left, and then left to right, while wiping Windex over a French door.
>
> (ibid.: 97)

The growth in the proportion of parents paying for child-care has also inspired interest from sociologists, who have identified how social divisions impact on who purchases child-care and on who provides it. The purchasers are invariably middle-class women who are themselves in employment. Working-class couples rarely use formal child-care, depending instead on family and friends, shift working, and shift parenting. In a qualitative study of how dualearner working-class parents managed their child-care in the UK, Warren *et al.* (2007) found some extremely complicated child-care arrangements. Mothers tended to work during the evenings and at weekends, and patchworked their care arrangements around intricate combinations of paid, formal care; family members, with complementary child-care frequently supplied by grandparents (themselves often in paid work); part-time preschool or nursery combined with some child-care from friends; and 'tagteam' parenting where couples worked 'opposite' hours to fit around child-care.

An absorbing development in the study of the provisioning of domestic work is its expansion to also consider the domestic work of the workers who are providing the domestic work for other families. The study of domestic workers and child-care providers also offers a fascinating insight into the realities of a globalisation of work, that we discussed in Chapter 6. In 'Love and Gold', Arlie Russell Hochschild demonstrates the resonance of global care chains via the story of the Bautista family from a farming village in the Philippines. The mother Rowena works in the USA as a nanny. For this, she receives the same pay that a small-town doctor would receive in the Philippines. The father is no longer involved with the family. Rowena's own children live:

> in a four-bedroom house with her parents and twelve other family members – eight of them children, some of whom also have mothers who work abroad. The central figure in the children's lives – the person they call 'Mama' – is Grandma, Rowena's mother. But Grandma works surprisingly long hours as a teacher – from 7.00 am to 9.00 pm . . . So, she [Rowena] has hired Anna de la Cruz, who arrives daily at 8.00 am to cook, clean and care for the children. Meanwhile Anna de la Cruz leaves her teenage son in the care of her eighty-year-old mother-in-law.
>
> (Hochschild 2002: 16–17)

For Hochschild, Rowena's life reflects a global trend towards the importation of care work from poor countries to rich ones in which the poor countries experience a care (as opposed to brain) drain.

Other social divisions

We have looked at how vital it is to incorporate gender, class and 'race' in the study of domestic work. But other social divisions have begun to enter the study too. For example, Gillian Dunne's work into how lesbian couples share domestic and other forms of work is revealing. In a project that drew upon the experiences of thirty-seven lesbian couples as well as on larger quantitative surveys on time use and on domestic work, Dunne (1992, 1998) was interested in the work time patterns of the women and in how children had impacted upon the paid and unpaid working of the birth mothers and co-parents. She asked whether domestic work is more equally shared than within heterosexual couples. Examining core routine domestic tasks like washing-up, ironing and bathroom cleaning, Dunne found high levels of negotiation around domestic work among the women and little evidence of one partner shouldering the bulk of all the tasks:

> Lesbian partners have greater flexibility in negotiating divisions of labour for a number of reasons. They occupy a similar position on the gender hierarchy, and share comparable gender ideologies and experience. Therefore the logic underpinning specialisation in heterosexual relationships cannot automatically make sense. This, together with their placement outside conventionality encourages reflexivity. Their discussions about work in interviews almost always indicated a holistic conceptualisation that made little distinction between the values, pleasures and obligations flowing from both 'workplaces'. This encourages the construction of more balanced approaches to paid employment and homelife, which do not necessarily link a primary domestic and caring role with biological motherhood.
>
> (Dunne 1998: 292)

Sociology has also seen an emerging interest in age divisions in the provisioning of domestic work. Bridget Anderson's *Doing the Dirty Work?* showed how domestic work is regarded as suitable employment for young girls. For Anderson, globally it is one of the most common forms of intensive and exploitative migrant child labour. In Europe, it is most likely to involve young women in the 'au pair' system. In the UK, unmarried persons between 17 and 27 can enter as au pairs from certain countries. At the time of her study, au pairs were supposed to help the family for no more than five hours a day, with two free days a week, and the Home Office suggested £35 a week pocket money. All the au pairs Anderson interviewed were working full days, permanently on call, and often subjected to sexual harassment. Young people and children are an emerging interest in others aspects of the sociology of domestic work too, with researchers exploring the performance and attitude to housework by young people of different ages, and also how they view the housework that their parents perform. The number of studies is limited currently but UK research by Julia Brannen has shown that the range of jobs performed expands as girls and boys grow older and are deemed more responsible, but girls spend more time on housework than boys and they do different and largely gender-differentiated jobs (Brannen 1995; Brannen *et al.* 2000). Even in more gender-equal Sweden, Marie Evertsson's (2006) analysis of the 'Swedish Child Level of Living Survey' showed the persistence of a gendering of children's housework.

Linking work in the public and private spheres

We end this chapter by returning to the crucial ways in which the study of domestic work has highlighted the artificial separation of public and private spheres. Sociologists have continued to demonstrate how the tasks that women undertake in the home contribute to their male partners' employment. Christine Delphy and Diane Leonard (1992) went on to differentiate between the direct and indirect contributions that women make to their partners' jobs. They might work directly alongside the man as a secretary, doing the books, working in a family business. We know that many Black and Asian women are involved closely in the businesses of their self-employed husbands, for example. But the women might offer hospitality and dinners, as well as 'backup work' like taking messages, and 'peripheral work' like remembering the names of clients. Women also provide moral support or emotional labour for men: carrying out work on their relationship, observing and moderating their partner's emotions, arranging his relaxation, supplying his personal needs, offering trouble-free sex, making a house a home, and maintaining contact with extended family. This is all in addition to doing – or managing the doing of – domestic work.

In Judy Wacjman's *Managing Like a Man* (1998), she argues that the whole idea of the worker – especially one high in the employment hierarchy – is underpinned by the marriage contract in which women offer free labour to men in return for financial support. In high-level jobs, a 'corporate wife' is assumed. In her sample of male and female managers, the majority of men had a corporate wife but the majority of women did not. That is, 40 per cent of the male managers had wives who were full-time housewives and 31 per cent had wives who worked part-time, while 88 per cent of the partners of the female managers were employed full-time. Since women managers could not offer a corporate wife to their employer, they were at a double disadvantage: they offered fewer 'total' hours than men and had to expend energy on – or organising for someone to do – their own domestic work. So while men are seen to bring two people to work, themselves and their corporate wife, women are bringing less than one.

Reflecting Pahl's stress on the linkages between all types of work, Miriam Glucksmann (2006), in her development of the *The total social organization of labour*, (TSOL), aims to provide an examination of the interconnections between different kinds of work activities, including paid work, informal and formal work and domestic labour, as well as different temporalities and spatialities of work and place. She argues, as do we in this book, that accepting the fundamental linkages between all forms of work is the only way to reach a full understanding of who does what work, why and with what consequences. Cockburn and Ormrod's *Gender and Technology in the Making* (1993) is a nice illustration of an attempt to combine an analysis of domestic and paid work spheres through the study of the microwave oven. In the book the authors study the way this one piece of technology is conceptualised, designed, built, transported, purchased and used. In doing so they examine in minute detail the gendered division of labour created in its construction and in its use.

The necessary linkages between work performed in the public and the private spheres have also been picked up by contemporary writers aiming to facilitate a cross-national comparison of variation, and similarities, in how breadwinning work and caring work are arranged. A range of models have been conceptualised, identifying the most and least gender-equal arrangements of the division of labour. At one extreme is the most gender-differentiated of possible arrangements in which the man is the sole worker and the woman the sole carer. This has been termed a family wage ideal by Nancy Fraser in the USA (1997), a housewife gender contract by Yvonne Hirdmann in Sweden (1998), a strong male-breadwinner régime by Jane Lewis in the UK (1992), and a male breadwinner/female carer gender arrangement by Birgit Pfau-Effinger (1998). Nancy Fraser (1997) has categorised a range of alternatives and considered their potential for gender equity (see Text box 10.3).

TEXT BOX 10.3 NANCY FRASER'S ALTERNATIVES TO THE FAMILY-WAGED MODEL

1 *The universal-worker model.* Women and men enter the labour market to the same extent. Caring work is provided by the state or the market. Problems: accepts and builds on a male norm in which labour market work is full-time in 'standard' employment, and caring work is provided by someone else.

2 *The caregiver parity arrangement.* Caring work remains in the home but it is valued and rewarded. Problem: caring still tends to be female-dominated and gender-differentiated work roles persist.

3 *The universal-caregiver model.* Balances caring and working, without over-prioritising either, and is not based on starkly gender differentiated tasks. Women and men engage equally in both paid and primary caring work.

While many countries remain close to the family wage/male breadwinner ideal, it is true to say that no one country has yet met the characteristics of the universal-caregiver model in full, although the Nordic countries are by far the closest (even here though, Warren (2001) shows how there are variations by class and 'race' in the extent to which different families 'fit' the societal model). Accordingly, the Nordic countries have received a wealth of attention from sociologists and other academics, as well as from policy-makers and campaigning groups, who have all tried to identify what is particular about, say, the Swedish model, and to consider whether any of its successes in the gender division of labour could be transferred to other less gender-equal societies.

Finally, the long tradition of home working, or carrying out paid work within the home, reveals further how inaccurate the separate spheres narrative has been. Recent qualitative (Phizacklea and Wolkowitz 1995) and mixed methods studies (Felstead and Jewson 2000) add to older evidence (Hakim 1987; Pahl 1984) to help assert the importance and persistence of home-working.

CONCLUSION

This chapter has examined how sociology approaches domestic work. After overcoming its initial reluctance to see domestic work as worthy of sociological attention, the discipline has been enhanced in many ways by its examination. First, a selection of fascinating and innovative studies has resulted into how domestic work is organised and experienced, and how the social divisions of class, gender and 'race' feature fundamentally in this. But the study of domestic work has also deepened the sociological understanding of how 'work' should be defined in a broader sense. Finally, paying more serious attention to domestic work has helped sociologists consider how all forms of work, within and outside the home, waged and unwaged, are inextricably linked.

FURTHER READING

Ann Oakley's *The Sociology of Housework* (1974) remains a classic text.

Barbara Ehrenreich and Arlie Hochschild's *Global Women: Nannies, Maids and Sex Workers in the New Economy* (2002) is a valuable edited collection exploring class, gender and 'race' within a global analysis.

Bridget Anderson's *Doing the Dirty Work?* (2000) also examines the intersections of class, gender and 'race' in who does the dirty work for whom.

Nicky Gregson and Michelle Lowe's *Servicing the Middle Classes: Class, Gender and Waged Domestic Labour in Contemporary Britain* (1994) brought in a class dimension to the outsourcing of domestic work.

Oriel Sullivan's article 'Time waits for no (wo)man: an investigation of the gendered experience of domestic time' (1997) is a sophisticated quantitative analysis of who spends what time on domestic work.

WEB SOURCE

The Women's Library in London has a large and important collection of material on the domestic division of labour:

http://www.londonmet.ac.uk/thewomenslibrary/

STUDENT PROJECTS AND ESSAY QUESTIONS

1 How has the distinction between work and home served to naturalise domestic work, with what implications?
2 How does an understanding of intersecting social divisions shape how we view domestic work?
3 How would you go about carrying out a project into who undertakes domestic work in households? Would you focus on a certain household type? Who within the household would you research, and how?
4 How would you carry out research into the working lives of paid domestic workers?

Unemployment and Work

▌ OVERVIEW

This chapter will:

- Look at why we need to examine questions of unemployment.
- Consider what the lack of paid work tell us about employment.
- Show how sociologists have tried to understand the absence of work in the past and in contemporary society.
- Ask what sociologists borrow and learn from other disciplines that examine this area.

▌ INTRODUCTION

In this chapter we want to examine the theme of unemployment. It may seem strange to focus on this issue in a book about work, but what we want to argue is that the relationship between work and non-work is a complex and interesting one. To fully understand the one, we have to have a deep understanding of the other. We want to argue that in studying unemployment, we can tap into some of the most important themes in this book, including what work means to people, and how (and if) they form their identity around work and employment. We can see too the way inequalities within the workplace are reflected in the treatment of those without work. We also want to explore what is sociologically important about unemployment. What is distinct about the way sociologists model and explain the absence of work, and how and in what ways do they borrow from other disciplines such as economics, social policy and psychology?

THE SOCIOLOGICAL MISSION

Often textbooks in the field of the sociology of work have rather neglected unemployment. In similar ways to debates about domestic work that we examined previously, unemployment has been viewed as the negative other to the state of paid work. It therefore occupies a difficult space within the sub-discipline. This is not to say that unemployment has been ignored within sociology. On the contrary, there has been a long tradition of interest in the area going back to the classical period of sociology. The first sociologists were interested in the changes wrought by industrial society, and unemployment was a key feature of this. But in tracing the sociological interest in unemployment, we want to suggest that the split between work and non-work has often been a damaging one. We also want to show the potential for both quantitative and qualitative methods in looking at this theme. By deploying quantitative approaches, we can build a picture of long-term trends, of the extent of problems, of the way certain groups in society are more exposed to the threat of unemployment than others, of movements into and out of unemployment, and also of people's views on work and its absence. In using qualitative research, we can gain a more in-depth understanding of the experiences and meaning of unemployment – and work – for people.

FOUNDATIONS

The founding father who feeds most directly into the sociology of unemployment is Karl Marx, in particular via his and Engels' consideration of the reserve army of labour and of the *lumpenproletariat*. They suggested that capitalism depended upon a reserve army of labour, which consisted of the unemployed and irregularly employed, that it could draw upon in times of boom and lay-off in slumps. The reserve army was also functional for capitalism as it controlled those who were in work, by reducing the power of their resistance and by forcing them to overwork for fear of losing their job. It kept wage levels in check too, curtailing the influences of worker campaigns for wage increases. Marx and Engels also coined the term 'lumpenproletariat' to describe a class separate from and below the working class. The group consisted of the long-term habitual unemployed, and of people who operated largely outside the formal economy (beggars, prostitutes and thieves): those without class consciousness – the rabble proletariat – labelled by Marx and

Engels the dangerous class, the social scum, the mob, the refuse of all classes (in *The German Ideology* 1845, and later works).

Emile Durkheim's interest in unemployment was focused very much on its potential consequences for the weakening of social ties. His concern with social order saw that unemployment disrupted a person's social integration, potentially leading to loss of norms and to suicide. The links between unemployment and suicide have generated a wealth of research in such disciplines as psychology and psychiatry, while sociologists have been interested in the broader impact of unemployment on a person's social belonging, including aspects of their health.

Weber's theorisation of the Protestant work ethic is his most important contribution to the later sociological studies of unemployment. It has influenced our understanding of the attitudes to work held by the unemployed and opinions about those who are unemployed too. Researchers have asked whether the unemployed hold a qualitatively different work attitude to people with jobs. The idea that the unemployed might be idle and work-shy, lacking a commitment to a work ethic, is a highly debated and contentious argument within sociology, as we will see in this chapter.

LATER DEVELOPMENTS

A range of disciplines in addition to sociology study unemployment. Economics, history and social policy have all played a significant part in the debates over how unemployment should be understood: over its causes, over whether it plays a function in society, over whether governments should try to reduce or control its level. In sociology, while sociologists have had a great deal to say about unemployment, its place within the sociology of work has been problematic as, by implication, lack of work is opposite to work. Thus the consideration of the absence of work occupies a broader approach, linking to other parts of sociology as well as allied and quite separate disciplines. This is particularly apparent in the post-war expansion of work sociology where what was studied were often problems of productivity or affluence (see Brown 1992).

The idle unemployed?

The broad understanding of unemployment in the nineteenth century was that it was the result of idleness or the moral failure of those without jobs. Even social reformer Charles Booth – who was carrying out pioneering work into poverty and working-class life – said in 1902 that the unemployed were a 'selection of the unfit' (in Ashton 1986: 29). The governmental approach to dealing with the unemployed in the nineteenth century reflected this viewpoint. Poverty relief mechanisms were set up by the New Poor Law of

1834 to force the unemployed to help themselves and to find work. Workhouses were made available but the conditions in them were made very harsh to ensure that they were not seen as an easy option for the idle unemployed. Gareth Stedman-Jones' *Outcast London* (1971) provides a wonderfully detailed historical account of employment, underemployment and joblessness in the Victorian labour market in London. He shows the power of the London economy to pull in massive population flows and the process by which many people experienced insecurity caused by the fluctuation of the market and the seasonality of demand.

Unemployment as a social problem

Around the start of the twentieth century, unemployment began to be viewed as a problem that required more substantial intervention, whether in terms of better supporting those without work or the attempt to regulate levels of joblessness. This period saw the development of a linked social policy and economics of unemployment. The dominant British policy view to emerge was influenced by social reformer and economist William Beveridge (whose later *Social Insurance and Allied Services* (1942) report was to act as the foundation for the development of the British welfare state). His view was that policy should be developed to reduce the sufferings experienced by the unemployed. Meanwhile, economists were concerned with developing theories to explain and potentially control levels and types of unemployment. Models of labour market supply and demand, and of the business cycle were developed. So-called 'supply side' theories focused on the characteristics of the unemployed to explain why they were not in jobs, while 'demand'-focused explanations looked at how the need for workers varied, perhaps as a result of fluctuations in the business cycle. The dominant economic view of unemployment after the wars in Britain was Keynesian. Here unemployment was not seen to be part of the normal functioning of the economy, as earlier classical economists had suggested, but a result of deficiencies in the operation of the market. Accordingly, the state could intervene to maintain full employment, if it so wished. The Keynesian and Beveridge post-war contract thus incorporated a commitment to full (male) employment and social support for the unemployed.

Flexibility and unemployment

After decades of relatively low levels of unemployment after the war, in the 1970s the UK and the USA were hit by poor performing economies and high inflation. Both countries also saw a growing dominance of belief in the importance of monetarism and of market forces. The associated policy approach was that the state had – or should have – no control over the level of unemployment. The 1980s saw very high levels of unemployment in the UK, Western Europe as well as in the USA, and these were escalated by deindustrialisation (see Chapter 6).

It was these high levels of unemployment that stimulated the real growth in the sociology of unemployment. A wealth of studies into the consequences of unemployment were to emerge, and these fed into a social policy literature concerned with alleviating the problems being faced by the unemployed and by communities impacted by mass unemployment. Before moving on to consider these, we recap briefly on the new dominant economic approach. The neo-liberal agenda in British politics in the 1980s saw unemployment as a supply-side issue. Influential British economists made recommendations to reduce levels of unemployment by limiting benefits and boosting the employability of the unemployed. In 1985, for example, Patrick Minford argued that too generous an unemployment benefit system distorts the natural operation of the labour market, pushes up wages to too high a level, and thus escalates unemployment. Wages were also seen to be pushed above their 'natural' level because it was felt that workers via strong trade unions had too much power. Two decades later, economist Richard Layard was similarly to make recommendations to reduce levels of unemployment via limiting the duration of eligibility for benefits, by strengthening tests for job searching among the unemployed, and via pursuing so-called active labour market policies to boost employability among the unemployed (Layard *et al.* 2005). The policy solution arising from this theoretical economic approach was to keep in check the welfare state. A parallel neo-liberal solution to promoting the smoother and more 'natural' functioning of the market was to reduce labour market rigidities by encouraging businesses to provide more diversity in the job market by expanding flexible work in temporary, casual and part-time employment (see Chapter 6).

The impact of unemployment

One of the main interests for the sociology of work has been the social impact of unemployment. What are the effects of unemployment on the unemployed person?; and how does their unemployment impact on their family and the community in which they live? Sociologists have also explored the effects of high levels of unemployment on those still in jobs, and on wider society too.

Unemployment and the individual

While there is substantial variation in reactions to the experience of being unemployed, many studies have confirmed its devastating impact on the individual. Social psychologists Marie Jahoda, Paul Lazarsfeld and Hans Zeisel's classic study of unemployment in Marienthal, a small town in Austria, in 1930, developed a range of topics that would emerge in many later accounts of unemployment (Jahoda *et al.* 1971). The closure of the small town's only factory had resulted in unemployment for the majority of households, and Jahoda and her colleagues carried out in-depth research looking at the experiences of mass unemployment for the unemployed, and their responses to unemployment. Published in English in 1982, Jahoda *et al.*'s study became particularly well known for examining what people gain from work, aside from income. The researchers identified that work gives a time structure, provides social relations beyond the family and neighbours, gives a sense of purpose and achievement as well as social status, clarifies personal identity and gives regular activity. For Jahoda, 'work is . . . the very essence of being alive' (1982: 8).

A range of classic British studies in the 1970s and 1980s such as *Workless* by Dennis Marsden (1982), Adrian Sinfield's *What Unemployment Means* (1981), as well as John Westergaard *et al.*'s *After Redundancy* (1989), provided valuable qualitative material on the lives of the unemployed. The focus in these accounts was largely on unemployed men, and the studies covered a broad range of topics including the men's memories of the work that they had lost, how they had looked for or were now looking for work; and the impact of job loss on their identity. A varied selection of topics was also covered in the edited collections by Stephen Fineman (1987) and Sheila Allen *et al.* (1986) which include a focus on the experiences of men and women as well as the family unit and community (see below. Also see Seabrook 1982). From these studies, we review briefly finances, time and health.

Financial

The financial costs of unemployment: growing poverty, loss of savings and mounting debt emerged from these fascinating and often desperately sad sociological accounts. Reductions in income also impact negatively on the other aspects of unemployed people's lives including their time use, mental and physical health, and social lives. Basically, the studies revealed how having less income makes lives harder in many and interlinking ways.

Time

Marie Jahoda suggested that key functions of paid work included providing a temporal structure to the day, week and year, as well as regular activities. Without work setting the correct times to do things, many of the unemployed in Marienthal felt disorientated (see Chapter 9 on time too). Some used strategies to improve the temporal structure of their day, like dedicating themselves to housework tasks. Because of this, and their low participation in housework, it was working-class men who had the most problems with the temporal structure of unemployment. Studies since have reiterated that men's inactivity is often very high when they are unemployed, they sleep in, watch telly, and spend little of this free time socialising, compounded by financial insecurity.

Health

The study of unemployment has shown a close association between being unemployed and having poor health. Anxiety, lack of morale, problems with sleeping, eating problems, depression are all recounted in the ethnographies, while quantitative research has demonstrated strong correlations between employment status and a range of indicators of poor health. Social psychologists have led the way in exploring the impact of unemployment on aspects of mental health, largely through quantitative studies. For Warr and colleagues, for example (Warr 1983; Warr and Jackson 1985), unemployment is associated with high levels of distress, low psychological health, anxiety, depression, low self-esteem and self-confidence. Sociological studies, from Durkheim onwards, have also revealed the negative impact of unemployment on mental health.

Multiple impacts

A range of negative effects of unemployment on the unemployed person have been identified. They face a reduction in the decision-making in the lives; they have less say over their life-styles and are less able to consider making major purchases. They have suffered a major loss of prestige and might well be being treated like second-class citizens. They might be facing constant rejections from job applications. They invariably feel insecure about their future and that of their families. Such is the level of unemployment-related multiple disadvantage that many political and policy debates moved on from an early focus on poverty and onto the 'social exclusion' experienced by unemployed people and unemployed communities (Byrne 1999; Social Exclusion Unit 2006). One of the largest interdisciplinary studies of unemployment, and employment, in Britain was carried out under the Social Change and Economic Life Initiative in the 1980s. A collection of papers on the experience of unemployment were collated by sociologists Duncan Gallie, Catherine Marsh and Carolyn Vogler (1994). The team's conclusion was that unemployment should be seen as an extreme case of labour market insecurity. This feeds well into the approach that we are advocating in this chapter, that unemployment should be integral to the sociology of work and employment.

Unemployment, family and community

These studies of unemployment also revealed its impact on family and wider communities (e.g. Westergaard *et al.*'s (1989) analysis of ex-Sheffield steel workers in 1979; David Clark's (1987) research into redundancies in South London; Harris' (1987) study of South Wales). (See also Coffield *et al.* 1986; Jenkins and Sherman 1979; Jordan 1982; Seabrook 1982.) An area of real interest to sociologists studying the impact of mass unemployment was the closure of mines in Britain in the 1980s (Bennett *et al.* 2000). Mining communities have been termed 'occupational communities' because one occupation, and often one employer, so fully dominated the local area, providing jobs for the bulk of the male working-class population (see Dennis *et al.* 1956). Seen as archetypal working-class communities, the changing experiences of those living in the (former) mining communities stimulated some rich ethnographic accounts in the sociology of work. For Martin Bulmer:

> The social ties of work, leisure, neighbourhood and friendship overlap to form close-knit and interlocking locally based collectivises of actors. The solidarity of the community is strengthened . . . by a shared history of living and working in one place over a long period of time.
>
> (1975: 87–8)

In the USA, the advent of deindustrialisation during the 1970s was marked by the influential publication of Bluestone and Harrison's *The Deindustrialisation of America* (1982). While neither of the authors was a sociologist, Bluestone was an economist and Harrison an urban studies scholar, they nonetheless put the social consequences of plant closure at the heart of their analysis and has provided a model which many others working in the field have orientated themselves around (see Cowie and Heathcott 2003). Many of the sociological accounts also demonstrated how it was not only the unemployed men whose lives were impacted by unemployment, but that partners and children experienced problems too. Moving from a focus on the individual showed, for example, that unemployment runs in households. Joan Payne (1987) discussed how if the 'head' was unemployed, then commonly so were the partner and any adult children.

A family-level analysis also raised issues of gender work relations within the home. Sheila Allen *et al.* (1986) demonstrate how sociology had only really problematised the unemployment of adult men, and that women's own experiences of unemployment were rarely being explored. Women's roles in unemployed households and communities were a more researched topic, however. The review by Gallie and Marsh (1994) identifies how the sociological study of the wives of unemployed men focused on examining the division of domestic work; stress and friction between couples; and women's leisure and networks. We looked at domestic work in detail in the previous chapter. There we showed that studies by Pahl (1984) and by Wheelock (1990) reported few changes in the domestic division of labour when men became unemployed, with only small if any increases in men's contribution to housework. Gallie and colleagues (1994) did find some shifting of tasks but they suggested that any changes were more strongly linked to women's rather than men's employment status: if the women were employed, then men increased their participation somewhat more.

What we touched on in the previous chapter too is how male unemployment might increase women's domestic burden. Women's role in managing household money thus intensifies on male unemployment, women having to work extra hard to make ends meet. Studies like those by Susan Hutson and Richard Jenkins (1989) showed that the family strain of male unemployment fell largely onto women. Women were found to restrict their own personal spending, and more so than men. It was women who faced debts, arrears and bill juggling, hunted down bargains, made economical meals, refused treats to the children, and patched clothes. Many women aimed to protect men from these extra worries, since they were already anxious about loss of work. The impact on women's friendships was also negative: since men were at home, there was less chance for women to maintain their largely home-based social lives. Relationships between couples were also impacted by the pressures of financial need. If the women were full-time housewives, spending day-in day-out together created tensions. If women had jobs, then different tensions emerged from the stereotype of the kept man, seen as a failure by family and friends. Richard Berthoud (1979) recounts how one unemployed man who had been a manager could not face telling his wife he had lost his job, and travelled daily to London until his season train ticket expired.

Roderick Martin and Judith Wallace's (1984) research is one example where unemployed women were themselves examined (see Angela Coyle's *Redundant Women* (1984) too). They explored the impact of being unemployed on women, in particular on their social activities. They found that women filled their time by doing more home duties, including visiting family. As with men, their social contacts with friends declined especially those involving expenditure such as meals out. As with men, isolation resulted.

CONTEMPORARY ISSUES AND FUTURE TRENDS

Definitions

Before we look at more contemporary developments in the sociological study of unemployment, we begin by noting a growing debate over how best to define this key concept. Changes in the definitions used over the years and variation between societies both mean that comparing levels of and trends in unemployment is fraught with difficulty. Governmental approaches have tended to focus problematically on some version of a 'claimant unemployment' definition: those who are officially registered as looking for work (see Text box 11.1 for an example of the limitations with this). The International Labour Organisation (ILO) has formulated a more inclusive definition of unemployment, and it is this one that shapes much social research (see Text box 11.2). In general, then, sociologist Marsh (1988a) suggested that to be seen as 'unemployed' is not just to be without paid work, it is also that someone would participate in the formal economy if they could find work and were able to work. Unfortunately, even this broader definition of unemployment still ignores those people who have been so unsuccessful in finding a job, and for so long, that they have simply given up looking – the 'discouraged workers'. And it does not take into account those who are underemployed, who do not have enough work, as we see later in the chapter. Notwithstanding its definitional difficulties, the ILO approach shows that nearly 191.8 million people were unemployed around the world in 2005, translating into a world unemployment rate of 6.3 per cent (see Table 11.1).

TEXT BOX 11.1 OFFICIAL UNEMPLOYMENT STATISTICS

Edward Fieldhouse and Emma Hollywood's (1999) *Life After Mining* critiques official statistics on levels of unemployment in the British coalfields, arguing that they do not reflect the reality of job losses in the 1980s and 1990s. Many ex-miners had disappeared from unemployment statistics by being registered not as 'unemployed' but as early retired or permanently sick.

TEXT BOX 11.2 ILO DEFINITION OF UNEMPLOYMENT

10. (1) The 'unemployed' comprise all persons above a specified age who during the reference period were:
(a) 'without work';
(b) 'currently available for work', i.e. were available for paid employment or self-employment during the reference period;
and
(c) 'seeking work', i.e. had taken specific steps in a specified recent period to seek paid employment or self-employment.

(ILO 1982)

Table 11.1 Unemployment rates, 2005

Region	%
Middle East and North Africa	13.1
Sub-Saharan Africa	9.9
Central and Eastern Europe (non-EU) and CIS	9.5
Latin America and the Caribbean	7.4
Developed Economies and European Union	7.1
South-east Asia and the Pacific	6.2
South Asia	4.7
East Asia	3.7
World	6.3

Source: Taken from ILO (2006) January, Table 3.

Table 11.2 Proportion of long-term unemployed

	Germany	Sweden	Denmark	Neth	Belgium	France	UK	Ireland	Italy	Greece	Spain	Portugal
1995–97	36.7	18.4	20.5	36.2	46	29.5	30.5	44.4	48.9	40.9	39.8	39.8

Source: Taken from Gallie and Paugam (2000), Table 1.1.

The unequal distribution of unemployment

It is widely accepted that the burden of unemployment falls unequally on different social groups. Table 11.1 shows how levels of unemployment vary between countries, and Table 11.2 shows that the composition of the unemployed varies too. In Sweden and Denmark, for example, around 20 per cent of the unemployed were long-term unemployed in 1995–97, compared with 49 per cent in Italy and 46 per cent in Belgium. Studies in Britain show that those who have been identified as being hit most by unemployment include unskilled men, Pakistani and Bangladeshi men, lone mothers, people with disabilities, the list goes on. The risk of unemployment varies over the life-course too, with the young and old hit hardest, but again different groups are more at risk at different times in their lives. For the higher non-manual salariat, for example, the risk of unemployment is higher at the start of their working lives, and approaching retirement. For unskilled people, it is most severe during peak working ages. The rate of unemployment has also varied substantially across regions within Britain, reflecting the geographical dispersion of available jobs. While elements of old distinctions like the North–South divide have persisted in Britain, inequality within regions has grown over time according to the skill of workers, an urban/rural split, and so on. In this section, we look to the main social divisions of the book: class, gender and 'race' to highlight this issue of inequality.

Class and unemployment

An association between class and unemployment is central throughout the history of the sociology of unemployment, and it permeates much of this chapter. The level and experiences of unemployment vary by class. Quantitative research has shown clearly that the working classes are most hit by unemployment and by its long-term dimension too. Qualitative research has added to this picture by demonstrating the class variation in the experiences people report when unemployed. Higher-level occupations offer longer notices of redundancy and better packages for people who are being laid off, for example. The impact of unemployment on a person's identity has been found to vary according to class, with debate over whether financial security is more important than identity issues for the working-class unemployed. The classed impact at the individual level accumulates at the household level and numerous sociological and economic accounts have revealed the polarisation between work-rich and work-poor households, in which members of couples – and adult children too – either all do or do not have paid work (Gregg and Wadsworth 1996; Pahl 1984).

Perhaps the most highly contested class-based debate on unemployment in the 1990s was whether the unemployed, or parts of the unemployed, could be seen to have formed or be forming an underclass. Elements of the underclass debate hark back to Marx's lumpenproletariat, and draw on the historical notions of the idle unemployed that we discuss earlier: the scum, the non-respectable poor, the unruly and dangerous mob with an antipathy to the work ethic. Lydia Morris' (1994) *Dangerous Classes* discusses the origins of underclass ideas in Malthus's (1766–1834) notions of over-breeding among the lowest classes, and traces it to the campaigns by the Eugenics Movement to restrict its growth.

The idea of an underclass, a class below the working class, had emerged in British sociology in the 1960s in relation to minority ethnic workers. Minority ethnic workers had found that they were excluded from white trades unions and had to rely instead on their own community for support. The suggestion was that due to racism, the black working classes were forming a separate class with poorer occupational chances and living standards (Chapter 7). In the 1990s, the underclass debate moved more towards the effects of long-term unemployment on communities. Did the unemployed face such multiple deprivations that they were becoming a separate underclass apart from the working class?

This reworked underclass debate was influenced by the work of Charles Murray, an American writer who came to Britain at the invitation of *The Sunday Times* newspaper and the Institute of Economic Affairs, a right-wing think-tank. He had been studying the underclass in the inner cities of USA. Looking at Britain in the 1990s, Murray argued that too generous state benefits were encouraging members of the underclass not to work but to live off the state; that children (particularly those in lone mother households) were being brought up without working role models and were not being socialised into a work ethic. Murray's ideas attracted severe criticism from sociologists. He has been criticised methodologically for drawing on limited data, including his dependence on anecdotal evidence. But it is the 'blaming the victim' that lies at the heart of his thesis that has caused the most reaction.

We can summarise the dominant sociological interpretation of whether there is an underclass in contemporary Britain by saying that, yes, persistent unemployment exists and this is associated with cumulative disadvantage in terms of finances, health and housing, and so on, but the majority of the unemployed are work committed and are actively seeking work. Sociological studies using diverse methodologies, such as those of Duncan Gallie (1994), Lydia Morris (1994), Gary Pollock (1997), Rob Macdonald (1996), found little difference between the work attitudes of the unemployed and those in paid jobs. Furthermore, studies have shown that rather than celebrating joblessness, shame is a recurring theme in the narratives of the unemployed. In a large multi-methods study of long-term unemployment in the mid-1990s, Jochen Clasen and colleagues (1998) carried out interviews with unemployed people aged between 30 and 45 and their partners in three cities in Britain, Germany and Sweden. The men felt embarrassed in front of their children, and some children were clearly ashamed of having an unemployed dad:

I was ashamed. I couldn't buy them anything. We couldn't go to the cinema or to McDonald's. It wasn't easy for me to look the children in the eye.

(Unemployed man in Germany, Clasen *et al.* 1998: 140)

She actually makes things up, she feels embarrassed. When she's at school and she has to fill things in, what does your dad do and your mum, she writes things in. I can understand it. I obviously don't tell her off or anything but it brings a bit of a wry smile . . . I think if I was in her position I'd probably do the same thing . . . because you know what kids are like; 'your dad hasn't got a job' and 'you haven't got this and that'.

(Unemployed man in Britain, ibid.: 185)

Gender and unemployment

We saw earlier that the impact of male unemployment on female partners has been of interest to sociology. Recent research by Paul de Graaf and Wout Ultee (2000) shows how unemployment tends to come in couples. They show that this is true in all EU countries, partly because of regulations concerning claiming unemployment benefits that tend to restrict how much work and income women can bring to the home without reducing the man's benefit income, and partly because of the inability of women's lower wages to support a family. But also, and linked, it relates to the challenges 'employed female/unemployed male' present to ideologies of the gender division of labour and the family wage. The impact of unemployment for women and men is shaped by the social policy framework within a country and by the societal gender régime – including views about appropriate gender roles – that feed into this framework. Helen Russell and Paolo Barbieri (2000: 333) demonstrate that gender régimes influence women's own experiences of unemployment, and establish too whether the economic and subjective impact of unemployment is gendered, varying for women and men.

'Race' and unemployment

Sociological research into unemployment among different ethnic groups has been less prevalent, but what has been done reveals clearly that certain ethnic groups are hardest hit both by unemployment and long-term unemployment (see Chapter 7). Examining the extensive PSI surveys in Britain, Tariq Modood *et al.* (1997) discuss how men of Bangladeshi, Caribbean and Pakistani origin are over-represented in unemployment, while men from African Asian and Indian backgrounds have made significant gains over time into jobs and into higher levels of the occupational structure. The Fourth Survey of Ethnic Minorities revealed variation in the proportions of women unemployed too, with higher levels experienced by Bangladeshi and Pakistani as well as Caribbean women, increasing for those within each ethnic group who had fewest educational qualifications. Qualitative and quantitative research by Angela Dale and colleagues (2002a, 2002b) also demonstrated that even if they have higher-level qualifications, Pakistani and Bangladeshi women still have high levels of unemployment. Tracey Warren and Nadia Joanne Britton (2003), analysing the large Family Resources Survey, confirmed high levels of unemployment for Bangladeshis and Pakistanis, revealing a far higher dependence of Bangladeshi families on income from the state rather than paid work (Table 11.3. See also Commission on Multi-Ethnic Britain 2000; Karn 1997; Luthra 1997). Part of the reason for such high levels of unemployment for these ethnic groups is that they live in areas with high unemployment,

Table 11.3 Family income levels and sources by ethnic group

	Minority Ethnic	White	All	Minority Ethnic groups							
				Black-Caribbean	Black-African	Black-Other	Indian	Pakistani	Bangladeshi	Chinese	Other
a) Level of family income* (£s)	190.6	262.8	259.0	201.7	185.2	196.2	224.3	139.6	136.2	302.0	207.0
Working age families	199.2	314.1	307.3	217.0	184.3	193.6	247.1	140.5	135.7	312.0	213.4
b) Proportion of income of working age families coming from:											
Work	70	81	80	67	64	68	77	64	39	75	70
State	21	11	12	27	29	28	14	29	55	5	18
Occ. Pension	2	3	3	2	0	0	2	0	3	2	1
Investment	2	3	3	1	2	0	2	3	0	3	1
Other**	5	2	2	2	4	4	4	3	3	15	10
Number of families	1,513	29,614	31,127	314	137	54	376	179	73	70	310

Notes: * Gross equivalised weekly median of benefit units.
** Including student grants, income from odd jobs, maintenance from a former partner.
Source: Family Resources Survey, 1995/96, in Warren and Britton (2003).

inner cities, for example. But still, within each area, the Bangladeshis, Caribbeans and Pakistanis have been shown to fare worse:

> The rate of unemployment, then, is associated with a number of factors. Most of these factors, say, manual work, lack of qualifications and inner city location, are linked . . . However, the scale of impact varies between groups. For whites, African Asians and Indians the presence or absence of each adverse characteristic has a significant impact, but makes relatively little difference to the unemployment rates of Caribbeans, Pakistanis and Bangladeshis. Similarly, although each group experiences the impact of particular disadvantages, the most disadvantaged ethnic groups always have higher unemployment rates than the more advantaged groups, even where they have similar characteristics.
>
> (Modood *et al.* 1997: 97)

The severe labour market disadvantage faced by some minority ethnic groups in Britain stimulated accounts of the structural underclass thesis that identified immigrant minority ethnic workers as a separate class with poorer occupational chances and living standards, as we saw earlier. We outlined Murray's ideas on the underclass earlier. They did not hold much of a 'racial' dimension in the UK, but his account of the underclass in the USA in his *Losing Ground* (1984) had been heavily and problematically 'racialised'. In marked contrast, sociologist William Julius Wilson's interpretation of 'race' and the underclass in the USA, in *The Truly Disadvantaged* (1987), argued that an underclass did exist among the inner-city black unemployed but it was a structural underclass. How this differs from and is a vastly more sophisticated argument than the Murray account is that, for Wilson, the underclass is caused by the extreme levels of economic deprivation and spatial ghettoisation faced by inner city black residents. It is not caused by an over-generous welfare state that encourages a culture of worklessness among these groups.

The impact of unemployment on workers and society: insecurity and risk

Contemporary sociology has been concerned too with how unemployment affects the whole society, and not just those who are actually unemployed. This brings us back to our argument at beginning of this chapter that we need to examine unemployment alongside an analysis of work and employment. Sociologists, in theoretical and empirical-based accounts of insecurity, have considered the impact of unemployment on those who are in paid work. Many fear becoming unemployed themselves, with some groups of workers in precarious jobs living daily under a very real threat of unemployment. As an example, Tom Gill (2001) has written an ethnographic study of day labourers in Japan and focuses on how the group deal with uncertainty. Precarious jobs are concentrated in but not confined to working-class occupations. Indeed, Martin Roderick's (2006) research showed how uncertainty characterises the working lives of professional footballers.

That those in relatively secure jobs are affected by the fear of unemployment has stimulated interesting sociological debates (see Text box 11.3). Marx had argued that one of the effects of unemployment is to police workers: stopping them complaining about the conditions of their work and making workers stick close to the firm. Amid fears of the uncertainty inherent in job changes, in areas of high unemployment people might stay in jobs that they are unhappy with simply because they have a job. If people are accepting less satisfying and downgraded jobs then this means there is less room for those coming into the market. A Marxian analysis also highlights how the unemployed cause those in work to overwork to keep their jobs, and even to work to sustain the company if it is struggling.

TEXT BOX 11.3 A RISING FEAR OF UNEMPLOYMENT?

Kevin Doogan (2001) found that between 25 per cent and 50 per cent of workers in the late 1990s feared being made redundant. At this time the actual overall rate of redundancies in the UK was very low (0.7 per cent: 435). Doogan showed too a growth in the proportions of workers who were actually in long-term employment. How can we explain the apparent contradiction? An answer, for Doogan, lies in how fears about job insecurity are shaped. He cites highly selective reporting of job gains and losses in the media that fuelled fears over job insecurity in the UK.

For Brendan Burchell *et al.* (2002) we must also broaden the scope of our research if we are to better understand the relationship between feelings of job insecurity and the reality of job loss. Workers not only fear losing their jobs. They might fear loss of aspects of their jobs that they value such as promotion opportunities, usual pay increases and control over their hours, and these fears are all feeding into how they feel about the security of their jobs.

Sociological studies have demonstrated that high levels of unemployment have numerous wide-reaching consequences. Employers invest less in providing apprenticeships for young workers, with longer-term implications that include shortages of skilled manual trades people like bricklayers and plumbers (Brown 1997). With high levels of unemployment, employers can more readily pick and choose their workers, with implications for discrimination in recruitment on the grounds of 'race' and ethnicity, gender and age. Sarah Vickerstaff (2003) has shown problems for the youth-to-adult, or school-to-work, transition if jobs are not available for young people and they are forced to remain living at home, partially dependent on their families. High levels of unemployment are also associated with the production of a secondary labour market or informal economy, as we discuss later.

Underemployment

We have dedicated this chapter to unemployment but the very closely related issue of underemployment has also received attention from sociologists. Discussing it here is not to say that underemployment is a brand new issue, indeed, it is as long-standing as unemployment. For Marx, for example, the reserve army consisted of the irregularly employed as well as the unemployed. It is as important as unemployment too because underemployment provides us with a direct bridge between the study of paid work and of having no paid work at all. We discuss it here to stress that the sociology of work should be looking at all forms of work, how they interlink and how they relate to different gradations of a lack of work.

In simple terms, being underemployed means being in paid work but not having enough of it. This can be interpreted in numerous ways, however. It can include not having paid work that matches your skill level sufficiently. But the most widespread understanding of underemployment is as 'time-related underemployment' – or not working as many hours as you like or need. Since the 1980s, the ILO has been working to develop an internationally agreed understanding of underemployment that would facilitate comparisons across time and place. Its definition of time-related underemployment 'includes all persons in employment whose hours of work are insufficient in relation to an alternative employment situation in which the person is willing and available to engage' (ILO 2005). People who are underemployed, under this definition, might be working part-time involuntarily or might want to increase their hours in a full-time job. They might want an additional job too, or want a new job with more hours. Of course, there are also many workers who would like to reduce their hours and are overworking in long hours cultures (see Chapter 9).

One of the most important and highly debated topics in the sociology of underemployment is whether those working part-time hours take part-time jobs voluntarily or whether they would prefer to work more hours. Researchers of work time preferences have analysed the 1998 'Employment Options' survey (a representative survey of 30,000 people aged 16–64 in the 15 EU countries and Norway). Here, working hours of economically active individuals in Europe averaged 39. Harold Bielenski *et al.*'s (2002) analysis showed a preference for a 'new shorter working time norm', with 71 per cent of respondents preferring to work between 30 and 40 hours a week, including overtime. Colette Fagan (2001b) found that employed men preferred a working week of 37 hours, and employed women 30. Women and men particularly disliked very long and very short hours.

The issue of preferences, and what constrains our enactment of preferences, harks back to long-standing theoretical debates over the role of agency and structure in shaping social lives and the formation of society. How these theoretical issues play out in the topic of working hours has generated a remarkably impassioned debate among sociologists in Britain. At the centre of the debate are the threefold facts that the bulk of those in part-time jobs in Britain are women (usually with dependent children); that these part-time jobs are largely low waged and offer few benefits or opportunities; that, still, the female part-time employees express very high levels of satisfaction with their jobs and the hours that they work. How can we explain why so many women enter and seem to be satisfied with such objectively poor jobs in Britain?

In 1991, Catherine Hakim first proposed her idea of a heterogeneous female labour force in which it is 'home-centred' women who enter such part-time jobs. For Hakim, these are the women who prioritise home life over paid work, demonstrating an instrumental approach to their jobs and choosing to restrict their hours to part-time. She went on to develop a 'preference theory' (2000), arguing that preferences determine women's but not men's work–lifestyles in the UK, over-riding the influences on women's choices exerted by demographic, social, economic and institutional factors. A large number of sociologists, while recognising the importance of preferences and choices, emphasised instead that structural constraints on women's lives (including a lack of adequate and affordable child-care in Britain and gender ideologies on good mothering) shape the formation and enactment of work-life preferences (Crompton 2006; Duncan et al. 2004; Ginn et al. 1996). For Sally Walters (2005) and for Tracey Warren (2001) – who carried out qualitative interviews and analysis of large-scale survey data respectively to explore the topic of female part-timers' hours – it is important to remember that part-time employment for women in Britain invariably means short hours in manual jobs, and that these jobs are largely taken by women from working-class backgrounds. Accordingly, for Walters, when they express satisfaction with their jobs and the part-time hours that they are working, these women are invariably 'making the best of a bad job'. For Warren, part-time manual work in Britain represents working-class jobs for working-class mothers, and so 'it is meaningless to look at women's employment choices without reference to the opportunities and constraints women from different classes have encountered and continue to experience in their educational and working lives' (Warren 2000: 6.5).

Hidden work

Not having enough paid work brings us neatly onto the topic of hidden work. Throughout the chapter we have looked at the effects of the absence of paid work. In this scenario, the unemployed undertake no work activities at all, aside from housework tasks for some. However, the sociology of work has also been interested in hidden work, the type of work that goes on for some form of remuneration but is not officially recorded. The extent of an informal economy, the role it plays and – here – whether the unemployed are involved in it, are all questions that have fascinated sociologists. How 'fiddly', 'off the books' or 'cash in hand' work operates has stimulated some absorbing sociological accounts. The fear that some people on state benefits might be working cash-in-hand without 'declaring' this extra income fed into the underclass debates of the 1990s that we reviewed earlier. Notions of 'idle, thieving bastards' (Bagguley and Mann 1992), of 'dole scroungers' and of the 'something for nothing society' all abounded in the British tabloid press, and the parallel in the USA would be the 'welfare queens'. Robert MacDonald (1994) reports on findings from a qualitative project in Cleveland in the north-east of England that asked 214 working-class women and men who were outside formal employment whether they engaged in 'fiddly' jobs and, if so, why. MacDonald found those that were taking fiddly work were largely men, and they were doing so to support their families and to gain back some self-respect for themselves. These fiddly jobs involved long and low paid hours of work, and were part of a survival strategy in the face of restricted opportunities for legitimate employment in the region.

Importantly, Ray Pahl's (1984) influential research into forms of work that we draw upon often in this book had noted that there were actually more opportunities for those already in paid work to engage in cash-in-hand work since they had more contacts and they often had access to the work equipment that was necessary to 'moonlight'. Geographers Colin C. Williams and Jan Windebank have also been influential in shaping the sociological understanding of hidden work, and its existence beyond the unemployed. In one study exploring the 'uneven geographies of informal economic activities' (2002a, 2002b), they draw upon 511 interviews, conducted in higher- and lower-income neighbourhoods of one affluent and one deprived city in Britain, to explore self-provisioning, mutual aid and paid informal work. In another study in England (2006), they usefully point out gender differences in the type of hidden work that is carried out, with women's undeclared work being more like mutual aid since it was largely conducted for family, friends and neighbours, and less well viewed through the lens of employment. Fascinating and valuable comparative material is available too from studies in the United States, a useful example being Sudhir Alladi Venkatesth's (2006) account of the Maquis Park area of Chicago's South Side. Venkatesth looks at the way a whole community is networked and supported by informal and hidden work that is, as his title suggests, taking place almost entirely *Off the Books*. Although hidden, when sociologists examine this type of economy they portray the very real connections between people and offer a way of understanding how work is embedded in community and daily life and how community inter-penetrates work.

Voluntary work also has a long history but one that has been largely overlooked by the sociology of work with its emphasis on the employment relationship. This is unfortunate because historical accounts confirm the importance of volunteering for numerous groups. Charity work was really the only form of work deemed appropriate for upper middle-class women in Victorian times, aside from managing the servants of the household. The middle class male philanthropic volunteer also has a very long history. In her contribution to *A New Sociology of Work* (2006), Rebecca Taylor shows too how many early working-class organisations like co-operatives and friendly societies depended on the work of volunteers. In contemporary societies, the number and range of charities are vast, and all depend, to varying extents on volunteer workers. In her own research into voluntary organisations, Taylor asked why people do or do not volunteer to work there, identifying a range of reasons – including work ethos, family upbringing and financial circumstances – that made volunteering an option or not. Taylor argues for the importance of:

> rethinking definitions of work and re-examining forms of labour that have been excluded from the sociology of work . . . It [voluntary work] particu-larly raises the issue of remuneration and reward in how we understand work, suggesting that other forms of capital are as important as economic capital in defining and shaping work practices.
>
> (Taylor 2006: 135)

Unemployment and the meaning of work

Finally, sociologically one of the most important aspects of the rise of unem-ployment has been to raise a whole series of questions about what work means to people and what forms of identity they derive from it. Douglas Ezzy in his book *Narrating Unemployment* (2001) draws on Goffman's concept of the breaching experiment. This is the idea that to best understand normative behaviour in an individual or a group, one disrupts normality in some way or another. Ezzy suggests that the mass unemployment experienced in the Western industrial economies over the past three decades or so can be seen as just such a breaching experiment in that work meaning and identity were taken for granted, unacknowledged and perhaps unimportant. With the loss of work there is a re-evaluation of traditional forms of work and indeed work as a more general concept. Some of the best qualitative accounts of the loss of work through unemployment and deindustrialisation have been in a wave of studies which examine the experience of industrial change and the impact it has had on communities, families and individuals. Industrial anthropologist Kate Dudley has written two important books which deal with the experience of industrial decline. Her first, *The End of the Line* (1994), examines the process of closure and change in the automotive industry in Kenosha, Wisconsin. Dudley records the attempts former car workers made to come to terms with the loss of what many consider to be meaningless repetitive employment.

> The building itself is something I'll miss. That building is older than I am. My whole concept of this city is that this city has been that big factory downtown. When they tear it down, my whole concept of what this city is, physically as well as psychologically, is gonna be drastically altered. It's gonna be this huge gaping hole where this chunk of my life was . . . literally, just a huge gaping hole.
>
> (Bill Sorensen, tool and die-maker, quoted in Dudley 1994: 173)

Dudley's *Debt and Dispossession* (2000) was an equally evocative reflection on the loss of rural agricultural jobs during the 1990s. Such research also addresses the effect of change on those outside the immediate group of workers made redundant. Since the 1990s, a whole series of books have been published on different communities and industries such as Dublin's *When the Mines Closed* (1998); Fine's *The Story of REO Joe* (2004), dealing with the loss of vehicle building in Lancing, Michigan; Doukas' *Worked Over* (2003), dealing with corporate withdrawal along the old Erie Canal in New York State. As we saw earlier with the Marienthal study, one of the reasons why there has been so much interest in writing about deindustrialisation is that many communities were in company towns where one employer had dominated the labour market (see also Cowie and Heathcott 2003; High 2003).

In this context, end-of-work debates (see Chapter 6) highlighted the real importance of identity for the sociology of work and unemployment. Identity is not a new topic but we mention it here to highlight the most current developments around identity and unemployment in the discipline, and to refer the reader to Chapter 12. In a society with a strong work ethic, much value is attached to having a job. We have seen that unemployment is materially distressing, and that it is psychologically damaging too due to the stigma attached to being unemployed. The range of studies we have discussed in this chapter also picked up the negative impact of unemployment on a person's identity. The impact on identity does depend on other aspects of people's lives, such as whether their main identity is family-/home-based or work-based. Unsurprisingly, then, a recurring theme in the sociological literature has been the impact of unemployment on male identity. This has received even more attention in recent years due to the proliferation of research into masculinity within sociology, gender and men's studies (Chapter 7). In this research, the ideology of the male breadwinner is widespread: if they are not the worker and earner of the home, there are severe implications for men's legitimate sources of identity. Not having a job can make men feel less of a man.

Studies have gone on to suggest that unemployment for women is less traumatic than it is for men, in part because that it impacts less on their identities. According to Marshall (1984), for many women, their identity is connected less strongly to the world of paid work, and so the home and house-work offer an alternative source of acceptable identity formation. Similarly, in Nickie Charles and Emma James' (2003a, 2003b) research into job insecurity in South Wales, although they were looking at employed people, they found gender differences in both the experience and the perception of job insecurity. Women felt less insecure than men, and Charles and James explained this by reference to more jobs being available for women in the local area; that women were more prepared to take just any job; and the continuing strength of male breadwinner ideology.

CONCLUSION

We have argued that the reason we are looking at unemployment in a book on work is because the two issues are inseparable. Throughout the book, we are arguing for a more holistic approach to work, incorporating all dimensions of people's working lives. By looking at unemployment, we have been able to reflect on how important paid work is to people, to their families and communities, and to society. We have been able to see that paid work has a range of purposes. In addition to providing an income, paid work also provides a structure to life, on a daily and annual basis and across the life-course too. Having a job offers a form of social status and work is a source of identity for many. Without paid work, many of the unemployed suffer economic deprivation; feel disorientated and anxious and fall sick; and suffer shame. We hope we have shown just how sociology has tried to determine the severity of the cumulative disadvantages faced by the unemployed. Through a combination of methods, empirical sociological studies have built up a picture of long-term trends in unemployment and revealed the extent of problems faced by diverse social groups. In also showing how people view work and unemployment, the study of unemployment feeds directly into debates about emotion and identity that we examine in the next chapter.

FURTHER READING

Catherine Marsh's 'Unemployment in Britain' (1988a) remains useful for debates over the meaning of unemployment.

Duncan Gallie *et al.*'s edited collection *Social Change and the Experience of Unemployment* (1994) presents the results on unemployment from the 1980s SCELI project.

Adrian Sinfield's *What Unemployment Means* (1981) includes classic qualitative accounts of being unemployed.

Charles Murray's contentious writings are available in *Underclass + 10: Charles Murray and the British Underclass 1990–2000* (2001).

Lynne Pettinger *et al.*'s *A New Sociology of Work* for chapters on voluntary and community work, among others (2006).

WEB SOURCE

Social Exclusion Task Force:
  http://www.cabinetoffice.gov.uk/social_exclusion_task_force/#content

The ILO: Founded in 1919, the ILO 'formulates international labour standards in the form of Conventions and Recommendations setting minimum standards of basic labour rights: freedom of association, the right to organise, collective bargaining, abolition of forced labour, equality of opportunity and treatment, and other standards regulating conditions across the entire spectrum of work related issues'.
  http://www.ilo.org/

STUDENT PROJECTS AND ESSAY QUESTIONS

1 What is the relationship between unemployment and work, and what are the recent changes associated with unemployment in the UK?

2 Unemployment is a problem only for the unemployed. How far is this statement an adequate assessment of the consequences of high levels of unemployment?

3 How would you go about establishing how typical the current level of unemployment in your locality is of the national picture? What challenges would you face?

4 How might you research the impact of job loss in a region? What would be your 'unit of analysis'?: unemployed people, their partners or families, communities, the employed, employers.

Culture, Emotion and Identity at Work

OVERVIEW

This chapter will:

- Ask why sociologists should be interested in the issues of workplace culture, emotion and identity.
- Provide an overview of how the classical theorists thought about these issues.
- Examine what use later sociologists had for these concepts.
- Place into historical context the rise of interest in these issues over the last two decades.

INTRODUCTION

In this chapter we want to look in detail at a range of subjective factors that shape the way we think about work and employment. The issues of work culture, emotion and identity are often viewed as representing very contemporary concerns but in this chapter we want to show the way that sociology has long been interested in how people are attached, or detached from their work. Work sociologists have consistently asked questions about how workers socialise with one another, how norms and values are created and reproduced over time. This chapter is concerned with a series of tensions. As we will see, there has been a recurring debate within sociology about the ability of people to find meaning in their work. Modern paid work is for some defined by its mundane nature where employees simply work for money. But at the same time, capitalism also creates new identities as industries emerge, relocate and close down over time.

In recent years debates about work identity and meaning have again come to the fore in Western countries in particular. The processes of industrial change and the collapse in many traditionally male-dominated industries have led many to claim that work can no longer provide the basis for identity, for men in particular. Meanwhile, increases in women's participation in the labour market have led to questions about women's orientations to work. We want to suggest here that while there has been a long tradition of looking at the different but related issues of culture, identity and emotion contemporary debates about them often neglect the rich sociological heritage of analysis and conceptualisation.

THE SOCIOLOGICAL MISSION

The subjective aspects of work and employment are central to understanding how people interact in work. Sociology is in part defined by its attempt to understand how people cope with the corrosive effects of capitalism. The founding fathers suggested that modern work was defined by a process by which the intrinsic rewards of work (the enjoyment of the task) were being destroyed and were being replaced by the cash nexus where money was paid as a compensation for a lack of fulfilment. Sociology is almost uniquely placed to understand these interrelated concepts of culture, emotion, and workplace identity. Sociology provides the analytical tools as well as the research methods to understand the complex processes of social interaction and socialisation. This is not to say that sociologists cannot and do not draw on other perspectives and in this chapter we will examine research from economists, psychologists, geographers and others, but what is important is that sociology can understand both micro interaction in work while placing this in the context of wider structural forces.

FOUNDATIONS

It is tempting to think of the issues of this chapter as the concerns of the late twentieth and early twenty-first centuries but on closer inspection it is clear that they have exercised the sociological imagination in general, and sociology of work in particular for a long time. Each of the classical theorists had something to say about culture, emotions and identity, at work as they collectively identified the potential for modernity to alter the experience of work.

Marx saw work as fundamental to human experience, the act of labour and the social context in which it occurred were the defining aspect of human identity in any era. As we have seen in previous chapters, Marx saw capitalism as a dynamic system which was both creative and destructive. It was creative in that it brought into existence new industries and social relationships, and destructive in the sense that it superseded and transcended old habits, customs and traditions. This destructive tendency was witnessed in all aspects of social life but especially in the arena of paid work. Marx saw modern capitalism as a productive system which accelerated this process of change and identified the tendency for social relationships at work between employers and employees to take on an increasingly instrumental aspect. At its most developed, Marx thought that the capitalist mode of production reduced this employment relationship to one purely based on what he called the cash nexus, where there was no pretence of intimacy or emotion between parties. Instead modern work was based purely on the purchase and selling of labour for a wage determined by the market. In a separate but related sense Marx also suggested that there was an historic tendency within the capitalist labour process for deskilling to occur whereby work was increasingly stripped of its ability to provide intrinsic satisfaction – rewards based on enjoyment of work. In the context of modern work, effort was compensated by the extrinsic satisfaction of economic reward. As we saw in earlier chapters, these aspects were part of Marx's notion of the process of alienation in modern society where workers were gradually alienated, or estranged, from various aspects of their work, their co-workers and ultimately themselves. In modernity, therefore, the space for the emotions and the ability to derive identity from work was increasingly being eroded.

This long-term process of degredation could only be reversed by the eventual transcendence of the capitalist system. Marx argued that this process was not an unintended consequence of capitalist development but central to the system itself. As one of the keenest observers of the new epoch, Marx believed that the greater division of labour cruelly distorted an individual's humanity. He wrote in the first volume of *Capital*:

It converts the labourer into a crippled monstrosity, by forcing his [*sic*] detail dexterity at the expense of a world of productive capabilities... Intelligence in production expands in one direction, because it vanishes in many others.

(Marx [1867] 1954: 340–1)

Only under socialism or communism would non-alienating work be possible and with this the creation of non-alienating social relationships around work.

Like Marx, Max Weber saw capitalism and modernity as having ambiguous consequences both for individuals and groups. For Weber, the modern world was one marked by a process of rationalisation which could be seen in every aspect of social life, and work and modern organisations were no exception. Industrial modernisation created the need for increased levels of specialisation and expert knowledge. This, when coupled with the greater division of labour, produced greater efficiency but also a tendency to narrowness. As was the case with Marx's alienated workers, Weber suggested that this process of specialisation created less rounded workers. This situation was brought about by the need for complex divisions of labour and knowledge within ever-larger organisational structures. As part of this process of rationalisation Weber identified the growth of bureaucracy which was a specialisation of administrative and managerial functions. Within this structure Weber suggested could be seen wider trends. Most importantly for our purpose in this chapter is the way Weber identifies the *impersonality* of modern organisations. He suggested that there was a tendency for decreasing scope for emotion in organisations as relationships became increasingly subject to rules and calculation. As the following quote illustrates, in modern organisations there could be no place for the emotions: 'Bureaucracy develops the more perfectly, the more it is 'dehumanized', the more completely it succeeds in eliminating from official business love, hatred, and all purely personal, irrational and emotional elements which escape calculation' (Weber 1978, quoted in Albrow 1997: 93).

It is important straightaway to point out that Weber used the notion of pure bureaucracy in the sense of an ideal type. So this idea of the organisation completely devoid of all human emotion was an extreme example against which the reality could be modelled. Nonetheless he believed that this process of rationalisation was a long-term trend in modern societies. His glimmer of hope lay in the role of 'charismatic' leaders who could offer a way out of the 'iron cage' of bureaucracy.

Other aspects of Weber's writing are useful in a wider discussion of workplace culture and identity. His ideas suggest ambiguity in that modernity both creates new occupational identities, albeit less rounded and more specialist ones, while at the same time destroying older traditional ones. A related concept is that of the notion of the work ethic which he developed and thought was crucial to the explanation of why industrial capitalism emerged in Western Europe. This ethic was one of the most profound early statements about how sociologists could conceptualise and analyse individual and collective work identity and motivation (Marshall 1982; Rose 1985). The idea of the work ethic helps us examine orientations to work, it was taken up by researchers in the 1960s and 1970s as we will see later, but also helps us understand the profound attachment to work which is often cruelly emphasised when workers lose their jobs (see Chapter 11).

Durkheim is important here both for his insights into workplace identity as well as subsequent analysis which has taken his writing as an inspiration. Unlike Marx and Weber, Durkheim's writing was informed by the sense that social order could be realised in modern societies. The division of labour, and in particular the moral order created by workplace groups and professional bodies, played an important part in securing order. In his Preface to the second edition of his *Division of Labour*, he writes of the importance of occupational groups:

> What we especially see in the occupational group is a moral power capable of containing individual egos, of maintaining a spirited sentiment of common solidarity in the consciousness of all the workers, of preventing the law of the strongest from being brutally applied to industrial and commercial relations.
>
> (Durkheim [1893] 1964: 10)

Individual freedom and identity, therefore, emerged from a strong sense of shared values and ethics residing and produced simultaneously by the group. So we can see that Durkheim is important in each of the themes of this particular chapter, culture, identity and emotion. In terms of culture, Durkheim has been described as '*the* classical theorist of culture' (Emirbayer 1996, cited in Lincoln and Guillot 2006: 89). While often seen as a conservative thinker because of his emphasis on social order, the implications for his ideas on the autonomy of work groups are actually profoundly radical. Connected to this area are understandings about work identity. Both *The Division of Labour* and *Professional Ethics and Civic Morals* deal with different aspects of individual and work groups' identification with employment. Perhaps less obvious is the way Durkheim's writing informs a study of emotion within work. Here again his reflection on how modern work and society have the potential to integrate or equally estrange the individual is interesting for us to think about.

What should be clear from this brief discussion of the classical sociology thinkers is that they all held a common view distinct from economists. Early sociologists rejected simplistic ideas of 'economic man' where people's motives could be reduced to economic incentives. Marx, Durkheim and Weber all clearly understood the importance of workplace culture and identity. Each acknowledged that it was critical to place work culture in its social context. In the remainder of the chapter we will see how the work of each of the classical theorists has helped to shape the way later sociologists and others have thought about the attachment or detachment workers have for their work and the relationships they have with co-workers.

LATER DEVELOPMENTS

In many ways, the discussion of the way sociologists of work have looked at questions of emotion, identity and culture is one of recovery as at times reading material from the 1980s and 1990s gives the distinct impression that writers previously were unconcerned with these aspects of work. In what follows we try to give a flavour of a fascinating range of resources which we can draw on in looking at cultural and subjective aspects of work. We want to suggest that we need to draw critically on the insights these studies offer in trying to understand contemporary work.

If we cast our net wide enough it is possible to see the roots of a sociological concern with work culture, emotion and identity running in an uninterrupted line from the time the classical theorists were writing. We could even go back to before the era of Marx, Durkheim and Weber by examining the work of Adam Smith. As we saw earlier (see Chapter 5) Smith noted the ambivalent nature of modern work techniques, in particular the greater division of labour. Just as he recognised the efficiency of the ever-greater subdivision of tasks, he also acknowledged that these degraded the moral character of those involved in the production. In an earlier chapter we looked at the work of F.W. Taylor. In essence, his 'scientific' approach to management was based on the idea that there was a distinct culture residing in the workforce. But rather than study it, Taylor argued it was something which had to be marginalised from work organisations. Taylor believed the autonomous norms and values of the workers to be detrimental to the efficient and rational organisation and control of work tasks. Employees would, if left to their own devices, work at less than their full capacity. Implicit in Taylor's theory was an understanding of worker culture, expressed through their norms and values which new members of the group were socialised into.

This early concern with workplace culture can also be seen in Henry Ford's management techniques. While not sociological, nor particularly sophisticated, Ford was interested in worker motivation and values and his famous $5 a day can be read as an attempt to compensate workers for the loss of the intrinsic satisfaction of work as a result of production line techniques. Ford famously created his own corporate sociology department to better understand his workers' behaviour (Baritz 1960: 33, cited in Albrow 1997: 34). There were other attempts at a management science which examined worker motivation during the first couple of decades of the twentieth century which mixed ideas from various nascent disciplines including psychology (see Albrow 1997; Brown 1992; Rose 1988).

In the inter-war years, 1918–39, the most important attempt to understand more fully the way workers orientated themselves to work was to be found in the so called Hawthorne studies. Again, this set of experiments took as their starting point the idea that worker motivation could be explained and to some extent controlled through the use of non-monetary factors. While the experiments initially focused on the ambience of work – factors such as variations in lighting levels – it later became clear that the culture that existed in the selected work groups could help to explain productivity gains and losses (see Gillespie 1991; Mayo 1949).

There are other intimations of interest in work cultures during and immediately after the Second World War and the ways in which these could be harnessed in the quest for greater productivity. Indeed, post-war British industrial sociology in part can claim its roots in a concern for human relations in the workplace (Brown 1965, 1967, 1992). The period of the 1950s and 1960s was a fascinating and important time for the study of workplace identity as various research projects were carried out which were informed by very different ideas about the object of study.

On both sides of the Atlantic there were the beginnings of a sustained ethnographic study of the workplace. A classic example of this approach is Donald Roy's (1958) study of a machine shop. As we saw in an earlier chapter, Roy wanted to examine workplace cultures, norms and values. His writing is a complex and fascinating description of small group interaction. Studies such as Roy's, notably in his essay entitled 'Banana time', set out to explain game playing in a work setting, showing, among other things, the way workers attempted to get through the day by the enactment of small rituals. This type of material can be seen in Jack Haas' 'Learning real feelings' ([1977] 2003) which is a good example of a sociologist attempting to embed themselves in a workplace culture, in this case, high steel construction workers. In his study, Haas was trying to understand the way workers coped with feelings of fear when they worked at great heights with minimal safety precautions:

> The discrepancy between my feelings and the lack of meaning of their unusually confident behaviour raised a question in my mind; was I attempting to interpret their actions according to my relevance structure? I had assumed that, sharing the same experience, we would have the same feelings about it; their actions, however, suggested we were not defining the situation similarly, and, in fact, they had overlooked what was, in my assessment of the situation, frightening. This perplexing discrepancy between the meaning of their behaviour and my own definition of the situation led me to attempt to understand why their behaviour would be appropriate to such a situation.
>
> (Haas 2003: 231)

The ethnographic approach was repeated by other work sociologists in a variety of occupations with varying degrees of success. At their best, such studies tell us something about how individuals and collective groups identify with their work and others, how they make it meaningful and how they understand it. In the UK, there were various ethnographic accounts of the workplace, or examples that at least drew on this method as part of a wider study. Classics of the genre include Huw Beynon's *Working for Ford* (1984), Ruth Cavendish's *Women on the Line* (1982) and Anna Pollert's *Girls, Wives, Factory Lives* (1981). In the USA these are complemented by studies such as Michael Burawoy's *Manufacturing Consent* (1979) (see Harper and Lawson 2003; Hodson 2001).

At the same time that Roy and others were carrying out this type of ethnographic study, some sociologists of work and organisations were approaching the subject from a rather different angle. Inspired by Parsonian functional sociology, various writers assumed that workers had certain needs which, if provided for, would result in contented workers and orderly workplaces (see Brown 1992; Hassard 1993, for a summary). It was largely against this type of thinking that one of the most important studies of the post-war period was undertaken. The Affluent Worker study was research based on industries in Luton, Bedfordshire, and was designed to test the idea, popularly held, that as workers became more affluent they increasingly took on the characteristics of the middle class – the so-called embourgeoisement thesis. The main research team of four led by John Goldthorpe (Goldthorpe *et al.* 1968a, 1968b, 1969) took as their starting point the idea that sociologists had to take seriously the ideas and motivations of the workers themselves in understanding why they undertook work in a particular trade, profession or workplace. Drawing on Weberian sociology, the team developed a set of typologies around certain orientations to work, which they labelled Traditional Proletarian, Deferential and Privatised/Instrumental Workers. Goldthorpe and his colleagues argued that these typologies emerged from a combination of the type of communities in which workers lived as well as the nature of the work undertaken. In a series of books and papers they argued that the instrumental orientation to work was likely to be increasingly seen in modern industry as traditional social and work based ties diminished in importance (see Brown 1992; Goldthorpe *et al.* 1968a, 1968b, 1969; Devine 1992).

Another strand of industrial sociology which is of interest to us here is the literature which grew up in the 1960s and 1970s concerned with occupational identity and in particular in the UK on occupational communities. These are interesting for us in that they examine the importance of place in the formation of work-based identity, and in addition some studies also highlight the centrality of class. A good example of this type of approach is Graeme Salaman's *Community and Occupation* (1974) which was a comparative study of architects and train drivers. He examined questions of socialisation, place, social networks and the culture of both groups. Another classic study of this type was Norman Dennis *et al.*'s *Coal Is Our Life* (1956), which mapped in detail the social relationships in a coal-mining community. There is a very real sense in which sociologists were trying to discover what was different and specific about different occupational groups and in doing so they tried to classify key variables likely to influence identity formation (see Strangleman 2004b). A flavour of this approach can be gained from the following quote from Bensman and Lilienfeld:

> There is no doubt in our minds that such occupational groups as medicine, architecture, teaching law, steamfitting, cobbling, taxicab driving, and ragpicking produce unique and peculiar combinations of attitudes appropriate to the craft as well as to the societal and social position, ideological and material interests, and commitment to the society at large. Every occupation, every skill at every substantive level produces such attitudes.
>
> (1975: 187)

This quote clearly echoes the ideas of the classical theorists. In trying to make sense of these studies in the context of the present chapter it is important to see them as part of a wider sociological tradition. During the 1960s, sociology was itself a far more coherent and homogeneous subject so that there was a sense in which research in the workplace was being used to throw light on a whole series of sociological themes other than simply work. The writing on occupational communities therefore needs to be seen equally as part of a sociological literature on class and community (see Savage 2005).

In the 1960s and 1970s, there was a further interesting developments which are relevant to our story. From the early 1960s, there was an upsurge in interest in social history, or what some have called history from below. Social historians such as E. P. Thompson and Raphael Samuel, as well as cultural critics such as Richard Hoggart and Raymond Williams, were at the forefront of this trend and they argued that popular culture and values had to be taken seriously in understanding the development of the working class. Thompson's research was a painstaking attempt to reconstruct popular ideas and values in order to understand social action among the common people in the eighteenth and nineteenth centuries (Thompson 1968, 1991). Raphael Samuel founded the History Workshop movement which spawned a variety of studies which often examined employment cultures of groups such as those working in the extractive industries: railways, agriculture and fishing (Samuel 1975; see also McKenna 1980; Thompson *et al.* 1983). This led to important developments in women's history and other more marginalised groups. The influence of this tradition is perhaps diffuse rather than direct on work sociology.

There is one further strand of sociological thinking which we should acknowledge before we move on and that is the sociological literature on professions. Like other disciplines, branches of sociology often explore similar areas to one another with little in the way of obvious cross-over. Those working in the professions field are interested in questions of identity largely in terms of how one group achieves occupational closure (see MacDonald 1995; Freidson 2001).

CONTEMPORARY ISSUES AND FUTURE TRENDS

In the 1980s, there was an upswing in interest in questions of culture, identity and emotion. This was due to a number of distinct and interrelated factors. First, there was the intellectual impact of the so-called 'cultural turn' (Chaney 1994; Jameson 1998; Ray and Sayer 1999) which stimulated debates on each of the issues focused on here. This trend attempted to understand and problematise the assumptions which lay behind cultures, stressing the need to question the taken-for-granted assumptions about social life and the social constructed nature of identities of all sorts. Second, there were the changes in the economy which we have looked at elsewhere in this book. These dramatic shifts in economic life have brought questions of identity and culture into sharp relief because of the loss of large swathes of heavy industry and occupational communities, the growth in new industries, and fundamental change in the division of labour. Finally, these issues have been firmly embraced by management theorists and writers who see culture and identity as answers to the challenges facing organisations.

In this next section we want to look at the three distinct but interrelated themes of culture, emotion and identity. For the sake of clarity we address these separately before looking at what can be said about them as a contemporary trend in the sociology of work.

Culture

As we have seen, a great deal of qualitative sociology has been concerned with the issue of 'culture', however, over the past two or more decades there has been a huge upswing in the interest in workplace and organisational culture. Interestingly this has not been led by those working in a sociological tradition, who apply the insights we have talked about above. Rather, this focus has originated in management writing and this is profoundly important in understanding the type of analysis adopted, the questions asked and the conclusions arrived at. This interest in organisational cultures from a management perspective is not new, from F. W. Taylor onward there has been a constant recognition of the importance of human factors in looking at the workplace. During the 1980s, however, this interest took a slightly different turn with the publication of a series of books which urged managers and their companies to take culture seriously in order to improve their business.

Perhaps the best-known example of this can be found in Peters and Waterman's *In Search of Excellence* (1982) and Deal and Kennedy's *Corporate Cultures: The Rites and Rituals of Corporate Life* (1988) (see also Ouchi 1981; Ouchi and Wilkins 1985. And for summaries, see Dingwall and Strangleman 2005; Parker 2000; Strangleman 2004b). The management literature suggested that successful companies either possessed or created the 'right culture'. 'Culture' now acquired a substantive and evaluative sense that it had not previously possessed. Managers were encouraged to learn how to create and direct culture. A small industry grew up to market the idea that culture was a variable that should be managed and to train managers how to do this (Anthony 1994; Bate 1995; Frost *et al.* 1985; Hickman and Silva 1985; Louis 1985; Lessem 1990; Wilson 1992).

Work culture in the social sciences

The reaction to this management-inspired literature on culture has been a fruitful one for the sociology of work. Essentially, social scientists take as their starting point the idea that cultures are incredibly complex things which are not amenable to crude manipulation. Raymond Williams (1976: 87) famously described 'culture' as 'one of the two or three most complicated words in the English language'. At the heart of the sociological understanding of culture is that it is an emergent property of a social group. This is not to say that it is completely sealed off from the outside world, but that it is not open to simplistic manipulation as some management writers would argue, or managers themselves would wish. Susan Wright, an organisational anthropologist, noted the way that this latter approach turned culture 'from being something an organization *is* into something an organization *has*, and from being a process embedded in context to an objectified tool of management control. The use of the term culture itself becomes ideological' (1994: 4).

Such a use of 'culture was alien and troubling to many social scientists (Alvesson 2002; Grint 1995; Lynn-Meek 1988; Wright 1994). Managerial writers also borrowed liberally from structural functional theory, although, by this time, it had been intensively criticised by social scientists. Management writers were, however, attracted by its straightforward dichotomies between good/bad; functional/dysfunctional; healthy/unhealthy. They could declare themselves the arbiters of what was and was not good/functional/healthy. As Lynn-Meek puts it: 'Any theory that assumes that culture is the internalisation of dominant norms and values, must also assume that all members must hold the dominant value system or else be "outside culture"' (1988: 458). This illustrates the gulf between sociological (and anthropological) writers and managerial theorists. For the former, the 'is' in the context of culture is the belief that culture is an emergent property of actions that simultaneously orient to and reproduce an organisation. Culture expresses the interaction of groups among themselves and with their environment. This view of organisations is predicated on an understanding that social life is fundamentally reflexive and therefore subject to change and open to unintended consequences of action. Culture is not simply a variable that can be altered to achieve a specified outcome.

For the critical sociologist of work, the exploration of work cultures is one of the most important aspects of what we do. We are interested in how workers make sense of their workplaces, how they interact with each other and how norms and values are created, reproduced and changed over time. Perhaps one of the crucial differences between sociologists and those working in a management tradition is that for the former the object of study is to understand more fully how social groups work, and for the latter it is to better understand how to control them (see Albrow 1997).

Emotion at work

As we saw at the beginning of this chapter, the founding fathers of sociology thought that modern industrial capitalism limited the role of emotion in organisation. Modern organisations and their members were becoming subject to greater levels of formal rules and less governed by the arbitrary power of particular individuals. Weber's work in particular has been interpreted by some management theorists as an argument for the *unemotional* organisation, or that the emotions were not a proper subject for study. In response to these suggestions, there has been a fruitful re-examination of Weber's analysis of emotions in organisational life (see Albrow 1997; Du Gay 2000, 2005; Ray and Reed 1994). In the 1980s and 1990s, greater attention was paid to the emotional aspects of work and organisation and it is important that we identify these. In the following sections we want to highlight some of the different ways in which writers have discussed this aspect of work.

Hochschild and 'emotional labour'

One of the most important and influential interventions in this debate was the work of Arlie Russell Hochschild (1983) and her book, *The Managed Heart: Commercialization of Human Feeling*. Hochschild aimed to explore the way employers attempted to manage emotions in the workplace – perhaps most notably in service sector jobs, she looked at female and male airline stewards and also debt collectors.

TEXT BOX 12.1 HOCHSCHILD'S DEFINITION OF EMOTIONAL LABOUR

- Feeling management which is performed as part of paid work, serving the interests of an employer in maximising surplus value
- Management of employees' own emotion (suppression or exaggeration of response).
- Management of others' emotion, predominantly undertaken during social interaction within the workplace – the product of emotional labour is often the state of mind or feeling within another person (customer or client).
- There must be some managerial attempt to prescribe, and or supervise and measure employee performance of emotional labour.

What Hochschild identified was a growing management interest in this type of work and the way human feelings, both those of the workers and customers, were subject to manipulation and commercialisation. In the case of the airline industry, emotional labour was seen as *the* potential difference in the services airlines could offer. Essentially there was little difference between the service offered by airlines, if what is being purchased was travel. But what Hochschild argued was that, by using emotional management techniques, airlines could differentiate their product from others. Managers therefore tried to train their staff to consistently present a particular persona in their interactions with customers in order to increase loyalty.

Hochschild's work is important in a number of ways not least because she set out to systematically analyse how companies were trying to exploit this form of labour. Emotional labour had two aspects to it. First, it can be seen in the ways that employees attempt to elicit responses from clients and customers. Second, emotional labour could describe the management of the employees' own emotions. In this latter case, Hochschild further differentiated between 'surface acting' (where responses are fairly superficial) through to 'deep acting' where workers internalise a whole set of roles. Hochschild suggested that there were psychological dangers in the application of emotional labour in that it represented a new form of estrangement, or even alienation, as workers denied their own feelings while acting into a managerial prescribed role. These elements of emotional labour were applicable across the service sector and beyond. Hochschild suggested that this type of emotion management was becoming more prevalent because of the growth in the relative size of the service sector where 'customer-facing' jobs were becoming increasingly common.

- *Surface acting* – 'to feel what we do not . . . we deceive others about what we really feel, but we do not deceive ourselves'.
- *Deep acting* – 'deceiving oneself as much as deceiving others . . . we make feigning easy by making it unnecessary'.

There have been a number of attempts to apply Hochschild's work by other sociologists. Steve Taylor used her ideas in his study of call centre workers where operators had to suppress feelings of boredom and sometimes anger in order to avoid being rude to clients on the phone (see Taylor 1997, 1998). Here is a quote from one of the telephone operators Taylor interviewed about their job and how they cope with disrespectful clients:

> If you have a rude or ignorant customer, you are supposed to pretend that something awful has just happened to them . . . 'always feel sorry for the ignorant customer, do not hate him [*sic*]' . . . this is what they tell you to do, 'put sympathy on to him and not yourself'.
>
> (Taylor 1998: 91)

But, while it is important to acknowledge that Hochschild coined the term emotional labour, attempts to manage the emotions of employees predates the 1980s and this type of control can be seen in many forms of work across time and space. If we consider virtually any form of work, it is possible to use the notion of emotional labour in its analysis. Think, for example, of the classic Fordist production line, what kinds of emotional labour do workers have to operationalise in order to cope with what is often mundane and repetitive tasks?

According to Hamper:

> The one thing that was impossible to escape was the monotony of our new job. Every minute, every hour, every truck and every movement was a plodding replica of the one that had gone before. The monotony gnawed away at Roy. His behaviour began to verge on the desperate. The only way he saw to deal with the monotony was to numb himself to it.
>
> (1986: 41)

Similarly, at the turn of the nineteenth century, there were over a million domestic servants in the UK (Bradley 1989), we can only imagine the range of emotions that may have had to have been suppressed or heightened in order to keep jobs. But it would be a mistake to think that the management of emotions is something which is solely pushed by management on to reluctant workers. Think, for example, of nurses who have to very directly manage emotion in dealing with what are often very difficult circumstances. The last thing a patient needs is an over-emotional nurse caring for them, and nurses themselves would quickly become exhausted if they were unable to manage their emotions to a great extent.

Another aspect of this interest in emotions at work is evidenced in Melissa Tyler and Pamela Abbott's (1998) writing on flight attendants and Lisa Adkins' (1995) research into leisure industry workers. Both demonstrate well how gender and sexuality are central to emotional work. As discussed in Chapter 8, a key element of the work expected from female flight attendants and leisure workers was that they should make customers feel special, and this often includes feeling sexually attractive. The workers are expected to have the 'right' appearance and to perform as sexualised actors, with flirting with customers a core element of their jobs. The work performed by prostitutes is also attracting growing attention in the study of emotional labour. A fundamental part of a prostitute's work role is to exchange the 'skilled emotional labour of sex' for a cash payment (Kong 2006). Like nurses, doctors and other workers who engage routinely in emotional labour, prostitutes have been found to 'manufacture' a work identity as a form of self-protection, as well as using this work identity – usually based upon heterosexual imagery – to attract customers (Sanders 2005).

The bulk of debates over emotion in work have looked at paid employment. But what we stress in this book is that work activities are also carried out within the home, often unpaid and largely by a woman for herself and her family. Emotion can be seen to be integral to the work relationship here. Indeed, it has been argued that ironing a shirt for a lover can better be seen as an act of love than an act of work (Pahl 1984). A great deal of sociological attention has been dedicated to understanding caring work. Care-giving work includes the work undertaken in unpaid domestic and personal services, but sociology now also distinguishes between the 'caring for' and 'caring about' dimensions of caring work: 'caring for' includes feeding, washing, lifting, protecting, representing and comforting, while 'caring about' concerns feeling affection for someone (Daly 2002; Tronto 1987; Ungerson 1983).

Of course, not all care work is provided for and by family members. Nevertheless, research has shown that those providing care work have long been expected to display affection and even love. When we examined slavery, we saw that house slaves in particular were expected to show love to their owners. Contemporary studies of domestic work have found that the 'best' nannies were the ones who displayed affection for their charges.

Indeed, some migrant nannies reported feeling more love for their charges than for their own children, whom they had not seen for many years (Hochschild 2002).

Emotions in organisations

In the past two decades there has been an upsurge in ideas around the emotional organisation distinct from those explored above. Stephen Fineman in the Introduction to his collection on emotion in organisations wrote: 'Emotions are within the texture of organizing. They are intrinsic to social order and disorder, working structures, conflict, influence, conformity, posturing, gender, sexuality and politics. They are the products of socialization and manipulation' (Fineman 1993: 1). Fineman and the others in the same collection see the organisation as being shot through with emotions, and as emotional arenas. But Fineman and the others in the collection perhaps overstate the way emotions have been ignored – certainly this is not true in sociology, particularly industrial sociology. In a series of books and papers, various sociologists in the past decade or so have tried to explore and rediscover classical sociology's insight into emotion and affectivity in organisations. These were important as they showed how the sociological imagination could be applied anew to the contemporary workplace on issues such as leadership, charisma, authority, bureaucracy, emotion and affect (see Albrow 1997; Bryman 1992; Du Gay 2000, 2005; Ray and Reed 1994).

While these interventions have largely been of a more theoretical kind, it is possible to see the emotional aspects of work discussed in a range of more empirically focused research. For example, almost all ethnographic work in industrial sociology reflects an interest in informal work cultures, and while they may not use the term 'emotion', they nonetheless talk about the affectual aspects of work. If you look at Beynon's *Working for Ford* or Cavendish's *Women on the Line*, you probably won't find the term emotion, certainly not in the index, but you will find discussions of the way workers come to terms with working on a very tedious line for years on end and how they cope with it.

One of the most interesting aspects of emotions within organisations is in terms of the way workers find meaning in their work and form attachments to it and come to develop an occupational or work identity and it is to this aspect we now turn.

Attitudes to work

The sociology of work has a long-standing interest in researching and understanding people's feelings about work. This interest appears throughout a range of linked debates on attitudes, orientations, commitments, satisfactions and preferences about work (see Text box 12.4), and it appears in other disciplines like psychology and economics too. For sociology, a central question is the part that attitudes play in how people live their working lives. Do people's preferences shape their work behaviour absolutely or do constraints impact on the decisions they make, such as whether they take a paid job or not; what type of job and for how many hours?

TEXT BOX 12.4 ASKING ABOUT WORK COMMITMENT

A range of work studies have employed the so-called 'lottery question'. Assuming you won or inherited enough money so that you did not need to work for financial reasons, would you continue to work?

One of the drivers behind sociological research into attitudes to work is an interest in the orientations to work held by different social groups. If differences do exist, what are they, why have they emerged, and what might be the consequences? We saw already how sociologists like Goldthorpe and colleagues were interested in potential class differences in work orientations, asking if working-class men were becoming increasingly instrumental and more middle class over time. Sociologists with an interest in class and 'race' have also examined work attitudes to reject elements of the underclass thesis that proposed a growth in work-shy and criminal communities in inner cities of the UK and the USA (MacDonald 1996; Wilson 1987). However, the major boost to debates about work attitudes in recent years came from researchers interested in gender who have returned to the question of whether women hold a different work ethic to men and ask too whether certain types of women are more 'male-like' in their attitudes than others.

One of the central questions in this contemporary attitudinal research is the issue of causation: to what extent do attitudes, orientations and preferences *shape* work behaviour. As economist Shirley Dex argues, the complexity of exploring the 'interplay between attitudes, orientations, constraints and behaviour' (1988: 152) has been well recognised in the study of work for many years. Nevertheless, debates over causation were reawakened in the 1990s when sociologist Catherine Hakim attached causal importance to the role of attitudes, choices and preferences in people's lives. Hakim's particular argument, as we see in the section on underemployment in Chapter 11, was that attitudes and preferences have shaped the types of work that women and men do: 'the majority of women (as well as men) still accept and even prefer the sexual division of labour that allocates domestic responsibilities to the wife and the income-earning role to the husband' (Hakim 1996: 38). For Hakim (2000), in Western Europe, women – but not men – have a range of work–life-style options freely open to them. Women are thus able to act out their (diverse) work–life preferences and it is this that explains the greater degree of heterogeneity in women's working patterns than in men's.

Hakim's writings have fed into longer-standing debates about the reality of ideal types of woman such as the 'traditional home-maker' and 'career woman', but it is the emphasis on preferences in her work that stimulated the most heated debates in the sociology of gender and work in Britain. The Hakim-inspired debate caused sociologists to ask: how do we interpret findings if, say, women express satisfaction with what would seem to be far more restricted work-life opportunities than men experience? Back in 1952, Ferdinand Zweig had argued:

> When a woman told me that she didn't like going out to work, so she stayed at home, I was inclined to take the statement at its face value, but in the course of the inquiry it was clear that the opinions, values and actions were really the outcome of different situations.
>
> (Zweig 1952: 10)

Most contemporary writers argue that the constraints that women face, particularly when they have children and when good quality and afford-able child-care provision is lacking, as it is in the UK, mean that women cannot simply act out their preferences (Crompton 2006 provides a useful review).

Hakim's research has reinvigorated debates over how sociologists can best carry out research into feelings about and attitudes to work, work commit-ment, satisfaction, and so on. The bulk of her analysis is based on data obtained from quantitative surveys. Attitudes to work and family roles are examined routinely in government-sponsored large-scale surveys like the British Social Attitudes Survey and British Household Panel Survey, as well as one-off surveys like the (1980) Women and Employment Survey. Many of Hakim's critics drew on research from qualitative studies to argue for a more complex case (though not all. McRae 2003 and Warren 2000 both used survey data to the same end), and to show that women are constrained, not free, in their work–life choices.

Finally, it is useful to note that outside academic debate, opinion polling organisations like Gallup, ICM, the NOP and MORI regularly collect data and publish findings on people's subjective understandings and experiences of work. Although the data collected is not exhaustive (it has been estimated that only about 35 per cent of these polls ever reach the public eye; Marsh 1988a: 277) and polls do not have 'pure' motives since they are invariably sponsored by commercial organisations, they still provide a fascinating insight into people's attitudes to and experiences of work.

Identity

In the past few decades, identity has emerged as one of the main concepts in the social sciences (Du Gay 1996, 2007). What has developed is a set of understandings which go beyond the idea that 'individual identity could simply be read off from social structural location' to one where 'multiple and competing discursive constructions of who we could be would play themselves out between and within individuals' (Halford and Leonard 2006: 1). In part, this shift was based on a very narrow reading of an older sociological tradition, where categories such as work are seen as the overwhelming factor influencing identity formation – so, for example, a coal miner would be socialised in a particular way and develop a common shared set of uniform characteristics with all other miners, with perhaps some space for regional difference (Dennis *et al.* 1956).

There was also a sense that to some extent questions of identity and subjectivity had been largely ignored by some working in the field. A long-standing debate of this type centres on Braverman's *Labor and Monopoly Capital* (1974) which its detractors argue stressed the structural determination of monopoly capitalism over questions of agency and subjectivity (see Burrell 2006, for a summary). In many ways this shift was itself part of a wider cultural turn within sociology and the social sciences, which could be labelled postmodern or post-structural. As we saw in the chapter on theory, this approach rejected overarching explanations of the type found in the writing of the founding fathers and tended instead to focus on a set of interests often remote from material reality and structural constraint. Part of the problem with such a situation has been the creation of a vacuum whereby work is often ignored or downplayed as a source of identity and where those studying work have not developed some of the intellectual tools and insights of the cultural turn.

There is a certain irony in the fact that while in the past two decades there has been such an increase in the study of social identity while identities derived from people's work have seen to be under threat or, in the more extreme interpretation, have disappeared altogether. Many of the points we make here echo those made in the chapter on post-industrial society but it is worth looking again about what is being said about identity.

At its most simple, there is a set of authors who have claimed that employment can no longer act as a source of identity as it once did. Catherine Casey is fairly typical of this approach when she writes:

> The industrial legacy of the centrality of production and work in social and self formation hovers precipitously with the post-industrial condition in which work is declining in social primacy. *Social meaning and solidarity must, eventually, be found elsewhere.*
>
> (Casey 1995: 2; emphasis added)

This is a clear and dramatic statement about what work can and cannot provide, essentially the conditions under which people, usually men, used to make sense and find meaning in the world has radically altered. There are several things to note about this passage which have great implications for this chapter. First, that work was once the main source of identity for men. Second, that work was important for both individuals and wider social groups. And, finally, that social actors have to increasingly derive identity from other aspects of their life outside the workplace such as lifestyle, consumption or family. But Casey is certainly not alone in this analysis, in fact, some of the biggest names in contemporary sociology and social theory have argued that the identification with work is either disappearing altogether or is becoming more marginal (see, for example, Bauman 1998; Beck 2000; Gorz 1999; see Strangleman 2007, for a summary). But why has there been this change? As we saw in previous chapters there have been dramatic changes in the world of work in the past three decades or more with many of the taken-for-granted certainties of social life being questioned and work here is no different. Some of these changes are highlighted in Text box 12.5.

TEXT BOX 12.5 CHANGES IN THE ECONOMY WHICH INFLUENCE WORK IDENTITY

- Unemployment
- Globalisation
- Feminisation of work
- Deindustrialisation and the growth of service-based employment
- Loss of traditional (often male work)
- Ending of established patterns of work education (craft apprenticeship)
- The rise of insecurity at work
- Individualisation at work.

All these factors have been seen to contribute to a breakdown of established patterns of work and employment and, importantly, these have implications both inside as well as outside the workplace. So instability in employment is seen as one of the factors affecting a loss of community in wider society more generally. As Ulrich Beck puts it: 'Paid employment is becoming precarious; the foundations of the social-welfare state are collapsing; normal life-stories are breaking up into fragments' (2000: 3).

Richard Sennett has talked about the intelligible narratives that people used to construct around their work identity and suggests that this is being made increasingly difficult to maintain in contemporary society. In a series of books and articles, he notes the way that what he calls the 'new capitalism' no longer affords the employed the ability to construct life narratives through their work (Sennett 1998, 2003, 2006). This, he argues, is due to the speeding up of capitalism and the ever-shorter time horizons in which shareholders expect return on their investments. Sennett sees this situation as one which damages the individual, their families, communities as well as the nature of work. He suggest that the new capitalism both isolates and individualises people by making them act in a highly selfish way, one where long term commitment to other workers, the organisation or the place you live is disadvantageous to career advancement. The 'good worker' under this new capitalism is one who does not invest themselves in anything other than their narrow career progression. What this creates for Sennett is what he describes as a 'corrosion of character', a degraded work identity which is the poorer for adopting such an instrumental attitude to work.

Gender and work identity

Many of the ideas on the end of work cited above are often implicitly discussing male work identity when they lament loss. The influence of post-structuralist theorists of identity, like Judith Butler, have moved sociology beyond the focus on class identity and on to examine how identities of gender, sexuality, ethnicity, and so on are formed (see Taylor and Spencer 2004). Innovative work on gender and class by sociologists like Beverley Skeggs has also introduced us to the notion of 'spoiled' identities. While men have long had recourse to respected and respectable sources of identity formation like breadwinner, and when working-class men in even the lowest status occupations had a heroic working-class masculinity to draw upon (Skeggs 1997), much of women's work has been trivialised and has offered a weaker source of identity formation (see also McDowell 2003). The trivialisation of the work performed by women in the home is reflected in women's statement: 'I'm just a housewife'. This takes us back to Oakley's classic research into housework that, although not using the contemporary language of a spoiled identity, revealed such problems with the 'housewife' identity for women.

While women's sources of identity might be found via a home life as mother or wife, men's identity has been dominated by male breadwinning. Accordingly, a sociological and psychological literature has highlighted the threat posed to male identity by unemployment and redundancy (Goodwin 2002; Jahoda 1982). As shown in Chapter 11, being unemployed makes many men feel less man-like: 'The man is the breadwinner. This is how you're brought up anyway. If the man hasn't got a job it's not just the job insecurity, he feels less of a man, doesn't he?' (Charles and James 2005: 547).

These contemporary debates about work identity are important because of the way they portray work now, as well as work identity in the past. Often in examining the instability of the present, writers are explicitly or implicitly suggesting a fixed past where work identity was static and homogenous. As we have tried to suggest in this and other chapters, this is a problematic viewpoint and one which the sociology of work needs to challenge in a variety of ways. In the remainder of this chapter we want to suggest ways in which this challenge might be mounted and identify some of the resources which could be used. In doing so we want to draw together the discussions we have had in this chapter.

A new cultural sociology of work?

In examining questions of work identity, meaning, emotion and culture we want to suggest that the renewed interest in these aspects of work is welcome and important. As we pointed out, the stimulus for such discussions often comes from outside rather than from within the sociology of work – social theory and management, for example. But we do not wish to suggest that this renewal is something which should be undertaken from outside the sociology of work. We believe that there are some very interesting developments that could be drawn upon here.

More recently, there has been a renewed interest in what some would call the moral aspects of work, which relate centrally to this chapter's topic. As part of this literature there is a focus on notions of dignity at work, and two American sociologists have recently published books on this subject. Michelle Lamont's *The Dignity of Working Men* (2000) is a detailed examination of the moral universe of blue-collar male workers in France and the USA. Lamont attempts to understand from the workers' own standpoint their worldview, the way they think about their work, their careers and co-workers. The value of this research is the way it takes seriously the subjective and collective moral interpretations of the workplace from the viewpoint of the shop floor. Hodson's book, *Dignity at Work* (2001), is very different in that it tries to examine many of the same issues by reanalysing qualitative material from many of the ethnographic studies of the workplace carried out by sociologists over the past forty or more years using quantitative approaches. Hodson's aim is to understand how workers try to achieve a sense of dignity and moral worth in the context of organisations and hostile management. In the UK, Andrew Sayer (2005) has written a number of pieces about moral economy and working-class understandings of work. Sayer's work is more overtly theoretical than the other pieces but what he provides is a potential framework and argument for taking working-class people's position seriously and is something which sociologists carrying out more empirically focused research could adopt as a useful model.

This alerts us to a wider issue for the sociology of work: that of the continued need to carry out ethnographic studies in the workplace in order to better understand emerging, stable as well as declining work cultures. Fincham (2006) has noted the decline in the number of work ethnographies. It would be a shame if this tradition were to die out as they offer one of the best ways of accessing notions of culture, identity and emotional attachment. This type of evidence can also be uncovered by sensitive and highly qualitative interviews. A model for this approach can be seen in Bourdieu *et al.* (1999) and in the work of Valerie Walkerdine (2005) which is informed by a detailed psychosocial approach. This work can supplement the long established sociological tradition of rigorous quantitative research into work identity and attitudes to and meanings of work, using primary and secondary data sets (see Chapter 3).

CONCLUSION

In this chapter we looked at the questions of identity, culture and emotion in work. While these are seen as very contemporary concerns we have argued here that they have their roots in the questions generated by classical sociology. We saw how these concerns informed later developments within sociology of work and related disciplines and tried to place the contemporary in this context. These themes help us understand how and why people and groups work as they do.

FURTHER READING

Robin Leidner's essay 'Identity and work' (2006) in the Korczynski *et al.* collection *Social Theory at Work* is a useful contemporary overview of some of the issues addressed in the chapter.

Douglas Harper and Helene Lawson's *The Cultural Study of Work* (2003) is a very useful collection of ethnographies which look at work culture and identity.

Arlie Russell Hochschild's *The Managed Heart* (1983) remains a foundational classic in discussions of emotions and work.

Paul du Gay has written a series of books on work and identity. His early work, including *Consumption and Identity at Work* (1996), links more directly to work sociology while his later work, including *Organizing Identity* (2007), engages more directly with management and organisational studies.

STUDENT PROJECTS AND ESSAY QUESTIONS

1 Does work still shape social identity?
2 How and in what ways is work identity gendered?
3 Compare and contrast the different type of evidence one would gain from qualitative and quantitative study in to work identity and attitude.
4 'All work is emotional' – discuss.

CHAPTER 13

▓ The changing nature
of work

▓ The changing nature of
the study of work

▓ The future for the
sociology of work

Conclusion

▓ THE CHANGING NATURE OF WORK

Recent decades have seen an amazing transformation in the way paid work is carried out and organised. Older certainties about this work have been lost, replaced by confusion but also a sense of possibility. In these years, the Western industrial economies have seen deindustrialisation and high levels of unemployment, the explosion of service industries, the increasing participation of women in the labour market, the impact of globalisation and huge changes in the application of information technology to work and work tasks.

As we have noted throughout *Work and Society*, many commentators have suggested that we are witnessing unprecedented changes in the organisation of paid work, to the extent that some proclaim the 'end of work', or that pregnant within the current crisis is the possibility that we can fundamentally rethink what work could be, that there is an opportunity to redistribute labour and to ensure that work becomes more rounded and fulfilling for all. Others suggest that very little has changed in these years, indeed, that work has changed very little since the nineteenth century. They argue that it is still embedded in a fundamentally unequal system and that, if anything, this is becoming even more polarised than was the case at the birth of sociology.

Contemporary debates have also paid increasing attention to those forms of work that stand outside the employment relationship, and in particular to unpaid labour carried out within the home. Questions of change characterise these debates too but commentators have identified more continuity than transformation in who performs unpaid domestic work and for whom. What marks these discussions is the recognition of the necessary interlinkages between unpaid and paid forms of work, inside and outside the home, and the need to see a more holistic picture of the division of all forms of labour.

THE CHANGING NATURE OF THE STUDY OF WORK

In *Work and Society*, we have been keen to stress both continuities and change in the way work in all its forms has been organised. Equally, we aim to understand how and why sociologists have looked at work in the ways they have. In the book we have taken as a starting point the basic idea that the ideas of the classical theorists are a powerful backdrop against which we can understand current developments and preoccupations. They provide us with a set of questions which are still incredibly fruitful in the analysis of work. We still want to know how people cope with economic change, how they understand their work and how or if they identify with it. We still seek new ways to understand why work is unequally distributed in the way it is. Above all we want to chart the social relationships which are created through work and in turn, how work creates new social relationships.

In the book we have tried to put forward the idea that the study of the sociology of work has not been an even process of unfolding improvement. Rather we have suggested the crablike progress of those in the area. The sociology of work is a label that can be attached to many researchers and writers concerned with the study of social relations in work. We also need to be aware of other parts of sociology which impinge on this area, as well as a whole range of other fields of study. We have focused our attention on the flaws and drawbacks of some of this writing and suggest what new directions they might take in the future.

In *Work and Society*, we have emphasised the need to see work as a very broad concept, one that encompasses paid and unpaid labour. We have argued that the sociology of work needs to integrate domestic work as well as unemployment in order to fully understand its subject matter. Running through the book has also been a concern to recognise that any form of work is always underpinned and embedded in a complex nexus of social divisions such as class, gender and 'race'. As sociologists of work we need to understand how these are formed, produced and are transformed over time, we need to ask questions about how the social is realised in the context of work and economic life. It is hoped that the reader of *Work and Society* also understands that work, like any aspect of social life, is complex, and that we need to apply the sociological imagination flexibly and broadly. This means that we cannot enjoy the luxury of 'one' theory or 'one' method which will tell us all we need to know. We suggested instead that a variety of theories and methods offers the researcher different cuts into a complex and shifting world of work. It is a sense of the dynamism and flow that we have tried to capture here. So the question is, what is the future for the sociology of work?

THE FUTURE FOR THE SOCIOLOGY OF WORK?

One place to start answering this question would be to ask, what is good about what we have already? The sociological imagination when applied to work is unique from other disciplines in that it provides us with a special set of tools. We can understand small-scale interaction through to the analysis of global shifts in the economy. We can understand how work, in its myriad forms, is organised and allocated at a number of levels with societies as well as make comparative and historical parallels. We also can be proud of the classic legacy of theory rooted in sociological understandings of the world and especially of work. So the argument of the book has been that we need to be aware of the tremendous set of resources that we can draw upon, but equally be aware that these have not always been brought to bear on all aspects of socio-economic life. One of the reasons why we have laid so much stress here on an historical perspective within work sociology is so that the reader can understand how and why writers have worked in the way they have. Equally, to be able to engage as sociologists in self-criticism it helps to be able to understand what has been done in the past under the title of the sociology of work. A disciplinary self-confidence allows the constructive borrowing and adaptation from other disciplines. So a future sociology of work is one sure of its past and able to critically engage with other disciplines which may be very close or more distant.

The great challenge for the sociology of work is to remain focused on the social relations of work and work organisation, and to above all recognise the humanity of all those who work. We hope that *Work and Society* has engaged its readers but, more than that, it has inspired them to go out and research the world of work. We hope that the reader is both aware of the traditions of work sociology and prepared to apply these tools in new and exciting ways.

BIBLIOGRAPHY

Abrams, F. (2002) *Below the Breadline: Living on the Minimum Wage*, London: Profile.

Acker, J. (1990) 'Hierarchies, jobs, bodies: a theory of gendered organizations', *Gender and Society*, 4(2): 139–58.

Acker, J. (2004) 'Gender, capitalism and globalization', *Critical Sociology*, 30(1): 17–41.

Ackroyd, S. and Thompson, P. (1999) *Organizational Misbehaviour*, London: Sage.

Adam, B. (1990) *Time and Social Theory*, Cambridge: Polity.

Adam, B. (1995) *Timewatch: The Social Analysis of Time*, Cambridge: Polity.

Adkins, L. (1995) *Gendered Work: Sexuality, Family and the Labour Market*, Buckingham: Open University Press.

Aitken, I. (ed.) (1998) *The Documentary Film Movement: An Anthology*, Edinburgh: Edinburgh University Press.

Albrow, M. (1997) *Do Organizations Have Feelings?*, London: Routledge.

Allen, S. (1971) *New Minorities, Old Conflicts: Asian and West Indian Migrants in Britain*, London: Random House.

Allen, S., Purcell, K., Waton, A. and Wood, S. (eds) (1986) *The Experience of Unemployment*, Basingstoke: Macmillan.

Alvesson, M. (2002) *Understanding Organizational Culture*, London: Sage.

Amin, A. (ed.) (1994) *Post-Fordism: A Reader*, Oxford: Blackwell.

Anderson, B. (2000) *Doing the Dirty Work? The Global Politics of Domestic Labour*, London: Zed Books.

Anderson, B. (2002) 'Just another job? The commodification of domestic labor', in B. Ehrenreich and A. Hochschild (eds) *Global Women: Nannies, Maids and Sex Workers in the New Economy*, London: Granta.

Anthias, F. (2001) 'The concept of "social division" and theorising social stratification: looking at ethnicity and class', *Sociology*, 35(4): 835–54.

Anthias, F. and Yuval-Davis, N. (1983) 'Contextualising feminism: gender, ethnicity and class divisions', *Feminist Review*, 15: 62–75.

Anthony, P. (1994) *Managing Culture*, Buckingham: Open University Press.

Ashton, D. (1986) *Unemployment under Capitalism*, Brighton: Wheatsheaf.

Austrin, T. and West, J. (2005) 'Skills and surveillance in casino gaming work, consumption and regulation', *Work, Employment and Society*, 19(2): 305–26.

Bagguley, P. and Mann, K. (1992) 'Idle thieving bastards? Scholarly representations of the "underclass"', *Work, Employment and Society*, 6(1): 113–26.

Bales, K. (1999) *Disposable People: New Slavery in the Global Economy*, Berkeley, CA: University of California Press.

Banton, M. (1967) *Race Relations*, New York: Basic Books.

Baritz, L. (1960) *The Servants of Power*, Middletown: Wesleyan University Press.

Barrett, M. and MacIntosh, M. (1980) 'The family wage: some problems for socialists and feminists', *Capital and Class*, 11: 51–72.

Barringer, T. (2005) *Men at Work: Art and Labour in Victorian Britain*, New Haven, CT: Yale University Press.

Basso, P. (2003) *Modern Times, Ancient Hours: Working Lives in the Twenty-first Century*, London: Verso.

Basu, A. and Altinay, E. (2003) *Family and Work in Ethnic Minority Businesses*, Bristol: The Policy Press.

Bate, P. (1995) *Strategies for Culture Change*, Oxford: Butterworth-Heinemann.

Bauman, Z. (1992) *Intimations of Post-modernity*, London: Routledge.

Bauman, Z. (1998) *Work, Consumerism and the New Poor*, Buckingham: Open University Press.

Baxter, J. (1997) 'Gender equality and participation in housework: a cross-national perspective', *Journal of Comparative Family Studies*, 28(3): 220–47.

Baxter, J. (2002) 'Patterns of change and stability in the gender division of household labour in Australia, 1986–1997', *Journal of Sociology*, 38(4): 399–424.

BBC News Online (2002) Wednesday, 24 April.

Beale, D. (1994) *Driven by Nissan?: A Critical Guide to New Management Techniques*, London: Lawrence and Wishart.

Beatty, C. *et al.* (2002) *The Real Level of Unemployment*, Sheffield: CRESR, Sheffield Hallam University.

Beck, U. (2000) *The Brave New World of Work*, Cambridge: Polity.

Becker, G. (1985) 'A theory of the allocation of time', *Economic Journal*, 75: 493–517.

Beechey, V. (1977) 'Some notes on female wage labour in capitalist production', *Capital and Class*, 3(12): 45–66.

Beechey, V. and Perkins, T. (1987) *A Matter of Hours: Women, Part-time Work and Labour Markets*, Cambridge: Polity Press.

Bell, D. (1973) *The Coming of the Post-Industrial Society: A Venture in Social Forecasting*, London: Peregrine.

Bello, W. and Rosenfeld, S. (1990) *Dragons in Distress: Asia's Miracle Economies in Crisis*, London: Penguin.

Bennett, K., Beynon, H. and Hudson, R. (2000) *Coalfields Regeneration: Dealing with the Consequences of Industrial Decline*, Bristol: Policy Press.

Bensman, J. and Lilienfeld, R. (1975) 'Craft and consciousness', in G. Esland, G. Salaman and M. Speakman (eds) *People and Work*, Edinburgh: Holmes McDougall.

Berman, M. (1982) *All That Is Solid Melts into Air: The Experience of Modernity*, London: Verso.

Berthoud, R. (1979) *Unemployed Professionals and Executives*, London: Policy Studies Institute.

Berthoud, R. (2000) 'Ethnic employment penalties in Britain', *Journal of Ethnic and Migration Studies*, 26(3): 389–416.

Beynon, H. (1973) *Working for Ford*, Harmondsworth: Penguin.

Beynon, H. (1988) 'Regulating research: politics and decision making in industrial organizations', in A. Bryman (ed.) *Doing Research in Organizations*, London: Routledge.

Bhavnani, R. (1994) *Black Women in the Labour Market: A Research Review*, Manchester: EOC.

Bhopal, K. (1998) 'How gender and ethnicity intersect: the significance of education, employment and marital status', *Sociological Research Online*, 3(3): http://www.socresonline.org.uk.

Bielenski, H., Bosch, G. and Wagner, A. (2002) *Working Time Preferences in Sixteen European Countries*, Dublin: European Foundation for the Improvement of Living and Working Conditions.

Biernacki, R. (1995) *The Fabrication of Labor: Germany and Britain, 1640–1914*, Berkeley, CA: University of California Press.

Bittman, M. (2004) 'Parenting and employment', in N. Folbre and M. Bittman (eds), *Family Time: The Social Organisation of Care*, London: Routledge.

Björnberg, U. (1998) 'Family orientation among men: a process of change in Sweden', in E. Drew *et al.* (eds) *Women, Work and Family in Europe*, London: Routledge.

Blair, A., Leopold, J. and Karsten, L. (2001) 'An awkward partner? Britain's implementation of the Working Time Directive', *Time and Society*, 10(1): 63–76.

Blauner, R. (1964) *Alienation and Freedom: The Factory Worker and His Industry*, Chicago: University of Chicago Press.

Bloch, A. (2004) 'Labour market participation and conditions of employment: a comparison of minority ethnic groups and refugees in Britain', *Sociological Research Online*, 9(2): <http://www.socresonline.org.uk/9/2/bloch.html>

Bluestone, B. and Harrison, B. (1982) *The Deindustrialization of America: Plant Closing, Community Abandonment, and the Dismantling of Basic Industry*, New York: Basic Books.

Bolton, A., Pole, C. and Mizen, P. (2001) 'Picture this: researching child workers', *Sociology*, 35(2): 501–18.

Bone, J. (2006) *The Hard Sell: An Ethnographic Study of the Direct Selling Industry*, Aldershot: Ashgate.

Booth, C. (1889) *Life and Labour of the People in London*, London: Macmillan and Co.

Bosch, G. (2000) 'Working-time reductions and employment – lessons from Europe', in P. Peltola (ed.) *Working Time in Europe: Towards a European Working Time Policy*, Report of an International Conference, 11–12 October 1999, Helsinki, Ministry of Labour.

Bosch, G., Dawkins, P. and Michon, F. (1993) *Times Are Changing: Working Time in 14 Industrialised Countries*, Geneva: Institute for International Labour Studies.

Bottero, W. (2004) 'Class identities and the identity of class', *Sociology*, 38(5): 985–1003.

Bottero, W. (2005) *Stratification: Social Division and Inequality*, London: Routledge.

Bourdieu, P. *et al.* (1999) *The Weight of the World: Social Suffering in Contemporary Society*, Cambridge: Polity.

Bradley, H. (1989) *Men's Work, Women's Work*, Cambridge: Polity.

Bradley, H. (1996) *Fractured Identities: Changing Patterns of Inequality*, Cambridge: Polity.

Bradley, H. (2004) 'Catching up? Changing inequalities of gender at work and in the family in the UK', in F. Devine and M. C. Waters (eds) *Social Inequalities in Comparative Perspective*, Oxford: Blackwell.

Bradley, H., Erickson, M., Stephenson, C. M. and Williams, S. (2000) *Myths at Work*, Cambridge: Polity Press.

Bradshaw, D. J. and Ozment, S. (eds) (2000) *The Voice of Toil: 19th-Century British Writing about Work*, Athens, OH: Ohio University Press.

Brah, A. (1994) ' "Race" and "culture" in the gendering of labour markets: South Asian young Muslim women and the labour market', in H. Afshar and M. Maynard (eds) *The Dynamics of Race and Gender: Some Feminist Interventions*, London: Taylor and Francis.

Braham, P., Rhodes, E. and Pearn, M. (eds) (1981) *Discrimination and Disadvantage in Employment: The Experience of Black Workers*, London: Harper and Row Ltd.

Brandth, B. and Kvande, E. (1998) 'Masculinity and child care: the reconstruction of fathering', *Sociological Review*, 46(2): 293–313.

Brannen, J. (1995) 'Young people and their contribution to household work', *Sociology*, 29(2): 317–38.

Brannen, J., Heptinstall, E. and Bhopal, K. (2000) *Connecting Children: Care and Family Life in Later Childhood*, New York: Routledge/Falmer.

Brannen, J. and Moss, P. (1991) *Managing Mothers: Dual Earner Households after Maternity Leave*, London: Unwin Hyman Ltd.

Braverman, H. (1974) *Labor and Monopoly Capitalism: The Degradation of Work in the Twentieth Century*, New York: Monthly Review Press.

Braybon, G. (1982) *Women Workers in the First World War: The British Experience*, London: Croom Helm.

Braybon, G. and Summerfield, P. (1987) *Out of the Cage: Women's Experiences in Two World Wars*, London: Pandora Press.

Breton, R. (2005) *Gospels and Grit: Work and Labour in Carlyle, Conrad, and Orwell*, Toronto: University of Toronto Press.

Breugel, I. (1979) 'Women as a reserve army of labour', *Feminist Review*, 3: 12–23.

Breugel, I. (1996) 'Whose myths are they anyway?: A comment', *British Journal of Sociology*, 47(1): 175–7.

Breugel, I. and Perrons, D. (1998) 'Deregulation and women's employment: the diverse experiences of women in Britain', *Feminist Economics*, 4(1): 103–25.

Brewer, J. (2000) *Ethnography*, Buckingham: Open University Press.

Brooks, D. (1975) *Race and Labour in London Transport*, Oxford: Oxford University Press.

Brown, C. (1984) *Black and White Britain*, London: Heinemann.

Brown, E. (2005) *The Corporate Eye: Photography and the Rationalization of American Commercial Culture, 1884–1929*, Baltimore, MD: The Johns Hopkins University Press.

Brown, M. and Taylor, B. (1993) *Art of the Soviets: Painting, Sculpture and Architecture in a One-Party State, 1917–1992*, Manchester: Manchester University Press.

Brown, R. K. (1965) 'Participation, conflict and change in industry: a review of research in industrial sociology at the Department of Social Science, University of Liverpool', *Sociological Review*, 13(3): 273–95.

Brown, R. K. (1967) 'Research consultancy in industrial enterprises: a review of the contribution of the Tavistock Institute of Human Relations to the development of industrial sociology', *Sociology*, 1(1): 33–60.

Brown, R. K. (1988) 'The employment relationship in sociological theory', in D. Gallie (ed.) *Employment in Britain*, Oxford: Blackwell.

Brown, R. K. (1992) *Understanding Industrial Organisations: Theoretical Perspectives in Industrial Sociology*, London: Routledge.

Brown, R. K. (ed.) (1997) *The Changing Shape of Work*, London: Macmillan Press.

Brown, R. K. and Brannen, P. (1970) 'Social relations and social perspectives amongst shipbuilding workers: a preliminary statement', *Sociology*, 4: 71–84.

Brubaker, R. (1991) *The Limits of Rationality: An Essay on the Social and Moral Thought of Max Weber*, London: Routledge.

Bryan, F. (2003) *Rouge: Pictured in its Prime*, Dearborn: Ford Books.

Bryman, A. (1992) *Charisma and Leadership in Organizations*, London: Sage.

Bryman, A. (2004) *Social Research Methods.* Oxford: Oxford University Press.

Bryman, A. and Bell, E. (2007) *Business Research Methods*, Oxford: Oxford University Press.

BSA (2002) 'Statement of Ethical Practice for the British Sociological Association', Durham: BSA.

Bulmer, M. (1975) 'Sociological models of the mining community', *Sociological Review*, 23: 61–92.

Bulmer, M. (ed.) (2002) *Sociological Research Methods*, London: Macmillan.

Burawoy, M. (1979) *Manufacturing Consent: Changes in the Labor Process under Monopoly Capitalism*, Chicago: University of Chicago Press.

Burawoy, M. (2000) *Global Ethnography: Forces, Connections, and Imaginations*, Berkeley, CA: University of California Press.

Burchell, B., Ladipo, D. and Wilkinson, F. (eds) (2002) *Job Insecurity and Work Intensification*, London: Routledge.

Burnett, J. (ed.) (1994a) *Useful Toil: Autobiographies of Working People from the 1820s to the 1920s*, London: Routledge.

Burnett, J. (ed.) (1994b) *Idle Hands: The Experience of Unemployment, 1790–1990*, London: Routledge.

Burrell, G. (2006) 'Foucauldian and postmodern thought and the analysis of work', in M. Korczynski, R. Hodson and P. Edwards (eds) *Social Theory at Work*, Oxford: Oxford University Press.

Byrne, D. S. (1999) *Social Exclusion*, Buckingham: Open University Press.

Casey, C. (1995) *Work, Self and Society after Industrialism*, London: Routledge.

Castles, S. (2003) 'Towards a sociology of forced migration and social transformation', *Sociology*, 37(1): 13–34.

Castles, S. and Kosack, G. (1973) *Immigrant Workers and Class Structure in Western Europe*, London: Oxford University Press.

Cavendish, R. (1982) *Women on the Line*, London: Routledge and Kegan Paul.

Centre for Contemporary Cultural Studies (CCCS) (eds) (1982) *The Empire Strikes Back: Race and Racism in 70s Britain*, London: Hutchinson.

Chaney, D. (1994) *Cultural Turn: Scene-setting Essays on Contemporary Cultural Theory*, London: Routledge.

Charles, N. (1990) 'Women and class: a problematic analysis?', *Sociological Review*, 38(1): 43–89.

Charles, N. and James, E. (2003a) 'Job insecurity, work orientations and gender', *British Journal of Sociology*, 54(2): 239–57.

Charles, N. and James, E. (2003b) 'The gender dimensions of job insecurity in a local labour market', *Work, Employment and Society*, 17(3): 531–52.

Charles, N. and James, E. (2005) ' "He earns the bread and butter and I earn the cream": job insecurity and the male breadwinner family in South Wales', *Work, Employment and Society*, 13(2): 205–24.

Chateauvert, M. (1998) *Marching Together: Women of the Brotherhood of Sleeping Car Porters*, Urbana, IL: University of Illinois Press.

Clark, D. (1987) 'Families facing redundancy', in S. Fineman (ed.) *Unemployment: Personal and Social Consequences*, London: Tavistock.

Clark, T. (1997) *Art and Propaganda in the Twentieth Century*, London: Everyman.

Clasen, J., Gould, A. and Vincent, J. (1998) *Voices Within and Without: Responses to Long-term Unemployment in Germany, Sweden and Britain*, Bristol: Policy Press

Cockburn, C. ([1983] 1991) *Brothers: Male Dominance and Technological Change*, London: Pluto Press.

Cockburn, C. (1985) *Machinery of Dominance: Women, Men and Technical Know-how*, London: Pluto Press.

Cockburn, C. and Ormrod, S. (1993) *Gender and Technology in the Making*, London: Sage.

Coffield, F., Borrill, C. and Marshall, S. (1986) *Growing up at the Margins*, Buckingham: Open University Press.

Cohen, L., Hancock, P. and Tyler, M. (2006) 'Beyond the scope of the possible: art, photography and organisational abjection', *Culture and Organization*, 12(2): 109–25.

Coles, N. and Zandy, J. (eds) (2007) *American Working Class Literature: An Anthology*, Oxford: Oxford University Press.

Collinson, M. and Collinson, D. L. (1996) 'It's only Dick: the sexual harassment of women managers in insurance sales', *Work, Employment and Society*, 1(10): 29–56.

Commission on Multi-Ethnic Britain (2000) *The Future of Multi-Ethnic Britain*, London: Runnymede Trust and Profile Books.

Comte, A. (1855/1974) *The Crisis of Industrial Civilization*, ed. R. Fletcher, London: Heinemann Educational.

Connell, R. W. (1987) *Gender and Power: Society, the Person and Sexual Politics*, Cambridge: Polity.

Connell, R. W. (2000) *The Men and the Boys*, Cambridge: Polity.

Connell, R. W. (2002) *Gender*, Cambridge: Polity.

Constantine, S. (1986) *Buy and Build: The Advertising Posters of the Empire Marketing Board*, London: HMSO.

Corti, L., Foster, J. and Thompson, P. (1995) 'Archiving qualitative research data', *Social Research Update*, Issue 10. http://www.soc.surrey.ac.uk/sru/SRU10.html.

Coupland, D. (1991) *Generation X: Tales for an Accelerated Culture*, London: Abacus.

Cowie, J. (1999) *Capital Moves: RCA's Seventy-Year Quest for Cheap Labor*, New York: The New Press.

Cowie, J. and Boehm, L. (2006) 'Dead man's town: "Born in the USA," social history and working-class identity', *American Quarterly*, 28(2): 353–78.

Cowie, J. and Heathcott, J. (eds) (2003) *Beyond the Ruins: The Meaning of Deindustrialisation*, Ithaca, NY: Cornell University Press/ILR.

Coyle, A. (1984) *Redundant Women*, London: Women's Press.

Craig, C., Rubery, J., Tarling, R. and Wilkinson, F. (1982) *Labour Market Structure, Industrial Organisation and Low Pay*, Cambridge: Cambridge University Press.

Craig, G., Corden, A. and Thornton, P. (2000) 'Safety in social research', *Social Research Update*, Issue 20: http://sru.soc.surrey.ac.uk/SRU29.html.

Craig, L. (2006) 'Children and the revolution: a time-diary analysis of the impact motherhood on daily workload', *Journal of Sociology*, 42(2): 125–43.

Crompton, R. (1997) *Women and Work in Modern Britain*, Oxford: Oxford University Press.

Crompton, R. (1999) 'The decline of the male breadwinner: explanations and interpretations', in R. Crompton (ed.) *Restructuring Gender Relations and Employment: The Decline of the Male Breadwinner*, Oxford: Oxford University Press.

Crompton, R. (2002) 'Employment, flexible working and the family', *British Journal of Sociology*, 53(4): 537–58.

Crompton, R. (2006) *Employment and the Family*, Cambridge: Cambridge University Press.

Crompton, R., Devine, F., Savage, M. and Scott, J. (2000) *Renewing Class Analysis*, Oxford: Blackwell.

Crompton, R. and Jones, G. (1984) *White-collar Proletariat: Deskilling and Gender in Clerical Work*, London: Macmillan.

Cross, S. and Bagihole, B. (2002) 'Girls' jobs for the boys? Men, masculinity and non-traditional occupations', *Gender, Work and Organization*, 9(2): 204–26.

Dabakis, M. (1999) *Visualizing Labor: American Sculpture*, Cambridge: Cambridge University Press.

Dale, A., Arber, S. and Proctor, M. (1988) *Doing Secondary Analysis*, London: Unwin Hyman.

Dale, A., Fieldhouse, E., Shaheen, N. and Kalra, V. (2002a) 'The labour market prospects for Pakistani and Bangladeshi women', *Work, Employment and Society*, 16(1): 5–25.

Dale, A. and Holdsworth, C. (1998) 'Why don't minority ethnic women in Britain work part-time?', in J. O'Reilly and C. Fagan (eds) *Part-time Prospects*, London: Routledge.

Dale, A., Lindley, J. and Dex, S. (2006) 'A life-course perspective on ethnic differences in women's economic activity in Britain', *European Sociological Review*, 22(3): 323–37.

Dale, A., Shaheen, N., Kalra, V. and Fieldhouse, E. (2002b) 'Routes into education and employment for young Pakistani and Bangladeshi women in the UK', *Ethnic and Racial Studies*, 25(6): 942–68.

Daly, M. (2002) 'Care as a good for social policy', *Journal of Social Policy*, 31(2): 251–70.

Daniel, P., Foresta, M., Stange, M. and Stein, S. (1987) *Official Images: New Deal Photography*, Washington, DC: Smithsonian Institution Press.

Daniel, W. W. (1968) *Racial Discrimination in England*, London: Penguin.

Daniels, J. (2003) *Show and Tell: New and Selected Poems*, Madison, WI: University of Wisconsin Press.

Danon, R. (1985) *Work in the English Novel: The Myth of Vocation*, London: Croom Helm.

Darley, G. (2003) *Factory*, London: Reaktion.

Davis, K. and Moore, W. (1953) Some principles of stratification', *American Sociological Review*, 18: 387–94.

Deal, T. and Kennedy, A. (1988) *Corporate Cultures: The Rites and Rituals of Corporate Life*, London: Penguin.

Deetz, S. (1998) 'Discursive formations, strategized subordination, and self-surveillance: an empirical case', in A. McKinlay and K. Starkey (eds) *Foucault, Management and Organizational Theory*, London: Sage.

de Graaf, P. and Ultee, W. (2000) 'United in employment, united in unemployment? Employment and unemployment of couples in the European Union in 1994', in D. Gallie and S. Paugam (eds) *Welfare Regimes and the Experience of Unemployment in Europe*, Oxford: Oxford University Press, pp. 265–85.

Delamont, S. (2003) *Feminist Sociology*, London: Sage.

Delphy, C. (1977) *The Main Enemy*, London: Women's Research and Resources Centre.

Delphy, C. and Leonard, D. (1992) *Familiar Exploitation*, Cambridge: Polity.

Delphy, S. (1977) *The Main Enemy: A Materialist Analysis of Women's Oppression*, London: Women's Research and Resources Centre Publications.

Denning, M. (1987) *Mechanic Accents: Dime Novels and Working-Class Culture in America*, London: Verso.

Dennis, N., Heniques, F. and Slaughter, C. (1956) *Coal Is Our Life: An Analysis of a Yorkshire Mining Community*, London: Eyre and Spottiswoode.

Denzin, N. K. (1989) 'Strategies of multiple triangulation', in N. K. Denzin (ed.) *The Research Act*, 3rd edn, Englewood Cliffs, NJ: Prentice Hall.

Devine, F. (1992) *Affluent Workers Revisited: Privatism and the Working Class*, Edinburgh: Edinburgh University Press.

Devine, F. and Heath, S. (1999) *Sociological Research Methods in Context*, London: Macmillan.

Devine, F., Savage, M., Crompton, R. and Scott, J. (eds) (2005) *Rethinking Class: Identities, Cultures and Lifestyles*, London: Palgrave.

Devine, F. and Waters, M. C. (eds) (2004) *Social Inequalities in Comparative Perspective*, Oxford: Blackwell.

Dex, S. (1987) *Women's Occupational Mobility*, London: Macmillan Press Ltd.

Dex, S. (1988) *Women's Attitudes towards Work*, Basingstoke: Macmillan.

Dicken, P. (1998) *Global Shift (Transformation of the World Economy)*, London: Paul Chapman Publishing.

Dickens, R., Gregg, P. and Wadsworth, J. (2003) *The Labour Market under New Labour: The State of Working Britain*, Basingstoke: Palgrave Macmillan.

Dingwall, R. and Strangleman, T. (2005) 'Organisational cultures in the public sector', in E. Ferlie, L. Lynn and C. Pollitt (eds) *The Oxford Handbook of Public Management*, Oxford: Oxford University Press.

Disney, R. and Hawkes, D. (2003) 'Why has employment recently risen among older workers in Britain?', in R. Dickens, P. Gregg and J. Wadsworth (eds) *The Labour Market under New Labour: The State of Working Britain*, Basingstoke: Palgrave Macmillan.

Ditton, J. (1979) *Part-time Crime*, London: Macmillan.

Dobash, R. E. and Dobash, R. P. (1979) *Violence against Wives: A Case Against the Patriarchy*, New York: Free Press.

Dobash, R. E., Dobash, R. P., Cavanagh, K. and Lewis, R. (2004) 'Not an ordinary killer – just an ordinary guy: When men murder an intimate woman partner', *Violence against Women*, 10(6): 577–605.

Doogan, K. (2001) 'Insecurity and long-term employment', *Work, Employment and Society*, 15(3): 419–41.

Doss, E. (2002) 'Design, culture, identity: the Wolfsonian Collection', *The Journal of Decorative and Propaganda Arts*, 24: 230–57.

Doukas, D. (2003) *Worked Over: The Corporate Sabotage of an American Community*, Ithaca, NY: Cornell University Press.

Downs, L. (1999) *Diego Rivera: The Detroit Industry Murals*, New York: W. W. Norton.

Dublin, T. (1998) *When the Mines Closed: Stories of Struggles in Hard Times*, Ithaca, NY: Cornell University Press.

Dudley, K. M. (1994) *The End of the Line: Lost Jobs, New Lives in Postindustrial America*, Chicago: University of Chicago Press.

Dudley, K. M. (2000) *Debt and Dispossession: Farm Loss in America's Heartland*, Chicago: University of Chicago Press.

Du Gay, P. (1996) *Consumption and Identity at Work*, London: Sage.

Du Gay, P. (2000) *In Praise of Bureaucracy: Weber, Organization, Ethics*, London: Sage.

Du Gay, P. (ed.) (2005) *The Values of Bureaucracy*, Oxford: Oxford University Press.

Du Gay, P. (2007) *Organizing Identity: Persons and Organizations 'After Theory'*, London: Sage.

Du Gay, P. and Salaman, G. (1992) 'The cult(ure) of the customer', *Journal of Management Studies*, 29(4): 616–33.

Duncan, S. (1995) 'Theorising European gender systems', *Journal of European Social Policy*, 5(4): 263–84.

Duncan, S. and Edwards, R. (1999) *Lone Mothers, Paid Work and Gendered Moral Rationalities*, London: Macmillan.

Duncan, S., Edwards, R., Reynolds, T. and Alldred, P. (2004) 'Mothers and child care: policies, values and theories', *Children and Society*, 18(4): 254–65.

Dunne, G. A. (1992) 'Balancing homelife and employment commitments in lesbian households', in G. A. Dunne, J. Jarman and R. M. Blackburn (eds) *Inequalities in*

Employment, Inequalities in Home-Life, Cambridge: University of Cambridge: The Sociological Research Group.

Dunne, G. A. (1998) ' "Pioneers behind our own front doors": new models for the organization of work in partnerships', *Work, Employment and Society*, 12(2): 273–95.

Durkheim, E. ([1893] 1964) *The Division of Labour in Society*. New York: The Free Press.

Durkheim, E. ([1912] 1965) *The Elementary Forms of Religious Life*, New York: Free Press.

Durkheim, E. (1992) *Professional Ethics and Civic Morals*, London: Routledge.

Dyer, R. (1997) *White: Essays on Race and Culture*, London: Routledge.

Edensor, T. (2005) *Industrial Ruins: Space, Aesthetics and Materiality*, Oxford: Berg.

Edgell, S. (1980) *Middle Class Couples: A Study of Segregation, Domination and Inequality in Marriage*, London: George Allen and Unwin.

Edwards, R. (1979) *Contested Terrain: The Transformation of the Workplace in the Twentieth Century*, London: Heinemann.

Ehrenreich, B. (2001) *Nickel and Dimed: On (Not) Getting By in America*, New York: Owl.

Ehrenreich, B. (2002) 'Maid to order', in B. Ehrenreich and A. Hochschild (eds) *Global Women: Nannies, Maids and Sex Workers in the New Economy*, London: Granta.

Ehrenreich, B. and Hochschild, A. (eds) (2002) *Global Women: Nannies, Maids and Sex Workers in the New Economy*, London: Granta.

EIRO (2002) 'Working time developments – annual update 2001', *EIRO Online*, 21 June, http:www.eiro.eurofound.ie.

Eldridge, J. E. T. (1968) *Industrial Disputes: Essays in the Sociology of Industrial Relations*, London: Routledge and Kegan Paul.

Elger, T. (1982) 'Braverman, capital accumulation and deskilling', in S. Wood (ed.) *The Degradation of Work?*, London: Hutchinson.

Elger, T. and Smith, C. (eds) (1994) *Global Japanization?: The Transnational Transformation of the Labour Process*, London: Routledge.

Elias, N. (1992) *Time: An Essay*, Oxford: Blackwell.

Ellingwood, K. (2004) *Hard Line: Life and Death on the U.S.–Mexico Border*, New York: Vintage.

El-Sawad, A. and Korczynski, M. (2007) 'Management and music: the exceptional case of the IBM songbook', *Group and Organization Management*, 32(1): 79–108.

Eltis, D. (2003) 'Labour and coercion in the English Atlantic world from the seventeenth century to the early twentieth century', in G. Heuman and J. Walvin (eds) *The Slavery Reader*, London: Routledge.

Emirbayer, M. (1996) 'Useful Durkheim', *Sociological Theory*, 14: 109–30.

Engels, F. ([1845] 1973) *The Condition of the Working-class in England: From Personal Observation and Authentic Sources*, London: Progress Publishers.

Engels, F. ([1884] 1972) *The Origin of the Family, Private Property and the State*, Harmondsworth: Penguin.

Epstein, C. (1990) 'The cultural perspective and the study of work', in K. Erikson and S. P. Vailas (eds) *The Nature of Work: Sociological Perspectives*, New Haven, CT: Yale University Press.

Epstein, C. F. and Kalleberg, A. L. (2001) 'Time and the sociology of work: issues and implications', *Work and Occupations*, 28(1): 5–16.

Esping-Anderson, G. (1990) *The Three Worlds of Welfare Capitalism*, 2nd edn, Cambridge: Polity Press.

Evans, M. (2003) *Gender and Social Theory*, Milton Keynes: Open University Press.

Evertsson, M. (2006) 'The reproduction of gender: housework and attitudes towards gender equality in the home among Swedish boys and girls', *The British Journal of Sociology*, 57(3): 415–36.

Ezzy, D. (2001) *Narrating Unemployment*, Aldershot: Ashgate.

Fagan, C. (2001a) (with Warren, T. and McAllister, I.) *More or Less Work? Gender, Employment and Working-time Preferences in Europe*, Luxembourg: European Foundation on Living and Working Conditions.

Fagan, C. (2001b) 'Time, money and the gender order: work orientations and working-time preferences in Britain', *Gender, Work and Organization*, 8(3): 239–66.

Fagan, C. and Lallement, M. (2000) 'Working time, social integration and transitional labour markets', in J. O'Reilly, I. Cebrián and M. Lallement (eds) *Working-time Changes: Social Integration through Transitional Labour Markets*, Cheltenham: Edward Elgar.

Fagnani, J. and Letablier, M. T. (2004) 'Work and family-life balance: the impact of the 35-hour laws in France', *Work, Employment and Society*, 18(3): 551–72.

Fahey, T. and Spéder, S. (2004) *Fertility and Family Issues in an Enlarged Europe*, Luxembourg: Office for Official Publications of the European Communities.

Faludi, S. (1991) *Backlash: The Undeclared War against Women*, London: Chatto and Windus.

Feldberg, R. and Glenn, N. E. (1979) 'Male and female: job versus gender models in the sociology of work', in J. Siltanen and M. Stanworth (eds) *Women and the Public Sphere*, London: Hutchinson and Co. Ltd.

Felstead, A. and Jewson, N. (2000) *In Work, at Home: Towards an Understanding of Homeworking*, London: Routledge.

Felstead, A., Jewson, N. and Walters, S. (2005) *Changing Places of Work*, London: Palgrave.

Fenton, S. (2003) *Ethnicity*, Cambridge: Polity.

Ferri, E. and Smith, K. (1996) *Parenting in the 1990s*, York: Joseph Rowntree Foundation.

Fieldhouse, E. and Hollywood, E. (1999) 'Life after mining: hidden unemployment and changing patterns of economic activity amongst miners in England and Wales, 1981–1991', *Work, Employment and Society*, 13(3): 483–502.

Fielding, N. and Lee, R. (eds) (1991) *Using Computers in Qualitative Research*, London: Sage.

Filby, M. (1992) 'The figures, the personality and the bums: service work and sexuality', *Work, Employment and Society*, 6(1): 23–42.

Finch, J. (1983) *Married to the Job: Wives' Incorporation in Men's Work*, London: Allen and Unwin.

Finch, J. and Mason, D. (1993) *Negotiating Family Responsibilities*, London: Routledge.

Fincham, B. (2006) 'Back to the old school: bicycle messengers, employment and ethnography', *Qualitative Research*, 6(2): 187–205.

Fine, L. (2004) *The Story of REO Joe: Work, Kin, and Community in Autotown U.S.A.*, Philadelphia, PA: Temple University Press.

Fineman. S. (ed.) (1987) *Unemployment: Personal and Social Consequences*, London: Tavistock.

Fineman, S. (ed.) (1993) *Emotion in Organizations*, London: Sage.

Fineman, S. (2003) *Understanding Emotion at Work*, London: Sage.

Fisher, K., McCulloch, A. and Gershuny, J. (1999) *British Fathers and Children*, working paper, Institute for Social and Economic Research, University of Essex.

Foner, P. and Schultz, R. (eds) (1985) *Art and the Labour Movement in the United States*, London: Journeyman Press.

Foucault, M. (1975) *Discipline and Punish*, London: Penguin.

Fox, A. (1966) *Industrial Sociology and Industrial Relations*, Royal Commission on Trade Unions and Employers' Associations, Research Paper No. 3, London: HMSO.

Fox, A. (1985) *History and Heritage: The Social Origins of the British Industrial Relations System*, London: Allen and Unwin.

Fox, A. (2004) *A Very Late Development: An Autobiography*, 2nd edn, Keele: BUIRA.

Fox, P. (1994) *Class Fictions: Shame and Resistance in the British Working-class Novel, 1890–1945*, Durham, NC: Duke University Press.

Fraser, J. A. (2001) *White-Collar Sweatshop: The Deterioration of Work and Its Rewards in Corporate America*, London: W. W. Norton.

Fraser, N. (1997) *Justice Interruptus: Critical Reflections on the Postsocialist Condition*, London: Routledge.

Frederick, C. (1913) 'The new housekeeping. Efficiency studies in home management', originally published in Ladies Home Journal, Sept.–Dec. 1912. http://nationalhumanitiescenter.org/pds/gilded/progress/text4/frederick.pdf. Last consulted 24-1-08.

Freidson, E. (2001) *Professionalism: The Third Logic*, Cambridge: Polity Press.

Friedmann, A. (1977) *Industry and Labour: Class Struggle at Work and Monopoly Capitalism*, London: Macmillan.

Frost, P., Moore, L., Louis, M., Lundberg, C. and Martin, J. (eds) (1985) *Organizational Culture*, Beverly Hills, CA: Sage.

Gaetz, S. and O'Grady, B. (2002) 'Making money: exploring the economy of young homeless workers', *Work, Employment and Society*, 16(3): 433–56.

Gallie, D. (1994) 'Are the unemployed an underclass? Some evidence from the social change and economic life initiative', *Sociology*, 28(3): 737–57.

Gallie, D. (2003) 'The quality of working life: is Scandinavia different?', *European Sociological Review*, 19(1): 61–79.

Gallie, D. and Marsh, C. (1994) 'The experience of unemployment', in D. Gallie, C. Marsh and C. Vogler (eds) *Social Change and the Experience of Unemployment*, Oxford: Oxford University Press.

Gallie, D., Marsh, C. and Vogler, C. (eds) (1994) *Social Change and the Experience of Unemployment*, Oxford: Oxford University Press.

Gallie, D. and Paugam, S. (2000) *Welfare Regimes and the Experience of Unemployment in Europe*, Oxford: Oxford University Press.

Gallie, D., Marsh, C. and Vogler, C. (eds) (1994) *Social Change and the Experience of Unemployment*, Oxford: Oxford University Press.

Garhammer, M. (1998) 'Time poverty in modern Germany', *Society and Leisure*, 21(2): 327–352.

Garrahan, P. and Stewart, P. (1992) *The Nissan Enigma: Flexibility at Work in a Local Economy*, London: Mansell.

Gauthier, A., Smeeding, T. and Furstenberg, F. (2004) 'Do we invest less time in children? Trends in parental time in selected industrialised countries since the 1960s', *Population and Development Review*, 30(4): 647–71.

Geertz, C. (1973) *The Interpretation of Cultures: Selected Essays*, London: Fontana.

Genovese, E. D. (1989) *The Political Economy of Slavery: Studies in the Economy and Society of the Slave South*, Middletown: Wesleyan University Press.

Gershuny, J. (1999) 'The work/leisure balance and the new political economy of time', *Millennium Lectures 10 Downing Street Magazine*, http://www.number10.gov.uk/output/page1484.asp.

Gershuny, J. (2000) *Changing Times: Work and Leisure in Postindustrial Society*, Oxford: Oxford University Press.

Gershuny, J. and Miles, I. (1983) *The New Service Economy: The Transformation of Employment in Industrial Societies*, London: Pinter.

Gershuny, J. and Robinson, J. P. (1991) 'The household division of labour: multinational comparisons of change', in European Foundation (ed.) *The Changing Use of Time*, Luxembourg: Office for Official Publications of the European Communities.

Gershuny, J., Godwin, M. and Jones, S. (1994) 'The domestic labour revolution: a process of lagged adaptation', in M. Anderson, F. Bechhofer and J. Gershuny (eds) *The Social and Political Economy of the Household*, Oxford: Oxford University Press.

Gill, T. (2001) *Men of Uncertainty: The Social Organization of Day Laborers in Contemporary Japan*, New York: SUNY.

Gillespie, R. (1991) *Manufacturing Knowledge: A History of the Hawthorne Experiments*, Cambridge: Cambridge University Press.

Gilroy, P. (1987) *There Ain't No Black in the Union Jack: The Cultural Politics of Race and Nation*, London: Hutchinson.

Ginn, J., Arber, S., Brannen, J., Dale, A., Dex, S., Elias, P., Moss, P., Pahl, J., Roberts, C. and Rubery, J. (1996) 'Feminist fallacies: a reply to Hakim on women's employment', *British Journal of Sociology*, 47(1): 167–74.

Gioia, T. (2006) *Work Songs*, Durham, NC: Duke University Press.

Glucksmann, M. (1990) *Women Assemble: Women Workers and the 'New Industries' in Inter-war Britain*, London: Routledge.

Glucksmann, M. (1995) 'Why "work"? Gender and the total social organisation of labour', *Gender, Work and Organization*, 2(2): 63–75.

Glucksmann, M. (1998) ' "What a difference a day makes": a theoretical and historical explanation of temporality and gender', *Sociology*, 32(2): 239–58.

Glucksmann, M. (2000) *Cottons and Casuals: The Gendered Organisation of Labour in Time and Space*, Durham: Sociology Press.

Glucksmann, M. (2006) 'The total social organisation of labour', in L. Pettinger, J. Parry, R. Taylor and M. Glucksmann (eds) *A New Sociology of Work*, Oxford: Blackwell.

Goffman, E. (1961) *Asylums*, London: Penguin.

Goldthorpe, J. H. and Hope, K. (1974) *The Social Grading of Occupations: A New Approach and Scale*, Oxford: Clarendon Press.

Goldthorpe, J. H., Lockwood, D., Bechhofer, F. and Platt, J. (1968a) *The Affluent Worker: Industrial Attitudes and Behaviour*, Cambridge: Cambridge University Press.

Goldthorpe, J. H., Lockwood, D., Bechhofer, F. and Platt, J. (1968b) *The Affluent Worker: Political Attitudes and Behaviour*, Cambridge: Cambridge University Press.

Goldthorpe, J. H., Lockwood, D., Bechhofer, F. and Platt, J. (1969) *The Affluent Worker in the Class Structure*, Cambridge: Cambridge University Press.

Goodrich, C. (1975) *The Frontier of Control: A Study of British Workshop Politics*, London: Pluto.

Goodwin, J. (2002) 'Irish men and work in North-County Dublin', *The Journal of Gender Studies*, 11(2): 151–66.

Goodwin, J. and O'Connor, H. (2005) 'Exploring complex transitions: looking back at the "golden age" of youth transitions', *Sociology*, 39(2): 197–200.

Gorman, J. (1986) *Banner Bright: An Illustrated History of Trade Union Banners*, Buckhurst Hill: Scorpion.

Gornick, J. C. and Meyers, M. K. (2003) *Families that Work: Policies for Reconciling Parenthood and Employment*, New York: Russell Sage Foundation Publications.

Gorz, A. (1999) *Reclaiming Work: Beyond the Wage-based Society*, Cambridge: Polity.

Graham, L. (1995) *On the Line at Subaru-Isuzu: The Japanese Model and the American Worker*, Ithaca, NY: Cornell University Press/ILR Press.

Gray, A. (2006) 'The time economy of parenting', *Sociological Research Online*, 11, 3, <http://www.socresonline.org.uk/11/3/gray.html>.

Green, A. (ed.) (1993) *Songs about Work: Essays in Occupational Culture for Richard A. Reuss*, Bloomington, IN: University of Indiana.

Gregg, P. and Wadsworth, J. (1996) 'More work in fewer households?', in J. Hills (ed.) *New Inequalities: The Changing Distribution of Income and Wealth in the United Kingdom*, Cambridge: Cambridge University Press.

Gregg, P. and Wadsworth, J. (eds) (1999) *The State of Working Britain*, Manchester: Manchester University Press.

Gregson, N. and Lowe, M. (1994) *Servicing the Middle Classes: Class, Gender and Waged Domestic Labour in Contemporary Britain*, London: Routledge.

Grey, C. (1994) 'Career as a projection of the self and labour process discipline', *Sociology*, 28(2): 479–97.

Grint, K. (1995) *Management: A Sociological Introduction*, Cambridge: Polity.

Grint, K. (ed.) (2000) *Work and Society: A Reader*, Cambridge: Polity.

Haas, J. ([1977] 2003) 'Learning real feelings: a study of high steel ironworkers' reactions to fear and danger', in D. Harper and H. Lawson (eds) *The Cultural Study of Work*, Lanham, MD: Rowman and Littlefield.

Hakim, C. (1979) *Occupational Segregation*, London: HMSO.

Hakim, C. (1982) *Secondary Analysis in Social Research*, London: George Allen and Unwin.

Hakim, C. (1987) 'Homeworking in Britain', *Employment Gazette*, 95(2): 92–104.

Hakim, C. (1991) 'Grateful slaves and self-made women: fact and fantasy in women's work orientations', *European Sociological Review*, 7(2): 101–21.

Hakim, C. (1993) 'The myth of rising female employment', *Work, Employment and Society*, 7(1): 97–120.

Hakim, C. (1996) *Key Issues in Women's Work: Female Heterogeneity and the Polarisation of Women's Employment*, London: The Athlone Press Ltd.

Hakim, C. (1998) 'Developing a sociology for the twenty-first century: preference theory', *British Journal of Sociology*, 49(1): 137–43.

Hakim, C. (2000) *Work-lifestyle Choices in the 21st Century: Preference Theory*, Oxford: Oxford University Press.

Hakim, C. (2003) *Models of the Family in Modern Societies: Ideals and Realities*, Aldershot: Ashgate.

Halford, S. and Leonard, P. (2006) *Negotiating Gendered Identities at Work: Place, Space and Time*, Basingstoke: Palgrave.

Hall, C. (1980) 'The history of the housewife', in E. Malos (ed.) *The Politics of Housework*, London: Allison and Busby.

Hall, S., Critcher, C., Jefferson, T. and Clarke, J. (1979) *Policing the Crisis: Mugging, the State and Law and Order*, London: Macmillan.

Hamper, B. (1986) *Rivethead: Tales from the Assembly Line*, New York: Warner Books.

Hantrais, L. (1989) 'Approaches to cross-national comparisons', in L. Hantrais (ed.) *Franco-British Comparisons of Family and Employment Careers*, Cross-national Research Papers Special Issue, Aston Modern Languages Club, Birmingham: Aston University.

Hantrais, L. (2005) 'Combining methods: a key to understanding complexity in European societies?', *European Societies*, 7(3): 399–421.

Hapke, L. (2001) *Labor's Text: The Worker in American Fiction*, New Brunswick, NJ: Rutgers University Press.

Harding, S. (1987) *Feminism and Methodology: Social Science Issues*, Milton Keynes: Open University Press.

Hardy, F. (ed.) (1979) *Grierson on Documentary*, London: Faber.

Hardyment, C. (1988) *From Mangle to Microwave: The Mechanization of Household Work*, Cambridge: Polity.

Harkness, S. (2005) 'Employment, work patterns and unpaid work: an analysis of trends since the 1970s', Research Project report, Bristol: Department of Economics, University of Bristol.

Harper, D. (1986) 'Meaning and work: a study in photo elicitation', *Current Sociology* 34(3): 24–46.

Harper, D. (1987) *Working Knowledge: Skill and Community in a Small Shop*, Berkeley, CA: University of California Press.

Harper, D. (1998) 'An argument for visual sociology', in J. Prosser (ed.) *Image-based Research: A Sourcebook for Qualitative Researchers*, London: Routledge/Falmer.

Harper, D. (2001) *Changing Works: Visions of a Lost Agriculture*, Chicago: University of Chicago Press.

Harper, D. and Lawson, H. (eds) (2003) *The Cultural Study of Work*, New York: Rowman and Littlefield.

Harris, C. C. (1987) *Redundancy and Recession in South Wales*, Oxford: Blackwell.

Harris, W. J. (ed.) (1992) *Society and Culture in the Slave South*, London: Routledge.

Hartmann, H. (1979) 'The unhappy marriage of Marxism and Feminism: towards a more progressive union', *Capital and Class*, 8: 1–33.

Harvey, D. (1989) *The Condition of Postmodernity*, Cambridge: Polity.

Harvey, M. (1999) 'Economies of time: a framework for analyzing the restructuring of everyday relations' in A. Felstead and N. Jewson (eds) *Global Trends in Flexible Labour*, London: Macmillan.

Hassard, J. (1989) 'Time and industrial society', in P. Blyton *et al.* (eds) *Time, Work and Organization*, London: Routledge.

Hassard, J. (1993) *Sociology and Organization Theory, Positivism, Paradigms and Postmodernity*, Cambridge: Cambridge University Press.

Hassard, J. (2000) 'Images of time in work and organization', in K. Grint (ed.) *Work and Society: A Reader*, Cambridge: Polity.

Hassard, J. and Holliday, R. (eds) (1998) *Organization Representation: Work and Organizations in Popular Culture*, London: Sage.

Hearn, J. and Parkin, W. (2001) *Gender, Sexuality and Violence in Organizations*, London: Sage.

Heath, C., Luff, P. and Sanchez Svensson, M. (2002) 'Overseeing organizations: configuring action and its environment', *British Journal of Sociology*, 53(2): 181–201.

Held, D., McGrew, A., Goldblatt, D. and Perraton, J. (1999) *Global Transformations: Politics, Economics and Culture*, Cambridge: Polity.

Hirdmann, Y. (1998) 'State policy and gender contracts: the Swedish experience', in E. Drew, R. Emerek and E. Mahon (eds) *Women, Work and the Family in Europe*, London: Routledge.

Heuman, G. and Walvin, J. (eds) (2003) *The Slavery Reader*, London: Routledge.

Hewitt, P. (1993) *About Time: The Revolution in Work and Family Life*, London: Rivers Oram Press.

Hickman, C. R. and Silva, M. A. (1985) *Creating Excellence*, London: Unwin.

High, S. (2003) *Industrial Sunset: The Making of North America's Rust Belt, 1969–1984*, Toronto: University of Toronto Press.

Hilton, L. (2005) 'Made in China', in I. Jack (ed.) *The Factory*, London: Granta.

Himmelweit, S. (1995) 'The discovery of unpaid work; the social consequences of the expansion of work', *Feminist Economics*, 1(2): 1–20.

Hirdmann, Y. (1988) 'Genussystemet – reflexioner kring kvinnors sociala underordning', *Kvinnovetenskaplig Tidskrift*, 3: 49–63.

Hirdmann, Y. (1998) 'State policy and gender contracts: the Swedish experience', in E. Drew, R., Emerek and E., Mahon (eds) *Women, Work and the Family in Europe*, London: Routledge.

Hobsbawm, E. (1964) *Labouring Men: Studies in the History of Labour*, London: Weidenfeld and Nicolson.

Hobsbawm, E. (1984) *Worlds of Labour: Further Studies in the History of Labour*, London: Weidenfeld and Nicolson.

Hochschild, A. R. (1983) *The Managed Heart: Commercialisation of Human Feeling*, London: University of California Press.

Hochschild, A. R. (1989) *The Second Shift*, New York: Aron Books Inc.

Hochschild, A. R. (1997) *The Time Bind: When Work Becomes Home and Home Becomes Work*, New York: Henry Holt and Company.

Hochschild, A. R. (2002) 'Love and gold', in B. Ehrenreich and A. Hochschild (eds) *Global Women: Nannies, Maids and Sex Workers in the New Economy*, London: Granta.

Hochschild, A. R. (2003) *The Commercialization of Intimate Life: Notes from Home and Work*, London: University of California Press.

Hodson, R. (2001) *Dignity at Work*, Cambridge: Cambridge University Press.

Hoecker-Drysdale, S. (1992) *Harriet Martineau, First Woman Sociologist*, New York: Berg.

Holdsworth, C. and Dale, A. (1997) 'Ethnic differences in women's employment', *Work, Employment and Society*, 11(3): 435–57.

Holgate, J. (2005) 'Organizing migrant workers: a case study of working conditions and unionization in a London sandwich factory', *Work, Employment and Society*, 19(3): 463–80.

Holgate, J. and Wills, J. (2007) 'Placing labour in London: trade union strategy and practice', in L. Turner and D. Cornfield (eds) *Seeking Solidarity: Labor and the Politics of Urban Coalition Building*, Ithaca, NY: Cornell University Press.

Hollowell, P. G. (1968) *The Lorry Driver*. London: Routledge and Kegan Paul.

Honey, M. (1999) *Black Workers Remember: An Oral History of Segregation, Unionism, and the Freedom Struggle*, Berkeley, CA: University of California Press.

hooks, b. (2000) *Feminist Theory: From Margin to Centre*, London: Pluto Press.

Humphries, J. (1977) 'Class struggle and the working class family', *Cambridge Journal of Economics*, 1: 241–58.

Humphries, J. (1981) 'Protective legislation, the capitalist state and working class men: the case of the 1842 Mines Regulation Act', *Feminist Review*, 7: 1–34.

Hurley, F. J. (1972) *Portrait of a Decade: Roy Stryker and the Development of Documentary Photography in the Thirties*, Baton Rouge, LA: Louisana State University Press.

Hutson, S. and Jenkins, R. (1989) *Taking the Strain*, Milton Keynes: Open University Press.

Hyman, R. (1987) 'Strategy or structure? Capital, labour and control', *Work, Employment and Society*, 1(1): 25–55.

Iganski, P. and Payne, G. (1996) 'Declining racial disadvantage in the British labour market', *Ethnic and Racial Studies*, 19(1): 113–33.

Ikuko, N. (1997) 'The "civilization" of time: Japan and the adoption of the Western time system', *Time and Society*, 6(2/3): 237–59.

ILO (1982) 'Resolution concerning statistics of the economically active population, employment, unemployment and underemployment, adopted by the Thirteenth International Conference of Labour Statisticians', http://www.ilo.org/public/english/bureau/stat/download/res/ecacpop.pdf, Accessed 17 August 2007.

ILO (2005) *The 20 Key Indicators of the Labour Market*, http://www.ilo.org/public/english/employment/strat/kilm/indicators.htm#kilm8).

ILO (2006) *Global Employment Trends Brief*, http://www.ilo.org/

Irwin, S. (2003) 'Interdependencies, values and the reshaping of difference: gender and generation at the birth of twentieth-century modernity', *British Journal of Sociology*, 54(4): 565–84.

Jacobs, J. (2002) 'Foreword', in U. Sinclair, *The Jungle*, New York: Random House.

Jacobs, J. A. and Gerson, K. (1998) 'Who are the overworked Americans?', *Review of Social Economy*, 56(4): 442–59.

Jacobs, J. A. and Gerson, K. (2001) 'Overworked individuals or overworked families? Explaining trends in work, leisure and family time', *Work and Occupations*, 28(1): 40–63.

Jahoda, M. (1982) *Employment and Unemployment*, Cambridge: Cambridge University Press.

Jahoda, M., Lazarsfeld, P. F. and Zeisel, H. ([1933] 1971) *Marienthal: The Sociography of an Unemployed Community*, London: Tavistock.

Jameson, F. (1998) *Cultural Turn: Selected Writings on the Postmodern 1983–1998*, London: Verso.

Jary, D. and Jary, J. (1991) *Collins Dictionary of Sociology*, Glasgow: W. Collins.

Jefferson, T. and King, J. E. (2001) '"Never intended to be a theory of everything": domestic labor in neoclassical and Marxian economics', *Feminist Economics*, 7(3): 71–101.

Jeffery, I. (1981) *Photography: A Concise History*, London: Thames and Hudson.

Jenkins, C. and Sherman, B. (1979) *The Collapse of Work*, London: Methuen.

Jennings, H. (1985) *Pandaemonium: The Coming of the Machine as Seen by Contemporary Observers*, London: Picador.

Jermier, J. M., Knights, D. and Nord, W. R. (eds) (1994) *Resistance and Power in Organization*, London: Routledge.

Jerrold, B. and Doré, G. (2005) *London: A Pilgrimage*, London: Anthem Press.

Jones, T. (1986) *Britain's Ethnic Minorities*, London: PSI.

Jordan, B. (1982) *Mass Unemployment and the Future of Britain*, Oxford: Blackwell.

Joyce, P. (1980) *Work, Society and Politics: The Culture of the Factory in Later Victorian England*, Cambridge: Cambridge University Press.

Joyce, P. (ed.) (1987) *The Historical Meanings of Work*, Cambridge: Cambridge University Press.

Kalra, V. (2000) *From Textile Mills to Taxi Ranks: Experiences of Migration, Labour and Social Change*, Ashgate: Aldershot.

Kanigel, R. (1997) *The One Best Way: Frederick Winslow Taylor and the Enigma of Efficiency*, London: Abacus.

Karn, V. (1997) *Employment, Education and Housing amongst Ethnic Minorities in Britain*, London: The Stationery Office.

Keating, P. J. (1971) *The Working Classes in Victorian Fiction*, London: Routledge and Kegan Paul.

Kefalas, M. (2003) *Working-Class Heroes: Protecting Home, Community and Nation in a Chicago Neighborhood*, Berkeley, CA: University of California Press.

Kemmis, S. and McTaggart, R. (1988) *The Action Research Planner*, Geelong: Deakin University Press.

Kerr, C., Dunlop, J. T., Harbison, F. H. and Myers, C. A. (1960) *Industrialism and Industrial Man: The Problems of Labor and Management in Economic Growth*, Cambridge, MA: Harvard University Press.

Kirk, J. (2003) *Twentieth-century Writing and the British Working Class*, Cardiff: University of Wales Press.

Kirkpatrick, I. and Martinez Lucio, M. (eds) (1995) *The Politics of Quality in the Public Sector: The Management of Change*, London: Routledge.

Kitterød, R. H. and Pettersen, S. V. (2006) 'Making up for mothers' employed working hours? Housework and childcare among Norwegian fathers', *Work, Employment and Society*, 20(3): 473–92.

Klein, N. (2000) *No Logo*, London: Flamingo.

Klein, V. (1965) *Britain's Married Women Workers*, London: Routledge and Kegan Paul.

Klingender, F. ([1947] 1972) *Art and the Industrial Revolution*, St Albans: Paladin.

Knights, D. and Willmott, H. (1989) 'Power and subjectivity at work: from degradation to subjugation in social relations', *Sociology*, 23(4): 535–58.

Knights, D. and Willmott, H. (eds) (1990) *Labour Process Theory*, London: Macmillan.

Kong, T. S. K. (2006) 'What it feels like for a whore: the body politics of women performing erotic labour in Hong Kong', *Gender, Work and Organization*, 13(5): 409–34.

Korczynski, M. (2003) 'Music at work: toward a historical overview', *Folk Music Journal*, 8: 314–44.

Korczynski, M. (2004) 'Music and meaning on the shopfloor', *Work and Occupations*, 34(3): 253–98.

Korczynski, M., Hodson, R. and Edwards, P. (eds) (2006) *Social Theory at Work*, Oxford: Oxford University Press.

Kristeva, J. (1981) 'Women's time', *Signs*, 1: 16–35.

Kuhn, A. and Wolpe, A. M. (eds) (1978) *Feminism and Materialism: Women and Modes of Production*, London: Routledge and Kegan Paul.

Kumar, K. (1978) *Prophecy and Progress: The Sociology of Industrial and Post-Industrial Society*, London: Penguin.

Kumar, K. (2005) *From Post-Industrial to Post-Modern Society*, 2nd edn, Oxford: Blackwell.

Lamont, M. (2000) *The Dignity of Working Men: Morality and the Boundaries of Race, Class, and Immigration*, New York: Russell Sage Foundation/Harvard University Press.

Land, H. (1980) 'The family wage', *Feminist Review*, 6: 55–77.

Lane, T. (1974) *The Union Makes Us Strong*, London: Arrow.

Langer, F. (1998) *Lewis W. Hine: The Empire State Building*, London: Prestel.

Larkin, S. (2005) *American Impressionism: The Beauty of Work*, London: Bruce Museum of Arts and Science.

Laurie, H. and Gershuny, J. (2000) 'Couples, work and money', in R. Berthoud and J. Gershuny (eds) *Seven Years in the Lives of British Families*, Bristol: The Policy Press.

Layard, R. G., Nickell, S. J. and Jackman, R. (2005) *Unemployment: Macroeconomic Performance and the Labour Market*, Oxford: Oxford University Press.

Lee, R. M. (1993) *Doing Research on Sensitive Topics*, London: Sage.

Lehman, J. M. (1995) 'Durkheim's theories of deviance and suicide: a feminist reconsideration', *The American Journal of Sociology*, 100(4): 904–30.

Leidner, R. (2006) 'Identity and work', in M. Korczynski, R. Hodson and P. Edwards (eds) *Social Theory at Work*, Oxford: Oxford University Press.

Lengermann, P. M. and Niebrugge-Brantley, J. (1998) *The Women Founders: Sociology and Social Theory, 1830–1930: A Text with Readings*, Boston: McGraw-Hill.

Leonard, M. (2001) 'Old wine in new bottles? Women working inside and outside the household', *Women's Studies International Forum*, 24(1): 67–78.

Lessem, R. (1990) *Managing Corporate Culture*, Aldershot: Gower.

Lewis, J. (1992) 'Gender and the development of welfare regimes', *Journal of European Social Policy*, 2(3): 159–73.

Lewis, S. and Lewis, J. (1996) *The Work-Family Challenge: Rethinking Employment*, London: Sage.

Lincoln, J. and Guillot, D. (2006) 'A Durkeimian view of organizational culture', in M. Korczynski, R. Hodson and P. Edwards (eds) *Social Theory at Work*, Oxford: Oxford University Press.

Linkon, S. and Russo, J. (2002) *Steeltown USA: Work and Memory in Youngstown*, Lawrence, KS: University of Kansas.

Littler, C. (1978) 'Understanding Taylorism', *British Journal of Sociology*, 29(2): 185–202.

Lockwood, D. (1958) *The Black Coated Worker: A Study in Class Consciousness*, London: George Allen and Unwin.

Lockwood, D. (1975) 'Sources in variation in working-class images of society', in M. Bulmer (ed.) *Working-class Images of Society*. London: Routledge and Kegan Paul.

Loretto, W., Vickerstaff, S. and White, P. J. (eds) (2007) *The Future for Older Workers: New Perspectives*, Bristol: Policy Press.

Louis, M. (1985) 'Sourcing workplace cultures', in R. H. Kilmann, M. Saxton, R. Sherpa and Associates (eds) *Gaining Control of Corporate Culture*, San Francisco, CA: Jossey-Bass, pp. 126–36.

Lovejoy, P. P. and Rogers, N. (eds) (1994) *Unfree Labour in the Development of the Atlantic World*, Essex: Frank Cass and Co. Ltd.

Lown, J. (1990) *Women and Industrialisation: Gender at Work in Nineteenth Century England*, Cambridge: Polity.

Lucas, R. (1997) 'Youth, gender and part-time work – students in the labour process', *Work, Employment and Society*, 11(4): 595–614.

Lucie-Smith, E. and Dars, C. (1977) *Work and Struggle: The Painter as Witness 1870–1914*, New York: Paddington Press.

Luthra, M. (1997) *Britain's Black Population: Social Change, Public Policy and Agenda*, Aldershot: Ashgate.

Luxton, M. and Corman, J. (2001) *Getting by in Hard Times: Gendered Labour at Home and on the Job*, Toronto: University of Toronto Press.

Lynn-Meek, V. (1988) 'Organizational culture: origins and weaknesses', *Organization Studies*, 9: 453–73.

Lyotard, J.-F. (1984) *The Postmodern Condition: A Report on Knowledge*, Manchester: Manchester University Press.

Mac an Ghaill, M. (1999) *Contemporary Racisms and Ethnicities*, Buckingham: Open University Press.

MacColl, E. (1990) *Journeyman: An Autobiography*, London: Sidgwick and Jackson.

MacDonald, K. M. (1995) *The Sociology of the Professions*, London: Sage.

MacDonald, R. (1994) 'Fiddly jobs, undeclared working and the something for nothing society', *Work, Employment and Society*, 8(4): 507–30.

MacDonald, R. (1996) 'Welfare dependency, the enterprise culture and self-employed survival', *Work Employment and Society*, 10(3): 431–47.

Mace, R. (1999) *British Trade Union Posters: An Illustrated History*, Stroud: Sutton Publishing.

Maharidge, D. (1986) *Journey to Nowhere: The Saga of the New Underclass*, New York: Hyperion.

Malthus, T. R. (1986) *An Essay on the Principle of Population*, London: Penguin.

Mann, K. (1991) *The Making of an English 'Underclass'? Social Divisions of Welfare and Labour*, Buckingham: Open University Press.

Marglin, S. (1980) 'The origins and functions of hierarchy in capitalist production', in Theo Nichols (ed.) *Capital and Labour: A Marxist Primer*, London: Fontana.

Marsden, D. (1982) *Workless*, Harmondsworth: Penguin.

Marsh, C. (1988a) 'Unemployment in Britain', in D. Gallie (ed.) *Employment in Britain*, Oxford: Blackwell.

Marsh, C. (1988b) *Exploring Data: An Introduction to Data Analysis for Social Scientists*, Cambridge: Polity.

Marshall, G. (1982) *In Search of the Spirit of Capitalism: An Essay on Max Weber's Protestant Ethic Thesis*, London: Hutchinson.

Marshall, G. (1984) 'On the sociology of women's unemployment, its neglect and significance', *The Sociological Review*, 32(2): 234–59.

Martin, J. and Roberts, C. (1984) *Women and Employment: A Lifetime Perspective*, London: HMSO.

Martin, R. and Wallace, J. (1984) *Working Women in Recession: Employment, Redundancy, and Unemployment*, Oxford: Oxford University Press.

Marx, K. ([1867] 1954) *Capital*, vol. 1, London: Lawrence and Wishart.

Marx, K. and Engels, F. ([1845] 1970) *The German Ideology*, Part One, London: Lawrence and Wishart.

May, T. (1994) 'Transformative power: a study in a human service organisation', *Sociological Review*, 42(4): 618–38.

May, T. (2001) *Social Research: Issues, Methods and Process*, Buckingham: Open University Press.

Mayhew, H. ([1851] 1985) *London Labour and London Poor*, London: Penguin.

Mayo, E. (1949) *The Social Problems of an Industrial Civilization*, London: Routledge and Kegan Paul.

McDowell, L. (1997) *Capital Culture: Gender at Work in the City*, Oxford: Blackwell.

McDowell, L. (2003) *Redundant Masculinities? Employment Change and White Working Class Youth*, Oxford: Blackwell.

McKee, L. and Bell, C. (1985) 'Marital and family relations in times of male unemployment', in B. Roberts, R. Finnegan and D. Gallie (eds) *New Approaches to Economic Life*, Manchester: Manchester University Press.

McKenna, F. (1980) *The Railway Workers, 1840–1970*, London: Faber and Faber.

McKinlay, A. and Starkey, K. (eds) (1988) *Foucault, Management and Organization Theory*, London: Sage.

McRae, S. (2003) 'Constraints and choices in mothers' employment careers: a consideration of Hakim's Preference Theory', *British Journal of Sociology*, 54(3): 317–38.

Meakin, D. (1976) *Man and Work: Literature and Culture in Industrial Society*, London: Methuen.

Menard, S. (1991) *Longitudinal Research*, Newbury Park, CA: Sage.

Merton, R. K. (1984) 'Socially expected durations: a case study of concept formation in sociology', in W. Powell and R. Robbins (eds) *Conflict and Consensus*, New York: Free Press.

Metcalf, H., Modood, T. and Virdee, S. (1996) *Asian Self-employment: The Interaction of Culture and Economics in England*, London: Policy Studies Institute.

Middleton, C. (1979) 'The sexual division of labour in Feudal England', *New Left Review*, 113–14: 147–68.

Middleton, C. (1988) 'Gender divisions and wage labour in English history', in S. Walby (ed.) *Gender Segregation at Work*, Milton Keynes: Open University Press.

Miles, R. (1982) *Racism and Migrant Labour*, London: Routledge and Kegan Paul.

Milkman, R. (1997) *Farewell to the Factory: Auto Workers in the Late Twentieth Century*, Berkeley, CA: University of California Press.

Mills, C. W. (1959) *The Sociological Imagination*, Oxford: Oxford University Press.

Mincer, J. and Polacheck, S. (1974) 'Family investment in human capital: earnings of women', *Journal of Political Economy*, 82(2): 76–108.

Minford, P. (1985) *Unemployment: Cause and Cure*, London: Blackwell.

Mirza, H. (1992) *Young Female and Black*, London: Routledge.

Modood, T. *et al.* (eds) (1997) *Ethnic Minorities in Britain: Diversity and Disadvantage*. London: PSI.

Morgan, D. H. J. (1972) 'The British Association scandal: the effects of publicity on a sociological investigation', *Sociological Review*, 20(2): 185–206.

Morris, L. (1994) *Dangerous Classes: The Underclass and Social Citizenship*, London: Routledge.

Murray, C. (1984) *Losing Ground: American Social Policy 1950–1980*, New York: Basic Books.

Murray, C. (2001) *Underclass + 10: Charles Murray and the British Underclass 1990–2000*, Trowbridge: The Cromwell Press.

Murray, R. (1989) 'Fordism and post-Fordism', in S. Hall and M. Jacques (eds) *New Times*, London: Lawrence and Wishart.

Nelson, B. (2001) *Divided We Stand: American Workers and the Struggle for Black Equality*, Princeton, NJ: Princeton University Press.

Nichols, T. and Beynon, H. (1977) *Living with Capitalism: Class Relations and the Modern Factory*, London: Routledge and Kegan Paul.

Nichols, T. and Cam, S. (2005) *Labour in a Global World: Case Studies from the White Goods Industry in Africa, South America, East Asia and Europe*, London: Palgrave.

Nolan, J. (2002) 'The intensification of everyday life', in B. Burchell, D. Ladipo and F. Wilkinson (eds) *Job Insecurity and Work Intensification*, London: Routledge.

Noon, M. and Blyton, P. (2002) *The Realities of Work*, London: Palgrave.

Nye, D. (1985) *Image Worlds: Corporate Identity at General Electric*, Cambridge, MA: MIT Press.

O'Connell Davidson, J. (1993) *Privatization and Employment Relations: The Case of the Water Industry*, London: Mansell.

O'Connell Davidson, J. (2005) *Children in the Global Sex Trade*, Cambridge: Polity.

O'Connell Davidson, J. and Layder, D. (1994) *Methods: Sex and Madness*, London: Routledge.

Oakley, A. (1972) *Sex, Gender and Society*, London: Maurice Temple Smith.

Oakley, A. (1974) *Housewife*, London: Lane.

Oakley, A. (1979) *Becoming a Mother*, Oxford: Martin Robertson.

Oakley, A. (1981) 'Interviewing women: a contradiction in terms', in H. Roberts (ed.) *Doing Feminist Research*, London: Routledge.

Oakley, A. (1974) *The Sociology of Housework*, Oxford: Basil Blackwell.

Oakley, A. (1986) *From Here to Maternity*, Harmondsworth: Penguin.

ONS (2006) *Social Trends Number 36*, London: HMSO.

Orvell, M. (1995) *After the Machine: Visual Arts and the Erasing of Cultural Boundaries*, Jackson: University Press of Mississippi.

Orvell, M. (2003) *American Photography*, Oxford: Oxford University Press.

Orwell, G. (1989) *Down and Out in Paris and London*, London: Penguin.

Ouchi, W. G. (1981) *Theory Z*, Reading, MA: Addison-Wesley.

Ouchi, W. G. and Wilkins, A. L. (1985) 'Organisational culture', *Annual Review of Sociology*, 11: 457–83.

Pahl, J. (1985) *Private Violence and Public Policy: The Needs of Battered Women and the Response of the Public Services*, London: Routledge and Kegan Paul.

Pahl, J. (1989) *Money and Marriage*, London: Macmillan.

Pahl, R. E. (1984) *Divisions of Labour*, Oxford: Blackwell.

Pahl, R. E. (1988) *On Work: Historical, Comparative and Theoretical Approaches*, Oxford: Basil Blackwell.

Parker, M. (2000) *Organizational Culture and Identity: Unity and Division at Work*, London: Sage.

Parkin, F. (1974) 'Strategies of social closure in class formation', in F. Parkin (ed.) *The Social Analysis of Class Structure*, London: Tavistock.

Parkin, F. (1979) *Marxism and Class Theory: A Bourgeois Critique*, London: Tavistock.

Parmar, P. (1982) 'Gender, race and class: Asian women in resistance', in CCCS (eds) *The Empire Strikes Back: Race and Racism in 70s Britain*, London: Hutchinson.

Parsons, T. and Bales, R. F. (1955) *Family, Socialization and Interaction Process*, Glencoe, IL: The Free Press.

Pateman, C. (1983) 'Feminist critiques of the public/private dichotomy', in S. Benn and G. Gaus (eds) *Private and Public in Social Life*, London: Croom Helm.

Patterson, S. (1963) *Dark Strangers: A Sociological Study of the Absorption of a Recent West Indian Migrant Group in Brixton, South London*, London: Tavistock Publications.

Payne, G. (2006) *Social Divisions*, London: Palgrave Macmillan.

Payne, J. (1987) 'Does unemployment run in families? Some findings from the General Household Survey', *Sociology*, 21(2): 199–214.

Pedersen, J. E. (2001) 'Sexual politics in Comte and Durkheim: feminism, history and the French sociological tradition', *Signs*, 27(1): 229–63.

Perks, R. and Thomson, A. (eds) (1998) *The Oral History Reader*, London; New York: Routledge.

Perreñas, R. S. (2002) 'The care crisis in the Philippines: children and transnational families in the new global economy', in B. Ehrenreich and A. R. Hochschild (eds) *Global Women: Nannies, Maids and Sex Workers in the New Economy*, London: Granta.

Perrons, D., Fagan, C., McDowell, L., Ray, K. and Ward, K. (eds) (2005) *Gender Divisions and Working Time in the New Economy*, Guilford: Edward Elgar Publishing.

Peters, T. and Waterman, R. H. (1982) *In Search of Excellence: Lessons from America's Best-run Companies*, London: Harper and Row.

Pettinger, L., Parry, J., Taylor, R. and Glucksmann, M. (2006) *A New Sociology of Work*, Oxford: Blackwell.

Pfau-Effinger, B. (1998) 'Gender cultures and the gender arrangement: a theoretical framework for cross-national gender research', *Innovation*, 11(2): 147–66.

Phillipson, C. and Smith, A. (2005) *Extending Working Life: A Review of the Research Literature*, London: Department of Work and Pensions.

Phizacklea, A. (2003) 'Gendered actors in migration', in J. Andall (ed.) *Gender and Ethnicity in Contemporary Europe*, London: Berg.

Phizacklea, A. and Wolkowitz, C. (1995) *Homeworking Women: Gender, Race and Class at Work*, London: Sage.

Pilkington, A. (2003) *Racial Disadvantage and Ethnic Diversity in Britain*, London: Palgrave Macmillan.

Plantenga, J. (2002) 'Combining work and care in the polder model: an assessment of the Dutch part-time strategy', *Critical Social Policy*, 22(1): 53–71.

Pollert, A. (1981) *Girls, Wives, Factory Lives*, London: Palgrave.

Pollert, A. (1988) 'The "flexible firm": fixation or fact?' *Work, Employment and Society*, 2(3): 281–316.

Pollock, G. (1997) 'Uncertain futures: young people in and out of employment since 1940', *Work, Employment and Society*, 20(2): 205–21.

Portelli, A. (2001) *The Death of Luigi Trastulli and Other Stories: Form and Meaning in Oral History*, Albany, NY: SUNY Press.

Prandy, K. and Blackburn, R. (1997) 'Putting men and women into classes: but is that where they belong?', *Sociology*, 31(1): 143–52.

Presser, H. B. (1995) 'Job, family and gender: determinants of non-standard work schedules among employed Americans in 1991', *Demography*, 32(4): 577–98.

Pringle, R. (1989) *Secretaries Talk: Sexuality, Power and Work*, London: Verso,

Procter, M. (1993) 'Analysing other researchers' data', in N. Gilbert (ed.) *Researching Social Life*, London: Sage.

Purcell, K., Hogarth, T. and Simm, C. (1999) *Whose Flexibility? The Costs and Benefits of Non-standard Working Arrangements and Contractual Relations*, York: Joseph Rowntree Foundation.

Puwar, N. (2001) 'The racialised somatic norm in the Senior Civil Service', *Sociology*, 35(3): 651–70.

Ram, M. (1992) 'Coping with racism: Asian employers in the inner-city', *Work, Employment and Society*, 6(4): 601–18.

Ram, M., Abbas, T., Sanghera, B., Barlow, G. and Jones, T. (2001) 'Making the link: households and small business activity in a multi-ethnic context', *Community, Work and Family*, 4(3): 327–48.

Ramji, H. (2005) 'Exploring intersections of employment and ethnicity amongst British Pakistani young men', *Sociological Research Online*, 10(4): <http://www.socresonline. org.uk/10/4/ramji.html>.

Ransome, P. (2005) *Work, Consumption and Culture: Affluence and Social Change in the Twenty-First Century*, London: Sage.

Ray, L. and Reed, M. (eds) (1994) *Organizing Modernity: New Weberian Perspectives on Work, Organization and Society*, London: Routledge.

Ray, L. and Sayer, A. (eds) (1999) *Culture and Economy after the Cultural Turn*, London: Sage.

Reed, J. (1990) *Moving Images: Commemorating 40 years of British Transport Films*, London: Capital Transport.

Reeves, R. (2002) *Dads' Army: The Case for Father-friendly Workplaces*, London: The Work Foundation: http://www.theworkfoundation.com/Assets/PDFs/dads_army.pdf.

Reid, D. A. (1976) 'The decline of Saint Monday 1766–1876', *Past and Present*, 71: 76–101.

Reid, R. (1986) *Land of Lost Content: The Luddite Revolt 1812*, London: Cardinal.

Rex, J. (1973) *Race, Colonialism and the City*, London: Routledge and Kegan Paul.

Rex, J. and Moore, R. (1967) *Race, Community and Conflict: A Study of Sparkbrook*, London: Oxford University Press.

Rex, J. and Tomlinson, S. (1979) *Colonial Immigrants in a British City: A Class Analysis*, London: Routledge and Kegan Paul.

Reynolds, T. (2001) 'Black mothering, paid work and identity', *Ethnic and Racial Studies*, 24(6): 1046–64.

Reynolds, T. (2006) 'Caribbean families, social capital and young people's diasporic identities', *Ethnic and Racial Studies*, 29(6): 1087–103.

Rhodes, C. (2004) 'Utopia in popular management writing and the music of Bruce Springsteen: do you believe in the promised land?', *Consumption, Markets and Culture*, 7(1): 1–20.

Rich, A. (1980) 'Compulsory heterosexuality and lesbian existence', *Signs*, 5(4): 631–60.

Richardson, D. (ed.) (1996) *Theorizing Heterosexuality: Telling It Straight*, Buckingham: Open University Press.

Rifkin, J. (1995) *The End of Work: The Decline of the Global Labor Force and the Dawn of the Post-Market Era*, New York: Putnam.

Riis, J. ([1890] 1998) *How the Other Half Lives*, London: Penguin.

Ritzer, G. (1998) *The McDonaldization of Society*, Thousand Oaks, CA: Pine Forge Press.

Ritzer, G. (2000) *McDonaldization: The Reader*, London: Sage.

Roberts, H. (ed.) (1981) *Doing Feminist Research*, London: Routledge and Kegan Paul.

Roberts, H. (ed.) (1989) *Doing Feminist Research*, London: Routledge and Kegan Paul.

Roberts, H. (1993) 'Women and the class debate', in D. Morgan and L. Stanley (eds) *Debates in Sociology*, Manchester: Manchester University Press.

Roberts, I. (1993) *Craft, Class and Control*, Edinburgh: Edinburgh University Press.

Roberts, I. (2006) 'Taking age out of the workplace: putting older workers back in?', *Work, Employment and Society*, 20(1): 67–86.

Robinson, J. P. and Godbey, G. (1997) *Time for Life: The Surprising Ways Americans Use their Time*, Philadelphia, PA: Pennsylvania State University Press.

Roche, W. K., Fynes, B. and Morrissey, T. (1996) 'Work time and employment: a review of international evidence', *International Labour Review*, 135, 2, 129–57.

Roderick, M. J. (2006) 'A very precarious "profession": uncertainty in the working lives of professional footballers', *Work, Employment and Society*, 20(2): 245–65.

Rose, G. (2001) *Visual Methodologies: An Introduction to the Interpretation of Visual Materials*, London: Sage.

Rose, M. (1985) *Reworking the Work Ethic: Economic Values and Socio-cultural Politics*, London: Batsford.

Rose, M. (1988) *Industrial Behaviour: Research and Control*, London: Penguin.

Ross, A. (2004) *Low Pay High Profile: The Global Push for Fair Labor*, New York: The New Press.

Rothenberg, D. (1998) *With These Hands: The Hidden World of Migrant Farm Workers Today*, New York: Harcourt Brace.

Rowbotham, S. (1973) *Women, Resistance and Revolution: A History of Women and Revolution in the Modern World*, London: Allen Lane.

Rowbotham, S. and Beynon, H. (eds) (2001) *Looking at Class: Film, Television and the Working Class in Britain*, London: Rivers Oram Press.

Rowntree, S. (1901) *Poverty: A Study of Town Life*, London: Macmillan.

Roy, D. (1958) ' "Banana time": job satisfaction and informal Interaction', in D. Harper and H. Lawson (eds) (2003) *The Cultural Study of Work*, Lanham, MD: Rowman and Littlefield.

Rubery, J., Smith, M. and Fagan, C. (1998) 'National working-time regimes and equal opportunities', *Feminist Economics*, 4(1): 71–102.

Rubery, J., Smith, M. and Fagan, C. (1999) *Women's Employment in Europe: Trends and Prospects*, London: Routledge.

Rule, J. (1994) 'Saturday night and Sunday morning: time and the working classes', inaugural lecture, Southampton: University of Southampton.

Russell, A. (2000) *The TUC and the Working Time Question: Policy, Action and Outcomes in Twentieth-Century Britain*, Sussex: The Book Guild Ltd.

Russell, H. and Barbieri, P. (2000) 'Gender and the experience of unemployment', in D. Gallie and S. Paugam (eds) *Welfare Regimes and the Experience of Unemployment in Europe*, Oxford: Oxford University Press.

Russo, J. and Linkon, S. L. (eds) (2005) *New Working Class Studies*, Ithaca, NY: Cornell University Press/ILR.

Rutherford, S. (2001) 'Are you going home already? The long hours culture, women managers and patriarchal closure', *Time and Society*, 10(2/3): 259–76.

Salaman, G. (1974) *Community and Occupation: An Exploration of Work/Leisure Relationships*, Cambridge: Cambridge University Press.

Salgado, S. (1993) *Workers: An Archaeology of the Industrial Age*, New York: Aperture.

Samuel, R. (ed.) (1975) *Village Life and Labour*, London: Routledge and Kegan Paul.

Samuel, R. (1977) 'Workshop of the world: steam power and hand technology in mid-Victorian Britain', *History Workshop Journal*, 3, Spring: 6–72.

Samuel, R. and Thompson, P. (1990) *The Myths We Live By*, London: Routledge.

Sanders, T. (2005) ' "It's just acting": sex workers' strategies for capitalizing on sexuality', *Gender, Work and Organization*, 12(4): 319–42.

Sassen, S. (2002) 'Global cities and survival circuits', in B. Ehrenreich and A.R. Hochschild (eds) *Global Women: Nannies, Maids and Sex Workers in the New Economy*, London: Granta.

Savage, M. (1998) 'Discipline, surveillance and the "career": employment on the Great Western Railway 1833–1914', in A. McKinlay and K. Starkey (eds) *Foucault, Management and Organization Theory*, London: Sage.

Savage, M. (2000a) 'Sociology, class and male manual work cultures', in A. Campbell, N. Fishman and J. McIlroy (eds) *British Trade Unions and Industrial Politics*, Aldershot: Ashgate.

Savage, M. (2000b) *Class Analysis and Social Transformation*, Buckingham: Open University Press.

Savage, M. (2001) 'Class formation and localism in an emerging bureaucracy: British bank workers, 1880–1960', *International Journal of Urban and Regional Research*, 25(1): 284–300.

Savage, M. (2005) 'Working-class identities in the 1960s: revisiting the affluent worker study', *Sociology*, 39(5): 929–46.

Sayer, A. (2005) *The Moral Significance of Class*, Cambridge: Cambridge University Press.

Sayer, K. (1995) *Women of the Fields: Representations Of Rural Women in the Nineteenth Century*, Manchester: Manchester University Press.

Sayer, L., Bianchi, S. and Robinson, J. P. (2004) 'Are parents investing less time in children?', *American Journal of Sociology*, 110(1): 1–21.

Sayers, J., Evans, M. and Redclift, N. (1987) *Engels Revisited: New Feminist Essays*, London: Tavistock Publications.

Scales, J. and Scase, R. (2000) *'Fit and Fifty?': A Report Prepared for the Economic and Social Research Council*, Swindon: ESRC.

Schieffelin, B. B. (2002) 'Marking time: the dichotomizing discourse of multiple temporalities', *Current Anthropology*, 43, Supplement: s5–s17.

Schor, J. (1991) *The Overworked American: The Unexpected Decline of Leisure*, New York: Basic Books.

Schumpeter, J. ([1942] 1984) *Capitalism, Socialism and Democracy*, London: Harper.

Seabrook, J. (1982) *Unemployment*, London: Quartet Books.

Sennett, R. (1993) *Authority*, London: W. W. Norton.

Sennett, R. (1998) *The Corrosion of Character: The Personal Consequences of Work in the New Capitalism*, London: W. W. Norton.

Sennett, R. (2003) *Respect: The Formation of Character in an Age of Inequality*, London: Allen Lane.

Sennett, R. (2006) *The Culture of the New Capitalism*, New Haven, CT: Yale University Press.

Sillitoe, A. (1990) *Saturday Night and Sunday Morning*, London: Flamingo.

Sinclair, U. ([1906] 2002) *The Jungle*, New York: Random House.

Sinfield, A. (1981) *What Unemployment Means*, Oxford: Martin Robertson.

Sirianni, C. and Negrey, C. (2000) 'Working time as gendered time', *Feminist Economics*, 6(1): 59–76.

Sivanandan, A. (1982) *A Different Hunger: Writings on Black Resistance*, London: Pluto Press.

Skeggs, B. (1997) *Formations of Class and Gender: Becoming Respectable*, London: Sage.

Skeggs, B. (2004) *Class, Self and Culture*, London; Routledge.

Small, S. and Solomos, J. (2006) 'Race, immigration and politics in Britain: changing policy agendas and conceptual paradigms, 1940s–2000s', *International Journal of Comparative Sociology*, 47(3–4): 235–57.

Smith, A. ([1776] 1982) *The Wealth of Nations*, London: Penguin.

Smith, D. (1988) *The Everyday World as Problematic: Towards a Feminist Sociology*, Milton Keynes: Open University Press.

Smith, D. J. (1977) *Racial Discrimination in Britain*, London: Penguin.

Smith, D. J. (1981) *Unemployment and Racial Minorities*, London: PSI.

Smith, T. (1997) 'Pictured history: the matchgirls' strike 1888', in J. Evans (ed.) *The Camerawork Essays: Context and Meaning in Photography*, London: Rivers Oram Press.

Social Exclusion Unit (2006) http://www.socialexclusionunit.gov.uk/page.asp?id=213).

Solomos, J. and Back, L. (1996) *Racism and Society*, Basingstoke: Macmillan.

Sorokin, P. ([1943] 1963) *Sociocultural Causality: Space, Time, a Study of Referential Principles of Sociology and Social Sciences*, New York: Russell and Russell.

Spender, D. (1981) 'The gatekeepers: a feminist critique of academic publishing', in H. Roberts (ed.) *Doing Feminist Research*, London: Routledge and Kegan Paul.

Stallabrass, J. (1997) 'Sebastião Salgado and fine art photojournalism', *New Left Review*, 223: 131–60.

Stanko, E. A. (1988) 'Keeping women in and out of line: sexual harassment and occupational segregation', in S. Walby (ed.) *Gender Segregation at Work*, Oxford: Oxford University Press.

Stanton, E. C., Anthony, S. B. and Gage, M. J. (eds) (1989) *History of Woman Suffrage*, 2nd ed., vol. 1, Rochester, NY: Charles Mann.

Stead, P. (1989) *Film and the Working Class: The Feature Film in British and American Society*, London: Routledge.

Stedman-Jones, G. (1971) *Outcast London: A Study in the Relationship Between Classes in Victorian Society*, Oxford: Oxford University Press.

Strangleman, T. (2001) 'Networks, place and identities in post-industrial mining communities', *International Journal of Urban and Regional Research*, 25(2): 253–67.

Strangleman, T. (2004a) 'Ways of (not) seeing work: the visual as a blind spot in WES?, *Work, Employment and Society*, 18(1): 179–92.

Strangleman, T. (2004b) *Work Identity at the End of the Line?: Privatisation and Culture Change in the UK Rail Industry*, Basingstoke: Palgrave.

Strangleman, T. (2005) 'Sociological futures and the sociology of work', *Sociological Research Online*, 10(4): http://www.socresonline.org.uk/10/4/strangleman.html

Strangleman, T. (2007) 'The nostalgia for permanence at work?: The end of work and its commentators', *Sociological Review*, 55(1): 81–103.

Strangleman, T. *et al.* (1999) 'Heritage work: re-representing the work ethic in the coalfields', *Sociological Research Online*, 4(3): http://www.socresonline.org.uk/4/3/contents.html

Strauss, A., Schatzman, L., Ehrlich, D., Bucher, R. and Sabshim, M. (1963) 'The hospital and its negotiated order', in E. Friedson (ed.) *The Hospital in Modern Society*, London: Macmillan.

Sullivan, O. (1997) 'Time waits for no (wo)man: an investigation of the gendered experience of domestic time', *Work, Employment and Society* 31(2): 221–40.

Sullivan, O. (2000) 'the division of domestic labour: twenty years of change?', *Sociology*, 34(3): 437–56.

Sullivan, O. (2004) 'Changing gender practices within the household: a theoretical perspective', *Gender and Society*, 18(2): 207–22.

Sullivan, O. and Gershuny, J. (2001) 'Cross-national changes in time-use: some sociological hi(stories) re-examined', *Sociology*, 52(2): 331–47.

Swann, P. (1989) *The British Documentary Film Movement, 1926–1946*, Cambridge: Cambridge University Press.

Sydie, R. A. (1987) *Natural Women, Cultured Men*, Milton Keynes: Open University Press.

Taylor, G. and Spencer, S. (2004) *Social Identities*, London: Routledge.

Taylor, P. and Bain, P. (2005) 'India calling to the far away towns: the call centre labour process and globalization', *Work, Employment and Society*, 19(2): 261–82.

Taylor, R. (2006) 'Challenging the boundaries of the public and private spheres: rethinking voluntary work', in L. Pettinger *et al.* (eds) *A New Sociology of Work*, Oxford: Blackwell.

Taylor, S. (1997) '"Empowerment or degradation"? Total Quality Management and the service sector', in R. K. Brown (ed.) *The Changing Shape of Work*, London: Macmillan.

Taylor, S. (1998) 'Emotional labour and the new workplace', in P. Thompson and C. Warhurst (eds) *Workplaces of the Future*, London: Macmillan.

Terkel, S. (1972) *Working: People Talk About What They Do All Day and How They Feel About What They Do*, New York: Pantheon Books.

The Project on Disney (1995) *Inside the Mouse: Work and Play at Disney World*, London: Rivers Oram Press.

Theriault, R. (1995) *How to Tell When You're Tired: A Brief Examination of Work*, New York: W. W. Norton.

Thomas, K. (ed.) (1999) *The Oxford Book of Work*, Oxford: Oxford University Press.

Thomis, M. (1970) *The Luddites: Machine-Breaking in Regency England*, New York: Schocken Books.

Thompson, E. P. (1967) 'Time, work-discipline and industrial capitalism', *Past and Present: A Journal of Scientific History*, 38: 56–76.

Thompson, E. P. (1968) *The Making of the English Working Class*, London: Penguin.

Thompson, E. P. (1991) *Customs in Common*, London: Merlin.

Thompson, E. P. (1993) 'Time, Work-Discipline and Industrial Capitalism', in *Customs in Common: Studies in Traditional Popular Culture*, Harmondsworth: Penguin.

Thompson, P. (1978) *Voice of the Past: Oral History*, Oxford: Oxford University Press.

Thompson, P. and Smith, C. (1998) 'Beyond the Capitalist Labour Process', *Critical Sociology*, 24: 3: 193–215.

Thompson, P., Wailey, T. and Lummis, T. (1983) *Living the Fishing*, London: Routledge and Kegan Paul.

Tilly, L. and Scott, J. (1989) *Women, Work and Family*, London: Routledge.

Todhunter, C. (2001) 'Undertaking action research: negotiating the road ahead', *Social Research Update*, Number 34: http://www.soc.surrey.ac.uk/sru/SRU34.html

Toynbee, P. (2003) *Hardwork: Life in Low Pay Britain*, London: Bloomsbury.

Treuherz, J. (1987) *Hard Times: Social Realism in Victorian Art*, London: Lund Humphries.

Tronto, J. C. (1987) 'Beyond gender difference to a theory of care', *Signs, Within and Without: Women, Gender, and Theory*, 12(4): 644–63.

Tumin, M. E. (1953) 'Reply to Kingsley Davis', *American Sociological Review*, 18(4): 672–73.

Tunstall, J. (1962) *The Fisherman*, London: MacGibbon and Kee.

Tyler, M. and Abbott, P. (1998) 'Chocs away: weight watching on the contemporary airline industry', *Sociology*, 32(3): 433–50.

UK Data Archive. *SN 2798 – Social Change and Economic Life Initiative Surveys, 1986–1987*: http://www.data-archive.ac.uk/findingData/snDescription.asp?sn=2798, accessed 24 July 2007.

Ungerson, C. (1983) 'Why do women care?', in J. Finch and D. Groves (eds) *A Labour of Love: Women, Work and Caring*, London: Routledge and Kegan Paul.

Ungerson, C. (ed.) (2002) *Gender and Caring: Work and Welfare in Britain and Scandinavia*, Hertfordshire: Harvester Wheatsheaf.

Vanek, J. (1974) 'Time spent in housework', *Scientific American*, 231(5): 116–20.

Veblen, T. ([1899] 1963) *The Theory of the Leisure Class*, London: New English Library Limited.

Venkatesth, S. A. (2006) *Off the Books: The Underground Economy of the Urban Poor*, Cambridge, MA: Harvard University Press.

Vickerstaff, S. (2003) 'Apprenticeship in the "golden age": were youth transitions really smooth and unproblematic back then?', *Work, Employment and Society*, 17(2): 269–87.

Vickerstaff, S., Baldock, J., Cox, J. and Keen, L. (2004) *Happy Retirement? The Impact of Employer's Policies and Practice on the Process of Retirement*, Bristol: Policy Press.

Virdee, S. (1995) *Racial Violence and Harassment*, London: PSI.

Virdee, S. (2000) 'A Marxist critique of black radical trade union theories of trade union racism', *Sociology*, 34(3): 545–65.

Virdee, S. (2006) 'Race, employment and social change: a critique of current theoretical orthodoxies', *Ethnic and Racial Studies*, 29(4): 605–28.

Wajcman, J. (1998) *Managing Like a Man: Women and Men in Corporate Management*, Cambridge: Polity.

Walby, S. (1986) *Patriarchy at Work: Patriarchal and Capitalist Relations in Employment*, Cambridge: Polity.

Walby, S. (ed.) (1988) *Gender Segregation at Work*, Milton Keynes: Open University Press.

Walby, S. and Olsen, W. (2004) *Modelling Gender Pay Gaps*, Manchester: Equal Opportunities Commission.

Walkerdine, V. (2005) 'Freedom, psychology and the neoliberal worker', *Soundings*, 29: 47–61.

Walters, S. (2005) 'Making the best of a bad job? Female part-timers' orientations and attitudes to work', *Gender, Work and Organization*, 12(3): 193–216.

Walvin, J. (1993) *Black Ivory: A History of British Slavery*, London: Fontana.

Walvin, J. (2000) *Making the Black Atlantic: Britain and the Black Diaspora*, London: Cassell.

Ward, J. and Winstanley, D. (2006) 'Watching the watch: the UK Fire Service and its impact on sexual minorities in the workplace', *Gender, Work and Organization*, 13(2): 193–219.

Ward, R. and Jenkins, R. (1984) *Ethnic Communities in Business: Strategies for Economic Survival*, Cambridge: Cambridge University Press.

Warde, A. and Hetherington, K. (1993) 'A changing domestic division of labour? Issues of measurement and interpretation', *Work, Employment and Society*, 7(1): 23–45.

Warr, P. (1983) 'Work, jobs and unemployment', *Bulletin of the British Psychological Society*, 36: 305–11.

Warr, P. and Jackson, P. (1985) 'Factors influencing the psychological impact of prolonged unemployment and of re-employment', *Psychological Medicine*, 15(4): 795–807.

Warren, T. (2000) 'Women in low status part-time jobs: a gender and class based analysis', *Sociological Research Online*, 4(4): http://www.socresonline.org.uk/socresonline/>

Warren, T. (2001) 'Divergent female part-time employment in Britain and Denmark and the implications for gender equity', *Sociological Review*, 49(4): 548–67.

Warren, T. (2002) 'Gendered and classed working time in Britain: dual-employee couples in higher/lower level occupations', in G. Crow and S. Heath (eds) *Times in the Making: Structure and Process in Work and Everyday Life*, London: Palgrave.

Warren, T. (2003) 'Class- and gender-based working time? Time poverty and the division of domestic labour', *Sociology*, 37(4): 733–54.

Warren, T. (2004) 'Working part-time: achieving the ideal work–life balance?', *British Journal of Sociology*, 55(1): 99–121.

Warren, T. (2007) 'Conceptualising breadwinning work', *Work, Employment and Society*, 21(2): 317–36.

Warren, T. and Britton, N. J. (2003) 'Ethnic diversity in economic well-being: the added significance of wealth and asset levels', *Journal of Ethnic and Migration Studies*, 29(1): 103–19.

Warren, T. and Walters, P. (1998) 'Appraising a dichotomy: a review of the use of "part-time/full-time" in the study of women's employment in Britain', *Gender, Work and Organization*, 5(2): 102–18.

Warren, T., Pascall, G. and Fox, E. (2007) 'Innovative social policies for gender equality from Europe: implications for the work–life reconciliation of low-waged women in England', Working paper, presented at the Fourth International Gender, Work and Organization conference, University of Keele.

Waters, M. (1995) *Globalization*, London: Routledge.

Weber, M. ([1904] 1970) *The Protestant Ethic and the Spirit of Capitalism*, London: Unwin University Books.

Weber, M. (1978) *Economy and Society*, Translated by G. Roth and C. Wittich, Berkeley, CA: University of California Press.

Webster, F. (1995) *Theories of the Information Society*, London: Routledge.

West, C. and Zimmerman, D. H. (1987) 'Doing gender', *Gender and Society*, 1(2): 125–51.

Westergaard, J., Noble, I. and Walker, A. (1989) *After Redundancy: The Experience of Insecurity*, Cambridge: Polity.

Westwood, S. (1985) *All Day, Every Day: Factory and Family in the Making of Women's Lives*, Chicago: University of Illinois Press.

Whalen, J., Whalen, M. and Henderson, K. (2002) 'Improvisational choreography in teleservice work', *British Journal of Sociology*, 53(2): 239–58.

Wheelock, J. (1990) *Husbands at Home: The Domestic Economy in a Post-Industrial Society*, London: Routledge.

Whitehead, S. (2002) *Men and Masculinities*, Cambridge: Polity.

Whitehead, S. (2006) *Men and Masculinities: Critical Concepts in Sociology*, London: Routledge.

Wilkinson, A. and Willmott, H. (eds) (1995) *Making Quality Critical: New Perspectives on Organizational Change*, London: Routledge.

Williams, C. (2003) 'Sky service: the demands of emotional labour in the airline industry', *Gender, Work and Organization*, 10(5): 513–50.

Williams, C. C. and Windebank, J. (2002a) 'The uneven geographies of informal economic activities: a case study of two British cities', *Work, Employment and Society*, 16(2): 231–50.

Williams, C. C. and Windebank, J. (2002b) 'Why do people engage in paid informal work? A comparison of higher- and lower-income urban neighbourhoods in Britain', *Community, Work and Family*, 5(1): 67–83.

Williams, C. C. and Windebank, J. (2006) 'Rereading undeclared work', *Community, Work and Family*, 9(2): 181–96.

Williams, R. (1976) *Keywords: A Vocabulary of Culture and Society*, London: Fontana.

Willis, P. (1977) *Learning to Labour: How Working Class Kids Get Working Class Jobs*, Farnborough: Saxon House.

Wills, J. (2004) 'Campaigning for low paid workers: The East London Communities Organisation (TELCO) living wage campaign', in W. Brown, G. Healy, E. Heery and P. Taylor (eds) *The Future of Worker Representation*, Oxford: Oxford University Press.

Wilson, D. C. (1992) *A Strategy for Change: Concepts and Controversies in the Management of Change*, London: Routledge.

Wilson, W. J. (1987) *The Truly Disadvantaged: The Inner City, the Underclass, and Public Policy*, Chicago: University of Chicago Press.

Windebank, J. (2001) 'Dual-earner couples in Britain and France: gender divisions of domestic labour and parenting work in different welfare states', *Work, Employment and Society*, 15(2): 269–90.

Witz, A., Warhurst, C. and Nickson, D. (2003) 'The labour of aesthetics and the aesthetics of organisation', *Organisation*, 10(1): 33–54.

Wolkowitz, C. (2006) *Bodies at Work*, London: Sage.

Wollstonecraft, M. ([1792] 1985) *Vindication of the Rights of Woman*, London: Penguin.

Wood, S. (ed.) (1982) *The Degradation of Work?: Skill, Deskilling, and the Labour Process*, London: Hutchinson.

Wright, E. O. (1985) *Classes*, London: Verso.

Wright, S. (ed.) (1994) *Anthropology of Organisations*, London: Routledge.

Yllo, K. (1993) 'Through a feminist lens: gender, power and violence', in R. Gelles and D. Loseke (eds) *Current Controversies in Family Violence*, Newbury Park, CA: Sage.

Yochelson, B. (2001) *Jacob Riis*, London: Phaidon.

Young, M. and Willmott, P. (1973) *The Symmetrical Family: A Study of Work and Leisure in the London Region*, London: Routledge and Kegan Paul.

Yuval-Davis, N. (2006) 'Intersectionality and feminist politics', *European Journal of Women's Studies*, 13(3): 193–209.

Zaniello, T. (2003) *Working Stiffs, Union Maids, Reds, and Riffraff: An Expanded Guide to Films about Labor*, Ithaca, NY: ILR Press.

Zelizer, V. (1985) *Pricing the Priceless Child*, New York: Basic Books.

Zweig, F. (1952) *Women's Life and Labour*, London: Victor Gollancz.

INDEX

Note: Books are listed under their authors. Films and television programmes are listed under their individual names.